Competition, Competitive Advantage, and Clusters

incorporating The College of Law

Competition, Competitive Advantage, and Clusters

The Ideas of Michael Porter

Edited by
Robert Huggins and Hiro Izushi

OXFORD

UNIVERSITY PRESS

OXFORD

UNIVERSITY PRESS

Great Clarendon Street, Oxford OX2 6DP
United Kingdom

Oxford University Press is a department of the University of Oxford.
It furthers the University's objective of excellence in research, scholarship,
and education by publishing worldwide. Oxford is a registered trade mark of
Oxford University Press in the UK and in certain other countries

First Edition published in 2011
First published in paperback 2012
Reprinted 2013

British Library Cataloguing in Publication Data
Data available

Library of Congress Cataloging in Publication Data
Data available

ISBN 978-0-19-966042-1

Contents

Contents

Acknowledgments

We would like to thank the contributors to this book who all provided us with high-quality inputs to work with. We would further like to express our thanks to David Musson and Emma Booth, who gave us great support throughout the project. In addition, we would like to express our appreciation to Michael Porter, who gave us considerable help in providing certain materials, as well as being generous with his time and allowing us to interview him at length.

Robert Huggins
Hiro Izushi

List of Figures

List of Tables

Notes on Editors and Contributors

Editors

Robert Huggins is Professor of Economic Geography at the School of Planning and Geography, Cardiff University, and Director of its Centre for Economic Geography. He is the originator of the *European Competitiveness Index*, the *UK Competitiveness Index*, and the co-founder – with Dr Izushi – of the World Knowledge Competitiveness Index. He is also the author of *The Business of Networks* (2000) and *Competing for Knowledge* (2007), and more than fifty academic journal articles.

Hiro Izushi received his PhD from the University of California at Berkeley, and is now Senior Lecturer in Innovation for the Economics and Strategy Group at Aston Business School, Birmingham, UK. With Professor Robert Huggins he is a co-founding Director of the Centre for International Competitiveness, and co-founder of the *World Knowledge Competitiveness Index*. He has written more than twenty academic papers, and, with Professor Huggins, is co-author of *Competing for Knowledge* (2007).

Contributors (in chapter order)

Jay B. Barney is Professor of Management and Human Resources at Fisher College of Business, Ohio State University. His research focuses on the relationship between costly-to-copy firm skills and capabilities and sustained competitive advantage. He has published more than fifty articles in leading journals such as *Academy of Management Review, Management Science, Sloan Management Review*, and *Journal of Management*. He serves on the editorial boards of *Strategic Management Journal, Columbia Journal of World Business*, and *Journal of Business Venturing*, and has been associate editor of *Journal of Management* and senior editor of *Organization Science*. He has also authored three books, including *Organizational Economics: Toward a New Paradigm for Studying and Understanding Organizations; Managing Organizations: Strategy, Structure, and Behavior;* and *Gaining and Sustaining Competitive Advantage.* He has been honored for his research and teaching, including election as a Fellow of the Academy of Management.

J.-C. Spender is currently Svenska Handelsbanken Visiting Professor at the School of Economics and Management, Lund University (Sweden), Visiting Professor at the ESADE/Universitat Ramon Llull (Spain), Visiting Professor at the Cranfield School of Management, and Visiting Professor at the Open University Business School. He has previously served on the faculties of City University (London), York University (Toronto), the University of California at Los Angeles, and the University of Glasgow, and as Chair of Entrepreneurship and Small Business at Rutgers University (New Jersey). After a year's sabbatical with the Advanced Technology Program (US Department of Commerce) he was appointed Dean, School of Management, New York Institute of Technology, and then Dean, School of Business and Technology, Fashion Institute of Technology (SUNY), New York. He retired in 2003.

Jeroen Kraaijenbrink is an Assistant Professor at NIKOS – the Dutch Institute for Knowledge Intensive Entrepreneurship at the University of Twente. He is also research manager of the high-tech incubator program VentureLab Twente. He holds an MSc and a PhD in industrial engineering and management and an MSc in public administration from the University of Twente. He has co-edited a book on knowledge management for small and medium-sized enterprises, and has published internationally in various books and journals, including *Technological Forecasting and Social Change, Knowledge Management Research and Practice, Journal of Product Innovation Management,* and *Journal of Management.*

Robert E. Hoskisson is George R. Brown Professor of Management at the Jesse H. Jones Graduate School of Business, Rice University. He received his PhD from the University of California-Irvine. His research topics focus on corporate governance, acquisitions and divestitures, corporate and international diversification, corporate entrepreneurship, privatization, and cooperative strategy. He has co-authored several books, including *Downscoping: How to Tame the Diversified Firm* (1994), *Competing for Advantage* (2003), and *Strategic Management: Competitiveness and Globalization* (eighth edn., 2009). His research has appeared in more than ninety publications, including *Academy of Management Journal, Academy of Management Review, Strategic Management Journal, Organization Science, Journal of Management, Academy of Management Executive,* and *California Management Review.*

Michael A. Hitt is a Distinguished Professor and holds the Joe B. Foster Chair in Business Leadership and the C. W. and Dorothy Conn Chair in New Ventures at Texas A&M University. He received his PhD from the University of Colorado. He has authored or co-authored several books and book chapters, and numerous articles in journals such as *Academy of Management Journal*, *Academy of Management Review*, *Strategic Management Journal*, *Journal of Applied Psychology*, *Organization Science*, *Organization Studies*, *Journal of Management Studies*, and *Journal of Management*.

William P. Wan is an Associate Professor of Management, and currently holds the Trinity Company Professorship at Rawls College of Business, Texas Tech University. He received his PhD in strategic management from Texas A&M University. His research focuses on corporate and international strategy, corporate governance, international business, strategy in emerging economies, and international entrepreneurship. His research articles have appeared in *Academy of Management Journal*, *Accounting, Organizations and Society*, *Journal of International Business Studies*, *Journal of Management*, *Journal of Management Studies*, *Management International Review*, and *Strategic Management Journal*.

Daphne Yiu is an Associate Professor at the Department of Management, Chinese University of Hong Kong. She received her PhD in management from the Michael F. Price College of Business, University of Oklahoma. Her research interests lie in corporate and international strategy, strategies in emerging markets, international entrepreneurship, and corporate governance. Her publications have appeared in management journals such as *Entrepreneurship Theory and Practice*, *Journal of International Business Studies*, *Journal of Management*, *Journal of Management Studies*, *Organizational Science*, and *Strategic Management Journal*. She serves as a senior editor of *Asia Pacific Journal of Management*, and as a member of the editorial board of *Journal of Management Studies*.

Omar Aktouf is Professor of Management at HEC Montréal. Prior to joining HEC he held upper management responsibilities in several firms, including a major petroleum company. He has researched a number of complementary areas, including organizational culture, project management, symbolism, and speech within organizations, as well as epistemology, methodology, and pedagogy of administration 'sciences'. He is the author of numerous books and articles, and is the recipient of several awards and prizes, including 'Best French Canada Business Book Award' for 2003 (Stratégie de l'Autruche). He is an active international lecturer–speaker and consultant, and has provided consultative services for numerous large and small companies.

Miloud Chennoufi was a journalist in Algeria during the 1990s, and now teaches at the Canadian Forces College (Toronto, Canada). He is the author of 'Grandes puissances et Islamism', and co-author of 'Hannah Arendt, le totalitarisme et le monde contemporain'. His on-going research involves the application of hermeneutical interpretation in different fields such as organization theory, political science, and international relations.

W. David Holford is an Associate Professor of Management at the University of Quebec at Montreal. He has co-authored several articles on organizational sense-making and the humanistic dimension of management, and its ramifications on both risk/crisis creation and knowledge management. Prior to embarking on his studies, he worked for nineteen years in the aerospace industry (Pratt and Whitney Canada), including the last nine years with important responsibilities in several engineering management positions.

Nicolai J. Foss is a Professor at the Copenhagen Business School and the Norwegian School of Economics and Business Administration. As the director of the Center for Strategic Management and Globalization at Copenhagen Business School, he has published widely on strategy, economic organization, and methodology, and is a member of the editorial boards of a host of international journals.

Robert M. Grant is Eni Professor of Management at Bocconi University in Milan. He has also held positions at Georgetown University, City University, California Polytechnic, the University of British Columbia, London Business School, and the University of St Andrews. His area of expertise is strategy management, in which he studies organizational capability, knowledge and organization structure, and strategic planning. He was born in Bristol, England, studied at the London School of Economics, and now lives in Milan and London.

Jan Fagerberg is Professor of Economics at the University of Oslo, where he is affiliated with the Centre for Technology, Innovation and Culture (TIK). He has specialized in research on the impact of innovation and diffusion on trade, competitiveness, and growth, and has published extensively on these and related topics in books and major journals. A selection of his papers in this area was published in the book *Technology, Growth and Competitiveness* (2002). He is also an editor of the *Oxford Handbook of Innovation* (2005).

Brian Snowdon was Professor of Economics and International Business at Newcastle Business School, Northumbria University. Now retired, he is currently a part-time Senior Teaching Fellow at the Department of Economics and Finance, Durham University. His main research interests are in the areas of macroeconomics and international growth and development. As well as numerous articles in academic journals, he has authored or co-authored eleven books including: *Reflections on the Development of Modern Macroeconomics* (with H. R. Vane, 1997); *A Macroeconomics Reader* (with H. R. Vane, 1997);

Conversations with Leading Economists: Interpreting Modern Macroeconomics (with H. R. Vane, 1999); *Conversations on Growth, Stability and Trade* (2002); *An Encyclopedia of Macroeconomics* (with H. R. Vane, 2002); and *Modern Macroeconomics: Its Origins, Development and Current State* (with H. R. Vane, 2002). His latest book, *Globalisation, Growth and Development*, was published in 2007.

Christian H. M. Ketels is a member of the Harvard Business School faculty at Professor Michael E. Porter's Institute for Strategy and Competitiveness, and an Honorary Professor at EBS University in Wiesbaden. He holds a PhD (Econ.) from the London School of Economics, and other degrees from the Kiel Institute for World Economics and Cologne University. He is a Senior Research Fellow at the Stockholm School of Economics, and Director of The Competitiveness Institute (TCI) – a global network of professionals interested in competitiveness and cluster development. He has led cluster and competitiveness projects in many parts of the world, and has written widely on economic policy issues.

Edward J. Malecki is Professor of Geography at the Ohio State University. He was previously a member of faculty at the University of Oklahoma and the University of Florida. He was a visiting researcher in the Centre for Urban and Regional Development Studies (CURDS) at the University of Newcastle-upon-Tyne, and a Fulbright Fellow at the University of Economics and Business Administration in Vienna, Austria. He is the author of more than 100 published papers and several books, including *The Digital Economy: Business Organization, Production Processes and Regional Developments* (with Bruno Moriset, 2008) and *Technology and Economic Development* (1997), and is a co-editor of *Making Connections: Technological Learning and Regional Economic Change* (1999). He is also an associate editor of the journal *Entrepreneurship and Regional Development*, and is a member of the editorial boards of several other journals.

Ron Martin is Professor of Economic Geography and a Fellow of the Cambridge-MIT Institute. He is also a Research Associate of the Centre for Business Research attached to the Judge Business School, and he holds a Professorial Fellowship at St Catharine's College. He was awarded the British Academy's Senior Research Fellowship (1997–98), was elected as an Academician of the Academy of Social Sciences in 2001, and in 2003 was selected by the American Economic Association as one of the World's Most Cited Economists. He is a Leverhulme Major Research Fellow for 2007–10.

Peter Sunley is currently Professor of Human Geography. He has been a member of staff in the School of Geography at the University of Southampton since 2003, and has published widely in the field of economic geography – frequently in collaboration with Ron Martin.

1

Competition, competitive advantage, and clusters: the ideas of Michael Porter

Robert Huggins and Hiro Izushi

1.1 Introduction

Michael Porter, the Bishop William Lawrence University Professor at the Harvard Business School and the founder of Harvard's Institute for Strategy and Competitiveness, has been one of the most influential figures in strategic management research over the last three decades. He infused a rigorous theoretical framework of industrial organization economics with the then still embryonic field of strategic management, and elevated it to its current status as an academic discipline. Porter's 1980 book *Competitive Strategy* (Porter 1980a) was firmly anchored in industrial organization economics and remarkably state of the art, covering new developments in the discipline, such as market signaling, exit barriers, and commitment through irreversible investments. His 1985 book *Competitive Advantage* (Porter 1985a) was an attempt to account for the sources of competitive advantage in terms of 'cost', 'differentiation', and 'focus'. The two books represent Porter's application of industrial organization economics, particularly the structure–conduct–performance paradigm, to strategic management research.

Both these books became hugely influential and placed Porter at the forefront of strategic management. Indeed, he was by far the most cited author in *Strategic Management Journal* between 1980 and 2000, with *Competitive Strategy* ranking first in the frequency of citations (266 times) and *Competitive Advantage* ranking third (135 times) (Ramos-Rodríguez and Ruiz-Navarro 2004). A poll conducted by the Strategic Management Society at its 1999 annual meeting found that Porter was the most influential strategic management scholar over the previous twenty-five years. In a similar vein, recent bibliometric research by Nerur et al. (2008) identifies Porter as a critical node in strategic management research along with Jeffrey Pfeffer, Henry Mintzberg, and Oliver Williamson. Porter's influence also extends significantly beyond academia, with the *New York Times* stating that: 'Business school professors tend to be an anonymous breed, and their research is often denigrated as a blend of big words and small ideas. Yet Michael Porter of the Harvard Business School stands out as a genuine star. When he speaks, people in business and government listen – frequently paying handsomely to do so' (*New York Times*, September 19, 1992, cited in Cho and Moon 2000: 97). Furthermore, 'Porter is probably the only business academic to have graced the cover of a major magazine – *Fortune*' (*Management Today*, August 1989, cited in Cho and Moon 2000: 97).

Porter's Five Forces framework presented in *Competitive Strategy* and the Value Chain framework in *Competitive Advantage* are now the standard analytical tools of industries and firms, respectively, and are widely studied by business school students and practiced by managers across the world. His influence upon practitioners is enormous, partly due to his own consulting activity as well as the application of his frameworks by others. Porter is a co-founder of the Cambridge, Massachusetts-based Monitor Group, a strategic consulting group which he founded in 1983 with five other entrepreneurs and academics including Mark and Joseph Fuller. Many corporations across the world operating in a whole range of sectors – including Caterpillar, DuPont, Procter & Gamble, Royal Dutch Shell, Sysco, and Taiwan Semiconductor Manufacturing Company, to name a few – have sought Porter's advice on competitive strategy. Major management consulting firms use Porter's frameworks, and a Porter Prize is offered annually to a Japanese company for strategic excellence.

After the publication of the seminal *Competitive Strategy* and *Competitive Advantage* books, Porter further widened his area of analysis, crossing over the traditional compartments of academic disciplines. Through his appointment by Ronald Reagan to the Presidential Commission on Industrial Competitiveness in 1985, he tackled the subject of national economic development, through the development of his Diamond framework, in *The Competitive Advantage of Nations* (1990*a*), which was further followed by his involvement in the World Economic Forum's *Global Competitiveness Reports*. Porter then focused upon a central element of the Diamond framework – the cluster (*On Competition*, 1998*c*) – and applied it to regional economic development: a subject long studied by economic geographers, regional scientists, and local development planners. Porter has not only promoted the Diamond framework and the idea of clusters as analytical concepts but also as key policy tools. As the celebrated architect and promoter of the Diamond framework and the cluster concept, Porter has advised policymakers around the world to help them identify a nation's or region's key business clusters and design relevant economic development policies.

From the OECD and the World Bank, to national governments (such as the United Kingdom, France, Germany, the Netherlands, and New Zealand), to regional development agencies, and to local and city governments (including various US states), policymakers at all levels have been eager to receive his advice. The list of Porter's clients does not end there: an expanding array of developing countries in Asia, Latin America, the Middle East, and Africa (including Armenia, Colombia, Kazakhstan, Libya, Nicaragua, Rwanda, and Thailand) vie for his expertise in economic development policy. His consultancy work with developing economies has resulted in, for example, the formation of the Latin American Center for Competitiveness and Sustainable Development – a permanent institution based in Costa Rica.

With expert contributors from a range of disciplines including strategic management, economic development, and economic geography and planning, this book assesses the contribution Porter has made to these respective disciplines. It clarifies the sources of tension and controversy relating to all the major strands of Porter's work, and provides academics, students, and practitioners – managers and policymakers – with a key and critical guide to the application of his frameworks.

The rest of this introductory chapter takes the following structure. In the next section we briefly provide an overview of Porter's academic background, highlighting its interdisciplinary nature. This is followed by an introduction to Porter's key frameworks; the Five Forces (Porter 1980a), the Value Chain (Porter 1985a), the Diamond (Porter 1990a), and clusters (Porter 1998d). We argue that while Porter remains focused on the nature of competition, a number of significant changes are observed when comparing his thinking underlying the Diamond framework and the concept of clusters to that associated with the Five Forces and Value Chain frameworks. These changes include: (a) a focus upon innovation as a form of competitive advantage creation under the Diamond framework and the cluster concept, as opposed to innovation being only a marginal feature of the tactics Porter proposes under the Five Forces and Value Chain frameworks; and (b) a new emphasis upon cooperation as a source of advantage and its coexistence with competition under the Diamond framework and the cluster concept, as opposed to the sole focus upon competition under the Five Forces and Value Chain frameworks. Furthermore, his thinking becomes more interdisciplinary in its foundation over the course of developing these frameworks. Also, Porter has more recently made a foray into a number of other topics, including inner city development, environmental regulations, and health care services. We provide a short review of his work in these areas as well as a list of his academic publications accompanying and complementing his major books (Porter 1980a, 1985a, 1990a, 1998c). Finally, we conclude this chapter with an outline of the remaining chapters in this book.

1.2 Porter's academic background and work prior to *Competitive Strategy*

Born in Ann Arbor, Michigan, in 1947, Michael Porter traveled throughout the world as the son of a career Army officer. He received a BSE with high honors in aerospace and mechanical engineering from Princeton University[1] in 1969, and an MBA with high distinction in 1971 from Harvard Business School. In an interview, Porter reflects on his decision to do an MBA:

> I decided that engineering would be just too limiting for me....I then briefly thought of going into medical school. However, I very quickly abandoned that idea and decided to do an MBA degree, thinking that with my technical engineering background, this would be a good combination. (Stonehouse and Snowdon 2007: 260–1)

There was already a sign of Porter's interdisciplinary orientation in this decision, and the orientation continued in his subsequent studies for a PhD. He obtained a job in the Department of Transportation in the summer of 1970 after the first year of the Harvard MBA program. This drew him into policy issues and economics. Through discussions with Professor Roland Christensen at Harvard Business School, Porter became interested in pursuing an academic career and subsequently entered the PhD program in business economics at Harvard's Economics Department in 1971, obtaining a PhD under the supervision of Richard Caves and Jesse Markham in 1973. Although the degree was essentially a PhD in economics, he chose a business economics program in which he elected for business to be one of his subfields, and studied business policy in the first year of his PhD studies. He recalls this hybrid route as being essential to the development of his thinking:

> ...Harvard Business School was very practitioner oriented, emphasizing case studies and real industries. In contrast, across the river, the emphasis among the economists was in developing theoretical models and producing journal articles. ...a couple of weeks into the industrial economics course, I suddenly realized that the professors at both the Harvard Business School and the Department of Economics were talking about the same issues but they were coming from completely different perspectives....The idea of bridging these two fields led to my doctoral dissertation, which in turn ultimately led to my 1980 book on competitive strategy. (Stonehouse and Snowdon 2007: 261)

Most of Porter's early work, including joint-authored articles with Caves and others, was published in mainstream economics journals with an emphasis on quantitative analysis (Porter 1973, 1974, 1976a, 1979b; Caves et al. 1975, 1977, 1980; Caves and Porter 1976, 1977, 1978, 1980).

A major piece of work of this period is Porter's book *Interbrand Choice, Strategy, and Bilateral Market Power*, which published in 1976. In this book, Porter presents a 'framework for modeling the buyer's process of gaining information for his choice among brands and its implications for sellers' sales-promotion strategies and market performance' (Porter 1976*a*: 7). As a harbinger of *Competitive Strategy*, Porter positions the book as a bridge between the mainstream economics research in industrial organization and the business administration research preoccupied with the problems of the manager. Taking issue with both the former's assertion that the structure of an industry defines the strategy of the firm and the latter's assertion that the firm has discretion over its choice of strategy and can influence the structure of its industry through its behavior, Porter argues that treating one or the other as dominant is seriously misleading. In his view, 'the firm's strategy is constrained but not determined by the structure of its industry, and...firms' strategies within an industry differ in economically important ways' (Porter 1976*a*: 7). In the case of interbrand choice, this is translated into Porter's claim that the profitability of a producer (firm performance) through product differentiation is influenced by the buyers' process of interbrand choice and the power of the retail sector (industry structure), as well as also being affected by the marketing strategies that the producer adopts (particularly in nonconvenience goods).

While publishing articles in mainstream economics journals, Porter also wrote a couple of articles for management journals in the 1970s with a style that was more suitable for addressing general practitioners. In 1975 he wrote a short course note for teaching (Porter 1975) based on the idea of the Five Forces. In the following year he published his first article in a management journal, *California Management Review* (Porter 1976*b*), experimenting with an accessible language for practitioners. This was followed by 'How competitive forces shape strategy,' which was published in *Harvard Business Review* in 1979 and paved the way for his first landmark study: *Competitive Strategy*.

1.3 *Competitive Strategy* and *Competitive Advantage*

In *Competitive Strategy* (Porter 1980*a*) Porter poses two central sets of questions. First, observing persistent variations in profitability across industries, he asks what factors determine the attractiveness of industries for long-term profitability. Where profit potential in the industry is measured in terms of long-run return on invested capital, Porter finds that not all industries have the same potential. While no firms earn spectacular returns in industries like tires, paper, and steel, high returns are common in industries like oil-field equipment and services, cosmetics, and toiletries. Porter argues that industry structure has a strong influence in determining the competitive rules of the game, with the ultimate profit potential in an industry being determined by the collective strength of five forces: threat of new entrants, intensity of rivalry among existing competitors, threat of substitute products, bargaining power of buyers, and bargaining power of suppliers, as shown in Figure 1.1.

New entrants to an industry can either bid down prices or inflate costs for incumbents, reducing profitability. Rivalry among existing competitors, using tactics such as price competition, advertising battles, new product introduction, and improvements in customer service, may make all firms in an industry worse off when moves and countermoves escalate. Substitute products limit the potential returns for the industry by placing a ceiling on the prices which firms in the industry can profitably charge. Buyers can hurt industry profitability by forcing down prices, bargaining for higher quality or more services, and playing competitors off against each other. In a similar vein, suppliers can squeeze industry profitability by threatening to raise prices or reduce the quality of purchased goods and services. The underlying structure of an industry, reflected in the collective strength of the five forces, determines industry profitability.

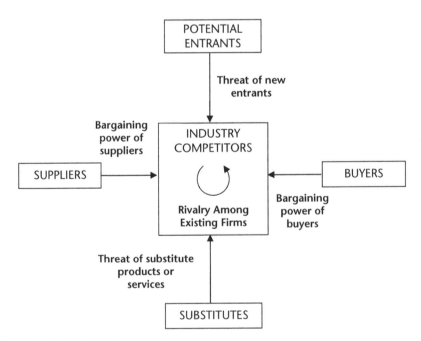

Figure 1.1. Five Forces framework

Source: Porter (1980a: 4)

Second, in addition to the cross-industry variations, in most industries some firms are much more profitable than others, regardless of what the average profitability of the industry may be. The second central question Porter asks in *Competitive Strategy* concerns the source of intra-industry variations in profitability. In Porter's view these arise from variations across firms in their ability to analyze the sources of each of the five forces, and their ability to find a position in the industry where they can best defend themselves against competitive forces or influence them in their favor. According to Porter (1980*a*) there are three internally consistent generic strategies for creating such a defensible position in the long run and outperforming competitors: overall cost leadership, differentiation, and focus. While cost leadership seeks to produce products at a lower cost than rivals, differentiation and focus refer to creating something perceived as being unique on an industry-wide basis, and to focusing on a particular buyer group, segment of the product line, or geographic market, respectively.

Porter follows up *Competitive Strategy* with *Competitive Advantage* published in 1985 (Porter 1985*a*). The central question in this sequel is how a firm actually puts the generic strategies laid out in *Competitive Strategy* into practice. Porter sees the ultimate goal of each generic strategy as being to create the value a firm is able to produce for its buyers. For instance, if a firm adopts a strategy of cost leadership, then the value the firm creates takes the form of lower prices than those of its competitors for equivalent benefits. In the case of differentiation, the value is created through the provision of unique benefits that more than offset a premium price. In Porter's view, the value a firm creates stems from the many discrete activities it performs in designing, producing, marketing, delivering, and supporting its product. The value a firm creates with cost leadership strategy may stem from such disparate sources as a low-cost physical distribution system, a highly efficient assembly process, or superior sales force utilization. In a similar vein, the value a firm creates with a differentiation strategy can derive from diverse sources, including the procurement of high-quality raw materials, a responsive order entry system, or a superior product design (Porter 1985*a*: 33). Of strategic importance here is the ability to accurately identify and map those activities which generate the value a firm seeks to create with the chosen generic strategy. To assist this process of identification and mapping, Porter presents the Value Chain framework in which he isolates nine generic categories of activity that are technologically and strategically distinct, as shown in Figure 1.2.

In *Competitive Strategy*, Porter suggests that intra-industry profitability variations at the level of individual firms, stemming from the choice of generic strategies, are within the bounds of the collective strength of the five forces at the industry level. This means that industry structure imposes some constraint upon the value a firm creates and captures as profits under the *Competitive*

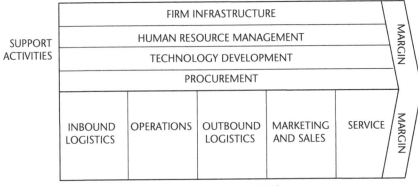

Figure 1.2. Value Chain framework

Source: Porter (1985*a*: 37)

Advantage framework. The value the firm creates for a buyer must be perceived by the buyer if it is to reward the firm with a premium price. In order to make this happen, the firm must communicate the value to the buyer through such means as advertising and the work of its sales force. Here, the firm and the buyer are in a position to divide the value between them through bargaining: the proportion of the value taken by the firm is its margin, while the rest of the value goes to the buyer in the form of either cost savings or greater satisfaction for the money the buyer pays. Porter suggests that industry structure determines the bargaining relationships between the firm and the buyer, and this is in turn reflected in the proportion of the value taken by each side. Similarly, bargaining takes place upstream between the firm and its supplier, deciding the proportion each side takes out of the value which the supplier creates. In this way, industry structure influences the configuration of the firm's value chain and how margins are divided with its buyers and suppliers (Porter 1985*a*: 59).

1.4 *The Competitive Advantage of Nations* **and** *On Competition*

In 1985 Porter was appointed by President Ronald Reagan to the President's Commission on Industrial Competitiveness, charged with examining the competitiveness of the United States. During the term of the Commission it became clear to Porter that there was no accepted definition and explanation of competitiveness. Macroeconomists see national competitiveness as a macroeconomic phenomenon, driven by exchange rates, interest rates, and government deficits. However, nations have enjoyed rapidly rising standards of living despite budget deficits, high interest rates, and appreciating currencies. To some economists, competitiveness is a function of cheap and abundant labor, yet nations such as Germany, Switzerland, and Sweden have prospered despite high wages and long periods of labor shortage. Another view is that competitiveness depends on possessing bountiful natural resources. However, the most successful trading nations have been countries with limited natural resources that import most raw materials (Porter 1990a: 3–4). The lack of a convincing explanation of the nation's influence on competitiveness led to the publication of *The Competitive Advantage of Nations* in 1990 (Porter 1990a).

The central question Porter asks in *The Competitive Advantage of Nations* is why firms based in a particular nation are able to create and sustain competitive advantage against the world's best competitors in particular industries or industry segments (Porter 1990a: 1). In Porter's view, a rising standard of living at the national level depends on the capacity of a nation's firms to achieve high levels of productivity and to increase productivity over time. Productivity is the prime determinant in the long run of a nation's standard of living, since the productivity of human resources determines their wages and the productivity of physical assets determines the return capital investments earn for investors. Here a nation does not have to succeed and raise productivity in every industry. International trade allows a nation to specialize in those industries and segments in which its firms are relatively more productive, and to import those products and services where its firms are less productive than foreign rivals, thus raising the average productivity level across the economy. Porter (1990a) finds that when one looks closely at any national economy, there are striking differences in competitive success across industries. Successful internationally competing firms in a nation are often concentrated in narrowly defined industries and even particular industry segments. Hence the question which must be asked concerns the sources of high levels of productivity and long-run productivity growth achieved by a nation's successful internationally competing firms in particular industries or industry segments.

Porter identifies four sets of determinants of such national advantage: (*a*) factor conditions, (*b*) demand conditions, (*c*) related and supporting industries, and (*d*) firm strategy, structure, and rivalry. These four sets of determinants are presented by means of the Diamond framework as shown in Figure 1.3 – a pictorial representation similar to that of the Five Forces framework.

Factor conditions refer to the availability of resources and skills necessary for competitive advantage in an industry. They are classified into two groups: basic factors and advanced factors. Whereas basic factors include natural resources, climate, location, unskilled and semi-skilled labor, and debt capital, advanced factors include information and communications infrastructure, highly educated labor such as graduate engineers and computer scientists,

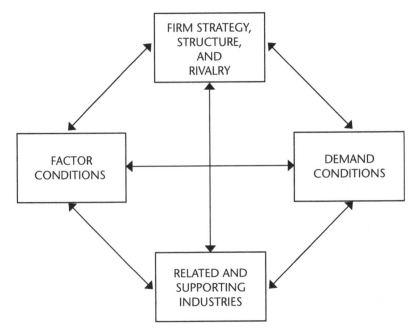

Figure 1.3. Diamond framework

Source: Porter (1990*a*: 72)

and university research institutes in sophisticated disciplines. Demand conditions within a nation can shape the rate and character of improvement and innovation by the nation's firms. A nation's firms gain competitive advantage if domestic buyers are the world's most sophisticated and demanding for particular products or services, allowing firms to perceive new needs and to engage in joint development work in ways that are difficult for foreign firms to match. Related and supporting industries concern the presence in a nation of supplier industries or related industries that are internationally competitive. Internationally competitive supplier industries in a nation not only provide efficient, early, rapid, and sometimes preferential access to the most cost-effective inputs, but also help firms perceive new methods and opportunities to apply new technology, often through ongoing coordination. The fourth set of determinants – firm strategy, structure, and rivalry – concerns (*a*) a match between the goals of the owners, managers, and employees, and the sources of competitive advantage in a particular industry; and (*b*) the pressures on firms to invest and innovate, which arise from vigorous domestic rivalry.

Porter presents the concept of clusters as part of the Diamond framework in *The Competitive Advantage of Nations* and deepens its understanding as an integral form of competitive advantage at the national and regional levels in a chapter of *On Competition*, published in 1998 (Porter 1998*d*). In Porter's view, competitive advantage in sophisticated industries and industry segments rarely results from only a single determinant. Usually, advantages in more than one determinant combine to create self-reinforcing conditions in which a nation's firms succeed internationally. The systemic nature of the Diamond promotes the geographical clustering of industries connected through vertical and horizontal relationships, with leading international companies within related industries often found in the same city or region of a nation. Porter defines clusters as 'geographic concentrations of interconnected companies, specialized suppliers, service providers, firms in related industries, and associated institutions (for example, universities, standards agencies, and trade associations) in particular fields that compete but also cooperate' (Porter 1998*d*: 197–8).

The concept of clusters helps to capture important linkages, complementarities, and spillovers of technology, skills, and information that cut across firms and industries. According to Porter, when compared with isolated firms located outside a cluster, firms in a cluster are often able to more clearly and rapidly perceive new buyer needs, new technological, operating, or delivery possibilities, as well as the actions and maneuvers of other firms. Benefits flow forward, backward, and horizontally, with people and ideas combining in new ways. Such interconnections among constituent firms and industries within a cluster facilitate productivity growth by increasing their capacity for innovation and stimulating new business formation that supports the cluster. Furthermore, many of the benefits of clusters are difficult to tap from a distance as they stem from the personal relationships which facilitate linkages, foster open communication, and build trust. Proximity, in geographic, cultural, and institutional terms, is considered by Porter to be interwoven and mutually reinforcing, and forms the basis of such personal relationships. Thus, Porter agues: 'Anything that can be efficiently sourced from a distance, however, has been essentially *nullified* as a competitive advantage in advanced economies. Information and relationships that can be accessed and maintained via fax or e-mail are available to anyone. . . . Paradoxically, then, the enduring competitive advantages in a global economy are often heavily local' (Porter 1998*d*: 236–7).

1.5 Developments in Porter's thinking

Porter's key ideas concern the nature of competition – a constant theme running through all of Porter's work. The words 'competitive' and 'competition' in the titles of the four books signify this. Porter has also continued to address business executives and managers – and increasingly policymakers – as a key part of his audience. Furthermore, he uses similar diagrams when presenting the Five Forces and Diamond frameworks (Figures 1.1 and 1.3, respectively). These may create an impression that the development of his thinking over time has been one-dimensional without any major leaps. However, we argue that his thinking has diversified into two strands, and the ideas underlying his Diamond framework and the cluster concept are significantly different from those underlying the Five Forces and Value Chain frameworks in two main ways: (*a*) the exclusive focus upon innovation as a means of creating competitive advantage under the Diamond and cluster frameworks, as opposed to innovation being only part of the tactics Porter envisages firms adopting under the Five Forces and Value Chain frameworks; and (*b*) a new emphasis on cooperation as a source of advantage and its coexistence with competition under the Diamond and cluster frameworks, as opposed to a restricted focus upon competition under the Five Forces and Value Chain frameworks. Within Porter's thinking, these two strands of ideas – the Five Forces/Value Chain and the Diamond/ cluster – coexist side by side as they are designed to answer different questions. Porter selectively applies these two strands of ideas to areas within his more recent work, such as inner city development, environment, corporate social responsibility, and health care, depending on the nature of questions under consideration. We examine the differences between the two strands of Porter's ideas below.

First, innovation is not highlighted in the Five Forces and Value Chain frameworks, particularly when compared with the focus it is given in both the Diamond framework and cluster concept. For instance, in *Competitive Strategy*, Porter (1980*a*) very briefly discusses three types of innovation – product innovation, marketing innovation, and process innovation – as a major source of industry structural change in a chapter on industry evolution (chapter 8). In *Competitive Advantage*, while Porter devotes a chapter (chapter 5) to discussing links between innovation and competitive advantage, he also provides a cautionary note that technological change may worsen a firm's competitive position and industry attractiveness (Porter 1985*a*: 165). By contrast, in *The Competitive Advantage of Nations*, innovation is given a central role. Porter writes in the book: 'Firms create competitive advantage by perceiving or discovering new and better ways to compete in an industry and bring them to market, which is ultimately an act of innovation' (Porter 1990*a*: 45). He then continues: 'Why are some companies able to perceive new ways to compete and others are not? Why do some companies do so earlier than others?... These fascinating questions will prove to be central ones in the chapters that follow' (Porter 1990*a*: 49). However, the publication of *The Competitive Advantage of Nations* and subsequent articles on clusters does not change Porter's view on innovation under the Five Forces and Value Chain frameworks. In a recent article he revisits the Five Forces framework and offers a critique of the blind pursuit of innovation: 'Faced with pressures to gain market share or enamored with innovation for its own sake, managers may trigger new kinds of competition that no incumbent can win. When taking actions to improve their own company's competitive advantage, then, strategists should ask whether they are setting in motion dynamics that will undermine industry structure in the long run' (Porter 2008a: 92).

The difference between Porter's view on innovation across the Five Forces/Value Chain and the Diamond/cluster paradigms is reflected in the choice of an indicator for competitive performance. Under the Five Forces/Value Chain profitability is the goal of firms, while under the Diamond/cluster the competitive performance of national and regional economies is measured by productivity levels and productivity growth. Profitability is a financial measure, comparing receipts and costs. There are a number of profitability measures, such as profits on a firm basis and profits as a percentage of assets or investments, but they are based on a common term of receipts less costs. By contrast, in fundamental terms, productivity is a measure of the output produced per unit input. When physical quantities of inputs (such as workers, labor hours) and outputs (such as tons, cubic feet) are used, it is a physical rather than a financial measure. Therefore, what influences physical productivity is essentially either technical efficiency or technological progress. It is not affected by a firm's pricing strategies, whereas profitability is, as can be seen in the case of monopolists charging higher margins. In practice, financial quantities of inputs (such as value of machinery and equipment) and outputs (such as turnover, value added) are often used to calculate productivity to account for their variations across inputs/outputs. However, such productivity measures run the risk of conflating technical efficiency and pricing strategies. Productivity is only one of several possibly idiosyncratic factors that determine profits (Foster et al. 2008). As Porter is concerned with cross-industry and within-industry profitability variations in *Competitive Strategy* and *Competitive Advantage*, innovation draws less attention in his discussions. By contrast, the choice of productivity as a performance indicator of nations pushes Porter to focus more on technical efficiency and technological progress – or innovation – in *The Competitive Advantage of Nations* and his subsequent writings on clusters.

Second, his conversion to an innovation stance has important implications concerning his views on inter-firm relationships. Ultimately, this 'new' focus leads Porter to identify knowledge spillovers as a key driver of the innovation taking place within clusters. As Porter notes, 'underlying the operation of the national "diamond," and the phenomenon of clustering, is the exchange and flow of information about needs, techniques, and technology among buyers, suppliers, and related industries' (Porter 1990a: 152), which subsequently facilitates innovation and productivity growth within a cluster. In addition, innovations diffuse rapidly through the conduits of suppliers or customers that have contact with multiple competitors, raising the level of productivity within a cluster as a whole. This centrality of knowledge spillovers as a cluster's innovation mechanism is evident in the way Porter draws the line of a cluster's border. As he argues: 'Drawing cluster boundaries is often a matter of degree, and involves a creative process informed by understanding the most important linkages and complementarities across industries and institutions to competition. The strength of these "spillovers" and their importance to productivity and innovation determine the ultimate boundaries' (Porter 1998*d*: 202). In other words, a cluster is defined by the presence of knowledge spillovers, which in turn forms the basis of the cluster's innovativeness.

The presence of knowledge spillovers as a cluster's underpinning feature adds a cooperation dimension to the Diamond framework and the cluster concept. In Porter's view, firms within a cluster 'share many common needs and opportunities and encounter many common constraints and obstacles to productivity.... The cluster provides a constructive and efficient forum for dialogue among related companies and their suppliers, government, and other salient institutions' (Porter 1998*d*: 205). Therefore, Porter suggests that a combination of both competition and cooperation exists within a cluster: 'Vigorous competition occurs in winning customers and retaining them. The presence of multiple rivals and strong incentives often accentuates the intensity of competition among clusters. Yet cooperation must occur in a variety of areas...Much of it is vertical, involves related industries and is with local institutions' (Porter 1998*d*: 222–3).

The coexistence of both competition and cooperation within a cluster is something Porter is at pains to point out. For instance, he argues there is a trade-off in a cluster's growth between greater access to information and specialized skills, on the one hand, and unwanted competition for, and increased costs of, employees and inputs, on the other. However, he assures us that this trade-off results in benefits for the cluster as whole: 'Any increases in competition comes with cluster benefits in productivity, flexibility, and innovation' (Porter 1998*d*: 256). Similarly, the coexistence of competition and cooperation rests on the assumption that either knowledge spillovers do not take place across competitors, or that the costs of knowledge spillovers across competitors are outweighed by the benefits from other forms of knowledge spillover.

By contrast, the view of inter-firm relationships presented in *Competitive Strategy* and *Competitive Advantage* is more straightforward, emphasizing rivalry and competition only. Under the Five Forces and Value Chain frameworks, profitability hinges on how total value is distributed among firms in an industry and their suppliers and buyers, and the extent to which firms in an industry are under pressure from the threat of substitutes, potential entrants, or existing rivals. In other words, Porter conceives competition as a power game between individual companies. In *Competitive Advantage*, Porter recognizes knowledge spillovers across firms through suppliers, consultants, ex-employees, and the reverse engineering of products. However, he suggests that a firm's sustainable advantage stems only from proprietary learning, not from total industry learning (Porter 1985a: 73–4). Hence, customers, suppliers, substitutes, and potential entrants are all competitors to firms in an industry under the Five Forces and Value Chain frameworks.

In sum, Porter's thinking has diversified into two distinct strands of ideas throughout his career. The two strands are distinct from each other in terms of the questions they pose, the performance indicators they use, the sources of competitive advantage on which they focus, and the inter-firm relationships they envisage. Between them, one does not supplant the other. As Porter comes to consider a wider range of issues, he selectively applies one of the two strands of his core ideas.

1.6 Porter's interdisciplinary orientation

Breakthrough insights occur when people see beyond their expertise, with an eye toward putting available materials together in new combinations. There is a tension between efficiency and creativity arising from the homogeneity of skills, approaches, and languages within a discipline. Efficient and effective communication takes place most frequently between members of a community who share common skills, approaches, and languages. The evolution of local 'languages' through iterative communication within a discipline allows speedier and more accurate exchanges of knowledge. Yet, homogeneity within a discipline may also stifle creativity. Creativity and insight can be incredibly vibrant through the cross-fertilization of different disciplines, and Porter has engaged with this creative process throughout his career. In an interview, Porter suggests:

> I think real innovation in ideas requires the bridging of different disciplines. I see my work as integrative. (Stonehouse and Snowdon 2007: 271)

As noted earlier, Porter's educational background is characterized by its cross-disciplinary orientation. He received his academic training in industrial organization economics (PhD in business economics in 1973), after studying engineering (BSE in aerospace and mechanical engineering in 1969) and business administration (MBA in 1971). His interdisciplinary orientation is evident in *Competitive Strategy*, bridging industrial economics and business policy.

Although he principally sees himself as an economist (Stonehouse and Snowdon 2007: 262), his interdisciplinary orientation remains unchanged and becomes even more strongly manifested as his work evolves, covering an increasing number of disciplines. For instance, *Competitive Advantage* cuts across many disciplines in management including marketing, finance, and operations, in addition to the business policy and industrial economics already covered in *Competitive Strategy*. He emphasizes that 'competitive advantage cannot be truly understood without combining all these disciplines into a holistic view of the entire firm' (Porter 1985a: xvi). In *The Competitive Advantage of Nations* he goes further to include a more diverse range of fields such as 'technological innovation, industrial economics, economic development, economic geography, international trade, political science, and industrial sociology, that are not usually combined' (Porter 1990a: xiii). Reflecting on this growing coverage of diverse disciplines in *The Competitive Advantage of Nations*, he stresses the limitations stemming from specialization: 'In studying national economic success, there has been the tendency to gravitate to clean, simple explanations and to believe in them as an act of faith in the face of numerous exceptions. The growing specialization of disciplines has only reinforced such a perspective. More can be done. Researchers in many fields of study are just beginning to recognize that traditional boundaries between fields are limiting' (Porter 1990a: 29).

1.7 Porter's other works

In addition to his four major books – *Competitive Strategy* (1980a), *Competitive Advantage* (1985a), *The Competitive Advantage of Nations* (1990a), and *On Competition* (1998c, updated and expanded edition, 2008b) – Porter has written numerous complementary or related articles. Those writings discussing or applying the ideas of the Five Forces and Value Chain frameworks include Porter (1980b, 1981, 1983, 1987a, 1996b) and McGahan and Porter (1997, 1999), as well as those publications prior to the 1980 *Competitive Strategy* (Porter 1975, 1976b, 1979a). Porter reviews the Five Forces, Value Chain, and Diamond frameworks in an article published in the *Strategic Management Journal* in 1991 (Porter 1991) and revisits the Five Force framework in a *Harvard Business Review* article in 2008 (Porter 2008a). An article with Harrigan (Harrigan and Porter 1983) concerns strategies for declining industries, while a series of articles and an edited book (Hout et al. 1982; Porter 1986a, 1986b, 1986c, 1987b) focus on competition in global industries, as a forerunner to *The Competitive Advantage of Nations*. Those writings discussing or applying the ideas of *The Competitive Advantage of Nations* include Porter (1990b, 1992, 2004), Porter, Council on Competitiveness, and Monitor Company (2005), Porter et al. (2008), and Furman et al. (2002). Case studies of specific countries include Porter and Ketels (2003) on the United Kingdom, and Porter and

Takeuchi (1999), Porter et al. (2000), Porter and Sakakibara (2004), and Sakakibara and Porter (2001) on Japan. There is also a series of writings on the cluster concept, including Porter (1994, 1996a, 1998a, 1998b, 2000b, 2000c, 2001b, 2003, 2005), Porter and Sölvell (1998), Porter and Stern (2001), Porter and Ketels (2009), and Porter et al. (2004).

After the publication of *The Competitive Advantage of Nations* (1990a), Porter further extended his research interests and has written on a number of new areas and topics. In these works, Porter often applies either of the Five Force/ Value Chain and the Diamond/cluster strands of ideas selectively in his analysis. For instance, following a joint-authored article with Victor Millar on information technology (Porter and Millar 1985), Porter (2001c) considers the impact of the Internet upon firm performance. Using the Five Forces/ Value Chain frameworks, he maintains the importance of strategy in the face of technical advances in ICT. He suggests: 'Because the Internet tends to weaken industry profitability without providing proprietary operational advantages, it is more important than ever for companies to distinguish themselves through strategy' (Porter 2001c: 63).

Increasingly, a significant proportion of Porter's time came to be occupied with issues of economic development. In an article published in *Harvard Business Review* in 1995, Porter deals with inner city development, and by applying the Diamond framework and the cluster concept he argues that the creation of economically viable companies is crucial to the development of inner cities in the United States. This article also shows a sign of his subsequent interest in corporate social responsibility: 'Countless companies give many millions of dollars each year to worthy inner-city social-service agencies. But philanthropic efforts will be more effective if they also focus on building business-to-business relationships that, in the long run, will reduce the need for social services' (Porter 1995: 66). In 1994 he founded the Initiative for a Competitive Inner City, a non-profit organization with a mission of fostering economic development in impoverished inner cities.

The environment has also become an area of key concern for Porter, particularly his work with Claas van der Linde (Porter and van der Linde 1995a, 1995b) and more recently with Forest Reinhardt (Porter and Reinhardt 2007). Porter criticizes the static view which argues that there is an inherent and fixed trade-off between the social benefits arising from environmental regulations and the private costs of prevention and clean-up. Through his research for *The Competitive Advantage of Nations*, Porter realizes that 'the costs of addressing environmental regulations can be minimized, if not eliminated, through innovation that delivers other competitive benefits' (Porter and van der Linde 1995a: 125). Hence he argues: 'Properly designed environmental standards can trigger innovation that lowers the total cost of a product or improves its value' (Porter and van der Linde 1995a: 120). As with his work on inner city development, Porter's thinking – that is, there is no inherent trade-off between social benefits and industry's private costs, and instead the pursuit of social benefits can make corporations more competitive – provides a natural conduit leading to his work on corporate social responsibility.

Corporate social responsibility is a subject Porter pursues with Mark Kramer (Porter and Kramer 1999, 2002, 2006). They work together as co-founders of the Center for Effective Philanthropy, a non-profit research organization located in Boston, as well as FSG Social Impact Advisors, an international non-profit consulting firm. In their view, the pursuit of social benefits through philanthropy can improve competitiveness by increasing productivity. They argue: 'Corporations can use their charitable efforts to improve *competitive context* – the quality of the business environment in the location or locations where they operate' (Porter and Kramer 2002: 58). There is a strong influence of the Diamond framework and the cluster concept upon this area of thinking, with its attention to location and emphasis on innovation in modern knowledge- and technology-based competition.

Another topic to which Porter has extended significant effort in recent years, jointly with Elizabeth Olmsted Teisberg, is health care services in the United States (Tesiberg et al. 1994a, 1994b; Porter and Teisberg 2006a, 2006b). Discussing health care reform, Porter and Teisberg apply the concept of generic strategies and argue that competition in the industry is currently undertaken at the wrong level, that is, reducing costs rather than improving quality. They suggest: 'The right goal is to improve value (quality of health outcomes per dollar expended), and value can only be measured at the disease and treatment level. Competing on cost alone makes sense only in commodity businesses, where all sellers are more or less the same. Clearly, this is not true in health care' (Porter and Teisberg 2006a: 67).

Between these works, Porter, with Jay Lorsch and Nitin Nohria, also wrote an article on the nature of leadership (Porter et al. 2004). Through a study of new chief executives of major companies, Porter and his colleagues identify seven surprises that new corporate leaders are most likely to face. They argue: 'How and how quickly new CEOs understand, accept, and confront them will have a lot to do with the executives' eventual success or failure' (Porter et al. 2004: 64).

1.8 Outline of the book

The rest of this book takes the following structure. Eleven chapters by expert contributors from strategic management, economics, and economic geography and planning are divided into three sections: Section 1 includes five chapters on *Competitive Strategy* and *Competitive Advantage*; Section 2 includes three chapters on *The Competitive Advantage of Nations*; and Section 3 includes three chapters on the cluster concept (*On Competition*). Following the three sections, the book ends with a concluding chapter by the editors.

Section 1 begins with a chapter by Jay B. Barney. In this chapter, Barney introduces the reader to the influence of Porter's thinking in the field of strategic management. The frameworks presented in Porter's seminal work, *Competitive Strategy*, addressed many of the central questions in what has since become the field of strategic management, such as: 'What is the appropriate dependent variable in strategic management research and practice?'; 'What is the proper theoretical framework for analyzing strategic management problems?'; 'What is the appropriate unit of analysis in this field?'; and 'What is the appropriate role of broader social issues in this field?' Barney suggests that after *Competitive Strategy*, strategic management became an academic discipline built around several well-articulated theories, all designed to address a single set of highly related questions.

Chapter 3 by J.-C. Spender and Jeroen Kraaijenbrink poses the question of why the book *Competitive Strategy* had such a huge impact and was so widely embraced by managers, policymakers, consultants, and strategy teachers, but at the same time was often criticized for its apparent shortcomings by strategy theorists. Spender and Kraaijenbrink consider the intellectual context and sources behind the book, and probe explanations of its impact. They explore the history of the industrial organization (IO) movement and its associated methodological issues and disputes. Through an examination of IO's relationship to contemporary business, Spender and Kraaijenbrink show that *Competitive Strategy*'s appeal to practitioners has little to do with the narrow logic of *homo economicus* or positivist notions of theoretical rigor. It is a framework to help strategists know what they should take into account as constraints on their options, so as to arrive at the 'managerial choices' for which their situation calls.

Chapter 4 by Robert E. Hoskisson, Michael A. Hitt, William P. Wan, and Daphne Yiu explores the influence IO economics has exerted on the theoretical and methodological frameworks of strategic management research, highlighting the significance of Porter's work in furthering its development. Applying the structure–conduct–performance framework of IO economics, Porter built a foundation for research on competitive dynamics: a description of the forces that determine the nature and level of competition in an industry, as well as suggestions for how to use this information to develop competitive advantage. Hoskisson, Hitt, and their colleagues show that strategic management has evolved into a firmly established field in the study of business and organizations, advancing from its 'humble' beginnings as the limited content of a capstone general management course in the business school curriculum.

The next two chapters offer a more critical examination of Porter's work in strategic management. In chapter 5, Omar Aktouf, Miloud Chennoufi, and W. David Holford suggest that while Porter's work is the basis of a systematic approach to strategy, it in no way guarantees the scientific rigor that he claims. They also offer a twofold critique concerning the 'real' reasons for the success enjoyed by Porter's work. At the ideological level, they argue that Porter's work legitimizes the current state of relations of force within and between firms operating in advanced capitalist economies, allowing dominant incumbents to draw arguments and reasons of a scientific nature to justify their domination. At the operational level, his work offers ease of comprehension, relative ease of implementation, and subsequent gratification from initial operational successes. In the view of Aktouf and his colleagues, operational successes derived from Porter's frameworks do not assure the achievement of a lasting, defensible, and non-easily imitable competitive advantage.

In chapter 6, Nicolai J. Foss shows that substantial changes have taken place in Porter's thinking from his PhD dissertation (Porter 1973) to his work on the role of location. While the doctrinal antecedents of the Porter industry analysis approach are clear and unambiguous – namely, IO economics in the Bain/Mason tradition – Porter has brought essentially resource-based insights into the frameworks of his later contributions, *Competitive Advantage* and *The Competitive Advantage of Nations*. Foss argues that this is not just a matter of Porter successively directing his attention to different analytical objects, it is also a matter of his attempting to approach different phenomena without applying the outgrowths of fundamental theory. According to Foss, the developments in Porter's thinking show that different theoretical alternatives are brought together in loose frameworks with no serious attempt to confront them and examine their logical relations; that is, in terms of whether they are consistent, complementary, or mutually exclusive.

Section 2 begins with chapter 7 by Robert M. Grant, who suggests that *The Competitive Advantage of Nations* has transformed thinking about the basis of national competitiveness and has had a substantial impact on public policies toward regional and national economic development. Grant argues that Porter's analysis of the impact of the national environment on international competitive performance demonstrates the potential for the theory of competitive strategy to rescue international economics from its slide into refined irrelevance, while simultaneously broadening the scope of the theory of competitive strategy to encompass both international dimensions and the dynamic context of competition. Nevertheless, Grant suggests that the breadth and relevance of Porter's analysis have been achieved at the expense of precision and determinacy. Grant points out that concepts are often ill defined, theoretical relationships poorly specified, and empirical data chosen selectively and interpreted subjectively.

In chapter 8, Jan Fagerberg focuses on one determinant of national advantage in the Diamond framework – demand conditions – and examines empirical evidence. Although the idea that the domestic market may affect competitiveness positively is by no means a new one, the publication of *The Competitive Advantage of Nations* led to increasing attention on the favorable impact that the domestic market, through 'advanced domestic users,' may have on the international competitiveness of a country. Fagerberg presents a critical appraisal of the theoretical and empirical evidence on the hypothesis that 'advanced domestic users' have a positive impact on the international competitiveness of a country. Examining evidence presented by three studies (Andersen et al. 1981*a*, 1981*b*; Fagerberg 1994, 1995; Beise-Zee and Rammer 2006), Fagerberg finds that their findings are consistent with the predictions made by Porter.

In chapter 9, Brian Snowdon assesses the contribution Porter made with *The Competitive Advantage of Nations* and his involvement in the World Economic Forum's *Global Competitiveness Report*. Snowdon focuses on Porter's attempt to bridge the gap between the micro-oriented strategic management literature and the economics literature relating to economic growth, development, and trade. As Snowdon indicates, Porter's analysis of the competitiveness of nations has proved to be an important and stimulating, if controversial, contribution. In particular, Porter has ignited a debate on the meaning and measurement of 'competitiveness' in the context of nations and regions. Snowdon also notes that Porter's leadership and research contribution to the World Economic Forum's (WEF) annual *Global Competitiveness Report* (GCR) has highlighted the importance of a nation's microeconomic fundamentals in providing the sound foundations necessary to foster sustained economic development and growth.

Section 3 begins with chapter 10 by Christian Ketels. In this chapter, Ketels looks at the origins of Porter's interest in clusters and identifies the key characteristics of his conceptual thinking and extensions of these core concepts in Porter's more recent work. Ketels then explores the policy implications that can be drawn from Porter's work on clusters. Discussing why Porter's work in this field has had such a profound impact, especially on practitioners, Ketels argues that Porter addresses the very specific needs of different practitioner constituencies, providing a framework and actionable ideas to which they can easily relate. Finally, Ketels turns to a number of open issues that will determine whether or not Porter's long-term impact on the practice and thinking in this field will reach its full potential. He suggests that in terms of academic scholarship, the future legacy of Porter's work on clusters will depend on whether his ideas will be reconnected to other related approaches in the field.

Chapter 11 by Edward J. Malecki traces the roots of Porter's cluster concept. Unusually for a business scholar, Porter has made important contributions to local and regional development. Malecki suggests that Porter's ideas are meshed with the emerging focus of economists, geographers, and regional scientists on innovation systems, inter-firm linkages, industry life cycle, and technological change. At the foundation of economic development, in its positive-sum, *generative* sense, are spillovers and increasing returns, which are exploited by the creation of local synergies among local actors and the integration of external connections into the local relational web. Although this is exactly what policymakers, regional development scholars, and Porter himself would like to generate, Malecki cautions that cluster policies run the risk of creating the illusion that the process is quick, rather than one that typically takes a long period of time to reach fruition.

Chapter 12 by Ron Martin and Peter Sunley offers a more critical account of the cluster concept than the other two chapters in this section. Clustering is claimed to be a key source of competitive advantage both for the firms involved and for the region where the cluster is located. Martin and Sunley examine the conceptual and empirical foundations for this argument. They outline the key elements in Porter's theory of 'clusters as drivers of competitiveness'. They then move on to the question of whether or not the available empirical evidence supports the model: 'Are firms inside clusters more competitive than their counterparts outside clusters?' This discussion then moves them on to consider how the cluster model differs from other modern reinterpretations of the concept of comparative advantage. Martin and Sunley argue that the cluster approach can be subsumed within a more general dynamic comparative advantage perspective on regional competitiveness. Some implications for cluster-based regional policies round off the chapter.

The book concludes with chapter 13, in which we not only provide an interpretation of the key perspectives and debates concerning Porter's contributions across the range of fields and disciplines into which he has delved, but also Porter's own views on his career, his contributions, and his critics. To this end, we draw on comments made by Porter in an interview he undertook with us at Harvard Business School in 2009. This interview provides a fascinating insight into the nature of Porter's thinking, especially in terms of seeking to connect the various strands that have contributed to his remarkable career.

Note

1. At Princeton he also played intercollegiate golf and was New England champion, and named to the 1968 NCAA Golf All-American Team. He was also an all-state high school football and baseball player in the state of New Jersey.

Section 1

Competitive Strategy and Competitive Advantage

2

Establishing strategic management as an academic discipline

Jay B. Barney

2.1 Introduction

The aim of this chapter is to review the influence of Porter's thinking in the field of strategic management, and how he helped to shape it as a distinct and credible academic discipline. There is little doubt that Michael Porter has been the most influential scholar in the field of strategic management over the last thirty years. The frameworks presented in his seminal work, *Competitive Strategy*, address many of the central questions in what has since become the field of strategic management. His answers to questions such as 'What is the appropriate dependent variable in strategic management research and practice?', 'What is the proper theoretical framework for analyzing strategic management problems?', 'What is the appropriate unit of analysis in this field?', and 'What is the appropriate role of broader social issues in this field?' continue to influence debates thirty years after *Competitive Strategy* was first published. Whether one agrees or disagrees with how Porter answered these questions, there can be no doubt that his answers have been influential.

Indeed, it would not be unreasonable to say that the publication of *Competitive Strategy* marked a fundamental change in the field of strategic management as we have come to know it. Before this book, the field was a loosely connected set of ideas built around some common organizing frameworks, with theories of limited scope and uncertain empirical implications. Since this book, the field has emerged as an academic discipline, built around several well-articulated theories, all designed to address a single set of highly related questions. Put differently, before *Competitive Strategy*, strategic management was not much more than an informed conversation. After *Competitive Strategy*, it became an academic discipline with important managerial implications.

2.2 Porter on the dependent variable

Before *Competitive Strategy* there was little consensus about the objective of strategic management practice or research. Some argued that strategic management should focus on how firms satisfy their customers, others that understanding the determinants of employee satisfaction should be the critical objective of the field, and still others that understanding how firms satisfy all their stakeholders should be the field's essential objective. Indeed, Porter provides a helpful summary of these different perspectives in the introduction to *Competitive Strategy*.

Porter's genius was to acknowledge the relevance of all these points of view, but then to focus on a single objective of strategic management research and practice that would facilitate the development of the field without entirely abandoning concerns for stakeholders besides a firm's equity holders. This objective was to understand the conditions under which a firm could obtain superior economic performance. Porter defined superior economic performance as a rate of return 'in excess of the return on government securities adjusted by the risk of capital loss' (Porter 1980a: 5) – what today we would call a rate of return in excess of a firm's cost of capital.

In this conceptualization of firm performance, equity holders are assumed to be a firm's residual claimants; that is, they appropriate all the profits generated by a firm after all other claims – by employees, customers, suppliers, and debt holders – are satisfied. Thus, in general, in order to maximize returns to its equity holders, a firm must pursue strategies that first satisfy all of its other stakeholders. In this sense, firm performance – as defined by Porter and others – is an outcome of the strategy-making process that is broadly consistent with the interests of all of a firm's stakeholders, not just its equity holders.

Of course, there will be circumstances where the interests of these different stakeholders will not be consistent and where simply maximizing returns to equity holders may hurt a firm's employees, customers, suppliers, or debt holders. This is an important economic issue that has led to some important research in its own right. For example, it has been addressed in several different literatures, including agency theory (Jensen and Meckling 1976), stewardship theory (Davis et al. 1997), and discussions of the balanced scorecard (Kaplan and Norton 1996). It is also a set of issues that Porter does not address in *Competitive Strategy*.

However, as important as these issues are, by focusing the field's efforts on understanding how firm strategies can generate a rate of return in excess of a firm's cost of capital, Porter helped set the stage for a revolution in the field of strategic management that continues to this day. By helping to create a consensus about the dependent variable in strategic management research and practice, Porter helped focus what had previously been a highly fragmented conversation. Without this focus, progress in theory or practice would have been difficult. Without this progress, current debates about the roles of different stakeholders in determining the performance of a firm would, themselves, probably have been less focused.

2.3 Porter on theory

Not only did Porter help the field settle on a dependent variable; he also made an argument about the kind of theoretical tools that would be most helpful in understanding that dependent variable: economic theory. The specific economic theory that Porter used is now well known: the structure, conduct, and performance paradigm. However, when *Competitive Strategy* was first published, the links between economic theory – any economic theory – and strategic management research and practice were not widely understood.

Porter's approach to applying the structure, conduct, and performance paradigm has also been influential. This paradigm was originally developed to help governments identify industries within which social-welfare-maximizing perfect-competition dynamics were not unfolding. *Competitive Strategy* turned this theory upside down and applied it to describe industries where firms could gain superior performance.

Other strategic management scholars have adopted a similar approach to applying economic theory to understanding strategic phenomena. For example, neoclassical price theory describes conditions under which competitive advantages enjoyed by a particular firm in an industry will be competed away through imitation. Resource-based logic turns neoclassical price theory upside down by altering one major assumption: that certain kinds of firm resources and capabilities are inelastic in supply. By altering this assumption, resource-based theory turns neoclassical logic from a theory that explains why competitive advantages cannot be sustained to a theory of why these advantages can be sustained.

Of course, Porter's emphasis on economic theory as the best way to analyze strategic management problems is not without critics. As a number of the following chapters in this volume illustrate, there is a growing recognition among many strategic management scholars and practitioners that a singular reliance on economic theory to develop the field has some important limitations. Questions about the impact of psychological and sociological phenomena on strategy formulation and implementation are receiving increased attention in both the research and practitioner literatures.

However, as was the case with the dependent variable in the field, that the field is moving away from a sole reliance on economic theory does not discount Porter's influence. Rather, without the rigor of economic theory being applied to the field of strategic management in the first place, it may have been more difficult to appreciate the psychological and sociological dimensions of strategy.

2.4 Porter on the unit of analysis

Porter's next key contribution, a focus on the industry as the unit of analysis, is derived directly from his choice of theoretical framework: the structure, conduct, and performance paradigm. Since that theoretical framework originally adopted the industry as the unit of analysis, it followed that applications of that framework – even turned upside down – would also adopt the industry as the unit of analysis. The choice of this unit of analysis enabled the development of one of the best known, and most widely applied, strategic management frameworks ever created: the Five Forces framework.[1]

In many ways, the choice of the industry as the unit of analysis in explaining why some firms are able to enjoy superior economic performance has been even more controversial than Porter's focus on economic performance as the dependent variable and his use of economic theory to develop the field of strategic management. At one level, no one can disagree with the assertion that the industry within which a firm operates should have a huge impact on the strategies that a firm pursues and on returns to those strategies. Moreover, no one can disagree with expanding the definition of competition to include a variety of individuals and institutions in an industry that seek to appropriate any superior performance of firms in that industry. However, an exclusive focus on industry determinants of firm performance can be quite problematic.

For example, such a focus suggests that, in the end, the most critical strategic choice a firm needs to make is in which industry or industries to operate. However, if the attractiveness of an industry is defined in ways that are independent of the resources and capabilities that a particular firm may possess – as is done when applying the Five Forces framework – then all competing firms will come to similar conclusions about which industries to enter, and entry into those industries cannot be expected to be a source of competitive advantage for any one firm.

Perhaps the best way to think about this emphasis on the industry as a unit of analysis is that Porter, in *Competitive Strategy*, was only beginning the conversation about how firms can apply economic logic to choose strategies that generate superior economic performance. Indeed, in the subsequent book *Competitive Advantage* (Porter 1985a), Porter develops a vocabulary that can be used to describe the resources and capabilities controlled by a particular firm. This vocabulary, called Value Chain analysis, helps focus attention on both the competitive environment within which a firm is operating and the specific business activities in which it engages to operate within that environment.[2]

2.5 Porter on social welfare

Still another implication of Porter's work in *Competitive Strategy* does not receive much emphasis in the book, *per se*, but has been the object of much debate and discussion ever since. This has to do with the role of social welfare in strategic management research and practice. In particular, the question posed by the arguments developed in *Competitive Strategy* is: 'Can prescriptions derived from the field of strategic management be consistent with maximizing social welfare, as it has traditionally been defined in economics, or are efforts to maximize both a firm's economic performance and broader social welfare inherently contradictory?'

The answer to this question in *Competitive Strategy*, once again, falls directly out of the theoretical apparatus that Porter used to develop the frameworks in that book: the structure, conduct, and performance paradigm. As suggested earlier, this framework was originally designed to identify industries where social-welfare-maximizing perfect-competition dynamics were not unfolding. By turning this logic upside down, Porter suggests that firms should focus their attention on industries where superior economic performance is possible.

Typically, these will be industries with low levels of rivalry, protected by barriers to entry, with few substitutes, and weak buyers and suppliers – industries that tend to be more monopolistic or oligopolistic in nature. Most economists agree that while firms in these kinds of industries can earn superior economic performance, the competitive processes in these industries are largely inconsistent with maximizing social welfare. Thus, in an important way, Porter's analysis in *Competitive Strategy* linked firms choosing strategies that can generate superior firm performance with actually reducing social welfare.[3]

Of course, an alternative to structure, conduct, and performance reasoning about industry structure and social welfare has existed in economics for some time. First introduced by Harold Demsetz, this approach suggests that the reason some firms in an industry may enjoy superior economic performance has less to do with their operating in a particular kind of industry and more to do with their differential ability to meet customer needs. Demsetz goes on to observe that the reasons these successful firms are successful 'may be very difficult to understand' (Demsetz, 1973). In this perspective, superior firm performance can, in fact, be consistent with maximizing social welfare, since firms with special resources and capabilities are simply using them to address customer needs efficiently and gain superior performance from doing so.

Demsetz (1973) further suggests that a firm's superior performance, far from being an indicator of anticompetitive forces in an industry, may actually result from competition itself.[4]

Any complete explanation of superior firm performance of course needs to recognize both the role of industry concentration, monopoly, and oligopoly, on the one hand, and the role of superior resources and capabilities, on the other. For example, a firm may gain superior performance initially because of its special resources and capabilities and, once it attains such a position, it may seek to sustain its competitive advantage through engaging in more monopolistic actions. In this sense, strategic management theory can be both inconsistent and consistent with maximizing social welfare in society, depending on the specific strategies a firm might pursue and the context within which they are pursued.

Porter has since discussed the social-welfare implications of his approach to strategic management more broadly. For example, in both his discussions of the competitive advantage of the inner city (Porter 1995) and the competitive advantage of nations (Porter 1990a), emphasis has shifted from engaging in activities that are inconsistent with social welfare to engaging in activities that are, in fact, consistent with social welfare. However, at a broader level, it is unlikely that the relationship between strategic management and social welfare would have arisen at all without the original and important work of Professor Porter published in *Competitive Strategy*.

2.6 A personal reflection

No one can have been a practicing strategic management scholar over the past thirty years without being deeply influenced by Michael Porter and his ideas. This is certainly true in my case. But I did not understand the magnitude of this influence until I attended a plenary session of the Strategic Management Society meetings held in Toronto, Canada, in the late 1980s.

There must have been over 500 people in the room – the best-known and most influential strategic management scholars and practitioners in the world. And in this unique setting, Michael Porter took much of his time discussing the limitations of a fledgling new theory with which I and several others were associated, a theory that has since come to be known as the resource-based view. I noted his criticisms and began developing, in my mind, how I some day would respond to them. What I had not anticipated was how my fellow strategic management scholars and practitioners would respond to Porter's criticisms. They congratulated me! While I was focusing on Porter's specific criticisms of the theory, they saw the bigger picture – that by criticizing the resource-based view, Porter was actually beginning to legitimate it as a theoretical perspective.

But only Michael Porter could have wielded such an influence, and this is what my colleagues recognized. The scholar who had set the stage for so much of the progress in the field of strategic management had, in a sense, invited us to begin to engage in a conversation about the future of the field. Once I realized what he had done, I was deeply honored by this recognition.

Acknowledgments

This is a revised version of Barney, J. B. (2002*b*) 'Strategic management: From informed conversation to academic discipline', *Academy of Management Executive*, 16(2), 53–7. I would like to thank the Academy of Management for permission to reproduce parts of the article.

Notes

1. Personally, I began to realize just how widely known this framework was when a colleague told me how his high-school sophomore had used the Five Forces framework to help his drama teacher decide which of several musicals to present that year.
2. In combination with the logic of competitive advantage developed in resource-based theory, Value Chain analysis is a very important tool that helps in identifying those firm-specific resources and capabilities that can be sources of sustained competitive advantage in a particular competitive environment. This perspective is developed in more detail in Barney (2002*a*).
3. These issues are discussed in more detail in Fried and Oviatt (1989) and Barney (2002*a*).
4. It also outlines the basic logic of what has since come to be known as the resource-based view of the firm.

3

Why *Competitive Strategy* succeeds – and with whom[1]

J.-C. Spender and Jeroen Kraaijenbrink

3.1 Introduction

Porter's extraordinary record of private, public, academic, and corporate accomplishment has diverse roots, but it is clear that the genesis, publication, and impact of *Competitive Strategy* shifted a promising career as a young award-winning Harvard economist into a very different gear. In this chapter we puzzle why the book has such impact and with whom – evidently widely embraced by managers, policymakers, consultants, and strategy teachers, though often criticized by strategy theorists for its shortcomings. At the same time it is impossible to overlook a curiosity – the disregard of Porter's work in the ongoing debates about the relevance of our field's research. For decades there has been rising concern about the gap between business school research and teaching and its value to the business community (Locke, 1996; Mintzberg, 2004, 2009; Starkey et al., 2004; Bennis and O'Toole, 2005; Spender, 2007). Hambrick's 1993 Presidential Address for the Academy of Management asked 'What if the Academy actually mattered?' (Hambrick 1994), and successive Academy Presidents have asked similar questions. In the breast-beating that followed (Ghoshal, 2005; Pfeffer, 2007), that Porter's work matters to a powerful constituency of business and national policy-makers has somehow been ignored. Thus, one of the lessons to be drawn from Porter's work is that some of our discipline's contributions do indeed matter – greatly (Brandenburger 2002). The question, of course, is why Porter's work matters when so much of our work does not.

In the following sections we summarize *Competitive Strategy*'s principal points and look at how the book was received by reviewers, management educators, theorists, and business practitioners. We consider the intellectual context and sources behind the book, and probe explanations of its huge impact. We conclude with some lessons for the rest of us.

3.2 The book

The iconic symbol of *Competitive Strategy* is the Five Forces framework diagram appearing on page 4 as Figure 1-1. Its comprehensiveness obscures that it is the book's point of departure, not its conclusion. Many readers of *Competitive Strategy* or its derivatives forget this, and for them the diagram becomes the book; there is little more to be said. But Porter has something very different in mind. His first sentence reads: 'The essence of formulating competitive strategy is relating a company to its environment' (Porter, 1980*a*: 1). This seems conventional enough – but does not explain why Porter finds it necessary to model the firm's environment in an unconventional way. Porter's Five Forces framework (hereinafter FFF) is this new model, configuring both the firm's industry and the competitors within it. It is a model of considerable subtlety with several levels, identifiable entities, and interactions. In contrast to microeconomic and marketing theory conventions, the FFF proposes that the firm's environment comprises of more than competitors. Likewise, 'industry' has little to do with industry as economists use the term; that is, Standard Industrial Classification (SIC) codes. Porter defines an industry very differently – as 'the group of firms producing products that are close substitutes for each other' (Porter, 1980*a*: 5). The point of doing this becomes evident in his next sentence: 'In practice there is often a great deal of controversy over the appropriate definition, centering around how close substitutability needs to be in terms of product, process or geographic market boundaries.' There is more than curious grammar here.

Defining products in terms of their substitutes might seem oblique. But it provides a novel way of analyzing the firm's environment. Porter's definition presumes a conceptual 'barrier' between products rather than any straightforward description of the goods and services the firm's production function generates. For instance, we know that inputs of glass, steel, plastic, leather, rubber, copper wire, computer parts, skilled labor, and so forth can produce many different types of automobile. Yet, though the engineering is closer than some would care to admit, a BMW is not like a Chevrolet when it comes to a competitive strategic analysis of the firms producing them. Strategizing based on microeconomics alone pays attention to manufacturers' pricing and its impact on the interplay between supply and demand, noting the maximization of revenue at the point of market equilibrium.

Porter goes well beyond such neoclassical thinking. The barriers he has in mind are not related to a single product market or industry; he presumes a multiplicity of interacting products and industries. Nor is an industry to be defined by its products—it is defined by 'barriers'. These vary from the impenetrable to the easily penetrated. As an extreme example, the distance between tableware and fashion garments is so great that it constitutes a barrier impenetrable even for Martha Stewart. In contrast, the barrier between automobiles and fashion is often penetrable; a Smart Car or a Maserati may be more of a fashion statement than a means of transport. More obviously, the barrier between motorized mowers and chain saws is highly permeable (Porter, 1983: 189). In *Competitive Strategy*, the barriers of interest are those between industries capable of interfering with each other – 'substitutability' being a term of art that implies interference with the firm's pursuit of its goals.

The analysis Porter offers stands on the material difference between competition as economists define it and what Porter refers to as 'rivalry' – the interactive situation managers should consider in their strategic choosing. Porter's analysis is for managers. For economists, competition is a structural matter, whether or not a firm has competitors, competition that can be measured in various ways – such as an industry concentration ratio or the Herfindahl Index. Much of the power of the FFF is that it reaches beyond the industry's incumbent firms to consider other entities. Porter argues that competitive strategy is a condition of 'extended rivalry' in which customers, suppliers, firms offering substitutes, and potential entrants are all rivals whenever they are able to influence or interfere with the focal firm's rent streams (Porter, 1980*a*: 8). This presumes economic power based on some economically significant sources or resources. Economists distinguish various types of rent – Ricardian, Paretian, entrepreneurial, Penrosian, and so on – some arising from Nature's randomly distributed gifts, others from Man's inventions, others resulting from government's actions, yet others from management-created entry barriers – and the relationships between these rent types are complex (Rumelt, 1987: 144; Mahoney and Pandian, 1992; Spender, 1994).

Porter glosses over these differences, as well as the way some rents are affected by factors beyond management's control – global warming, technological change, resource depletion, and so on. *Competitive Strategy* focuses directly on the rent-shaping behaviors influenced by a firm's management without identifying the rents in question, for Porter's attention is on rent-shaping rivalry and not on the rents themselves. While seldom able to influence the presence or absence of competition, managers can often alter an industry's degree of rivalry, particularly by engaging in or eschewing price competition. Even when there is plenty of competition in the sense of many suppliers and a low concentration ratio, there may be little or no rivalry. Competing firms often engage in collusion as a method of decreasing rivalry, while even a monopolistic firm can face rivalrous pressure from its customers and suppliers.

Porter's analysis begins by disaggregating the factors that influence rivalry into distinct categories – the 'five forces'. Having introduced these at an abstract level, Porter brings them into the context of practical management with a Bain-based discussion of the various kinds of entry barriers (Porter, 1980a: 7). For Porter, economies of scale are strategically significant – not because they can lead to lower production costs but because they can be both warning signals and practical impediments to entry by other firms that have not achieved such economies. Switching costs present a potential entrant with disincentives. To be denied access to distribution channels provides the potential entrant with no viable way of entering, and so on. The FFF's stress is on the dynamics of preventing others' strategic action rather than on determining the industry's structure and its consequences.

The analysis in *Competitive Strategy* becomes explicitly dynamic and akin to multi-period game theory, as Porter considers 'expected retaliation' as incumbents respond to an entrant's acts or threats to act. All of this leads to the FFF-based characterization of the firm's situation or state of rivalry it is experiencing (Porter, 1980a: 17). The FFF implies three levels of interaction: (*a*) the conventional microeconomist's level, between the industry's incumbent firms; (*b*) a well-defined extended level between the firm and its existing trading partners, and those already offering substitute products and services; and (*c*) a more nebulous extended level between the firm and the potential industry entrants offering new substitute products and services. *Competitive Strategy*'s primary objective is not to help managers see rivalry's importance – they know that well enough. It is to illuminate this three-level complex and thereby help managers get a handle on what exactly they might be able to manage.

In Porter's view, every firm is located in a lumpy rent-field mapped by barriers that separate various domains of economic activity – each offering different rent possibilities. Firms may make strategic moves from one domain to another, seeking the higher rents of a 'better position' in the strategic landscape by exiting one line of business or entering another. Thus, many put Porter's work in a 'positioning school' (Mintzberg, 1987, 1990a, 1990b; Bowman et al., 2002). This clouds the analysis actually offered in *Competitive Strategy*. In the FFF, barriers define the significant rivalrous entities. Managing them requires an understanding of the barriers defining the strategic situation – and the relevant entities and their relationships. The positioning metaphor suggests that the firm's strategic objective is to reposition itself from one domain to another. Boundaries are penetrable to the degree which rents in one domain are accessible to an entrant from another domain.

But Porter also argues that while strategic repositioning is possible, rivalry can be provoked and managed by many other means. The FFF's implicit question is not 'which domain to enter' in the pursuit of new rents. On the contrary, the emphasis is on protecting the firm's existing rent streams from interference (reduction) by the various other entities comprising the firm's extended rivalry network. Porter discusses 'force' in several ways – bargaining power and signaled threats as well as actual acts of domain entry (Porter, 1980a: 6). Force and barrier are thought to be complementary, force being required to penetrate a barrier. Forces describe the dynamic relationships between the entities, tilting the analysis toward an active process view and away from a static structural view.

The treatment of force and dynamic process gradually reveals the book's true objective – little to do with the one-directional arrows in the FFF diagram. While Porter's esthetic may be to show the firm under pressure from everyone else, the relationships are two-way. Quasi-monopolists such as Wal-Mart exert considerable pressure on their suppliers, perhaps forcing them into bankruptcy, and likewise rebut the power of their customers (Moreton, 2009). Other firms, such as Microsoft, pressure their customers directly. Moreover, having acquired 'business intelligence' and developed expectations that a specific potential entrant is planning a strategic move against it, a firm might negotiate an alliance with the potential entrant, to their mutual benefit, or reset its prices to act against it. Likewise, at the extended level of the analysis, when negotiating with a specific supplier, a firm might 'second source', looking into the market for alternative suppliers or substitutes.

Competitive Strategy not only shows managers how to view their rivalrous environment from the vantage point of identifying and protecting their own current rent streams, but also advises them to pay attention to goings-on that might affect their rents in the future. For instance, they should note the number of competitors and their balance or concentration, the presence or absence of switching costs, the lumpiness of productive and distributive capacity, the height and strategic location of the exit barriers, and so on. The point here is the diverse and contingent nature of these rivalry-defining characteristics revealed through the FFF as a sketch of the network of power relations. In short, *Competitive Strategy* is about the nature and management of the firm's economic power and the resulting rents, and how it might manage its responses to the actions and threats of powerful others. This power is contingent on the specifics of the firm's strategic and economic situation and the actions and strategic intentions of those able to engage in it. The multifaceted empirical details offered here cannot be summarized in overarching concepts, be they economic, structural, strategic, or behavioral. The FFF is a framework for selecting, viewing, and attending to these heterogeneous empirical realities. Porter's proposition is that a firm's managers must understand these different interactions and types of power if they are to deploy the power available to them effectively.

Aside from obvious questions about how to operationalize these ideas or make a specific strategic decision, there is some question about whether *Competitive Strategy* proposes a theory of strategy. Many presume that Porter's analysis eventually identifies a domain of strategic opportunity determined by the industry environment, and that the firm should then position itself there by selecting one of the three generic strategies (cost leadership, differentiation, and focus) (Porter, 1980a: 34). We think this interpretation is peripheral rather than central to the book, even though it has given rise to the principal academic critiques of *Competitive Strategy* (for example, Hendry 1990). More to the point, if strategy is about executives deciding what to pay attention to, given their limited attention, *Competitive Strategy* is very much about strategy even though a specific strategic prescription is not generated. Likewise, if strategy is about making actionable sense of a complex, uncertainty-driven situation that in practice cannot be grasped with a rigorous one- or two-dimensioned model, then *Competitive Strategy* is about strategy. Inasmuch as strategy is about formal analysis and decision-making, Porter's book pushes the discussion forward from obsessive concern with the market share held by the industry's other firms toward understanding the industry's attractiveness and growth rate. But it comes at some cost to clarity. How might a firm's capabilities be measured against those of unknown potential entrants at the third, most nebulous, level of the FFF's analysis? How might the possibilities opened up by its dynamic non-equilibrium analysis be reconciled with rigorous econometric models? Evidently, balancing the use value of the FFF against its clarity calls for some authorial strategic decision-making, and there seems no question that Porter's academic strategizing has proven successful.

3.3 Initial reception

To understand how *Competitive Strategy* was received we have to take Porter's earlier writings into account, in particular his 1976 article in *California Management Review* (CMR) and his 1979 article in *Harvard Business Review* (HBR). In the *CMR* piece, Porter deploys the list-making style so evident and perhaps overdone in *Competitive Strategy*. But after seven pages he moves to report his PIMS-based analysis of 310 firms with chronically low returns – candidates for industry exit whose non-exit indicated the presence of strategically significant exit barriers. Though he does not present the statistical tables typical of scholarly journals, he reports the statistical significance of the variables chosen and so on. We can see from Porter's earlier works that he was no stranger to statistical economic analysis (Porter, 1973, 1974, 1976a, 1979b). Likewise, his economics articles published jointly with Caves and others are academic (Caves et al., 1975, 1977, 1980; Caves and Porter 1976, 1977, 1978, 1980). In contrast, *CMR* is a practitioner-oriented journal, the West Coast equivalent of *HBR*, and Porter's 1976 piece is an attempt to write for a non-academic business audience that has its mind on the firm's performance. Its citations are also revealing – ten only and with the exception of Gilmour's DBA thesis on divestment decision-making, all practitioner-oriented.

Porter further polished his style of addressing practitioners in the *HBR* article 'How competitive forces shape strategy' (Porter, 1979*a*), which attracted considerable attention. Its revealing subtitle is 'Awareness of these forces can help a company stake out a position in its industry that is less vulnerable to attack', the active process view we find laid out in *Competitive Strategy*. In the light of the complex and multilayered nature of the concepts involved and the conceptual differences between price changes, bargaining power, and threats, the clarity and directness of the *HBR* article's language is striking. It completely eschews academic style and terminology and is a fine example of writing for the 'reflective practitioner'. Its sole citation is to Porter's earlier 1976 article on exit barriers in *CMR* (Porter, 1976*b*).

Clearly, Porter learned a great deal about writing for practitioners between the 1976 *CMR* and 1979 *HBR* articles. He also placed a version of the *HBR* article in the *Financial Analysts Journal* in the 1980s (Porter, 1980*b*). Both suggested a larger work in the background – *Competitive Strategy* – the manuscript of which was mentioned along with a co-authored work (Caves et al. 1990) in the bio details of the *HBR* article. During our interview, Porter told us he drafted the first version of *Competitive Strategy* around 1975, only to put it aside as clumsy and overly dependent on 'stylized' academic economics. Around the same time he began teaching a class on Industry Competitive Analysis (ICA). It became a hit with the MBA students. For these students he wrote the first of several versions of his 'Note on the structural analysis of industries' (Porter, 1975). This evolved into chapter 1 of *Competitive Strategy* and, as we have seen, it contains all the fundamental concepts of the book – with one notable exception: chapter 2's 'generic strategies' that, in our interview, Porter suggested was almost an afterthought. The Note was also the basis for the 1979 *HBR* article. Leveraging from what he was learning from teaching his ICA course, Porter spent three years rewriting the manuscript, fleshing out the 1975 Note written not to his economic colleagues or even the business practitioners he mentions in *Competitive Strategy*'s Preface, but to his students.

On the whole, *Competitive Strategy* was well received by academic reviewers. Most praised its usefulness to practitioners. The book was brought to the attention of the business world in October 1981 by Kiechel, who did a series on management strategies in *Fortune* (Kiechel III, 1981). He devoted three full pages to an upbeat executive summary, accentuating Porter's three generic strategies. Lewis, a consultant with Strategic Planning Associates, reviewed the book in *Strategic Management Journal* (*SMJ*). He began: 'Finally, the power of economic theory has been brought to bear on the practical problems of business strategy … *Competitive Strategy* promises to revolutionize the creative process underlying the selection and formulation of strategies' (Lewis, 1981: 93). Another important supportive comment by Shubik, the father of modern game theory, appeared in 1983: 'The book by Porter contains a useful checklist that to some extent puts the older economic studies of oligopoly theory and industrial organization on their heads and reviews their contributions from the viewpoint of the corporate planner' (Shubik, 1983: 170).

More critical was a 1981 three-part review by Steiner, Hertz, and Boyd that appeared in the *Journal of Business Strategy (JBS)*. Steiner of UCLA, then corporate strategy's leading academic, reported that Porter had introduced 'an important new frame of reference and new techniques that strategic managers will find of great value' and that the attention to competition, largely overlooked in the strategy literature of the time, was done 'superbly' (Steiner, 1981: 84). But he expressed concern about the enormity, time- and cost-wise, of a full-blown industry analysis. Hertz, likewise generally complimentary, noted that talking about competition was not new and that much of Porter's analysis arose out of management consulting practice – even though *Competitive Strategy* provided a road map to the strategy-choosing process, giving CEOs 'much needed comfort as well as a supportive basis for making hard decisions' (Hertz, 1981: 87). Boyd, a marketing academic, noted that the marketing literature is replete with analyses of the relationship between strategy and the specifics of product, price, channels, and promotions, and that previous work on product positioning and market segments had been particularly significant: 'What has been missing is a framework for developing an "optimum portfolio of product-market strategies" that would link market response to expenditures to obtain a "best yield"' (Boyd, 1981: 85). Then he added: 'The Porter book does not fill this void.' While he regarded several chapters as worth reading, he concluded that *Competitive Strategy* in its entirety could not be recommended to marketing practitioners.

The next issue of *JBS* had further reviews by Collier and Henderson. Collier's was a lengthy summary of the contents of each chapter, with little comment. He found *Competitive Strategy* a well-written book, useful for practitioners and students alike, that should be in the library of every practitioner of strategic planning (Collier, 1981: 85). The review by Henderson – founder of the Boston Consulting Group (BCG) and author of the BCG matrix – was very different. While he found it a 'monumental book' that should be in every executive's library as a reference, he also criticized the book for lacking the integration and systems analysis needed to qualify as a treatise on strategy: 'In spite of the title this book is not about strategy. It does not attempt to integrate this material into a system of relationships. . . . The substance of the book is a catalog of things to be considered in doing an analysis of the competitive situation. . . . But it evokes an underlying feeling of frustration. Which of these factors are critical? How do they trade off against each other?' (Henderson, 1981: 84–5).

MIT's Bowman reviewed the book in *Sloan Management Review* and offered mixed views that reflected some of Henderson's concerns in more academic language. After going through the contents and complimenting Porter on his pedagogical style, Bowman was explicitly critical. 'There are however some disturbing elements in this style carried throughout the book, which is perhaps explained by the point that it is the practitioner who is being addressed. The reader, at least this academic reader, is frequently left with a question: On what basis can the author make this statement?' (Bowman, 1981: 67). Noting Porter's evident academic talent and citing some of his economics publications, Bowman wrote: 'this reviewer hopes that Professor Porter will now write another book, not unlike this one, but addressed to his academic colleagues and their graduate students... my preference would have been a much more systemic inclusion of research findings in the chapters where appropriate. This would be more satisfactory for the scholar's epistemological search for "veritas"' (Bowman, 1981: 67–8).

Competitive Strategy also received attention in the marketing journals. Fox, a marketing academic, reviewed it in the *Journal of Marketing*. He concluded: 'This short review does not do justice to Porter's numerous findings and insights.... Inevitably in this comprehensive coverage, knowledgeable practitioners and academicians will recognize some familiar ideas. Other findings or conclusions may seem obvious in retrospect. The book could also be faulted for repetitiousness.... This reviewer found the contents highly stimulating and helpful' (Fox, 1982: 124). Another marketing-based review by Leo, an Assistant General Counsel for Scovill Inc., appeared in *Industrial Marketing Management*. Leo concluded: 'Much of the advice set forth... is given in a commonsense style that might be obvious to many. The strength of the book, however, is mainly in its comprehensive style rather than its innovativeness... the benefit of *Competitive Strategy* is assuring that each element is closely considered as a single factor interrelated with others in the industry environment' (Leo, 1982: 319).

Surprisingly, there were no reviews of *Competitive Strategy* in any *Academy of Management* journal until Gartner's appeared in the *Academy of Management Review* (*AMR*) (Gartner, 1985). But Porter's next blockbuster *Competitive Advantage* (Porter, 1985a) had already appeared, as had his *Cases in Competitive Strategy* (Porter 1983). In short, the FFF machine was rolling and its success undeniable. Gartner reviewed both *Competitive Strategy* and *Competitive Advantage*. He opened by noting that Porter's ideas come from industrial economics: 'Both books make accessible some of the ideas originating in the Industrial Organization (IO) literature, though Porter does not provide references to ground his ideas in the literature' (Gartner, 1985: 874). Seemingly unaware of Porter's 1981 article on IO's impact on strategy theory in *AMR*, Gartner continued: 'A disappointment with both of these books is their somewhat myopic or selective view of the strategic management literature. No recognition of other views of strategic typologies was given, though many thoughtful, empirically generated studies have been undertaken' (Gartner, 1985: 875).

What is to be made of these reviews? Did they foreshadow *Competitive Strategy*'s success? A common compliment is to Porter's non-academic writing style, and this was clearly important. A second is the recognition that *Competitive Strategy* was for practitioners – as Porter emphasized in its revealing Preface. Third is the book's comprehensiveness – lists of the contextual characteristics managers should pay attention to – lists, for some, to a fault, but for others, such as Bowman, still missing the firm itself and its people. Fourth, especially from the marketing scholars, a sense of *déjà vu* – old stuff, though nicely packaged. Fifth, for strategy theorists, a valuable correction to the one-dimensionality of much strategy literature and its obsession with market share. But there was nothing that would portend the book's success. Indeed, for some, there was a sense of frustration and pushback from those asking 'where is the theory?' This is explicit in Bowman. Henderson too is asking 'how does it come together into a prescription?' – a practitioner's way of talking about deterministic theory. For Porter this particular criticism was not new.

The term 'theory' is glaringly absent from Porter's *CMR* and 1979 *HBR* articles, as it is from *Competitive Strategy*. Likewise, Veendorp's 1978 review of Porter's earlier Wells Prize-winning *Interbrand Choice, Strategy and Market Power* asked the same question (Porter, 1976a). Veendorp wrote: 'The theoretical part of the book...is somewhat disappointing' (Veendorp, 1978: 671). Curiously, while in the 1976 book's chapter 8, Porter writes: 'These premises spawned the theory presented in Chapters 2 through 5' (Porter, 1976a: 232), there is actually no mention of theory in these chapters. We do, however, find the term 'framework' – and the difference between the two is crucial to Porter's thought and works. But the reviews also present us with a significant empirical fact, that is, the lack of a specifically testable theory, expressible as the hypotheses that characterize our scholarly journals, was clearly no impediment to the book's success and may, perhaps, have been a kind of cause.

In the next section we look at the commentaries on *Competitive Strategy* that have appeared since these early reviews. For these later authors, *Competitive Strategy*'s success is not to be doubted. Our agenda is to see if they throw any additional light onto why.

3.4 Impact

Getting a handle on *Competitive Strategy*'s impact – beyond citations – is not as simple as it might seem. Hearsay has it that the FFF is taught in most undergraduate and MBA strategy courses around the world (Shih, 2007). No question, it is wonderfully teachable and easily remembered – but so are SWOT, the

BCG matrix, and break-even analysis. How do FFF and other strategy tools actually impact strategic management or our research and publication practices? The bibliographic data presented by Furrer et al. (2008) are interesting. They researched the occurrence of keywords in four leading management research journals – *Academy of Management Journal, Academy of Management Review, Administrative Science Quarterly*, and the *Strategic Management Journal* – between 1980 and 2005. Bearing in mind Steiner's comment (1981) that *Competitive Strategy* brought 'competition' into the foreground of strategic analysis, we can hypothesize an association between the greater use of 'competition' and *Competitive Strategy*'s publication. Furrer et al.'s findings are that 'competition' occurred in 6.1 percent of papers between 1980 and 1985, but rose sharply to 16.2 percent in 1986–90, to be sustained at a similar rate in the 1991–5, 1996–2000, and 2001–5 intervals. 'Planning' plummeted from 26.7 percent in the 1980–5 period to 3.2 percent in the 2001–5 period. Other terms go up and down; there is a steady erosion of 'methodology' and 'mission' and a big increase in 'alliances' and 'capabilities'. 'Fit' almost disappears, and 'leadership' barely makes an appearance.

Bibliographic research reveals keyword usage but does little to explicate a term's meaning. Although objective measures are slippery, we can grasp part of *Competitive Strategy*'s impact from the way various writers who trace the evolution of the strategy field have – or have not – written about it. No question, Porter is recognized as a major influence in retrospective analyses of the strategy field (Caves, 1984; McKiernan, 1996, 1997; Hoskisson, et al. 1999; Gavetti and Levinthal, 2004). Yet the limited mention of his book in earlier studies reminds us of how slowly ideas percolate through our literature. Bower, one of Porter's colleagues at Harvard Business School (HBS), published a review of the business policy field in 1982. *Competitive Strategy* rates only four sentences with Bower arguing: 'the elaborated language of structural analysis does not solve the strategist's problem, though it makes its specification more precise' (Bower, 1982: 633). More generally, the early reviews of the strategy field revealed no signs of why *Competitive Strategy* might eventually become a major influence on strategy (Dutton et al., 1983; Hamermesh, 1983; Horovitz, 1984; Lamb, 1984; Eliashberg and Chatterjee, 1985; Ginsberg and Venkatraman, 1985; Enz, 1986; Bresnahan and Schmalensee, 1987).

Kiechel's 1981 *Fortune* article indicated that the book was already being widely read by managers, plus there were stories that every recruit to the rapidly expanding consulting and accounting firms would be handed a copy and told to read it as a way of getting to know what they were supposed to be doing. The rising sales would support this view. The book's uptake seemed immediate; managers found no difficulty with the concepts or the conclusions to which they led – nor have subsequent generations of undergraduate and graduate students. As mentioned already, Porter's disciplined communication skills and authorial talents, carefully honed throughout the years in which *Competitive Strategy* was gestating, as well as his two-pronged business and academic publishing strategy, were important contributing factors.

Gradually things changed, but only after the focus shifted and views of *Competitive Strategy* began to emphasize its different audiences. In the classroom the FFF took on a life of its own as a highly teachable strategy tool, to be set alongside SWOT, BCG matrix, scenario analysis, Seven-S, and so on. Practicing managers did not flock to *Competitive Strategy* because they were interested in the academic niceties of strategic group definition or the marketing theory behind generic strategies – they liked the FFF. Likewise, strategy teachers learned the value of presenting their students with the FFF, maybe as one tool in a strategic toolbox, together with cases on which to try it out. Here the FFF was immediately comprehensible with its implicit balance between industry-level opportunities and threats and firm-level resources and processes.

In contrast, an increasing number of strategic, economic, and legal academics took exception to *Competitive Strategy*'s assumptions, casting doubt on the rigor or clarity claimed for the FFF. While some thought the analysis novel and insightful, others felt that Porter had borrowed too liberally from Scherer's earlier theorizing (Scherer, 1970). Others echo some of the earlier academic reviewers' misgivings; that is, the principal criticism being methodological, with many of the points Porter makes lacking any justification; making the choice of forces seemingly arbitrary; and resulting in an inability to operationalize any analysis based on these forces (Speed, 1989: 9). There was also the matter of a missing chapter that might address the political, regulatory, and legal constraints on monopolistic activity and corporate form – a 'sixth force' perhaps (Fried and Oviatt, 1989).

Rumelt et al.'s examination (1991) of the relationship between strategic management and economics provided a substantial commentary. Reflecting the thinking developed in an earlier paper (Rumelt and Wensley, 1981), the authors argued: 'The most influential contribution of the decade [1980s] from economics was undoubtedly Porter's *Competitive Strategy*... In a remarkably short time, Porter's applications of mobility barriers, industry analysis, and generic strategies became broadly accepted and used in teaching, consultation, and many research projects' (Rumelt et al., 1991: 8). Considering the FFF along with the resource-based view (RBV) and its relatives, they continued: 'the single most significant impact of economics in strategic management has been to radically alter explanations of success.... success is now seen as sustained by mobility barriers, entry barriers, market preemption, asset specificity, learning, ambiguity, tacit knowledge, non-imitable resources and skills, the sharing of core competences, and commitment' (Rumelt et al., 1991: 13).

They also noted a shift in business school culture from behaviorism toward economics, impelled largely but not entirely by the success of Porter's approach. The historical analysis of this shift comprised a substantial part of their paper, leading to the hypothesis that *Competitive Strategy*'s success may have been less to do with its content than to changes in the business and academic environment. Khurana's analysis of the same shift – especially the widespread acceptance of shareholder value over social benefit as the principal aim of management – supported this (Khurana, 2007).

Just as academic reviews of *Competitive Strategy* began to criticize the lack of theory, Porter made an interesting move, reworking a 1979 Academy of Management Meeting paper into an *AMR* paper: 'Contributions of industrial organization to strategic management' (Porter 1981). Had *Competitive Strategy* been written toward academics rather than to practicing strategists and his ICA students, it would surely have included this paper's points in a theory and methodology chapter. It might also have included many of the academic arguments then evident in Porter's economic papers. Thus, the 1981 paper helped highlight the differences between the business and academic communities, not merely on the basis of their divergent interests and intellectual modalities, but also in terms of what was going on in their respective environments. *Competitive Strategy*'s core assumption was obviously not neoclassical in the sense of looking for an equilibrating microeconomic model. Rather it presumed the dynamism, heterogeneity, and uniqueness of each firm's situation – and academics and business practitioners have different responses to this. Academics look for generalizations across multiple situations, while practitioners look to the impact on their specific situation.

While managers and students revel in the FFF, the more closely the foundations of *Competitive Strategy* were scrutinized by academic researchers and theorists, the less supported they found it. But, interestingly, they fastened onto arguments about the generic strategies, pushing closer analysis of the FFF and the strategy making of Part III of *Competitive Strategy* to one side. The root question is about the nature of the goods in the *Competitive Strategy* package. If we focus on the FFF, *Competitive Strategy*'s principal contribution, the academic complaints about a lack of theory were sustained rather than rebutted. As Bowman anticipated, subsequent theorizing and research has not provided support that was not already available when the book was published. But if *Competitive Strategy*, or more precisely chapter 1 and Part III, the bits that managers take to immediately, did not offer a viable theory of corporate strategy in imperfect markets – those in which rents are presumed available – what did it offer? And why was what it offered so stunningly popular?

3.5 The success's roots

Our explanation of *Competitive Strategy*'s success requires a look at the background against which the FFF was formed and the theoretical sources on which Porter drew. We reveal how the terms Porter used gathered their meaning, making it possible for us to get behind and problematize them. We get into the history of the IO movement and its associated methodological issues and disputes. The idea here is not to develop an academic history of IO, an economic historian's activity. It is to probe *Competitive Strategy*'s appeal to practitioners via an examination of IO's relationship to contemporary business, and to show that it has little to do with the narrow logic of *homo economicus* or positivist notions of theoretical rigor.

Porter's 1981 *AMR* paper, the first part of the methodology theory chapter thought missing from *Competitive Strategy*, sets off from the Learned, Christensen, Andrews, and Guth (LCAG) (1965) framework that underpinned HBS casework in business policy and strategy at the time – a framework that goes back at least to McNair et al. (1949) and Smith (1951). This framework was HBS's imprimatur when Porter arrived there in 1969 to begin his MBA. It is often presented as the four-box diagram that appears as Figure 1 in Porter's 1981 paper and as Figure 1-2 in *Competitive Strategy*. It says that the strategist's task is to reconcile and synthesize four 'strategic elements': (*a*) company strengths and weaknesses, (*b*) industry-level economic and technical opportunities and threats, (*c*) the personal views of key implementers, and (*d*) broader societal expectations. Like the FFF, this diagram deals with complex matters in a disarmingly presentable way.

Porter wrote: 'LCAG offered a series of general but logically compelling consistency tests that could help a firm probe its strategy to see if it truly related these elements' (Porter 1981: 610). But he went on to criticize: 'The high-performing (high return on investment) firm in LCAG's framework was one that had found or created a position in its industry where such consistency was present. However, LCAG offered no help in assessing the "contents" of each of the boxes in Figure 1 in a particular situation. That was left to the practitioner' (Porter 1981: 610). Close acquaintance with the LCAG framework – first as an MBA student and then later using it himself in the classroom – led to its lack of theoretical substance becoming Porter's intellectual target. As he noted: 'I wanted to influence thinking on business strategy by establishing a more analytical approach' (Stonehouse and Snowdon 2007: 262).

Porter's use of IO was instrumental to his achieving this. He wrote: 'The essence of this [Bain/Mason] paradigm is that the firm's performance in the marketplace depends critically on the characteristics of the industry environment in which it competes. . . . Industry structure determined the behavior or conduct of firms whose joint conduct then determined the collective performance of the firms in the marketplace' (Porter 1981: 610–1). The resulting IO paradigm 'offers a systematic model for assessing the nature of competition in an industry – one aspect of the four-part LCAG framework: industry opportunity and threats. . . . Thus the model can help firms predict a level of performance that can reasonably be expected. Unlike the ad hoc approach to industry analysis embodied in most policy literature, Bain/Mason is potentially a systematic and relatively rigorous one backed by empirical tests. Bain/Mason does *not* help the strategist with the other three key elements identified by LCAG' (Porter 1981: 611). He then went into reasons why strategy theorists had to date not made much use of the paradigm – an important matter. But he left the relationship between the LCAG and Bain/Mason paradigms up in the air, though his preference for the comprehensiveness of the LCAG model was obvious. Importantly, it is not clear whether he considered the LCAG model to be part of, or even compatible with, the IO tradition.

Ghemawat's 2002 review of strategy teaching at HBS filled in some of the background to the LCAG paradigm and to the development of today's box of strategy consulting tools; but he paid no attention to the theoretical issues or the paradigm's sources (Ghemawat 2002). He noted that 'business policy' goes back to HBS's earliest days – in 1912 it was a required second-year course. He recited the policy teaching developments in the 1940s and 1950s that preceded the LCAG period (Ghemawat 2002: 40–1). He noted the influence of a 'Harvard School' of economists, presuming Mason was a member of the Harvard Economics department. While this was true for a while before World War II (Markham and Papanek 1970: viii), Mason was actually a political scientist and development economist, and from 1947 to 1958 was Dean of what is now the Kennedy School of Government. Likewise, though Bain spent a year at Harvard (1951–2), his entire academic career was spent at UC Berkeley. After World War II an informal group of American IO researchers emerged that followed Mason's intellectual lead, including Bain, Tennant, and the Harvard-based Markham, McKie, and Caves (de Jong and Shepherd 2007: 209).

Harvard's economics department is not on the same campus as HBS, so both Porter and Ghemawat told of rediscovering IO economics 'across the river' in the Business Economics PhD program (Stonehouse and Snowdon 2007: 261). They talked competition, rivalry, and price flexibility. As Porter said: 'I suddenly realized the professors at both the Harvard Business School and the Department of Economics were talking about the same issues but they were coming from completely different perspectives.... While one intellectual tradition focused on case studies, treating each study separately, the other tradition focused on theory and statistical analysis. The idea of bridging these two fields led to my doctoral dissertation, which in turn ultimately led to my 1980 book on competitive strategy. Looking back, I can now see how my being in the right place at the right time, with inspiring mentors, allowed me to make the connections that led to my later work' (Stonehouse and Snowdon 2007: 261).

While Mason was a major influence on three Harvard schools – HBS, Economics, and Government – the source of the LCAG paradigm remained unclear. Did it come from Mason or elsewhere? Was it in the IO tradition at all? The question is not mere academic nitpicking, for the answer is central to understanding *Competitive Strategy*'s genesis and impact – our chapter's problematic.

3.6 Connecting with the past

Probing the relationship between the IO and the LCAG framework takes us into the theoretical background of the IO movement – especially the differences between Bain and Mason (1939*a*, 1939*b*, 1959). Bain was one of Mason's PhD students, and though they are often mentioned together it is important to appreciate that their theorizing was toward different policy objectives. Bain was interested in distinguishing industries and their differing degrees of monopoly; discerning an industry's entry barriers remains crucial to effecting antitrust legislation. Mason pursued a general theory of government control of big business and, following Joan Robinson and Chamberlin (1954), ways of characterizing imperfect markets. Mason's focus was big business – corporate power – generally. His work was an attempt to theorize business's socioeconomic power and, where politically appropriate, the effective means of curbing it; an agenda that reflected a stream of progressive theorizing going back a century or more to Veblen's *Theory of the Business Enterprise* (1904) (Ganley 2004; Witt 2009). Mason argued that a firm has power to the extent that its strategic choices are not fully determined by its circumstances – not by market structure, technology, nor anything else. In particular, Mason's focus was on the constraints to a firm's agency or strategic choices. Bain's emphasis on 'industry' was different from Mason's focus on the firm (Phillips and Stevenson 1974).

While Bain stood back and saw industry structure as determining performance, Porter's FFF was closer to the firm – Mason's focus – emphasizing its strategic options within a domain framed and constrained by industry conditions. In his 1981 *AMR* paper, the first diagram Porter drew of the structure–conduct–performance (SCP) paradigm has one-directional fully determining arrows (Porter 1981: 611). He went on: 'The Bain view that strategic choices do not have an important influence on industry structure is nearly dead. It is now recognized that there are feedback effects of firm conduct on market structure' (Porter 1981: 615–16). Porter's corrective was to introduce feedback. In Figure 3 of the 1981 *AMR* paper, structure determines performance, while performance equally determines structure, the system embracing both industry and firm levels (Porter 1981: 616). Yet the diagrams inadvertently display a hint of determinism. The implicit determinism, unilateral or bilateral, overemphasized or not, denies the focal firm's agency along with that of the other entities implied in the FFF.

The denial seemed opposed to Porter's intuition. If HBS stands for anything, it is for the freedoms of the private sector and the economic and political viability of a business's agency. In contrast, Berkeley's radicalism probably stands for more constraint, evident in Bain's work. Mason sought a middle path or 'third way' acknowledging both inter-firm competition and its economically progressive impact, and the complementary need to constrain business freedom to ensure its social acceptability. Porter's unease was clear in *Competitive Strategy* when he spoke of the 'judgmental placement' of an industry's boundaries (Porter 1980*a*: 186) and, in a significant revision of the FFF, used two-way arrows in Figure 8-4 (Porter 1980*a*: 187). If Porter inadvertently underplayed the agentic core of Mason's thinking in some diagrams, a consequence of Caves' teaching perhaps, or through failing to restrain the deterministic systems thinking familiar to him as an engineering undergraduate or equally from neoclassical economic theory, what about the LCAG paradigm's treatment of agency? There can be no doubt that the LCAG framework sets up a discussion of the constraints to management's agency. The puzzle is to see how this is treated.

While the LCAG paradigm is often illustrated with the four-box diagram, it was not originally presented that way. Its authors noted the agentic dimension of executive judgment: 'The ability to identify the four components of strategy ... is nothing compared to the art of reconciling their implications in a final choice of purpose' (Learned et al. 1965: 21). Their distinction was between the 'four forces' being determinative versus merely framing the agentic act of their reconciliation. In the pages before this statement, LCAG laid out the act's constraints in a very different language. They spoke in terms of what the firm (*a*) might do, in terms of environmental opportunity, or (*b*) can do, in terms of ability and power (Learned et al. 1965: 20). They went on to (*c*) what the executives want to do, and finally (*d*) what the firm should do in terms of the ethical constraints on its actions. This fourfold 'might do, can do, want to do, and should do' characterization of the executive's agentic task had an important precedent in the work of John Commons.

In the *Legal Foundations of Capitalism*, Commons wrote: '... a working rule lays down four verbs for the guidance and restraint of individuals in their transactions. It tells us what the individuals must or must not do (compulsion or duty), what they may do without interference from other individuals (permission or liberty), what they can do with the aid of collective power (capacity or right), and what they cannot expect the collective power to do in their behalf (incapacity or exposure)' (Commons 1924: 6). So there seems little doubt the origins of LCAG's four boxes are the diagrams in chapter IV of Commons' book (Commons 1924: 65). Commons, along with Veblen and Mitchell, was one of the founders of the 'institutional' or 'evolutionary' economic paradigm that merged into IO. IO began as dissension from extreme laissez-faire and led to the founding of the American Economic Association in 1885. Among the movement's leading lights were Seligman, Adams, James (who played a major role in founding the Wharton School), and Ely. Because economics PhDs were not obtainable in the United States prior to the founding of Johns Hopkins, as the first of the US German-style research universities in 1876, all had trained in Germany and in its Historicist tradition of economic history.

When in 1880 Ely returned from Heidelberg, where he had been a student of Knies, he joined the faculty at Johns Hopkins—where Commons was studying – and where he also influenced Veblen. Ely entered into a methodological fight with Newcomb, a Johns Hopkins astronomer and mathematician, lost, and departed to Wisconsin, taking Commons with him. There the institutionalist economic agenda was competition, rivalry, and performance – and public control of big business or the Trusts. Ely's 1903 *Studies in the Evolution of Industrial Society* helped establish the terminology and concepts of competitive analysis, monopoly, and rivalry now associated with IO (Ely 1903).

The German Historicist data-driven tradition led directly to today's case studies, already legitimate at Harvard before the foundation of HBS in 1904, and HBS's first Dean, Edwin Gay, like the other IO founders mentioned, spent many years in Germany. These historical comments are to suggest that the IO tradition ran much further back than Mason, who studied Chamberlin's and Robinson's work at Oxford, at least as far back as the German Historicists Schmoller and Knies. Their impact on economics in America was profound – and not uncontested. Ely's fight with Newcomb was a North American replay of the fight which the German Historicists, especially Schmoller, had with marginalism and Menger – known as the *Methodenstreit* (Vaughn 1994). The battle-lines were methodological and lay between those who thought of theorizing in the deductive sense, from first principles to testable hypotheses, versus those who thought of theorizing inductively, the discovery of generalizations or patterns in accumulated data. Porter's work is clearly in the second tradition. That *Competitive Strategy* is grounded in 'detailed studies of hundreds of industries with all varieties of structures and at widely differing states of maturity' (Porter 1980a: xvi), and that Porter managed a team of researchers that he credited fully for working with him for over five years (Porter 1980a: x), is often overlooked. He notes: 'I didn't come to the conclusion that there were five forces until I had looked at hundreds of industries' (Argyres and McGahan 2002b: 46).

Competitive Strategy is, in this sense, a product of collaborative work in a data-intensive tradition and also of a research team applying techniques that ran back to HBS's founding and its German Historicist inheritance. In this sense, IO is in HBS's genes – a view that leads to a better understanding of the methodological tension between HBS's inductive theorizing and the deductive approach of the economics profession generally, ruled as it is by neoclassical notions of equilibrium or what Winter calls the Friedman Conjecture (Winter 2005: 517). The historicists were on the losing side in the *Methodenstreit*, and marginalism and mathematics won hands-down (Vaughn 1994: 31). Economic historians became mere historians, which, in America, normally means theoretically irrelevant. In a famous comment – that Williamson reprised later – Coase dismissed the 'old institutional economists' saying: 'without a theory they had nothing to pass on except a mass of descriptive material waiting for a theory – or a fire' (Posner 1996: 419n).

The development of IO took American economists to a fork on Method Road. Most appreciated they could start from axioms, such as *homo economicus*, and look for testable hypotheses – like the majority of their discipline – or they could work with voluminous data and seek out generalizations that would withstand empirical challenge – like 'behavioral economics'. With his dismissal of IO, Coase missed the 'third way' Porter sought in *Competitive Strategy* as he attempted to bridge economic theorizing and managerial practice, leveraging off the LCAG framing of the executive task as something only agency can inform. How agency crept into the economists' methodological picture is a longer story, buried in the development of American pragmatism (Delanty 1997). But it is clear that Commons – along with Dewey and James – absorbed agency and judgment into his thinking (Commons 1924: 342).

Thus, Porter appealed to the IO theorists' intuition that aside from the methodological options considered in the *Methodenstreit* – deductive versus inductive determinism – there was a third 'agentic' position, by definition central for management theorists. It captured the party silenced in the economists' discussion – the judging economic actor herself/himself. Theory, whether deductive or inductive, remains in the academic domain. Economic action lies in the practitioner's domain. It is the academics' conceit that theory alone is sufficient to frame and explain the actions of others. Bounded rationality denies this, ironically admitting the significance of agency. Agency presupposes that managers have options and market power that are never wholly determined.

3.7 Extending the theory

At this point it is useful to turn to Porter's 1991 *SMJ* paper and see it as the second half of the theory chapter missing from *Competitive Strategy*. Porter was remarkably parsimonious about 'theory', normally preferring 'framework'. His 1991 paper balanced the deductive, inductive, and agentic modes of analysis – the 'trading off' academic critics (and Henderson) sensed missing from *Competitive Strategy*. Few strategy theorists have tackled this issue, so Porter's paper is one of the few substantial discussions of the methodological issues confronting strategic management researchers who, focusing on strategic action rather than on modeling a determining economy, work the distinction between the deductive, inductive, and agentic methodologies. His paper contrasts with the bulk of our discipline's methodology texts that either ignore the echoes of the *Methodenstreit* and propose a dogmatic faith in statistical analysis – not even Schmoller believed data could be unproblematic – or paper over the gap between deductive and inductive methods with palliatives like 'triangulation' or 'commitment' (for example, Van de Ven 2007).

Instead of using the language of causality to push the agent out of the analysis, Porter wrote the strategist into its foreground: 'Given the goal of informing practice, the style of research in the strategy field, including my own, has involved a very different approach. . . . Instead of models, however, the approach was to build frameworks. A framework such as the competitive forces approach encompasses many variables and seeks to capture much of the complexity of actual competition. Frameworks identify the relevant variables and the questions that the user must answer in order to develop conclusions tailored to a particular industry and company. . . . In frameworks, the equilibrium concept is imprecise' (Porter 1991: 98). 'Frameworks' make no measurable presuppositions about the agent – rational, entrepreneurial, aware, or otherwise. They provide the grist to the agent's judgment mill and allow the managerial reader to sense the call for their own agency and active strategic contribution.

All this suggests that the FFF is more of a reconstruction of the LCAG paradigm rather than an upending of Bain's alleged SCP determinism – a conclusion that goes far deeper than focusing IO's analytic tools onto just one of that paradigm's four boxes. The underlying four-verb structure of the LCAG paradigm is not identical to the FFF, and some content realignment follows from the differing languages brought to the analysis. But the space created for the manager's agentic input is similar. While Porter's reconstruction of the LCAG framework introduced a potentially more rigorous language, stiffening the analysis, it reframed the implicit model of the firm. Instead of the single-firm context of the LCAG paradigm, the FFF put the firm into a multi-firm competitive industry context. As Steiner noted in his review, Porter placed competition front and center at a time when it was underemphasized, and even ignored (Steiner 1981: 84). It follows that *Competitive Strategy* made a place for a fifth force – rivalry – that seemed underemphasized or lost in the LCAG analysis. At the same time the FFF rebalanced the emphasis between LCAG's four boxes.

In short, *Competitive Strategy* was never advanced as a deterministic theory of corporate strategy, nor as a checklist of industry- or economy-wide decision-making heuristics (Spender 1989). It is precisely what Porter told us it is – a framework to help strategists note what they should take into account as constraints to their options and so arrive at the 'managerial choices' their situation calls forth. If this reading is correct, the nature and subtlety of *Competitive Strategy* becomes clear, and our chapter's question about its appeal is more or less answered. The FFF's very lack of prescriptive theory, in the conventional sense of presenting a theory grounded in some determining characteristics of the situation, frames a place for the executive's situated agency to generate closure – and does so in a way with which virtually all executives, familiar with the economy's call to their agency, can identify. They have no need to grasp *Competitive Strategy*'s intricacies to feel its tug. At the same time the book's IO discourse is crisp enough to appeal to those, such as strategy faculty and MBA students, who, knowing no such agentic demands, see the FFF as a general model for practical analysis.

3.8 Concluding comments

Behind Porter's successful exploitation of the methodological ambiguities buried within the IO tradition lie lessons for management students, faculty, researchers, and administrators alike. How was he able to 'get away with' a style of research that seems almost outlawed in today's Chicago-driven positivistic hegemony? When it came to the ICA note, the *CMR* and *HBR* papers, and *Competitive Strategy*, he took a huge gamble; but in a benign environment, presuming IO is indeed in HBS's genes. He was in a group that understood management as leadership and agency – in the Barnard (1968) and LCAG framework – that had little to do with rational analysis and decision-making. Luck and timing played their part. There was also the mixture of discipline and personal qualities that enabled Porter to attract the support of Christensen and MacArthur, the HBS Dean. Porter's reshaping of the agentic and IO principles on which HBS was founded paid off handsomely in ways appreciated far beyond its walls. But for most young researchers today, the balance between professional risk and identifiable return inclines them to be risk-averse – a posture frequently endorsed by their risk-averse supervisors and mentors. Under these circumstances, where are the next breakthroughs to come from, if not from able students encouraged to attempt something challenging?

There are also lessons to be learned about today's methodological prescriptions. It is a commonplace that practice-oriented consultants developed most of our strategy-toolbox's contents. Despite their varying emphases, most of these tools reflect the venerable distinctions underpinning the LCAG boxes, grounded in the Wisconsin IO tradition that emphasizes entrepreneurship, agency, and situatedness over a time- and space-denying neoclassical rigor and mathematical precision. If we look at what has happened to the strategy field since it became a discipline with HBS's founding, there are two outstanding contributors – Chandler and Porter. Both adopted inductive approaches: Chandler as a professional historian of business, and Porter as a dedicated case-writer, case-teacher, and case-analyzer. It is unlikely either would be able to get tenure for, or even publish, this material today. Gay's effort to establish business history as a distinctive discipline survived at Harvard, but remains almost invisible within the Academy of Management.

Yet we look in vain for significant discipline- or practice-shaping products from the deductivist or inductivist schools. The differing impact of Porter's academic articles and his books underlines the disparity between the audiences *Competitive Strategy* addresses – different products to meet different needs. Today's orthodoxies make the gulf between writing to an academic audience versus to a practitioner audience wider than ever – resulting in loss to both. Thus, the possibility of anyone repeating *Competitive Strategy*'s success and bridging the different methodologies seems increasingly remote. *Competitive Strategy*'s relevance to the broad and influential policymaking audience in either public or private sectors lies in its attention to agency – suggesting that the oft-noted irrelevance at the core of the rigor-and-relevance debate springs from its denial.

The subsequent evolution of Porter's work is likewise revealing. Our chapter's focus is on *Competitive Strategy* because it was the intellectual foundation to all of Porter's work. Up to his 1991 *SMJ* paper – in spite of the other work he was publishing – Porter seemed keen to stiffen up its theoretical dimensions. He had the incentive and the opportunity to create the book which *Competitive Strategy*'s first academic reviewers (along with Henderson) looked for. We have argued that his two methodology papers successfully clarified the book's objectives and methodology, sketching the missing methodological chapter that would have made it into the strategy discipline's most significant work to date. Some might argue that *Competitive Advantage* is this book, though we would disagree. But rather than push toward such theoretical high ground and retreat from the challenge of dealing with uncertainty and agency, Porter saw an alternative development path – to recover Mason's agenda and move from business policy toward regional and national economic policy, as discussed in later chapters of this volume.

Finally, it is curious to see how strategy theorists have shifted their attention away from the oft-ignored richness of Porter's work toward that of Barney and others who focus on the firm's 'resources and capabilities'. Porter's 1991 assessment of what has become our leading conversation, moving the field's researchers and students away from the FFF, is kind (Barney 2002*b*: 56), but a tad bewildered (Porter 1991: 107). One might note in passing that the RBV has had virtually no impact on business practice and has produced nothing that could be thought of as a candidate for the strategist's toolbox. This is not the place for a full analysis of the RBV which we have examined elsewhere

(Kraaijenbrink et al. 2010). Consequently, the RBV's dominance warrants some comment and, perhaps, concern.

The firm in *Competitive Strategy* is a dynamic reconciliation, as LCAG suggest, of the various three-level pricing, gaming, bargaining, market, and signaling processes identified in the FFF. To go beyond competition and embrace lobbying and negotiation, rounding out his attention to the three bases of social order – power, game theory, and institutionalization (Etzioni 1961) – would oblige Porter to spell out this reconciliation process. The result would be a significant extension, given *Competitive Strategy*'s overemphasis on economic force and underemphasis on how it is acquired – inevitable legacies of IO – as well as less than necessary attention to collaboration. Duly emended, the reconciliation has the potential to be a terrific description of the executive task in a democratic capitalist socioeconomy – an analysis with the potential to best even Barnard's classic work (1968).

Note

1. The Editors and J.-C. Spender interviewed Professor Porter while researching this chapter. He was generous, as ever. The discussion was especially appreciated in that it triggered thoughts about the methodological issues that form the core of this chapter.

4

Antecedents and precedents to Porter's *Competitive Strategy*

Robert E. Hoskisson, Michael A. Hitt, William P. Wan, and Daphne Yiu

4.1 Introduction

This chapter explores the influence industrial organization (IO) economics has exerted on the theoretical and methodological frameworks of strategic management research, highlighting the significance of Michael Porter in furthering its development. It reviews the development of the field and its current position, as well as examining changes in the primary theoretical and methodological bases through its history. Derivation of the field of strategic management can be traced to several different dates. Possible starting dates include 1980, 1978, 1962, and 320 BC, for example. In 1978, the first textbook for the field – Hofer and Schendel's *Strategy Formulation* – was published. The year 1962 marked Alfred Chandler's pioneering work on strategy. Also, the field's roots in military strategy were sown around 320 BC, by Sun Tsu. Among the dates, 1980 was a seminal year because it marked the publication of Porter's *Competitive Strategy* as well as the inception of the Strategic Management Society.

The work of Porter made one of the most significant contributions to the development of strategic management. Earlier work in the field tended to be fragmented, with few analytical techniques for gaining an understanding of industries and competition within them. Porter's work helped to fill the void. Applying the structure–conduct–performance (S–C–P) framework of IO economics, he built a foundation for research on competitive dynamics: a description of the forces that determine the nature and level of competition in an industry, as well as suggestions for how to use this information to develop competitive advantage. From its 'humble' beginnings as the limited content of a capstone general management course in the business school curriculum, strategic management is now a firmly established field in the study of business and organizations. During a relatively short period of time, this field has witnessed a significant growth in the diversity of topics and variety of research methods employed.

4.2 Early development of the strategic management field

During the period of the field's early development, a number of scholars made significant contributions to the later development of strategic management, known, at that time, as business policy. Among the most important works are Chandler's *Strategy and Structure* (1962), Ansoff's *Corporate Strategy* (1965), and Learned et al.'s *Business Policy: Text and Cases* (1965/1969).

Although not explicitly mentioned on most occasions, the footprints of the earlier classics in management can be found during this early period of work on the forerunner of strategic management. For example, Barnard's (1938) detailed exposition of the cooperation and organization in business firms, as well as the managerial functions and processes therein, provided a solid foundation upon which subsequent works in strategic management were built. The crucial importance of 'distinctive competence' and leadership emphasized in Selznick's study (1957) in administrative organizations coincided well with early strategy scholars' focus on firms' internal strengths and managerial capabilities. Penrose (1959) related firm growth and diversification to the 'inherited' resources, especially managerial capacities, a firm possesses. Her proposition complemented Chandler's findings (1962) on the growth of the firm. From a behavioral perspective, Herbert Simon's *Administrative Behaviors* (1945) and Cyert and March's *A Behavioral Theory of the Firm* (1963) also provided input into the early development of strategic management (Ansoff's, 1965, *Corporate Strategy* is a good example). They emphasized internal processes and the characteristics of organizations, such as decision-making processes, information-processing limitations, power and coalitions, and hierarchical structures. In many respects it is likely that the early development of strategic management thinking was influenced, at least to a certain extent, by these early classics' detailed expositions of the internal processes of organizations and focus on the important roles of managers.

An important year for the field of strategic management was 1962 when Chandler's seminal work, *Strategy and Structure*, was published (Rumelt et al. 1994). Chandler's work focused primarily on how large enterprises develop new administrative structures to accommodate growth, and how strategic change leads to structural change. According to Chandler, strategy is 'the determination of the basic long-term goals and objectives of an enterprise, and the adoption of courses of action and the allocation of resources necessary for carrying out the goals', while structure is 'the design of organization through which the enterprise is administered' (1962: 13–14). Changes in strategy are mainly responses to opportunities or needs created by changes in the external environment, such as technological innovation. As a consequence of change in strategy, complementary new structures are also devised. Moreover, the book also illuminates vividly the active role of managers in pursuing strategic changes and exploring new administrative structures.

In the preface to his book, Ansoff describes that its main focus is on strategic decisions, defined as 'decisions on what kind of business the firm should seek to be in' (1965: viii). He views strategy as the 'common thread' among a firm's activities and product-markets and comprises four components: product-market scope, growth vector (or the changes that a firm makes in its product-market scope), competitive advantage, and synergy.

Andrews and his colleagues considered business policy as 'the study of the functions and responsibilities of general management and the problems which affect the character and success of the total enterprise' from the viewpoint 'of the chief executive or general manager, whose primary responsibility is the enterprise as a whole' (Learned et al. 1965/1969: 3). More importantly, they define strategy as 'the pattern of objectives, purposes, or goals and major policies and plans for achieving these goals, stated in such a way as to define what business the company is in, or is to be in and the kind of company it is or is to be' (1969: 15). They also suggest that corporate strategy is composed of two interrelated, but practically separated, aspects: formulation and implementation. The challenge in formulation is to identify and reconcile four essential components of strategy: (*a*) market opportunity, (*b*) firm competence and resources, (*c*) managers' personal values and aspirations, and (*d*) obligations to segments of society other than the stockholders. This broad definition of strategy is in accord with that of Chandler, but incorporates Selznick's 'distinctive competence' (1957) and the notion of an uncertain environment (Rumelt et al. 1991). After the strategy is formulated, implementation is concerned with how resources are mobilized to accomplish the strategy and requires appropriate organization structure, systems of incentives and controls, and leadership. To Andrews and colleagues, implementation is 'comprised of a series of subactivities which are primarily administrative' (1969: 19).

The three seminal works by Chandler, Ansoff, and Andrews and his colleagues, respectively, provide the foundation for the field of strategic management (for example, Rumelt et al. 1991). Collectively, they help define a number of critical concepts and propositions in strategy, including how strategy affects performance, the importance of both external opportunities and internal capabilities, the notion that structure follows strategy, the practical distinction between formulation and implementation, and the active role of managers in strategic management. While there existed disagreements regarding these concepts that remained to be further specified and developed (Hofer and Schendel 1978), together these three works advanced the domain of strategy beyond the traditional focus of merely a capstone course about functional integration. Rumelt et al. provide an apt description: 'Nearly all of the ideas and issues that concern us today can be found in at least embryonic form in these key writings of the 1960s' (1994: 18). However, Rumelt et al. (1994) overlook the contributions of Thompson (1967). He first introduced the notion of cooperative and competitive strategies and coalition formation, a forerunner of network and strategic alliance strategies. Also, his work contributed to understanding the implementation of corporate strategy through his notion of interdependence between business units. Pooled, reciprocal, and serial interdependence are associated with the corporate strategies of unrelated diversification, related diversification, and vertical integration, respectively. Although these writings form a foundation for strategic management, they were mostly process-oriented to facilitate case examination, the main methodological tool of study at the time.

4.3 Early methodologies

Works by Ansoff and Andrews, among others during the period, emphasized the normative aspect of business knowledge and are chiefly interested in identifying and developing the 'best practices' that were useful for managers. The target audience of their work were managers and students aspiring to be managers. Their principal goal was to impart knowledge to practitioners, rather than to pursue knowledge for scientific advancement. In *Business Policy: Text and Cases*, Andrews and his colleagues described this viewpoint clearly. To them, it is impossible to 'make useful generalizations about the nature of these variables or to classify their possible combinations in all situations' because there are a large number of variables unique to a certain organization or situation that guide the choice of objectives and formulation of policy (1969: 5).

The study of business policy provides a familiarity with an approach to the problems, and together with the skills and attitudes, one can 'combine these variables into a pattern valid for *one* [italics added] organization' (1969: 5). The most appropriate method for accomplishing this objective is inductive in character: in-depth case studies of single firms or industries. Generalization is practically unfeasible, as each case is assumed to be too complex and unique. In addition, these authors were skeptical about the purposes of other academic disciplines, such as engineering, economics, psychology, sociology, or mathematics. These disciplines may not be appropriate for strategy studies because 'Knowledge generated for one set of ends is not readily applicable to another' (Learned et al. 1965/1969: 6). Therefore, they concluded that the most valid methodology to achieve their purpose was case studies, inasmuch as strategy research at the time had not yet advanced enough to capture significant attention.

In comparison, Chandler's *Strategy and Structure* is less normative or prescriptive in nature, although the research methods employed are still inductive (Rumelt et al. 1994). Chandler mainly used an historical approach to produce a detailed account of four large firms (Du Pont, General Motors, Standard Oil of New Jersey (later known as Exxon), and Sears Roebuck), considered to be representative to derive his thesis and propositions. Most of the information on the firms was gathered from publicly available sources, internal company records, and interviews. Interestingly, prior to the in-depth case studies of the four firms an extensive survey of a larger number of firms had been conducted to provide initial knowledge of the business patterns of large US enterprises. Subsequent to the case studies, Chandler extended the scope of the research to conduct a comparative analysis across the four firms to investigate which enterprises adopted or rejected the multidivisional structure, and why. Therefore, unlike Andrews and Ansoff, Chandler attempted to seek generalizations regarding his thesis across a wider population of firms.

Overall, the approaches used by prominent strategy scholars during this foundation period were mainly normative or prescriptive in purpose, with in-depth case analysis as the primary research tool. To the extent that generalization is one of the goals, it is primarily achieved through induction (Rumelt et al. 1991), perhaps facilitated by comparative studies of multiple cases similar to Chandler's approach. However, in many circumstances, generalization was not a goal nor was it deemed feasible, as maintained by Andrews and his colleagues.

Unfortunately, the heavy emphasis on the case approach and lack of generalization did not provide the base necessary for continued advancement of the field. As such, work in this area was not well accepted by other academic fields. The need for a stronger theoretical base and for empirical tests of the theory to allow generalization produced a swing of the pendulum. Furthermore, much of the early work examined firms largely as closed systems. However, businesses, as with all organizations, are open systems (Thompson 1967). Thus, an open-systems approach to understanding strategy was necessary. Because of its appropriate fit and advanced development, the swing moved toward use of economic theory to examine strategic management phenomena. Schendel and Hatten (1972) argued for a broader view of strategic management that emphasized the development of new theory from which hypotheses could be derived and empirically tested. An early example of this work was Rumelt's study (1974). Rumelt's large-sample study (1974) examined the relationship between the type of strategy and structure adopted, and firm performance. His research paved the way for many subsequent studies in this area using quantitative methods.

4.4 The shift toward industrial organization (IO) economics

During the next developmental period, strategic management departed significantly theoretically and methodologically from the early period. Although Jemison (1981a) advocated that strategic management could be an amalgam of marketing (Biggadike 1981), administrative behavior (Jemison 1981b), and economics (Porter 1981), the field moved primarily toward economics in theory and method. During this swing, the influence of economics, particularly industrial organizational (IO) economics, on strategy research was substantial, and in terms of methodology, strategy research also became much more 'scientific'. This swing changed strategy research from inductive case studies, largely focused on a single firm or industry, to deductive large-scale statistical analyses seeking to validate scientific hypotheses, based on models abstracted from the S–C–P paradigm (also known as the Bain/Mason (Bain 1956, 1968; Mason 1939b) paradigm). The most widely adopted IO framework in strategic management gave rise to the rich body of research on 'strategic groups'.

In the preface to the first edition of *Industrial Organization*, Bain stated that the book (or IO economics in general) was concerned with 'the economywide complex of business enterprises . . . in their function as suppliers and sellers, or buyers, of goods and services of every sort produced by enterprise' and 'the environmental settings within which enterprises operate and in how they behave in these settings as producers, sellers, and buyers'. He also suggested that his approach was basically 'external', and the primary unit of analysis was 'the industry or competing group of firms, rather than either the individual firm or the economywide aggregate of enterprises' (Bain 1968: vii). The central tenet of this paradigm, as summarized by Porter (1981), is that a firm's performance is primarily a function of the industry environment in which it competes; and because structure determines conduct (or conduct is simply a reflection of the industry environment), which in turn determines performance, conduct can be ignored and performance can, therefore, be explained by structure. Other research supports this argument, but also suggests that the industry environment has differential effects on large and small firms (Dean et al. 1998). The adoption of the S–C–P paradigm in strategic management naturally shifted the research focus from the firm to market structure.

Competitive dynamics (multi-point competition and competitive action–reaction), an increasingly popular research area in the current field of strategic management, also evolved partly from IO economics. This stream of research often draws heavily on works by IO economists, such as Edwards (1955) and

Bernheim and Whinston (1990), who introduced important concepts such as 'mutual forbearance' and 'spheres of influence', as well as game theoretical arguments (for example, Camerer and Weigelt 1988; Grimm and Smith 1997). In summary, this shift from the early development of the field to IO economics had a major effect on the field in terms of both theory and method.

4.5 Porter and beyond

Porter (1980a, 1985a) made the most influential contribution to the field employing IO economics logic. Using a structural analysis approach, Porter (1980a) outlines an analytical framework that can be used in understanding the structure of an industry. Structural analysis focuses on competition beyond a firm's immediate and existing rivals. Whereas the concept of industry structure remains relatively unclear in the field of IO economics, Porter's Five Forces model (1980a), by more clearly specifying the various aspects of an industry structure, provides a useful analytic tool to assess an industry's attractiveness and facilitates competitor analysis. The ability for a firm to gain competitive advantage, according to Porter (1980a, 1985a, 1996b), rests mainly on how well it positions and differentiates itself in an industry. The collective effects of the five forces determine the ability of firms in an industry to make profits.

To Porter (1980a, 1985a), the five forces embody the rules of competition that determine industry attractiveness and help determine a competitive strategy to 'cope with and, ideally, to change those rules in the firm's favor' (1985a: 4). Therefore, as a refinement of the traditional S–C–P paradigm, and also a significant contribution to the field of strategic management, Porter's framework specifies the competitive structure of an industry in a more tangible manner, as well as recognizes (albeit limitedly) the role of firms in formulating appropriate competitive strategy to achieve superior performance. Porter (1980a, 1985a) suggested generic strategies (low cost leadership, differentiation, and focus) that can be used to match particular industry foci and, thereby, build competitive advantage.

Building on the IO economics perspective, strategy researchers also developed the concept of 'strategic groups'. In his study of the white goods industry, Hunt (1972) first introduced strategic groups as an analytic concept. To date, although there has yet to be a universal definition of strategic groups in the literature, it is commonly defined as a group of firms in the same industry following the same or similar strategies (Porter 1980a: 129). This line of research disagrees with IO economics' assumption that an industry's members differ only in market share and, hence, suggests that the presence of strategic groups in an industry poses a significant effect on the industry's performance

(Newman 1978). The concept of strategic groups is closely linked to mobility barriers (Caves and Porter 1977), which insulate firms in a strategic group from entry by members of another group through means such as scale economies, product differentiation, or distribution networks. Mobility barriers represent crucial factors, in addition to industry-wide factors, in accounting for intra-industry differences in firm performance (Caves and Porter 1977; Porter 1979b). In this regard, industry is no longer viewed as an homogeneous unit to the extent that the concept of strategic groups exposes the 'structure within industries' (Porter 1979b).

Although Hunt, Newman, and Porter's research on strategic groups purports to explain firm performance, the focus is actually on groups, rather than on firms. For example, Newman's study (1973) is on thirty-four 'producer goods' industries that are all related to chemical processes, while Porter's focus (1973) is on thirty-eight 'consumer goods' industries. A series of studies conducted in the context of the brewing industry by Hatten (1974), Hatten and Schendel (1977), and Hatten et al. (1978) attempt to move the study of strategic groups to the firm level by emphasizing firm heterogeneity and conduct (strategy). As a result, these studies focus on strategic groups within one industry. In addition to using structural variables such as firm size and industry concentration ratios, these brewing studies employ manufacturing (such as the capital intensity of plants), marketing (such as the number of brands), and financial (leverage) variables, among others, as the basis for strategic group formation. Firm profitability is regarded as a function of both industry structure and strategic conduct (Hatten and Schendel 1977; Cool and Schendel 1987), thereby placing the IO economics strategic groups research squarely in strategic management.

However, despite the large number of studies on strategic groups, this stream of research faces some critical issues. Barney and Hoskisson (1990) challenged two untested assertions in strategic groups theory: (a) whether strategic groups exist, and (b) whether a firm's performance depends on strategic group membership. They argued that the existence of strategic groups in an industry rests on the researcher's presumption that strategic groups actually exist. Indeed, the resulting groupings may be merely statistical artifacts of the cluster analytic procedures used to create groups. To date, the concept of strategic groups lacks theoretical support. Furthermore, the relationship between group membership and firm performance depends critically on the existence of mobility barriers. To the extent that mobility barriers exist in an industry, there is no theory to define them in a particular industry. The attributes used for clustering strategic groups are considered mobility barriers if firm performance is different among the strategic groups.

Barney and Hoskisson (1990) show that different clusters of the same set of firms can produce significant differences in firm performance by group. Based on these two limitations, Barney and Hoskisson (1990) raise doubts about the contribution of strategic groups research to the field of strategic management. The concept of strategic groups, developed largely as a theoretical compromise between IO economics and strategic management, may lack theoretical validity. Wiggins and Ruefli (1995) found that stability of performance group membership is lacking, questioning the efficacy of mobility barriers and, thus, the predictive validity of strategic groups. The fundamental question is whether firms are acutely aware of their mutual dependence within their particular strategic groups (Porter 1979b) or are these groups an analytic convenience employed by researchers (Hatten and Hatten 1987).

Further developments in the strategic groups research point toward several perspectives. First, the dynamic characteristics of strategic groups have been examined (for example, Oster 1982; Mascarenhas 1989). This line of research found initial evidence that there is a low level of firm movement across strategic groups. Through an in-depth longitudinal study of the US insurance industry, Fiegenbaum and Thomas (1995) expanded this line of research by focusing on the influence of strategic groups as a reference point for firm-level competitive strategy decisions. Another recent development in strategic group research is based on a cognitive perspective. Instead of using secondary data, Reger and Huff (1993) rely on managers' cognitive classifications to categorize strategic groups. In a related vein, Porac et al. (1995) also use managers' cognitive perceptions to examine how firms define a reference group of rivals. Peteraf and Shanley (1997) advance cognitive strategic group research by proposing a theory of strategic group identity and distinguish between groups with strong identities from those with weak identities.

Similar to the research on strategic groups, organizational ecologists have emphasized an evolutionary perspective in which the population of strategically similar organizations are studied longitudinally, considering both their success and failure (Barnett and Burgelman 1996). Such research can account for dynamics in the relationships among firms. This approach allows the examination of how strategic outcomes develop. Thus, the theory developed predicts patterns of change, rates of change, and alternative paths of change (Barnett and Burgelman 1996). Additionally, an evolutionary perspective assumes potential variation in the strategies that firms pursue over time. In particular, based on the ecological perspective, an evolutionary approach examines how selection processes affect, and are affected by, the type and rate of strategic change (Barnett and Burgelman 1996). More empirical foci of the evolutionary approach include the evolution of technological capabilities (Stuart and Podolny 1996) and the iterated processes of resource allocation (Noda and Bower 1996). Scholars adopting this evolutionary perspective argue that it is not based on a single theory. Rather, it synthesizes many theoretical perspectives, such as economic efficiency, market power, organizational learning, structural inertia, transaction costs, and others

(Barnett and Burgelman 1996). They claim it provides an integrative framework in which firm success and failure can be understood (Schendel 1996).

While strategic group studies represented the first swing away from industry-level research, another research stream – competitive dynamics – further emphasizes the firm level in strategic management research. The essence of this stream is an explicit recognition that a firm's strategies are dynamic. Actions initiated by one firm may trigger a series of actions among the competing firms. The new competitive landscape in many industries, as described by Bettis and Hitt (1995), gives rise to the relentless pace of competition, emphasizing flexibility, speed, and innovation in response to the fast-changing environment. D'Aveni (1994) coined the term 'hypercompetition' to describe the condition of rapidly escalating competition characterizing many industries. The increase in competitive dynamics research signifies strategy researchers' acute awareness of the new competitive landscape in the environment. There are several areas that can be categorized as competitive dynamics research, all of which are characterized by an explicit concern for the dynamic nature of business competition. These different areas are individually known as multi-point (or multi-market) competition and competitive action–reaction.

The development of multi-point competition traces its primary theoretical origin to IO economics (mainly oligopoly theory). There are content areas in the IO economics literature concerned with competition across multiple markets (Gimeno 1994), to include strategic groups (such as Newman 1973, 1978; Greening 1980), mutual forbearance (such as Edwards 1955; Bernheim and Whinston 1990), and product-line rivalry (such as Brander and Eaton 1984; Bulow et al. 1985). While these three content areas focus on different mechanisms, the central prediction is that tacit collusion produces rivalry reduction and is more likely among firms sharing similar product-market scope because each of them realizes that intense rivalry will harm their individual performance. Porter (1980a, 1985a) and Karnani and Wernerfelt (1985) pioneered the concept of multi-point competition in the strategy literature. Illustrated with cases in the roasted coffee industry and the heavy machinery industry, Porter (1980a) discusses the analysis of 'cross-parry' conditions where a firm reacts to a move of a competitor by counterattacking another market of that competitor. Also relying on an inductive case study, Karnani and Wernerfelt (1985) developed two concepts – 'counterattack' and 'mutual foothold equilibrium' – in their framework of multi-market competition that emphasizes the role of multi-market retaliation.

Large-scale econometric studies on multi-market competition have begun to appear in the strategy literature since the late 1990s. Using data on more than 3,000 city-pair markets in the US airline industry, Gimeno and Woo (1996) examined the simultaneous role of strategic similarity and multi-market contact in competitive de-escalation. They found that strategic similarity moderately increases the intensity of rivalry, while multi-market contact strongly reduces it. Although prior literature found that strategic similarity reduces rivalry, the effect of strategic similarity on rivalry may be biased if multi-market contact is not appropriately controlled. Boeker et al. (1997), using a sample of hospitals located in California, found that the extent to which competitors compete in similar markets has a negative effect on market exit, providing additional evidence that market overlap results in decreased rivalry. Baum and Korn (1996) examined how market domain overlap and multi-market contact influence market entry and exit. In the context of the California commuter airline market, they found that market domain overlap increases the rates of market entry and exit, whereas increases in multi-market contact reduces them. This line of research provides new insight suggesting that close competitors are often not the most intense rivals, thus challenging the traditional assumption of firm rivalry.

Chen (1996) synthesized two crucial subjects in competitive dynamics: competitor analysis and interfirm rivalry. Drawing on different theories, Chen (1996) introduced two firm-specific concepts: market commonality (from multi-market competition) and resource similarity (from the resource-based view) to help elucidate the pre-battle competitive tension between two firms and to predict how firms may interact with each other as competitors. Chen's approach demonstrates the fruitfulness of integrating Porter's IO-based approach ('outside-in') and the resource-based approach ('inside-out') for understanding interfirm competition. Besides, unlike that of Porter's Five Forces framework (1980a) focusing on the industry level, analysis in Chen's model (1996) focuses on the firm, emphasizing a dyadic, pairwise analysis, yielding significant insights for competitive dynamics research.

The influence of the S–C–P paradigm has been enormous. From a firm-level analysis where the identification of 'best practices' was considered the goal, much research in the field suddenly embraced the crucial importance of industry structure and its effects: strategy and performance. Although Porter's influence on the field is widely regarded as substantial (Porter 1998c), his view about the significance of the industry is not without critics. Rumelt (1991) argued that interfirm heterogeneity within industries (business-specific effects) explains firm economic performance much more than industry membership. Roquebert et al. (1996), using a different database, also support this finding. Porter (1996b) reaffirmed the crucial significance of strategic positioning in business competition. A study by McGahan and Porter (1997), with a sample including service sectors, found that (a) industry represents an important factor in affecting firm economic performance and, more specifically, (b) industry effects are more important in accounting for firm performance in the service industry than in the manufacturing industry. Although a lot has been learned about performance determination over the years, it appears that much remains unanswered for strategy researchers.

Despite the effect of the S–C–P paradigm on the field of strategic management, the shift from the industry level to the firm level began gradually with the focus on strategic groups. The original conception of strategic groups was focused primarily on the industry level (for example, Newman 1978; Porter 1979*b*), but the concept's development by strategy researchers has been predominantly concerned with firm strategy within an industry (such as Purdue University's brewing industry studies). Interestingly, strategic groups research represents the first swing in the field back toward the firm level.

The ability of strategy research to internalize and develop diverse theories to study a variety of topics has enabled the field to experience exceptional development in its short history. Besides strategic groups, research on competitive dynamics clearly demonstrates the field's ability to integrate economics-based arguments with management theories and concepts, such as information processing, expectancy–valence theory, to create a unique body of research with a strong focus on the firm and competitive interaction. Therefore, although strategic management in this period was heavily influenced by economics, researchers were able to develop new, unique theories for the field.

4.6 IO and methodological development

Although normative, inductive case-based studies had dominated the early history of strategic management, positivistic, deductive empirical research became dominant during the ensuing period. Therefore, concern with explanation and prediction, rather than prescription, was strongly advocated by strategy scholars with the aim to elevate the field to a more rigorous, 'scientific' academic discipline.

In this regard, IO economics has had an important effect on strategy research beyond theoretical influence, by encouraging strategy researchers to adopt the methodologies used in economics. Porter (1981: 617) holds that because IO economics research has developed 'a strong empirical tradition built around the statistical analysis of populations of firms and industries', research on strategy would be able to supplement the more traditional case study with statistical methods. IO economics, as a sub-field of economics, utilizes the methodological framework of positive economics. In *Essays in Positive Economics*, Milton Friedman (1953) describes positive economics, unlike normative economics, as 'in principle independent of any particular ethical or normative prescriptions', whereas 'Its task is to provide a system of generalizations that can be used to make predictions about the consequences of any change in circumstances', and 'Its performance is to be judged by the precision, scope, and conformity with experience of the predictions it yields' (1953: 4). In this regard, economics appears to bear substantial influence on both the theoretical as well as methodological frameworks of strategic management, as it changed to become a more 'scientific', and hence more 'respectable', academic discipline.

While IO economics emphasizes industry-level phenomena, strategic management is concerned with firm-level strategies. Application of the IO paradigms brought new and important foci to the strategic management field. However, building on the early work of Ansoff and others, there remained some missing pieces of the puzzle. Research has shown that some firms perform better than others in the same industry and/or within the same strategic group. This suggests that firm-level phenomena are important. Furthermore, the competitive landscape for many industries began to change, particularly with the development of global markets (as opposed to domestic markets) (Hitt et al. 1998). Foreign firms entered domestic markets and, in some cases, armed with new ideas and strategies, began to capture significant market shares. Thus, strategic management scholars retrained their focus on the firm.

4.7 The rise of the resource-based view: back to the future

Recently, the popularity of the resource-based view (RBV) of the firm has returned our focus to inside the black box of the firm (for example, Wernerfelt 1984; Barney 1991, 2001; Conner 1991; Peteraf 1993). The significance of the RBV was recognized when Birger Wernerfelt's 'A Resource-based View of the Firm' (1984) was selected as the best 1994 paper published in the *Strategic Management Journal*. The RBV emerged as 'an important new conceptualization in the field of strategic management' and is 'one of the most important redirections of the (content of) strategy research in this decade' (Zajac 1995: 169). Theoretically, the central premise of RBV addresses the fundamental question of why firms are different and how firms achieve and sustain competitive advantage. Its research sub-streams focus on specific types of resources inside a firm, such as strategic leadership (for example, Cannella and Hambrick 1993; Kesner and Sebora 1994; Finkelstein and Hambrick 1996) and tacit knowledge (for example, Kogut and Zander 1992; Spender and Grant 1996). Methodologically, the RBV also has helped the field reintroduce inductive, case-based methods focused on a single or a few firms into the research to complement deductive, large-sample methods.

The RBV of the firm, however, is not new. Its footprints can be found in early management works. The relationship between a firm's special competencies (deploying its resources) and firm performance was embedded in some

classic management treatises. For instance, Selznick's idea (1957) of an organization's 'distinctive competence' is directly related to the RBV. Also, Chandler's notion (1962) of 'structure follows strategy', as well as Andrew's proposal
(1971) of 'an internal appraisal of strengths and weaknesses', led to the
identification of distinctive competencies. Additionally, Ansoff's definition
(1965) of synergy as 'one internally generated by a combination of capabilities
or competencies' is related to the RBV. Among these, the founding idea of
viewing a firm as a bundle of resources was pioneered in 1959 by Penrose in
her theory of the growth of the firm. Penrose viewed the firm as a collection of
productive resources – '[A] firm is more than an administrative unit; it is also a
collection of productive resources the disposal of which between different uses
and over time is determined by administrative decision' (1959: 24). She
further defined resources as 'the physical things a firm buys, leases, or produces for its own use, and the people hired on terms that make them effectively part of the firm' (1959: 67). Penrose argued that it is the heterogeneity,
not the homogeneity, of the productive services available or potentially available from its resources that gives each firm its unique character. The notion
that firms attain a unique character by virtue of their heterogeneous resources
is the basis of RBV.

Research into strategic leadership, one of the RBV's major sub-streams,
focuses on individuals (such as CEOs or division general managers), groups
(such as top management teams), or other governance bodies (such as boards
of directors). Studying the role of top executives has been an historical topic of
interest in the management literature (for example, Barnard 1938; Fayol 1949;
Selznick 1957; March and Simon 1958; Mintzberg 1973). Drawing on this,
Kotter (1982) helped to foster a formal stream of strategic leadership research
with his *The General Managers*. He was followed by Hambrick and Mason
(1984) who argued that an organization becomes 'a reflection of its top
managers'. Empirical evidence of strategic leaders' effects on organizational
outcomes is numerous. Organizational performance is found to be associated
with: executives' past performance record (Smith et al. 1984; Pfeffer and
Davis-Blake 1986); and top management team size, composition, and tenure
(Murray 1989; Haleblian and Finkelstain 1993; Smith et al. 1994).

The other major sub-stream of the RBV, research into tacit knowledge, as a
firm's resources, has its origin in Michael Polanyi's assertion (1966), 'We can
know more than we can tell' (p. 4). Polanyi classified knowledge into two
categories: explicit or codified knowledge, which refers to knowledge that is
transmittable in formal, systematic language; and tacit knowledge, which has
a personal quality and, thus, is difficult to formalize and communicate. Building on Polanyi's idea, Kogut and Zander (1992) view firms as a repository of
capabilities in which individual and social expertise is transformed into economically valuable products. This means that by its tacitness and social

complexity, a firm's stock of knowledge is an important determinant of its competitive advantage. Such a conceptualization of firms as bearers of tacit, social, and path-dependent organizational knowledge created a new paradigm called the knowledge-based view (KBV) of the firm (Foss 1996*a*). Notable studies of the KBV include Cohen and Levinthal (1990) who coined as 'absorptive capacity' the ability of a firm to recognize the value of new, external information, assimilate it, and apply it to commercial ends, and Nonaka (1994) who explained the interactive amplification of tacit and explicit knowledge through four phases of the 'knowledge spiral' ('socialization', 'combination', 'externalization', and 'internalization'). Lei et al. (1996) integrate the RBV and KBV by arguing that core competencies only maintain value through continuous development.

Re-emergence of internal firm characteristics is also evident in the emphasis placed by organizational economics on competitive dynamics and boundary relationships between the firm and its environment. Unlike classical microeconomics that treats the firm as a production function (or 'black box'), organizational economics is a sub-field of the economics discipline that ventures into the black box to unravel its inner structural logic and functioning. This primary interest in the 'organization' (or the 'firm') creates a strong affinity with strategic management. With a focus on boundary relationships, the field began to emphasize transaction costs analysis (Williamson 1975, 1985), which examines the firm–environment interface through a contractual or exchange-based approach. In a similar vein, agency theory suggests that the firm can be viewed as a 'nexus of contracts' (Jensen and Meckling 1976). Both transaction costs economics (TCE) and agency theory have their roots in Ronald Coase's influential essay (1937) 'The Nature of the Firm', with agency theory further evolving from the insights found in *The Modern Corporation and Private Property* (1932) by Adolf Berle and Gardiner Means. TCE has fostered much research on firm boundaries and markets versus hierarchies, such as work on the multidivisional structure (for a review, see Hoskisson et al. 1993), and vertical integration and strategic alliances (Kogut 1988). Additionally, a substantial amount of studies on corporate governance has been spawned by agency theory (Eisenhardt 1989; Hoskisson and Turk 1990). Both TCE and agency theory's focus on the 'firm' helps swing the strategic management pendulum further away from the industry-level emphasis of the S–C–P paradigm and toward a firm-level analysis.

4.8 Conclusion

From a Porterian and IO economics perspective, mobility barriers or market positions are the critical sources of competitive advantages that lead to superior performance. By contrast, organizational economics is more concerned with devising appropriate governance mechanisms or contracts to help reduce transaction or agency costs. Furthermore, the advance of RBV has refocused the field of strategic management on firms' internal characteristics and views firms' internal resources as the source of competitive advantage. While all three theoretical perspectives have significantly advanced our understanding of the sources of competitive advantages and hence firm performance, the sustainability of firms' competitive advantages has increasingly become an important question, with the new competitive landscape forcing firms to continue to evaluate the sustainability of their positions (Bettis and Hitt 1995; Porter 1996b; Hitt 1998). Consequently, some strategic management researchers are advocating the importance of dynamic core competencies (Lei et al. 1996) or the understanding of firms' market positions from a dynamic theoretical perspective (Porter 1991). The dynamic nature of firm resources, or more generally firms' strategic flexibility (Sanchez 1995; Hitt 1998; Hitt et al. 1998), makes the study of the sources and sustainability of competitive advantages an important research objective. As valuable knowledge and resources become transient, organizational learning (Nonaka 1991; Nonaka and Takeuchi 1995) – by definition a dynamic process – is likely to be incorporated into many theoretical models for the study of strategy.

Although the advent of the RBV in the 1990s and 2000s apparently takes the field back to our starting point, the level of theoretical and methodological sophistication and maturity currently exhibited underscores the extent to which the field has advanced over the last several decades. Empirical research on the RBV of the firm, and particularly resource-based corporate strategy, has been difficult because key concepts such as tacit knowledge or capabilities resist direct measurement (Farjoun 1994; Robins and Wiersema 1995). Nonetheless, RBV researchers have already made great strides in overcoming these empirical problems. Attempts to quantify empirically the nature and effects of resource-based constructs offer a fruitful avenue for future research. With each shift in its theoretical and methodological frameworks, the field of strategic management has made significant progress and will continue to flourish into the coming decades.

During the 1990s and since, rich streams of research emerged in such areas as competitive strategy (D'Aveni 1994; Gimeno 2004), corporate governance (Hoskisson et al. 2002; Daily et al. 2003), international strategy (Tallman 2001; Lu and Beamish 2004; Penner-Hahn and Shaver 2005), strategic leadership (Finkelstein and Hambrick 1996; Hambrick and Cannella 2004), and dynamic capabilities (Teece et al. 1997; Helfat and Peteraf 2003; Winter 2003). Emerging areas of strategic management research include strategic entrepreneurship (Amit and Zott 2001; Hitt et al. 2001, 2002), strategy process (Chakravarthy et al. 2003; Floyd et al. 2004), and network strategies (Dyer and Singh 1998; Gulati and Singh 1998; Ireland et al. 2002).

Strategic researchers will be increasingly challenged to respond to frequent, discontinuous changes and provide answers to new problems. In fact, the results of strategic management research will become increasingly important for current executives and in educating future executives. As such, the quality of this research and its ability to provide answers to critical strategy questions take on a new urgency within the highly dynamic competitive business landscape. Because the nature of strategy problems cannot easily be framed within a fixed paradigm, strategic management is necessarily a multi-paradigmatic discipline, requiring varied theoretical perspectives and methodologies. Therefore, the field of strategic management will likely experience increasing integration of multiple theoretical paradigms. Explanations of the future trends also suggest a balance between internal and external explanations of the complex relationships in this new competitive landscape.

Acknowledgments

We would like to thank Sage for permission to reproduce parts of the following article: Hoskisson, R. E., Hitt, M. A., Wan, W. P., and Yiu, D. (1999) 'Theory and research in strategic management: Swings of a pendulum', *Journal of Management*, 25(3), 417–56.

5

The strategic management framework: a methodological and epistemological examination

Omar Aktouf, Miloud Chennoufi, and W. David Holford

5.1 Introduction

What accounts for the phenomenal success of Porter's work? Assessing the contributions of Porter's Five Forces framework presented in *Competitive Strategy* (Porter 1980*a*), Brandenburger (2002) suggests that two factors account for the longevity and extent of Porter's influence. First, Porter's thinking 'gives a clear image of the essential activity of business. It depicts the whole vertical chain of economic activity running from suppliers (owners of resources) through businesses and on to customers. It highlights the central role of business in creating value but also emphasizes how businesses are interdependent with their suppliers and customers' (Brandenburger 2002: 58). Brandenburger adds that in contrast to canonical economic models, which assume atomized producers and consumers, Porter's model is more realistic in that it focuses on the reality of large firms that dominate many industries; that is, on situations of monopoly or oligopoly. Second, the very limited number of generic strategies that Porter advocates (low-cost leadership, product differentiation, and market specialization) is another element of clarity that attracts the attention of decision-makers, consultants, and academics to his work.

But clarity and accessibility is unlikely to guarantee the wide diffusion of a given work on management. Much of what is written about strategy is quite clear and accessible, yet little results in the success achieved by Porter. Porter frames matters differently, he claims, in terms of making a contribution to science and of scientific rigor. With regard to *Competitive Strategy*, he maintained in an interview which was quite revealing of the ins and outs of his thought: '... there was an opportunity to bring industrial organization thinking into the study of strategy, and vice versa' (Argyres and McGahan 2002*b*: 43).[1] As such, he was the first author to bring together two disciplines – industrial organization economics and strategic management – in order to provide a better discussion of the strategic choices made by firms. He went on to explain why this discussion also had to rid itself of neoclassical economic thought: '... *ceteris parabus* assumptions don't work. Managers must consider everything. I concluded that we needed frameworks rather than models' (Argyres and McGahan 2002*b*: 43). Lastly, with regard to scientific rigor, he added: 'We also needed a more disciplined way to think about strategy. We needed a more rigorous approach, a systematic way to look at industries and where firms stood in their industries' (Argyres and McGahan 2002*b*: 43–4).

In this chapter we attempt to show that while Porter's work is the basis of a systematic approach to strategy, it in no way guarantees the scientific rigor he claims, and furthermore does not assure the achievement of a lasting, defensible, and non-easily imitable competitive advantage. In addition, we try to shed further light as to why his work has been attractive for so long to a significant proportion of western managers, consultants, and academics. We discuss each of his two early pivotal works – *Competitive Strategy* (Porter 1980*a*) and *Competitive Advantage* (Porter 1985*a*) – in order to draw out their foundations, to reveal how their purported scientific rigor is non-demonstrable, and to point out the epistemological and methodological insufficiencies which seriously undermine Porter's claims to scientific rigor. We also visit another school of thought, namely the resource-based view (RBV) of the firm, which not only highlights practical and operational weaknesses in Porter's proposed frameworks but also serves to reinforce our view of the epistemological and methodological insufficiencies found in Porter's work. Our own arguments concerning the real reasons for the success enjoyed by Porter's work are twofold. At the ideological level his work legitimizes the current state of relations of force within and between firms operating in advanced capitalism. The legitimizing power of his thought makes it an ideal wellspring from which dominant incumbents can draw arguments and reasons of a scientific nature to justify their domination. At the operational level his work offers ease of comprehension, relative ease of implementation, and subsequent gratification from initial operational successes. However, in our view, operational successes derived from his frameworks are very often neither long-lasting nor easily defendable.

5.2 Doctrine of positioning and legitimating domination

In contrast to those researchers who preceded him in the field of strategic management, Porter is an advocate of the strategic positioning of a firm in a given industry (Porter 1979*a*, 1980*a*). At the time, this approach was novel in that previous strategic management researchers largely devoted their attention either to the elaboration of strategies or to strategic planning (Mintzberg et al. 1998). The notion of competitive advantage, which would come to occupy a central place in Porter's work, was absent and barely mentioned in the field.

According to Porter, strategic positioning derived from an exhaustive analysis of a certain number of factors which he baptized as 'the five competitive forces': competitive rivalry, bargaining power of suppliers, bargaining power of buyers, threat of new entrants, and threat of substitutes. These five forces, which, in Porter's words, 'emerged as an encompassing way to look at an industry' (Argyres and McGahan 2002*b*: 44), are supposed to be the most relevant and most significant indicators for any firm seeking to penetrate the industry which suits it best.

Logically, it is argued, the analysis of these indicators leads to a firm's strategic positioning in an industry in which

- there is little competition;
- there are suppliers and buyers with weak negotiating power;
- there are high entry barriers; and
- there are few substitute products.

Under these circumstances, Porter claims that a firm can maximize profits, as he says: 'I decided that fundamental to any theory of positioning had to be superior profitability' (Argyres and McGahan 2002*b*: 44). It should also be noted that Porter seeks to situate his theory in a normative perspective, something which he takes pains to stress: 'My work aims not to be descriptive but normative. What principles explain successful strategies? I believe strongly that managers can apply these principles prospectively, and that most do' (Argyres and McGahan 2002*b*: 45). Up to this point, firms are a kind of black box in Porter's work, inasmuch as he chose to situate his analysis at the mesoeconomic level; that is, the industry level. The criticisms of this choice led him, in *Competitive Advantage*, to integrate the microeconomic level into his framework via the notion of the Value Chain. We return to this point in the following section. For the moment, we discuss two major issues in the framework of strategic positioning – one epistemological in nature, and the other dealing with the framework's normative dimension.

Firstly, how does Porter justify his epistemological decision to set the level of analysis at the industry level? As we have learned from the science of complexity, the choice of the organizational level at which to analyze determines the scope of the results of the analysis. Why is the analysis of competitive forces at the industry level more relevant in strategy? In canonical management terms, why should the strategist's interest be focused on the firm's environment and only on the environment? To be sure, there was a real need in the field of strategic management to go beyond then-existing models, such as the BCG portfolio model or models based on an analysis of the advantages and disadvantages of individual firms, which limit themselves to the micro-economic level. However, this does not justify the epistemological choice made by Porter, who does not develop his argument about the choice any further. The question remains, and leads one to believe that there is a certain arbitrariness to this choice.

Moreover, one wonders what logic and which criteria underlie Porter's identification of the number and nature of competitive forces. The only argument invoked by Porter is that when he began his research he took his inspiration from industrial organization economics, which discussed phenomena such as monopsony (a situation in which there is only one customer for a firm's product). He also acknowledges that the notion of substitution already existed in economic thought. But he maintains that it was necessary to go further by imagining a series of factors integrated within the same kind of framework for analyzing industries. In the same interview quoted above, however, he presents two different arguments about the identification, the nature, and the number of these factors. On the one hand, he argues that 'these dimensions... have to be intuitively grounded' (Argyres and McGahan 2002*b*: 46). A little further on, on the other hand, he corrects himself and claims that: 'I didn't come to the conclusion that there were five forces until I'd looked at hundreds of industries' (Argyres and McGahan 2002*b*: 46).

Intuition and case studies are not mutually exclusive; they can even be complementary, with case studies confirming or invalidating the intuition. But this is not the problem. The real problem is that Porter displays positivism in spite of his use of case studies as a means for inferring his framework.[2] According to Popperian rigid positivism (Popper 1972), verification by one or several empirical experiences does not support the truthfulness of a proposition. Instead, a proposition is true for only so long as any example does not contradict it; that is, until it has been falsified. With respect to the competitive forces in Porter's framework of strategic positioning, it is not difficult to imagine a good number of industries in which other competitive forces are much more determinant than those identified by Porter: government in the arms and pharmaceutical industries; non-governmental organizations in the hydrocarbon industry, and so on. This points to the extreme fragility of the universality of Porter's Five Forces framework. Although the framework is presented as deriving from an heuristic approach consisting of induction, the basis of this induction is rather limited.

Furthermore, Porter's assertion of the framework's generality and scientific rigor creates an issue within those firms implementing it. According to Habermas's communicative ethics (1990), the morality of a given utterance depends on the dialogical exchange, consisting of a claim to validity by a speaker, objections to this claim by other speakers, and arguments by the speaker in response to these objections, all of which occur within the system of a space of free speech. There is a problem with Porter's framework here as his stance of generality presents the number and nature of competitive forces and the result of the ensuing analysis of industries as scientific truths. It is in this sense that Porter's framework can be a formidable instrument of domination against non-experts. When the framework is used by expert analysts and their constituents – senior management within a given business – there are no possible grounds of legitimacy for non-experts' questioning the framework's components and results. This element appears as an unacknowledged foundation running throughout Porter's thinking.

Continuing in an epistemological vein, Porter's thinking is characterized by environmental determinism, in that he glosses over an enactment phenomenon which has for some time been viewed as central in the analysis of the environment in management studies (Morgan 1997). The process of enactment is the process through which we proactively shape and structure our realities in an unconscious manner. Morgan states: 'Although we often see ourselves as living in a reality with objective characteristics, life actually demands much more of us than this. It requires that we take an active role in bringing our realities into being through various interpretive schemes, even though these realities may then have a habit of imposing themselves on us as "the way things are"' (Morgan 1997: 141). This phenomenon appears to produce at least as many projections (from the point of view and the interest of those conducting the analysis) about the characteristics of the environment under study as those which are really 'measured' or 'observed'. This is in addition to the inevitable changes brought about by any 'sector study', in any environment, when the study gives rise to strategies and the implementation of decisions that are likely to have an impact on the environment. In this event it is no longer the environment that determines corporate strategy, but the reverse.

Over forty years ago this position was seriously discussed, illustrated, and confirmed by Galbraith (1967) with concrete, edifying examples. In particular, he showed how the (strategic) planning of certain General Motors and Ford car models (his analysis focused on the Mustang, for which six years elapsed between the design phase and the marketing phase) contributed to determining – in defiance of all the so-called market laws – internal and external salaries as well as the price of products such as rubber, iron, coal, steel, and so on, for a number of years. This analysis demonstrates how the policies of large corporations to a large extent 'manufacture' domestic and international environments and completely distort the play of competition.

Secondly, the normative and prescriptive capacity of Porter's Five Forces framework is limited in its application and has ideological implications. For Porter's recommendations with regard to industry analysis to be normative and prescriptive, they have to permit an ex-ante identification of the industries which best suit a firm seeking to position itself. As we have seen, this industry must display competitive forces that are favorable to the firm. Is the ex-ante identification always possible? It is possible, but only in particular cases and given certain conditions. Positioning a firm in an industry through the analysis of competitive forces can occur in the case of an entrepreneurial situation in which the firm or its division does not yet exist. Here the decision to enter the industry hinges on the existence of favorable conditions for the firm to be able to exercise its domination. However, such favorable conditions for a new entrant would not exist unless firms already operating in the industry had never considered the possibilities offered by the industry. Then under what circumstances would pre-existing firms in an industry have never considered its possibilities? There can only be one explanation of this: it is when these pre-existing firms have not received the services of experts and consultants trained in Porter's industry analysis. This impasse brings us again to the true logical outcome of this framework: handing over the lion's share of power to experts and analysts.

The framework's limitation becomes clearer when a pre-existing firm employs it to analyze the industry in which it is situated. In the event of a firm already operating in a given industry, Porter's framework will lead it either to exit (inasmuch as the competitive forces are unfavorable) or to remain in the industry (inasmuch as the competitive forces are favorable). But the analysis will never enable the firm to know how to change its situation if it is precarious. As such, the normative and prescriptive capacity of Porter's Five Forces framework is limited. On the other hand, the framework will enable the ex-ante justification of a monopoly or oligopoly situation, since the analysis of the competitive forces will show that it is quite normal for a firm or firms to have a monopoly or oligopoly in an industry in which they have positioned themselves, as a function of competitive forces. It is for this reason that Porter's framework should be viewed as having the potential for legitimizing the domination by the most powerful companies with the help of a seemingly learned discourse.

5.3 *Competitive Advantage* and the expert's apology

Of all the inadequacies identified in *Competitive Strategy*, Porter is open particularly, if not exclusively, to a single criticism: determining the positioning of a firm in a given industry without inquiring into the firm's fit (in terms of its capacities, its resources, its abilities, and so on), resulting in firms entering industries which do not suit them at all. Porter felt obliged to turn to the microeconomic aspects of his doctrine, which resulted in the publication of *Competitive Advantage*. *Competitive Advantage* seeks to understand the nature of the specific, unique value that the firm produces to the benefit of different groups of consumers. It is for this reason that the firm 'needs to develop a unique set of skills that other organizations don't have' (Argyres and McGahan 2002*b*: 47). These abilities are supposed to be incorporated into the firm's activities, but attaining them requires a detailed analysis of these very activities, which Porter groups under another fundamental notion of his thinking – the Value Chain.

At first glance, Porter appears to have given a coherent response to the flaw in his earlier work. This at least is what is claimed by the mainstream literature in the field of strategic management. However, a closer examination of his discourse about competitive advantage, the Value Chain, and generic strategies reveals several tensions, which, as was the case with *Competitive Strategy*, bring seriously into question the scientific worth of his theory.

Porter's definition of competitive advantage is problematic, in that it is ambiguous, tautological, or marred by a serious ontological confusion. Porter writes that 'competitive advantage grows fundamentally out of the value a firm is able to create for its buyers that exceeds the firm's cost of creating it' (Porter 1985*a*: 3). As Klein (2001) notes, this in no way defines competitive advantage, unless, one might be tempted to suggest, one agrees to lump competitive advantage with value. In this case, and even if we ignore the problems engendered by this confusion, and bearing in mind that the question of value has divided theorists for decades, competitive advantage loses its relevance as a central notion in strategic thinking. Therein lies the ambiguity of this definition. Moreover, when Porter claims that 'competitive advantage is at the heart of a firm's performance in competitive markets' (Porter 1985*a*: XV), not only is the issue of the definition of competitive advantage glossed over, but Porter's claim is clearly tautological.

In addition, as Klein (2001) points out, defining something exclusively in terms of its consequences logically means that the consequences are known ex-ante and must have emerged prior to the thing itself – something which is a logical impossibility, especially when the reasoning is empirical in nature, as is the case with Porter. In other words, competitive advantage is defined as the source (or cause) of a firm's competitive performance, but this definition does not tell what makes such a source: the source of a firm's competitive performance is not defined, other than being called a 'competitive advantage', and thus remains ambiguous. In this light, Porter's claim that his theory is normative is devoid of meaning. It is for this reason that we feel justified in pointing to a profound contradiction pervading the entirety of the Porterian approach. His initial objective was to provide a normative framework for business strategy; however, its formalism yields an analytic approach which has no prescriptive power.

Let us take things further. For competitive advantage to be genuinely efficacious, it is absolutely necessary for it to be difficult, if not impossible, to imitate it. However, for this condition to be met, it is necessary that competitive advantage is difficult to identify unless the firm's competitive advantage is either protected from imitation in some way (such as protection of intellectual property by patents) or not available for purchase in the market. Otherwise all businesses would be able to carry out the analytical process leading to its identification and thereby procure the same competitive advantage. There is only one irrefutable way out of this logical impasse for Porter's theory. Its importance is crucial inasmuch as it clearly identifies both the implicit and never-stated implications of this theory and the underlying reasons for its success. What serves as a way out of the above impasse is not logical derivations from the analytical framework itself but the scientific status of its expertise which only 'high-powered' experts and consultants can operate effectively: not all firms receive the services of experts and consultants trained in Porter's Value Chain analysis. Leaving aside for the moment the intrinsic limitations of the reliance on experts and consultants, let us focus on how the scientific aura that Porter seeks to give his theory ultimately serves to legitimize the inordinate power accorded to experts and consultants, a group to which Porter himself belongs. We made the same discovery with regard to *Competitive Strategy*, and have come to the same conclusion with *Competitive Advantage*. This observation strikes us as one of the most significant reasons underlying the success of Porter's work among experts and consultants.

Porter firmly argues that there are three generic strategies: product differentiation, low-cost leadership, and market specialization. A fundamental question must be asked: What exactly does the notion of differentiation mean for Porter? What is differentiated – the firm or the product? According to Porter, it is the firm: 'A firm differentiates itself from its competitors when it provides something unique that is valuable to buyers beyond simply offering a low price' (Porter 1985a: 120). The phrase 'beyond simply offering a low price' clearly refers to competitive advantage. But as we showed above, the concept of competitive advantage is too ambiguous to signify anything precise. At best, differentiation means something different depending on whether one is in the position of a company director (in Porter's view) or that of an employee or the consumers (for whom 'differentiated' only concerns the product). As for low-cost leadership, it is neither more nor less than the reuse of an old neoclassical economic notion, and largely concerned with minimizing costs with a view to maximizing profits. Furthermore, in limiting himself to three formal generic strategies, Porter does not distinguish anything connected with emergent, creative, and innovative strategic notions.

Lastly, the value chain is a schematic representation of business activities, broken down into main activities and supporting activities, each one likely to contain value enabling the firm to acquire a competitive advantage. The task of the expert or consultant is to sketch this representation, study each activity on its own, and identify those that will give the firm the value to procure a competitive advantage. The analytical aspect of Porter's conception of strategy gains in strength and consolidates once again the influence of experts and consultants. In methodological terms, this way of doing things is akin to the Cartesian method of analysis and suffers from the same inadequacies. A Cartesian attitude toward a complex problem (determining the source of specific value within a firm with countless activities) involves subdividing it into a number of simple problems (breaking down the firm's activities into many easy-to-study activities) and to examine each activity on its own, without considering the others.[3]

Once all these simple problems are resolved, it is only a matter of reconstituting the whole. We now know that there is no validity to this kind of reasoning, given that it presupposes that the whole (the firm) is merely the sum of its parts (the firm's activities). Twentieth-century science has shown that the whole is made up of often complex relationships among the parts, and not merely the juxtaposition of the parts. In other words, it is less important to understand each part in its singularity than to understand the singularity of the relationships each part has with the other parts and the specificity of the relationships binding together the parts of the whole. In view of this, it is quite likely that the activity identified, after having been examined on its own, as yielding value (and hence a competitive advantage) will not necessarily be identified as yielding the same value if it is analyzed in relation to other activities. This indicates the extent to which Porter remains a prisoner of the linear, fragmented reasoning of classical science and the most simplistic elements it has to offer. However, if Porter's writings have been successful, it is because this simplified view is easy to present in the business and consulting worlds, neither of which are particularly familiar with epistemological reflection. It is thus not illegitimate to speak here in terms of the false representation of a stream of thought, the scientific value of which stems from the ignorance of those for whom it is intended.

In a similar vein and for the same reasons, no one – or almost no one – has identified another very serious limitation of Porter's ideas. Porter explicitly assumes the omniscience and the absolute rationality of experts and consultants who are able to find, fit together, and analyze a significant sum of data about competitive forces and about the components of the value chain. As such, Porter scorns the generally acknowledged observation in organizational theory regarding the limited rationality of individuals: namely, that there is a limit to the amount of information that human beings can process. Even computer simulations cannot resolve this problem. On the one hand, it is difficult to standardize, as we have seen, the determining factors common to all industries, and on the other hand, simulation is the application of a computer program designed on the basis of an algorithm constructed by human beings; that is, the same human beings characterized by their limited rationality.

One last, ontological remark in connection to this is necessary. Situating the value produced by a firm at the level of its activities is not at all obvious, and requires an argument to this end. However, Porter is content to claim this phenomenon, limiting himself to decreeing it in a self-referential discourse. The consequences of this are significant. Firstly, it amounts to a reification of the business through its activities. Secondly, the matter of rooting value in activities occludes the role that employees can play in the creation of value, which is wrongly attributed to the 'firm'. But this occlusion plays a highly ideological role – that of avoiding at all costs the social and political dimensions of the firm that is the object of the strategic analysis. Furthermore, it becomes evident that Porter's lack of attention to the role of the employee, worker morale, level of management leadership, and interpersonal skills poses serious limitations to the operational effectiveness of his framework in attaining a lasting, defensible, and not easily imitable competitive advantage.

5.4 Porter versus the resource-based theorists

In *Competitive Advantage* (1985a), Porter's Value Chain framework attempts to analyze the sources of competitive advantage by examining the activities a firm performs and the extent to which they are linked together. But intrinsic factors such as corporate culture, worker morale, level of communication and team spirit, level of management leadership, and interpersonal skills are not considered in his analysis. In 'Technology and competitive advantage' (1985b), Porter uses a similar approach to *Competitive Advantage* in identifying the primary and supporting technologies a firm may involve in the Value Chain. He then states how a firm identifies the core technologies that have significant impacts toward achieving a competitive advantage. Superficial attention is given to the significance of a firm's internal resources when he refers to 'relative technological skills', which he states is a function of many factors such as management, corporate culture, and organizational structure. He also adds that one of the actions used by a firm to strengthen its overall technological position is 'acquisitions or joint ventures to introduce new technological skills to the corporation, or to invigorate existing skills' (Porter

1985*b*, 78). But as in *Competitive Advantage*, intrinsic factors that can lead to the creation or further advancement of technology and innovation are hardly mentioned. Furthermore, the complexities and effects of corporate cultures that are encountered when integrating new technologies in situations of acquisitions are not addressed in any meaningful manner.

The RBV of the firm emerged with Prahalad and Hamel's (1990) article on 'core competence', followed by Stalk et al.'s (1992) article on 'capabilities-based competition'. Supporters of the resource-based approach take the view that the competitive environment of the 1990s and beyond has changed so significantly that the structural approach represented by Porter's competitive-forces framework is no longer effective. Prahalad and Hamel's definition of core competence is 'the collective learning in the organization, especially how to co-ordinate diverse production skills and integrate multiple streams of technologies' (Prahalad and Hamel 1990: 82). While Prahalad and Hamel focused on corporate-wide technologies and production skills in defining core competencies, Stalk et al. (1992) take a broader value chain or business-process view of the skill base in defining capabilities.

According to Stalk et al., the 'war of position' was a strategy that companies could follow when the economy was relatively static, characterized by 'durable products', stable consumer needs, well-defined national and regional markets, and clearly defined competitors. They contend that 'competition is now a "war of movement" in which success depends on anticipation of market trends and quick response to changing customer needs' (Stalk et al. 1992: 60). They add that: 'in such an environment, the essence of strategy is *not* the structure of a company's product and market but the dynamics of its behavior' (Stalk et al. 1992: 60). In contrast to Porter (1980*a*, 1985*a*), these RBV studies examine the behavior of 'how' a firm chooses to compete rather than the position of 'where' it chooses to compete. They also contend that competitive advantage should be found in resources and skills within the firm, as opposed to the general market environment 'outside' the firm.

In 'Towards a dynamic theory of strategy' (1991), Porter acknowledges the RBV as one of three 'promising' streams of research that attempt to address the challenge of developing a truly dynamic theory of strategy. He argues, though, that the RBV is but an intermediate step in understanding the true source of competitive advantage and that ultimately 'resources are not valuable in and of themselves', but 'are only meaningful in the context of performing certain activities to achieve certain competitive advantages' (Porter 1991: 108). For Porter, 'Competitive advantage derives from more than just resources. . . . It is the collective advantage gained from all sources that determines relative performance' (Porter 1991: 108). He concludes that it is even questionable how far we need to go up the chain of causality to generate a truly dynamic theory of strategy, or as he puts it: ' . . . we need to know how necessary or helpful it is to push even further back in the chain of causality . . . an important theoretical issue is where in the chain of causality to best cut into the problem. . . . It should be said that understanding the ultimate origins of advantage may not always be necessary for thinking about how to improve future advantage' (Porter 1991: 115–16).

In Porter's view, more emphasis should be put on 'crafting empirical research to make further progress in understanding these questions' (Porter 1991: 116). He seems to imply that understanding and harnessing the underlying fundamentals that foster competitive advantage is not as important as generating empirically based frameworks that may well work today, and surely he hopes will work tomorrow, without need for radical modifications. But as Stalk et al. stated back in 1992, the environment is now much more turbulent with unexpected perturbations. From a methodological point of view, it would seem that to deflect fundamental work and to depend only on continuous overlapping layers of empirical studies is a reactive strategy. This would be tantamount to increasing the magnitude of the 'day of reckoning' when conditions will be so dynamic and unpredictable that all empirical work will be as good as useless. For this reason' what is crucial is to conduct fundamental work toward trying to truly understand these conditions. In Porter's defense, one can say that when he wrote this article (Porter 1991), the RBV was still in its infancy and probably not advanced enough in trying to determine the true source of competitive advantage. In the ensuing years it suffered, as Nonaka and Takeuchi (1995: 48) point out, from a somewhat blurred focus, due to the lack of an agreed-upon and well-defined definition of terms. When looking at various articles on the RBV of the firm, we still see this fuzziness. Nonetheless, we will attempt to portray one type of philosophy within this view as being the fundamental building block toward competitive advantage.

In recent history, many scholars have identified a number of explicit attributes toward attaining competitive advantage. For example, there was Total Quality Management (TQM) from the 1980s to the early or mid-1990s, information technology (IT) roughly throughout the same period extending into the late 1990s, and knowledge management and innovation from the mid-1990s to the present day. But is there a more fundamental element which transcends all these attributes? If we look at TQM, many in the West lauded the Japanese mastery of quality and resulting competitive advantage, and, in response, proceeded to implement TQM methods. A study by Powell, however, examined the effectiveness of TQM as competitive advantage and noted: 'Potential TQM adopters may not appreciate that TQM success depends not only on adopting the TQM attributes, but also on the preexistence of complementary factors apparently unrelated to TQM, yet more difficult to imitate than TQM itself' (Powell 1995: 21). It appears to require a culture receptive to change, a motivation to improve, and people capable of understanding and implementing TQM's peculiar set of practices as well as corporate persever-ance. More fundamentally, Powell reports that TQM appears to require a complete restructuring of social relationships both within the firm and between the firm and its stakeholders. He states: 'Under TQM, firms must reconstitute all these relationships, in addition to relationships among em-ployees and between managers and employees. And they must reconstitute them more or less at the same time' (Powell 1995: 22). We agree with him that this social re-engineering is usually beyond the capabilities of most firms.

Powell's study (1995) concluded that firms who implement TQM proce-dures do not produce performance advantages if they do not create a culture within which these procedures can thrive; namely, executive commitment, an open organization, employee empowerment, and a good reputation with suppliers and customers. His overall conclusion is that although TQM can produce competitive advantage, 'adopting the vocabularies, ideologies, and tools promoted by the TQM gurus and advocates matters less than developing the underlying intangible resources that make TQM implementation success-ful' (Powell 1995: 31). As Aguayo (1990) illustrates in his book on quality implementation (chiefly inspired by the views and notions of W. Edwards Deming), much of what is required to implement quality within the workplace has less to do with metrics or sophisticated gadgetry and more with, as Deming (1986) once stated, 'pride of workmanship'. The source of competitive advan-tage seems to be pointing toward people: by people, we mean *employees, man-agement, and the social–corporate environment in which they work*. Even Nonaka and Takeuchi's work (1995) on knowledge management, which is primarily interested with the *process* of creating, harnessing, and managing knowledge and innovation, is really pointing back to the process of interaction and man-agement of people. Thus, our position is that people are the true source of competitive advantage.

Pfeffer (1994) advocates this view in 'Competitive advantage through peo-ple', in which he examines the five top-performing firms on the stock market in North America from 1972 to 1992 (in ascending order, Plenum Publishing with a return of 15,689 percent, Circuit City 16,410 percent, Tyson Foods 18,118 percent, Wal-Mart 19,807 percent, and Southwest Airlines 21,775 per-cent). These firms would have met the exact opposite criteria of what Porter's framework of five fundamental competitive forces recommends. The indus-tries in which these top firms are involved (retailing, airlines, publishing, and food processing) were 'characterized by massive competition and horrendous losses, widespread bankruptcy, virtually no barriers to entry (for airlines after 1978), little unique or proprietary technology, and many substitute pro-ducts or services. And in 1972, none of these firms was (and some still are not) the market-share leader, enjoying economies of scale or moving down the learning curve' (Pfeffer 1994: 10). He goes on to show that what these five firms have in common is how they manage their workforce. The reason why Southwest Airlines achieved a cost advantage comes from a 'very productive, very motivated, and by the way, unionized workforce' (Pfeffer 1994: 17).

This cost advantage is not easily imitable by competitors due to the fact that the culture and practices that enabled Southwest Airlines to achieve this success are not easily obvious. As Pfeffer argues: ' . . . it is often hard to comprehend the dynamics of a particular company and how it operates because the way people are managed often fits together in a system. It is easy to copy one thing but much more difficult to copy numerous things. This is because the change needs to be more comprehensive and also because the ability to understand the system of management practices is hindered by its extensiveness' (Pfeffer 1994: 18). In another article, Pfeffer and Veiga (1999) present in detail seven practices of successful companies:

1. Employment security.
2. Selective hiring.
3. Self-managed teams and decentralization as basic elements of organizational design.
4. Comparatively high compensation contingent on organizational performance (rather than individual performance).
5. Extensive training.
6. Reduction of status differences.
7. Sharing information.

They state that in general, firms have about a one-in-eight chance of succeeding at this since they often attempt 'piecemeal innovation' and therefore fail, or many of those that do try to integrate all these practices give up before results are forthcoming (Pfeffer and Veiga 1999).

In 'Creating advantages', Porter (1997) refers to the need and importance for innovation and how a firm needs to master technologies that it can apply and integrate (and not to just make the scientific breakthroughs). It is taken as a 'given' that this can be done irrespective of the organizational environment within the firm, once everyone at the executive and strategic level accepts that this is an important attribute for which to strive. It is an easy-to-adopt (and easy-to-imitate) concept as long as no extra effort is needed to instill the internal dynamics and conditions to make it happen. However, few firms which have adopted this approach have been able to distinguish themselves from their competitors in any significant or lasting manner in their respective industries, since the internal or intrinsic ingredient is the non-imitable portion of the formula.

Unlike the view presented by Porter and Stern (2001) in 'Innovation: location matters', innovation is primarily created by forces within the company as opposed to forces in the external environment. These forces are created by people within the firm. By primarily focusing on external forces, many managers have lost touch with people even though they know how important they are for achieving competitive advantage. As Bartlett and Ghoshal (2002) mention, 'Most managers see the strategic implications of the information-based, knowledge-driven, service-intensive economy.... They know that skilled and motivated people are key, and yet, a decade of delayering, destaffing, restructuring, and reengineering has produced people who are more exhausted or cynical than empowered ... developing internal resources and capabilities is more difficult to imitate.... Senior managers must move beyond slogans, and develop commitment to a set of beliefs that not only are articulated in clear terms, but also are reflected in daily actions and decisions' (Bartlett and Ghoshal 2002: 7–8).

To simply generate a strategy at the level which Porter advocated in his school of positioning in the 1980s and 1990s would be missing enormous fundamental issues which a firm needs to assess and harness in order to be truly successful in attaining a sustainable competitive advantage. But Porter's frameworks are attractive in both their relative simplicity to comprehend and, more importantly, relative ease of coordination to implement. A strategy of acquisition and positioning is much easier to implement (and imitate) than, as Pfeffer and Veiga (1999) point out, trying to put in place a culture and organization that seeks strength from within the firm. Ease of understanding and relative ease of implementation (notwithstanding the requirement for financial resources) is the reason why we believe many consultants to this day have been successful in attracting client firms to the Porterian view. However, it is another question as to whether firms have been truly successful in acquiring lasting advantages from this strategy.

5.5 Conclusion

We have attempted to reveal the inadequacies of Porter's strategic thinking from a methodological and epistemological point of view. We have also sought to show that his thinking misses enormous fundamental issues (as pointed out by the resource-based theorists) which a firm needs to come to terms with in order to be truly successful in attaining a lasting, defendable, and not easily imitable competitive advantage. Furthermore, guided by the question of why his frameworks have enjoyed so much success among academics, consultants, and management, we have suggested that the reason is not only to be found in its content (that is, ease of understanding and relative ease of implementation), but also in the ideological role it plays in legitimizing situations of domination at the firm and industry levels.

At the industry level, Porter's theory justifies and legitimizes three general trends inherent in the dominant paradigm of financial capitalism: domination by large corporations; the concentration of capital; and excessive centralization of power through hierarchies. As we have seen, Porter offers little help to small actors in a given industry, or to companies that want to draw more on their employees' knowledge and field experience in formulating their strategies.

At the firm level, a specific model of governance emerges from Porter's thinking, in which domination is exercised by management due to the exorbitant power accorded to experts and analysts. The degree of analytical expertise required by strategic positioning, competitive advantage, and the value chain reinforces the image of the consultant and management as 'the only' experts, and denies legitimacy for the participation of all the firm's other human components in the process of conceiving strategy or in questioning the strategy advocated. Indeed, experts are *a priori* immunized from criticism because of the supposedly 'scientific' nature of their reasoning, analyses, and decisions. As a result, employees are reified as blind system drones, confined to the role of performers, 'implementers' of strategies, which may lead one to think that Porter's thinking is merely another episode in the long history of orthodox management theories. Given the highly specialized character and the high-level position accorded to expert-strategists, it is an interdiction of any kind of movement toward participatory management. This potentially deprives organizations that adhere to Porterism of a significant competitive advantage enjoyed by organizations operating within the embrace of the RBV, which seek strength from within the firm by acknowledging the importance of employees, the management style employed, and the social–corporate environment that is cultivated.

Acknowledgments

This is a revised version of Aktouf, O., Chennoufi, M., and Holford, W. D. (2005) 'The false expectations of Michael Porter's strategic management framework', *Problems & Perspectives in Management*, (4), 181–200. We would like to thank Wiley for permission to reproduce part of the article.

Notes

1. We cite this interview often because it is one of the rare documents in which Porter discusses the methodological and epistemological aspects of his thought, which are

generally glossed over in his central works. See Argyres and McGahan (2002*a*) concerning the interview's background.

2. The same problem can be found in the Diamond framework presented in *The Competitive Advantage of Nations* (Porter 1990*a*).

3. This Cartesian attitude is somewhat toned down in an article published in 1991, as Porter argues: 'It is the collective advantage from all sources that determines relative performance' (Porter 1991: 108).

6

The evolution and eclecticism of Porter's thinking

Nicolai J. Foss

6.1 Introduction

There can be little doubt that economics has become a dominant voice in the contemporary conversation of strategy scholars. There are many reasons for this. Among the obvious ones are that economics provides a relatively clear-cut language and a number of useful established insights, it allows strategy scholars to interpret (long-lived) performance differences between firms, and more generally a number of the basic strategic issues rather naturally lend themselves to an economic treatment. Increasingly, therefore, concepts originally deriving from economics have become part of the discourse in strategy, and even strategy scholars, who might otherwise have difficulties with economic approaches to strategy, accept that the essence of strategy is the pursuit of economic rent.

Arguably, there are two overall approaches – each existing in different versions – that dominate contemporary economic approaches to strategy research. The first one is the *industry analysis approach* originally developed by Michael Porter (1980a) and later updated in the light of breakthroughs in game-theoretical, new industrial organization (IO) economics (Tirole 1988; Shapiro 1989) by Brandenburger and Nalebuff (1996), Ghemawat (1997), and others. The other dominant contender is the *resource-based view*, launched by a number of scholars in the mid-1980s (Teece, 1982; Wernerfelt, 1984; Barney, 1986a). In the *industry analysis approach*, Porter's contributions are outstanding. He helped to revive strategy when the field was suffering a setback in popularity and respect, as a result of strategic planning tools not being able to effectively deliver what was expected from them. By infusing the strategy discipline with IO economics, he has also done much to further conversations among strategy scholars.

However, looking at Porter's contributions over more than twenty years – from his PhD dissertation (Porter 1973) to his work on the role of location (Porter 1990*a*, 1994) – indicates that substantial changes took place in his thinking. This is not just a matter of Porter successively directing his attention to different analytical objects. It is also a matter of his explanatory approach significantly changing, which to a large extent is due to the impact of attempting to approach different phenomena without applying the outgrowths of fundamental theory. The central idea in *Competitive Strategy* (Porter 1980*a*) is that the IO economics of Joe Bain (1959) and Edward Mason (1939*a*, 1939*b*) provides a strong basis for strategic thinking. However, the external and industry-oriented perspective of the IO economics framework he uses is of relatively little *direct* use for theorizing firm strategy. In effect, it has to be modified, as Porter (1981) clearly recognized. In this chapter I ague that as Porter responds to unresolved issues and fills gaps introduced by 'importing' IO economics, he has made numerous *ad hoc* adjustments (meaning both extensions and modifications) to his IO framework. For instance, his attempt to incorporate the firm-side in his 1985 book *Competitive Advantage* (Porter 1985*a*), and his Schumpeterian focus on innovation as a form of a nation's competitive advantage creation in his 1990 book *The Competitive Advantage of Nations* (Porter 1990*a*, which is discussed in more detail in later chapters in this volume), result in an uneasy coalition of both IO-based and resource-based insights, without any theory playing a unifying role. The developments in Porter's thinking show that different theoretical alternatives are brought together in loose frameworks, with no serious attempt to confront them and examine their logical relations, that is, in terms of whether they are consistent, complementary, or mutually exclusive.

6.2 The IO connection

Although it is widely recognized that economic theory is important to management studies, and perhaps particularly to the strategy discipline, this has not always been the case. Consider the verdict issued by the prominent economist, Arthur Pigou:

> ...it is not the business of economists to teach woollen manufacturers to make and sell wool, or brewers how to make and sell beer, or any other business men how to do their job. If that was what we were out for, we should I imagine, immediately quit our desks and get somebody – doubtless at a heavy premium, for we should be thoroughly inefficient – to take us into his woollen mill or his brewery. (Pigou 1922: 463–4)

Most firms employ relatively few economists, and the influence of economics on management may arguably primarily manifest itself through the curricula of business school. Through this route, however, economics is bound to have an influence on the practical execution of firms' strategies. This is because economics supplies a body of well-corroborated knowledge that may serve as a foundational element for strategy research. For example, economics helps us better understand and answer questions such as the following: What are the sources of competitive advantage? How can competitive advantage be sustained? How sensitive is competitive advantage to environmental changes?

In the mid-1970s, economists-turned-strategy scholars, such as Richard Caves and Michael Porter, realized that the Bain–Mason structuralist approach in industrial organizations could be very usefully applied to the study of firm strategies, as well as for deriving practical recommendations. To Caves and Porter, basic IO concepts such as entry barriers and the collusion these barriers may foster offered an explanation of the observed persistence of above-normal profit. However, it was not entirely unproblematic to rely on IO in strategy research. The would-be importer of IO to the strategy field confronted basic translation problems, the most notable of which is the early (or 'old') IO's industry focus. The focus of early IO is clearly described by Bain (1959, 2nd edition 1968):

> I am concerned with the environmental settings within which enterprises operate and in how they behave in these settings as producers, sellers, and buyers. By contrast, I do not take an internal approach, more appropriate to the field of management science, such as would inquire how enterprises do and should behave in ordering their internal operations and would attempt to instruct them accordingly. . . . my primary unit for analysis is the industry of competing group of firms, rather than either the individual firm or the economywide aggregate of enterprises. (Bain 1968: Preface to the first edition, vii)

Given that Bain explicitly dissociates himself from any concerns of relevance to management science, and indeed defines away those features that would be relevant here, it is not surprising that Porter (1981: 609) could talk about communication problems (even 'suspicion') between strategy scholars and economists studying industrial organization. And one should in fact doubt whether the completely anonymous conceptualization of the firm in IO was an appropriate one for a field which is often thought to be about matching the *capabilities* of the firm to a changing environment in order to improve performance. The neoclassical theory of the firm, of which genus Bain's firm is a specie, is a very stylized entity. It is simply a step in the mental reasoning carried out for reaching conclusions about market phenomena.

This was a matter of some concern to Porter (1981), but in retrospect it is perhaps not so very surprising that he should decide in favor of IO after all. In fact, it was a quite logical thing to do in the mid-1970s for an economist who wished to approach strategy in terms of his own discipline. This is because it is doubtful whether there was really any other kind of economics other than IO that would at that time have been capable of performing a similar service for strategic thinking. Standard neoclassical price theory was still very much a matter of a fundamentally static and institutionless set-up, with fully informed and hyperrational agents almost completely separated from reality (compare with Loasby 1976). On the other hand, organizational economics and evolutionary economics were only in their infancy. From this perspective, IO had seemingly much more to offer. It had a rather direct empirical orientation, it could convincingly account for long-lived dispersals of returns, and it dealt directly with firms' strategies, and so on (cf., Porter 1981: 611, 617).

So it is not so strange after all that Porter considered that in the late 1970s there was 'increasingly clear evidence that much promise for cross-fertilization existed' between the strategy field and the IO structuralist tradition (Porter 1981: 609). However, numerous translation problems existed before IO could be applied to strategic thinking. In his 1981 article, 'The contributions of industrial organization to strategic management', Porter identified these translation problems as relating to differences in terms of, for example, whose interest is pursued (society versus firm owners), the unit of analysis (industry versus firm), temporal perspective (static versus dynamic), industry structure (exogenous versus endogenous), and theoretical scope (general ana-lytical categories versus detailed checklists). Such differences are of course fundamental and far-reaching, and the danger will always lurk around the comer that the 'translation' will be incomplete, partially flawed, and leave numerous gaps to be filled. For example, because of the inherently external and industry-oriented perspective of IO, a would-be translator may be seduced into putting much more emphasis on the Opportunities–Threat side of the overall SWOT framework than on the Strengths–Weaknesses side. One could argue that this is precisely what happened to Porter, at least initially, in his 1980 book *Competitive Strategy*.[1]

6.3 Porter's three key books

Porter's enormously influential 1980 book is firmly anchored in IO, and it is remarkably up to date with (then) newer developments in IO, such as market signaling, exit barriers, and commitment through irreversible investments. The structuralist whistle is blown from the beginning:

> The essence of formulating competitive strategy is relating a company to its environment....Industry structure has a strong influence in determining the competitive rules of the game as well as the strategies potentially available to the firm. Forces outside the industry are significant primarily in a relative sense; since

outside forces usually affect all firms in the industry, the key is found in the differing abilities of firms to deal with them. (Porter 1980a: 3)

This quotation also brings out the general tendency of the book: there is much about the 'environment,' but little about the 'company'. Capabilities enter the picture, for sure, but it is not organizational capital, such as 'core competencies' (or similar fashionable contemporary terms), that interests Porter. Rather, it is the ability to engage in tactical ploys dealing with 'outside forces' (competitors) which is of relevance (see, for example, Porter 1980a: 68) – an ability that presumably lies with top management. There is clearly a presumption in the book that the key capability is the skill with which top management analyzes its environment, reads signals (1980a: ch. 4), establishes commitment (1980a: ch. 5), and positions the firm in general. So although the firm level does enter the picture, the firm-specific components of competitive advantage are never seriously addressed. Or to express it somewhat differently: the underlying resource endowments that allow firms to carry out their strategic ploys are never seriously analyzed, and an analysis of how, why, and when firms should aim for which kinds of portfolios of resources is never undertaken.

In spite of its firm IO orientation, a form of eclecticism is already present in the 1980 book. For example, much of it (chapters 9–12) is taken up with discussing market and technology evolution in terms of product life-cycle theories or the Abernathy and Utterback product/process life-cycle (Utterback and Abernathy 1975; Abernathy and Utterback 1978). However, these evolutionary theories do not have any direct relation to the IO economics that is the 'formal' core of the book. In fact, they may even contradict it. This is because structural character-istics are generally seen in evolutionary theories as fundamentally endogenous, even in the short run, while in ('old') IO economics, structure is at least fixed in the short run. Partially as a result of this, evolutionary theories tend to interpret industry outcomes in terms of efficiency rather than market power, while IO does the reverse. Finally, the role of equilibrium is different: equilibrium is a crucial part of formal ('old' and 'new') IO, while it is not necessarily a feature factored in evolutionary models. This attempt to combine a basic IO influence with evolutionary insights continues to characterize Porter's thinking, and be-comes more evident in his later contributions. In particular, it shows a strong presence in the 1990 book *The Competitive Advantage of Nations*, in which he tries to combine (among other things) his Five Forces framework (1980a) with a strong focus on dynamic innovation capabilities clearly inspired by evolutionary economics.

The 1985 book *Competitive Advantage* is largely an attempt to further account for the sources of competitive advantage in terms of a decomposition of 'cost', 'differentiation', and 'focus'. However, the parsimony and precision of the 1980 book (Porter 1980a), which was due to its being anchored unequivocally in IO, is sacrificed in an attempt to address the complexities of the internal activities of the firm. Porter's 1985 approach to the firm is to understand it in terms of discrete 'activities', which refer to assembling, sales people making visits, and so on. The firm is a collection of such activities. It is not his intention to conceptualize the firm as a contractual entity (Porter 1985*a*: 53 n.) – as in transaction cost theory – but rather as a technological one, as in IO. Furthermore, there is no elaborate discussion of how resources and capabilities underpin activities; instead, activities should be understood as the link between resources and capabilities, on the one hand, and product-market positions on the other hand (de Man 1994). This implies that there is a difference in how competitive advantage is conceptualized in the 1985 book compared with the 1980 book. In the later book, competitive advantage stems from superior coordination of activities, while in the 1980 book it is a matter of erecting entry and mobility barriers and thus restricting supply. In other words, the conceptualization has changed from a (market) power perspective with an emphasis on entry deterrence, to one that emphasizes relative advantage (efficiency) and the sustainability of advantage through barriers to imitation (Porter 1985*a*: 268–9). However, as he admitted in 1991 (Porter 1991) there is no comprehensive discussion in the 1985 book of how activities are underscored by bundles of resources, and of the rent-yielding capacity of different bundles of resources.

The 1990 book is somewhat more explicit about the resource endowments of firms, and in general adopts a more dynamic view of the creation of (a firm's) competitive advantage through innovation and the sustainability of (a nation's) advantage through upgrading 'advanced factors'. What is noteworthy on the analytical level about *The Competitive Advantage of Nations* is that the perspective is now more explicitly evolutionary (there are several approving references to Joseph Schumpeter), though not in the formal sense of, for example, Nelson and Winter (1982). The IO heritage only directly reveals itself in one of the corners of the Diamond (namely, that relating to industry structure and competition). However, it may be present in other, more subtle and implicit ways. For example, although Porter places much emphasis on the creation and upgrading of factors through process and product innovation, the relevant factors/resources are mostly seen as located in the environment (clusters, as described by the Diamond framework) of the firm, not inside the firm. In other words, competitive advantage is still very much a matter of outside influences, and there is relatively little attention to individual firms' processes of resource accumulation.

6.4 Types of eclecticism in Porter's thinking

So, what has happened in the evolution of Porter's thinking? Overall level, it is fair to say that Porter's thinking has become increasingly eclectic, although eclecticism was certainly present from the beginning (such as the use of theories of industry evolution in some chapters of the 1980 book *Competitive Strategy*). However, eclecticism comes in a variety of forms, some of which are quite sensible, while others are not.

In terms of the first kind of eclecticism considered here, it may be (quite sensibly) argued that approaching some phenomenon by means of different analytical approaches within the same discipline, or approaching it in terms of different disciplines, may further our understanding of the relevant phenomenon. For example, the firm is conceptualized within economics as a production function in standard neoclassical price theory, as a contractual entity within modern contractual economics (for example, Williamson 1985), or as a repository of knowledge within evolutionary economics (for example, Nelson and Winter 1982). Although the problems treated by these theories are different, and although the more formal manifestations of these theories may even be incommensurable, they all arguably capture real aspects of firms, and may accordingly be used depending on the specific purposes at hand. To understand, say, the short-term impacts on profitability of outsourcing, the production of certain components, transaction cost economics may be the most helpful, while understanding how excessive outsourcing may harm the accumulation of resources may require a more long-run approach, perhaps best represented by an evolutionary approach.

I take this kind of eclecticism to be rather uncontroversial. This may be argued to be present in Porter's work to the extent that he chooses to conceptualize the firm in different ways depending on his actual purpose: as a production function (when analyzing industry-level phenomena; Porter 1980*a*), as a Value Chain (when trying to grapple with the firm-specific sources of competitive advantage; Porter 1985*a*), and as a repository of production knowledge and an innovating entity (when constructing his Diamond framework; Porter 1990*a*).

Another form of eclecticism refers to integration: seemingly different approaches are brought together, and, if the eclecticist is successful, shown to be in some way consistent. Again, successful eclecticism in this sense is rather uncontroversial; in fact, Larry Laudan (1977), the philosopher of science, argues convincingly that bringing seemingly incompatible approaches together and demonstrating that they are after all consistent is one important way in which science progresses. Now, less successful eclecticism of this form is the one where approaches or (related) disciplines are simply brought together without any serious attempt to examine their compatibility. There is an attempt to amass tools without examining whether they all really belong in the toolbox. Management studies as a whole may be representative of this kind of undisciplined eclecticism, and the strategy field certainly shows this quality. Many textbooks in strategy bring together insights from social psychology with insights from economics, political science, information theory, and so on, for the purpose of arriving at useful checklists, but do not make any attempt to examine whether these insights really fit with each other.

Clearly, Porter may be said to be an eclecticist in the sense of trying to integrate a diversity of approaches, although not a very successful one in the above sense. I discuss this issue in more detail later, so I restrict myself here to pointing out that integration remains on the level of loose frameworks, and there is no attempt to examine whether theories are compatible on deeper levels. For example, Porter does not present any arguments that the basic IO forming the core of the 1980 book is consistent with the industry evolution story in later parts of the book, nor does he draw on any basic research that has established this connection.[2] Furthermore, in his later contributions Porter's attempt to combine the basic IO with resource-based insights shows a more *ad hoc* approach, the third form of eclecticism discussed in the next section.

6.5 Progress and ad hock'kery

The third form of eclecticism refers to a situation in which a scientist or group of scientists make *ad hoc* adjustments of the underlying theoretical apparatus in an attempt to address more and more phenomena. Attempting to explain an increasing number of empirical phenomena is bound to produce problems for any theoretical approach (tradition, research program, etc.), some of which may be transitory, while others may be permanent. In Thomas Kuhn's well-known story (1962), it is the accumulation of serious, unsolved problems ('anomalies') that finally spells disaster for an established paradigm, and, through a process of the creative destruction of the intellectual domain, opens the door for establishing a new paradigm. However, what is largely neglected in this basic story is that the size and seriousness of problems will depend on whether the approach is expanded into related or unrelated areas, the speed of expansion, the maturity of the approach, and the number of scholars involved in the process of expansion.

What one means about '*ad hoc* adjustments' as a cause of such anomalies depends on one's position in the theory of science. Orthodoxy in the theory of science, perhaps best represented by Karl Popper's writings (1959), denounces *ad hoc* adjustment as merely 'immunizing stratagems' adopted by researchers to protect their hypotheses from negative empirical evidence. According to Popper (at least in his earlier writings), if a theory is confronted by a single refuting instance, it should be abandoned. It is well known that the basic trouble with this is that theories consist of complexes of hypotheses, and it is seldom possible unequivocally to single out the hypothesis (or hypotheses) that resulted in the theory being falsified (the so-called 'weak version of the Duhem–Quine thesis'). By contrast, proponents of a more 'holistic' view of science, such as Imre Lakatos, allow a certain degree of 'dogmatism', and do not demand that a theory should automatically be abandoned because of a single falsifying instance. Thus, adjustment of theories in the face of empirical anomalies is allowed. However, adjustments come in different guises (Lakatos 1970; Hands 1988). Some of them are consistent with the core propositions or the heuristic principles of the approach, others are not; that is, some are not *ad hoc* while others are. Specifically, Lakatos (1970) makes a distinction between three types of *ad hoc* adjustments, the first kind relating to adjustments which do not say anything theoretically new, the second kind relating to those that do not add any new empirical knowledge, and the third kind relating to adjustments which are in conflict with the core propositions and heuristics of the approach (or 'scientific research program'). When the latter kind of adjustments begins to cumulate, the approach is in trouble, since increasing fragmentation has begun.

I emphasize that we do not have to accept all of these rather orthodox positions in the theory of science to acknowledge the basic point that the successful development of approaches, theories, research programs, traditions, fields of knowledge, and so on, depends not only on whether they approach new phenomena (thus expanding their problem-solving capacity), but also on how they do this. Thus, in my opinion we need both Laudan's emphasis (1977) on problem-solving capacity, on the one hand, and the Lakatosian emphasis on the necessity of a close relation between new theoretical ideas and the core ideas of the research program, on the other hand, if there is to be a more adequate understanding of progress.

On common-sense grounds, therefore, I argue in favor of the normative implication that adjustments or extensions of an approach that keep intact its organizing core propositions are 'permissible' and 'better' than those which do not. This is so because such adjustments will not threaten the longer term viability of the approach. Moreover, such adjustments may (in retrospect) be 'sensible' in the sense that they help the approach develop. In contrast, adjustments that are inconsistent with the core propositions of an approach do not add anything new, or rely on entirely different heuristic principles for their construction are neither 'permissible' nor 'sensible', as they will only contribute to the disintegration of the approach. We now turn to applying these common-sense methodological considerations to evaluating the evolution of Porter's thinking.

6.6 The evolution of Porter's thinking

At least until *The Competitive Advantage of Nations* (Porter 1990*a*), IO has continuously been present in Porter's thinking as a theoretical legacy. When

IO was employed in the 1980 book *Competitive Strategy* it had to be modified in order to be of use in strategy research, as Porter himself was very well aware (Porter 1981). Specifically, and to summarize, the first adjustment to IO that Porter made was turning IO topsy-turvy so that it could be used as a normative framework for strategy. While it is debated whether this adjustment is 'sensible' (see, for example, Saloner 1991, 1994), this is clearly a 'permissible' adjustment in the sense that it does not contradict the core of IO. Crucial characteristics of IO did in fact carry over to his industry analysis approach in *Competitive Strategy*. An example is the black-box conceptualization of the firm that is characteristic of older IO. Another one is the focus on non-cooperative equilibria, where firms earn rents from their market power because of their ability to engage in tactics designed to build and maintain mobility and entry barriers.[3] The use of IO in the service of constructing the framework in *Competitive Strategy* keeps largely intact the core propositions of the old IO and thus is 'permissible'.

However, the adoption of IO sows the seeds of internal tension in Porter's approach. While these tensions remain virtually invisible in *Competitive Strategy*, they become more evident and problematic in the 1985 book *Competitive Advantage* and the 1990 book *The Competitive Advantage of Nations*. In these two later books, Porter continues to use the old IO as a fundamental part of his frameworks while addressing new phenomena (that is, the internal activities of the firm, the competitiveness of a national economy) with additional theoretical ideas (such as resource endowments of the firm, the creation of competitive advantage through innovation). The 1985 book *Competitive Advantage* adopted the activity-based view of the firm (Sheehan and Foss 2007, 2009) as a remedy for the lack of firms' internal aspects in the previous 1980 book, although his treatment of the strengths and weaknesses of firms in terms of their endowments of resources and capabilities is still limited. In the 1990 book *The Competitive Advantage of Nations*, Porter adopted a more dynamic view of the creation and sustainability of competitive advantage through learning and innovation. When adding these new insights, however, he does not make any serious attempt to examine how the IO conception of competitive advantage, as fundamentally a matter of market power and entry deterrence, squares with the (essentially resource-based) conception that seems to have become increasingly stronger in his thinking, namely, competitive advantage as a matter of accumulating and deploying asset-bundles with superior efficiencies to product-markets.

In Porter's own terms (1991), his thinking has increasingly moved away from relatively rigorous and unambiguous 'models' to much looser 'frameworks' (such as the Diamond in *The Competitive Advantage of Nations*). That is to say, he has become increasingly eclectic, in the sense that he has drawn on an increasing number of approaches and insights in the attempt to address an increasing number of objects of explanation. But that eclecticism has not been a very disciplined or successful one, since there has been little attempt to integrate and refine those approaches. The development that has taken place in Porter's thinking has been much more a matter of quickly reacting to the need to address new phenomena than it has been a matter of applying outgrowths of fundamental theory. That is, the evolution of his thinking has been much more practically driven than theoretically driven. Because fundamental theory (of any kind) seems to have been of declining importance in Porter's thinking, there has been an impression of increasing undisciplined eclecticism in his work.

Porter's own reflections (1991) on the strategy/economics nexus reveal that he has little desire to put any of the now prominent economic approaches to strategy at the center of his research effort. As he sees it, recent game–theoretic work 'stops short of a dynamic theory of strategy' (Porter 1991: 106). This critique is surely a bit surprising since *Competitive Strategy* in many respects dovetails with the new IO-inspired work on firm strategy. In a similar vein, the resource-based view (RBV) is criticized by Porter for being overly 'introspective' (Porter 1991: 107). Not only is this claim subject to criticism but it also ignores the increasingly evident presence of resource-based insights in his own contributions, *Competitive Advantage* and *The Competitive Advantage of Nations*.

It has been commonplace in the debate on the RBV to argue that it neglects the environment (for example Porter 1991; Verdin and Williamson 1994), and that this is one of the serious problems that besets this view. However, this judgment may be criticized. For example, Dierickx and Cool (1989) argue that product market positioning and unique resources work together to determine competitive advantage. Wernerfelt argues much the same, pointing out that product market positioning and the RBV '. . . should ultimately yield the same insights' (1984: 171). Thus, the environment is at least not completely neglected by the RBV (Foss 1998).

Furthermore, the activity-based view presented in Porter's *Competitive Advantage* is in many ways compatible with the RBV (Sheehan and Foss 2007, 2009). The activity-based view in the 1985 book follows a logic in which firms are not paid for products *per se*, but rather they are reimbursed for the activities they perform to provide products for consumers. While Porter's Five Forces framework (1980a) is firmly rooted in IO 'by turning the rough-and-ready Harvard School view of what imperfect competitors ought not do (for the sake of economic efficiency) into an account of what the smart manager ought to do (for the sake of profit)' (Langlois 2003: 285), the activity-based view in the 1985 book is closer to the Chicago IO perspective whereby rents are earned not due to exercising market power, but by being more efficient than rivals. Unlike the widely held association with Penrose (1959), the RBV draws inspiration from the Chicago perspective (Conner 1991;

Rumelt et al. 1991; Foss et al. 1995; Foss 1999). As Peteraf and Barney (2003) outline, both Porter and the RBV have similar definitions of competitive advantage and economic value.

What accompanies Porter's reluctance to acknowledge the adoption of essentially resource-based insights in his 1985 and 1990 books is his unwillingness to draw in a comprehensive manner on fundamental theory other than IO, coupled with his preference to continue working out home-grown frameworks. An outcome of this unwillingness is a lack of coherence in these contributions. Porter's 1980 book *Competitive Strategy* was an outgrowth of basic research, and this accounts for its relative coherence and perhaps also for its success.[4] However, the foundation of fundamental economic theory becomes evidently weak in his later contributions (Porter 1985*a*, 1990*a*). They are not to the same extent derived from basic research as *Competitive Strategy*, but made up of numerous *ad hoc* adjustments to the old IO-based approach. The theoretical foundation of those adjustments, many of which are essentially resource-based, are not confronted, and their logical relations to the old IO are not examined. As a result, his 1985 and 1990 books are significantly less coherent and less satisfactory.

6.7 Conclusion

The lack of an adequate theory of the firm has been a constant problem in Porter's thinking, and his attempts to incorporate the firm-side stop short of drawing on a fundamental economic theory. Metaphorically, Porter has only fully captured one of the scissor-blades of competitive advantage in his theorizing: only industry determinants of competitive advantage are comprehensively identified and discussed, while a comprehensive analysis of firm determinants is lacking. This, it should immediately be noted, may not necessarily be analytically wrong. For short-run purposes, 'black-boxing' the firm (and fixing industry structure) in this way may not be at all illegitimate. However, it can only provide a partial picture.

I have shown that Porter has brought essentially resource-based insights into the frameworks of his later contributions (Porter 1985*a*, 1990*a*). The activity-based view of the firm in *Competitive Advantage* is in many ways compatible with the RBV, and Porter's focus on resource-accumulation processes and the creation of competitive advantage through innovation in *The Competitive Advantage of Nations* bears a mark of the RBV. I have also argued that his old IO-based perspectives and resource-based insights are brought together in loose frameworks without examining their logical relations in terms of fundamental economic theory. The question is whether the kind of economics that underlies Porter's industry analysis approach is consistent with/complementary to the kind of economics beneath the resource-based insights.

While the doctrinal antecedents of the Porter industry analysis approach are clear and unambiguous, namely IO economics in the Bain–Mason tradition, things are different with respect to the RBV (Foss 1996c). The RBV has been argued to either stem from, rely on, or be compatible with a wide variety of economic approaches, such as that concerning the Chicago IO economics (Lippman and Rumelt 1982; Rumelt 1984; Barney 1986a, 1991; Conner 1991; Peteraf 1993; Foss 1999, 2000), the new IO à la Tirole (1988) and Shapiro (1989) (Ghemawat 1991), the Austrian school of economics (Wensley 1982; Jacobson 1992; de Man 1994; Foss and Ishikawa 2007), and evolutionary economics (Foss et al. 1995; Dosi 2000; Marengo et al. 2000). These economic approaches are distinguishable from each other in terms of a number of key assumptions (Foss 1996b, 1996c, 1999, 2000; Foss and Ishikawa 2007).

The Chicago IO economics and the new IO are both equilibrium approaches, although employing different assumptions to account for the observed persistence of above-normal profit. The Chicago IO approach was developed through the 1970s in open opposition to the Harvard industrial organization approach (the old IO) dominant in the 1960s and the main source of inspiration for Porter's early work (1980a). Whereas the Harvard approach argues that monopoly profits stem from the restriction of supply in product markets, on the basis of market power (such as entry barriers, collusion), the Chicago approach assumes informational asymmetry in factor markets (in other words, analysts on the supply side may not possess the same information as a firm on the demand side with respect to the net present value of a resource when applied in the operations of the demand-side firm). In the Chicago approach, entry barriers are informational (as assets in factor markets are not necessarily priced according to their value, due to inherent informational asymmetry), concentration is a result of efficiency, and high returns are returns to efficient underlying assets.

By contrast, the new IO has made formal the basic approach of the Harvard School; namely, that strategic positioning in price and quantity space allows firms to create anticompetitive effects and, by implication, competitive advantage and profit (Tirole 1988; Shapiro 1989). Strategic positioning, in this approach, means engaging in a game in which influencing rivals' expectation of one's future behavior is able to influence significantly the behavior of those rivals to the benefit of the strategizing firm. Specifically, a game between competing firms is specified and solved using the concept of Nash equilibrium or one of its refinements. A high degree of rationality (in other words, smart agents) is assumed in models of this approach. Given a common lineage in the old IO, the new IO shares many assumptions with the Porter industry analysis framework. In this sense, the new IO has an affinity with Porter's early work

(1980*a*). However, both the Chicago approach and the new IO are equilibrium-oriented. They start out from an otherwise perfect neoclassical world and introduce selected imperfections in factor markets in order to generate the desired results: the existence of rents (namely, above-normal profits) in equilibrium. As a result, neither the new IO nor the Chicago approach places any significant prominence on the role of learning, innovation, or entrepreneurship.[5]

The Austrian school of economics and evolutionary economics, by contrast, assume a disequilibrium-oriented view of productive activities. In the Austrian school, disequilibrium derives from its emphasis on the subjectivity of knowledge and expectations, as well as the role of the entrepreneur (Lachmann 1956, 1976). Within this view, resource attributes such as characteristics, function, and possible use are neither objectively given nor 'inherent', but are first constructed as part of entrepreneurial appraisal activities, which may then become actualized when entrepreneurial plans are implemented. Lachmann argues that experience is the 'raw material out of which all expectations are formed' (Lachmann 1956: 21). Expectations are formed as a result of a process through which a former expectation is revised through experience. The expectation that triggers entrepreneurial judgment might be different for each person, implying that estimates of the net present value of a resource differs widely across agents. Entrepreneurs discover hitherto undiscovered opportunities for profitable trade, causing disequilibrium in production activities (Kirzner 1973). However, the Austrian school does not feature innovation in the Schumpeterian sense of introducing new processes of production, new products, forms of organization, and so on.

Evolutionary economics, in contrast to the Austrian school as well as the Chicago IO economics and the new IO, is explicitly concerned with processes of technological change and development (Dosi et al. 1988). An important characteristic of modern evolutionary economics (Nelson and Winter 1982; Dosi et al. 1988; Metcalf and Gibbons 1989; Andersen 1994) is its orientation toward *population dynamics*, implying a view of heterogeneity of the (rather inflexible) members of a population as driving the evolutionary process. This process is characterized by analogies to three central mechanisms of evolutionary biology: variation; heredity; and selection. In evolutionary economics, the firm is seen as a knowledge-creating entity. The firm's path-dependent and 'sticky' knowledge endowment makes it differ in important respects from other firms, and allows it to articulate rent-seeking strategies that differ from those of other firms.

If those adjustments Porter introduced in his later contributions (Porter 1985*a*, 1990*a*) to account for the firm-side were possibly seen as deriving from the new IO, it would provide some consistency with his early industry analysis framework (Porter 1980*a*), mainly due to their common origin in the old IO. It would also provide new dimensions for his industry analysis framework, such as the heterogeneity of firms (in other words, firms may differ in terms of their cost structures, reputations, and so on) and resource indivisibility and immobility (which helps firms to sustain competitive advantage). However, this interpretation is difficult, if not impossible, to maintain. The equilibrium-oriented new IO finds it difficult to accommodate resource-accumulation processes, particularly the creation and upgrading of factors through process and product innovation featured in *The Competitive Advantage of Nations*. Processes of resource accumulation, in particular the accumulation of 'invisible' resources of competence, involve path-dependence, (collective) learning, and unanticipated consequences – notions which are hard to make consistent with basic equilibrium methodology (Nelson and Winter 1982; Dosi et al. 1988). Unless the new IO incorporates Schumpeterian perspectives, such as the models of creative destruction highlighted in the endogenous growth literature (for example, Segerstrom et al. 1990; Aghion and Howitt 1992), the resource-accumulation processes through process and product innovation remain theoretically unsupported *ad hoc* adjustments. In a similar vein, the Chicago IO economics is ruled out because of its equilibrium orientation.

The Austrian school and evolutionary economics are capable of accounting for processes such as learning, entrepreneurship, and innovation to a partial or fuller extent respectively. However, if the resource-based insights featured in Porter's later contributions (Porter 1985*a*, 1990*a*) are seen to derive from either the Austrian school or evolutionary economics, their frameworks are based on an uneasy alliance between two vastly different economic approaches – the old IO on the one hand, and the Austrian school or evolutionary economics on the other. Given the theoretical distance separating the old IO from the Austrian school and evolutionary economics, the frameworks in Porter's later contributions contain significant if not non-conciliatory tensions. Therefore, whatever economic approach those resource-based insights Porter introduced in his 1985 and 1990 books are seen to be based upon, these later contributions most probably represent the third kind of Lakatosian eclecticism: the compatibility between those adjustments introduced at later stages and the core propositions and heuristics of the pre-existing approach – namely, the old IO upon which Porter's industry analysis framework was originally built – is suspect.

Acknowledgments

I would like to thank Wiley for permission to reproduce parts of the following article: Foss, N. J. (1996*b*) 'Strategy, economics, and Michael Porter', *Journal of Management Studies*, 33(1), 1–24.

Notes

1. We should, however, not think of Porter as a mere translator; he is also a contributor to IO economics in his own right. For example, together with Richard Caves he anticipated later work on endogenous sunk cost (cost sunk in advertising and R&D) (Caves and Porter 1978) and on endogenous entry barriers (Caves and Porter 1977).
2. To be fair, it should be emphasized that Porter's 1980 book is still much more coherent than the average strategy textbook.
3. All this was stated in qualitative terms, with the equilibrium focus in *Competitive Strategy* being more implicit than explicit. The upsurge in work on the new IO that took place at the beginning of the 1980s changed this, expressing Porter's 'intuition' explicitly with the use of mathematical models.
4. However, Langlois (2003) is even critical of the 1980 book for a lack of depth in its theoretical foundation. He argues: '... economic theory arguably played a "deep background" role in Porter's analysis, whereas much of the action in his framework actually comes from the eclectic outer core – both his own and that of the Harvard School – rather than from anything flowing directly from the logic of neoclassical industrial organization' (Langlois 2003: 285).
5. In the new IO, agents may formally learn in Bayesian games, but their learning *functions* never change (O'Driscoll and Rizzo 1985: 37).

Section 2
The Competitive Advantage of Nations

7

National economic development and *The Competitive Advantage of Nations*

Robert M. Grant

7.1 Introduction

If Porter's *Competitive Strategy* and *Competitive Advantage* established the foundations for strategic management, *The Competitive Advantage of Nations* has transformed thinking about the basis of national competitiveness, and has had a massive impact on public policies toward regional and national economic development. *The Competitive Advantage of Nations*, therefore, is clearly an important book. Among Porter's books it is the broadest in scope and the most ambitious in intent. It addresses a question which lies at the heart of economic and managerial science: 'Why do some social groups, economic institutions, and nations advance and prosper?' (Porter 1990*a*: xi). This is no new issue: the same question stimulated Adam Smith's *Wealth of Nations* in 1776 and has been a central theme motivating the development of economic science since then. This chapter assesses Porter's answer to this question, and, in doing so, the contribution which the book makes to international economics and strategic management.

The book signified a milestone both in Porter's intellectual odyssey and in the development of the strategic management field as a whole. It represents a sharp departure from his *Competitive Strategy* (Porter 1980*a*) and *Competitive Advantage* (Porter 1985*a*). In addition to shifting the attention from the performance of the firm to the performance of the nation, the orientation of *The Competitive Advantage of Nations* was positive rather than normative; the primary mission was a predictive and explanatory theory of the international pattern of competitive advantage. In developing this theory, Porter combined inductive and deductive analysis. Beginning with established theories of competitive strategy and international economics, together with ideas conceived during his membership of the US President's Commission on Industrial Competitiveness, Porter developed his analytical framework through studying the performance of ten countries (United States, West Germany, Italy, United Kingdom, Sweden, Switzerland, Denmark, Japan, Korea, and Singapore); with each involving between five and nineteen industry cases. The book attests to the potential for inductive analysis using multiple, comparative case studies to develop innovative, empirically relevant theory.

The book also represented a partial redress of the imbalance of trade between strategic management and economics. While strategic management traditionally imported concepts and theories from economics, organization theory, systems theory, psychology, and population ecology, in *The Competitive Advantage of Nations* the primary flow of ideas is in the opposite direction. Porter uses the concepts and theories drawn from strategic management to extend and reformulate the theories of international trade, direct investment, and economic development.

At the level of academic research, *The Competitive Advantage of Nations* has provided a major stimulus to the field of economic geography and has fueled interest in the spatial aspects of strategy. As a result of subsequent research, particularly that into the role of industry clusters (or 'industrial districts'), several areas of Porter's core 'diamond' model have developed in depth, sophistication, and empirical validation. In particular, research into the dynamics through which local competitive advantage develops has focused attention on the role of knowledge transfer, social networks, and entrepreneurship. One of the outcomes of this research has been to narrow the geographical focus from the nation state to much smaller localities: Hollywood in the case of movies, Bangalore for IT services, Greenwich CT for hedge funds, and Antwerp for diamond cutting.

7.2 The theory

While the primary objective of the book was to explain why particular countries succeed in particular industries, in Porter's analysis it is firms rather than nations which are the principal actors. The influence of the nation on the international competitive performance of firms occurs through the ways in which 'a firm's proximate "environment" shapes its competitive success over time' (Porter 1990a: 29). The primary role of the nation is the 'home base' which it provides for the firm. Since firms typically develop within a domestic context prior to expanding internationally, the home base plays a key role in shaping the identity of the firm, the character of its top management, and its approach to strategy and organization, as well as having a continuing influence in determining the availability and qualities of the resources available to the firm:

> The home base is the nation in which the essential competitive advantages of the enterprise are created and sustained. It is where a firm's strategy is set and the core product and process technology (broadly defined) are created and maintained. Usually, though not always, much sophisticated production takes place there.... The home base will be the location of many of the most productive jobs, the core technologies, and the most advanced skills. (Porter 1990*a*: 19)

This view of the nation as a set of contextual variables which influences the competitive performance of firms and industries has several advantages from an analytic perspective. First, it permits Porter's analysis of industrial performance at the national level to draw upon recent contributions to the theory of competitive advantage at the firm level. The volume's second chapter restates the strategic theory of competitive advantage within an international context. Although well known in the strategic management area, this analysis offers powerful insights into the determinants of national competitive performance. For example, the theory of international trade has been preoccupied with cost differentials as the basis for trade. Recognition that differentiation advantage through quality, technological sophistication, design, and product features is at least as important a determinant of trade and overseas investment, particularly between the industrialized nations, is an essential ingredient of a richer and more predictively valid theory.

Second, it facilitates a dynamic approach to the analysis of competitive performance at the national level. These dynamic considerations include the role of innovation in creating competitive advantage, the role of imitation in eroding it, and the need to upgrade the sources of advantage if it is to be sustained over time.

Finally, Porter's analysis of national competitive performance encompasses both trade and direct investment. Exports and direct investment are closely related both as substitutes and complements, but their flows tend to be highly correlated and are driven by the same national determinants, including 'national economic structures, values, cultures, institutions, and histories' (Porter 1990*a*: 19). Hence, Porter does not distinguish international competitive advantage based upon direct investment from that based upon exports. International competitive advantage is measured by 'either (1) the presence of substantial and sustained exports to a wide array of other nations and/or (2) significant outbound foreign investment based on skills and assets created in the home country' (Porter 1990*a*: 25). An empirical benefit of this inclusiveness is that Porter's model can be applied as easily to national competitiveness in services (where competitive success tends to be through multinational expansion by companies rather than through exports) as it can to tangible products.

This view of the importance of national environments in firm success runs counter to most prevailing thinking which emphasizes the increasing dissociation of multinationals from their home bases. The 'globalization' of markets implies the globalization of the strategies and structures of multinational corporations (Levitt 1983). Even if nations retain a distinctiveness either in customer preferences or in the conditions of resource availability, to adjust to and exploit these differences requires that firms shake off the constraints of their 'home base' and move either toward a global orientation (Ohmae 1990) or a 'transnational' structure (Bartlett and Ghoshal 1989). Thus, while multinationality permits access to global-scale economies and the resource advantages available in different countries, this is quite consistent with Porter's basic proposition that national environments exercise a powerful influence on the competitive advantage of companies and industries. In the case of multinational corporations, the notion that the home base exercises a dominant national influence upon the company as a whole is more contentious. However, casual observation suggests that with the possible exception of the Shell Group, Unilever, and Nestlé, all leading multinationals are strongly influenced by their parent company's nationality. Indeed, Shell and Unilever may be exceptions that prove the rule to the extent that both possess dual nationality.

7.3 National influences on competitive advantage: the 'diamond'

Porter's theory of national competitive advantage is based upon an analysis of the characteristics of the national environment which identifies four sets of variables which influence firms' ability to establish and sustain competitive advantage within international markets. These interacting determinants form what Porter refers to as the 'national diamond', which forms the core of the book's theoretical contribution. The key features of the 'diamond' are as follows:

- *Factor conditions*: Factor endowments lie at the center of the traditional theory of international comparative advantage. Porter's contribution here is to analyze in much greater detail the characteristics of factors of production, the processes by which they are created, and their relationship to firms' competitiveness. He recognizes 'hierarchies among factors', distinguishing between 'basic factors' (such as natural resources, climate, location, and demographics) and 'advanced factors' (such as communications infrastructure, sophisticated skills, and research facilities). Advanced factors are the most significant for competitive advantage and, unlike factors whose supply depends upon exogenous 'endowment', advanced factors are a product of investment by individuals, companies, and governments. The relationship between basic and advanced factors is complex. Basic factors can provide initial advantages which are subsequently extended and reinforced through more advanced factors; conversely, disadvantages in basic factors can create pressures to invest in advanced factors. An example is the Italian steel industry's pioneering of mini-mill technology as a response to the disadvantages of the high capital costs, energy costs, and lack of raw materials. Similarly, expensive, difficult-to-fire labor provided important incentives for the development and adoption of automated equipment in Germany, Sweden, and Japan. In analyzing the relationship between factor conditions and national competitive advantages, Porter stresses the need to disaggregate factors of production to a fine level. A fundamental flaw of most empirical tests of factor–proportions theories of trade is their propensity to lump factors of production into broad categories such as land, labor, and capital. Porter observes that:

One of the least aggregated trade studies, Leamer (1984), includes capital, three types of labor, four types of land, coal, minerals, and oil. But even this level of aggregation is far too broad to capture the differences among nations that lead to competitive advantage. (Porter 1990a: 782)

The advanced factors which provide the most enduring basis for competitive advantage tend to be specialized rather than generalized, which inevitably implies a close interaction between industry success and the creation of the specialized factors of production necessary to that success.

- *Demand conditions*: Since the creation of advanced factors such as sophisticated skills and new technologies plays such an important role in establishing and sustaining national advantages, it is essential to understand the features of the national environment which are conducive to such investment. Within his 'Diamond' framework, Porter places particular emphasis on the role of home demand in providing the impetus for 'upgrading' competitive advantage. Firms are typically most sensitive to the needs of their closest customers; hence the characteristics of home demand are particularly important in shaping the differentiation attributes of domestically made products and in creating pressures for innovation and quality. Porter places particular emphasis on the role of sophisticated and demanding domestic customers, noting the influence of highly discerning home buyers on the development of the Japanese camera industry, and the German passion for durable, high-performance cars as a factor in German dominance of the world luxury-car market.

- *Related and supporting industries*: An industry's investments in advanced factors of production are likely to have spillover benefits beyond the confines of that industry. One of the most pervasive findings of the study is the tendency for the successful industries within each country to be grouped into 'clusters' of related and supporting industries. One such cluster is centered upon the German textiles and apparel sector which includes high-quality cotton, wool, and synthetic fabrics, women's skirts, dyes, synthetic fibers, sewing machine needles, and a wide range of textile machinery. Economies which are external to individual firms and industries are internalized within the industry cluster. Technological leadership by the US semiconductor industry during the period up until the mid-1980s provided the basis for US success in computers and several other technically advanced electronic products.

- *Firm strategy, structure, and rivalry*: Porter identified systematic differences in the characteristics of the business sectors of different countries which are important determinants of the industry pattern of competitive advantage within each country. These characteristics include strategies, structures, goals, managerial practices, individual attitudes, and intensity of rivalry within the business sector. For example, in the past the large number of small, family-owned companies in Italy has been conducive to the success of design-orientated, craft-based industries where entrepreneurial responsiveness and flexibility in adjusting to fashion changes are important sources of competitive advantage. German management style, with its emphasis on strong hierarchical control and methodical product and process improvement, has been particularly successful in engineering industries where manufacturing excellence and commitment to reliability and technical product performance are key buyer considerations. Within this broad set of influences, the most interesting relationship which Porter identifies is between domestic rivalry and the creation and persistence of competitive advantage. Rivalry is critically important in pressuring firms to cut costs, improve quality, and innovate. Because competition between domestic firms is more emotive and personal, and because domestic rivals compete from a common national platform, their rivalry tends to be more intense than with foreign competitors. Hence, domestic rivalry is particularly effective in promoting the upgrading of competitive advantage. Porter notes the intense domestic rivalry present in the Japanese automobile, camera, audio equipment, and facsimile industries (Porter 1990a: 412), and contrasts the success of these industries with the failure of most 'national champions' outside their domestic markets.

7.4 Dynamics of the national diamond

These four sets of national influences on competitive advantage operate inter-dependently rather than individually. For the 'diamond' to positively impact competitive performance usually requires that all four sets of influences are present. The interaction gives rise to some complex dynamics; for example, upgrading of competitive advantage through investment in product innovation, sophisticated labor skills, and process improvements is encouraged by a high level of domestic rivalry. At the same time, domestic rivalry is stimulated by the availability of factors of production which facilitate new entry, and by a domestic market which is large, growing, and discerning.

The intensity of interaction between the four corners of the diamond determines the extent to which the national environment is conducive to international success. The strength of interaction depends upon two primary factors. The first is industry clustering. The creation of 'advanced factors' such as technologies, sophisticated employee skills, design capabilities, and infrastructure is greatly facilitated by vertical and horizontal linkages between successful industries. The demand conditions created by successful downstream industries encourage development and upgrading by supplier industries, and entry by successful firms in related industries contributes to strong rivalry. Tight clustering of successful industries was observed to be a characteristic of all the successful smaller nations, including Switzerland, Sweden, Denmark, and Singapore, as well as Japan and Italy. By contrast, the relative decline of Britain as an industrial nation owes much to a failure to maintain and build closely related clusters:

> Britain's strong cluster of financial services and trade-related industries was highly self-reinforcing. In industrial businesses, however, there has been a gradual unwinding of clusters, in which only pockets of competitive advantage remain. (Porter 1990a: 502)

The strength of interaction between the determinants of national competitive advantage also depends upon geographical concentration of the industry. A general feature of successful industries within a country was their tendency to be located within particular cities and regions: 'The vast majority of Italy's woolen textile producers, for example, are located in two towns. . . . British auctioneers are all within a few blocks in London. Basel is the home base for all three Swiss pharmaceutical giants' (Porter 1990a: 154–5). Such proximity accelerates diffusion of innovation, facilitates investment in skills, and encourages the development of supporting industries. As later chapters in the volume cover, geographical concentration also raises the issue of whether the nation state is too aggregated a unit for studying the influence of industry location on competitive advantage. Porter observes that: 'the underlying issues are even broader than the role of nations (or locales). What I am really exploring here is the way in which a firm's proximate "environment" shapes its competitive success over time' (Porter 1990a: 29). Although a national perspective obscures the true localization of competitive advantage in particular industries, at this stage in his thinking Porter maintains that the characteristics of nations are sufficiently important that it is the country rather than the city or region which is the relevant unit of analysis.

The final stage of Porter's analysis extends his theory of competitive advantage to explain economic development within nations, and national differences in prosperity and growth. National prosperity, in Porter's analysis, is closely linked to the 'upgrading' of competitive advantage. Sustained competitive advantage depends upon firms upgrading their competitive advantages through innovation and investment in 'advanced' factors of production. At the national level these processes enhance labor productivity and increase real income per head of population. In addition, upgrading involves a changing national composition of industries and activities. Firms lose competitive position in the most price-sensitive industries as they develop more capital and technology-intensive industries. Within industries, firms move toward more differentiated segments, they shift many of their lower technology activities overseas, and within their home bases concentrate on activities which require the highest levels of skill and expertise. Porter identifies a four-stage development process. The characteristics of each are summarized in Table 7.1.

Table 7.1. The stages of national competitive development

Driver of development	Source of competitive advantage	Examples
Factor conditions	Basic factors of production (such as natural resources, geographical location, unskilled labor)	Canada, Australia, Singapore, South Korea before 1980
Investment	Investment in capital equipment, and transfer of technology from overseas. Also requires presence of large home market, acceptance of risks, and national consensus in favor of investment over consumption	Japan during 1960s, South Korea during 1980s
Innovation	All four determinants of national advantage interact to drive the creation of new technology	Japan since late 1970s, Italy since early 1970s, Sweden and Germany during most of the post-war period
Wealth	Emphasis on managing existing wealth causes the dynamics of the diamond to reverse: competitive advantage erodes as innovation is stifled, investment in advanced factors slows, rivalry ebbs, and individual motivation wanes	United Kingdom during post-war period; United States, Switzerland, Sweden, and Germany since 1980

7.5 Contribution to international trade and investment theory

The main contribution of *The Competitive Advantage of Nations* was in extending the theories of international trade and direct investment to explain more effectively observed patterns of trade and investment between developed countries. Porter's ability to dramatically expand the scope of existing theory concerning international trade and investment derives from his integration of the theory of competitive strategy with that of international trade and investment. By dispensing with the economist's fiction of trade being transactions which occur between countries ('Assume a two-country, two-commodity world...'), Porter was able to explore an unprecedentedly broad range of national-level influences upon firms' competitive performance within world markets.

As a result, Porter broadened and integrated contemporary contributions to the theory of international trade. For instance, the Diamond framework assigns a prominent role to a country's stock of productive factors in determining competitive advantage in particular industries. Porter's contribution is the detail with which he examines the characteristics of factors of production, and his analysis of the determinants of a country's stock of resources. His detailed analysis of the roles of education, infrastructure, technical knowledge, and the incentives provided by factor disadvantages represents a considerable advance on the simplistic theoretical and empirical analyses associated with traditional Heckscher–Ohlin models.

Similarly, Porter's discussion of the links between domestic demand conditions and national competitive advantage extended prior analysis of the scale advantages associated with a large home market (Grubel 1967; Krugman 1980), and of the role of domestic demand in driving trade and the location of production through the product life cycle (Vernon 1966). Whereas the earlier theories focused upon particular aspects of the domestic market (its size, and the existence of an early market for new products), Porter's theory identifies a broad range of demand variables which influence the international competitive performance (including the rate of growth of domestic demand, its segment composition, the sophistication of home customers, and the early saturation of the home market).

Porter's greatest departure from previous theories of international trade and investment was probably in emphasizing dynamic aspects of competitive advantage. The central characteristic of internationally successful firms and industries is their commitment to internal investment in the products, processes, and skills needed to continuously upgrade their sources of advantage. Hitherto, technology has played a minor role in trade theory, and most models which incorporate it are of a 'technology gap' type where technology differences between countries are exogenous (Krugman 1990: 152–64). Porter's analysis of the competitive advantages of nations directs attention at national and industry-level influences upon innovation within firms. Particularly interesting and insightful are his analyses of domestic rivalry and selective factor disadvantages as drivers of innovation. The analysis of the relationship between rivalry and innovation has long antecedents in the industrial economics literature. It is worth noting that his unambiguous finding that rivalry is conducive to sustained success in international markets contrasts with the inconsistent findings of prior research with regard to the relationship between industry structure and innovative activity (Greer and Rhoades 1976; Kamien and Schwartz 1982).

The breadth of Porter's theory is a consequence of the goals of the book. Because his primary objective is to explain important real world phenomena rather than to construct elegantly logical theory, the book contrasts with much recent work in the international trade area and returns to the tradition represented by Smith and Ricardo. Although international trade theory has developed rapidly in recent years due to the application of industrial organization theory to trade issues (developments closely associated with the work of Brander (1981) and Krugman (1990)), little new light has been shed upon the determinants of international competitive performance. Most of the recent research has been concerned with explaining the existence of international trade between countries with similar resource profiles. While this work has interesting implications for trade policy (Helpman and Krugman 1989), it has not contributed substantially to explaining and predicting the patterns of trade between nations.

At the same time, the breadth and relevance of Porter's theory do not come without cost. The ambitious theoretical and empirical sweep of the analysis has been achieved at the expense of precision and determinacy. Lack of precision is apparent in the wooly definitions of some of the key concepts and in the specification of relationships between them. For example, a key contribution which Porter makes to the analysis of national competitive advantage is his view of the creating and sustaining of advantage as a dynamic process. This process involves the 'upgrading' of competitive advantage. But his concept of 'a *hierarchy* of sources of competitive advantage in terms of sustainability' (Porter 1990a: 49) lacks clarity. 'Upgrading' is not only about greater sustainability of competitive advantage. It also involves greater complexity and sophistication in technology, skills, and customer relationships. Later 'upgrading' is interpreted to mean 'achieving higher-order competitive advantages in existing industries and developing the capability to compete successfully in new, high-productivity segments and industries' (Porter 1990a: 544). But sustainability, factor complexity, and productivity tend not to be perfectly correlated. Saudi Arabia's competitive advantage in the supply of crude oil is based upon the very basic advantage of natural resource endowment, yet seems quite sustainable. Conversely, many recent product innovations in the securities and financial services industries appear to require quite complex skills and systems, yet are quickly imitated by rivals. The links between the upgrading of competitive advantage and national economic development are also tenuous. Many of the countries at the first (factor-driven) development stage such as Canada, Nauru, and the United Arab Emirates are among the world's most prosperous.

Reliance upon broad but ill-defined concepts such as the 'upgrading of competitive advantage' reflects a more general failure to perfectly reconcile microlevel analysis of competitive advantage of firms and industries with macrolevel analysis of national development and prosperity. There is inconsistency in the definition and measurement of competitive advantage as the analysis moves from the industry to the national level. Competitive advantage at the firm and industry level is measured in terms of exports and outbound foreign investment, while 'the only meaningful concept of competitiveness at the national level is national productivity' (Porter 1990a: 6). Porter presumes the existence of some invisible hand whereby firms' pursuit of competitive advantage translates into increasing national productivity and prosperity. This presumption is unwarranted. Since 1985 a combination of real wage erosion and dollar depreciation has improved US competitiveness in several industries; however, these developments have not been accompanied by corresponding growth in US productivity and living standards. Part of the problem is Porter's attempt to treat exports and outward direct investment as part of the same phenomenon, and to ignore their complex interrelationships. Thus, the competitive advantage of British companies in publishing, accounting, and certain processed foods is revealed mainly in multinational growth which has made little contribution to the upgrading of competitive advantages in the domestic economy.

Lack of precision is also apparent in the 'National Diamond' framework. At its most basic, the diamond is a taxonomy for classifying the various national influences on firm and industry competitiveness. Yet the categories overlap to such a degree that it is not clear that the various influences would not be better represented by a triangle or pentagon rather than a diamond. For example, the role of supporting and related industries in promoting competitive advantage appears to be largely through their effects on factor conditions and demand conditions. Successful upstream industries are a resource for domestic firms, successful downstream industries provide stimulating demand conditions, and horizontally related industries contribute to factor creation through investment in skills and technology.

Some corners of the diamond become so all-embracing that the variables included and their relationships to national competitive advantage are widely diverse. In particular, 'firm structure, strategies, and rivalry' is an awkward catch-all category which comprises: national differences in management and practices and approaches; attitudes towards authority; social norms; the orientation of firms towards competing globally; goals and motivations; national prestige and priority; and domestic rivalry (Porter 1990a: 108–17). These variables do not form a coherent group nor are they related in similar ways to national competitive advantage. Domestic rivalry is an industry-level variable which is clearly defined and its relationship to pressure for improvement and innovation is precisely specified. Management training and practices, and employee attitudes and motivations on the other hand, appear to be national characteristics which relate to factor conditions.

Indeterminacy of the relationships in the Porter 'diamond' model stems from three sources. First, some variables have an ambiguous impact on competitive performance. An abundant supply of highly productive factors of production is generally conducive to competitive advantage in industries which make intensive use of such factors. However, in certain instances, it is disadvantages in the supply of basic factors which create incentives for upgrading competitive advantage. Porter fails to clearly define the conditions under which advantages in the supply of basic factors of production are an advantage, and the conditions under which they are a disadvantage. Second, the relationship between each corner of the diamond and national competitive performance is complicated by the interactions between the different variables. Porter analyzes how changes in each of the four corners of the diamond are influenced by each of the other determinants, yet he acknowledges: 'In such an environment, cause and effect relationships among the determinants become blurred' (Porter 1990a: 179).

Finally, determinacy is further weakened by two-way relationships between each of four corners of the diamond and national competitive performance. While Porter's model seeks to explain national advantage in terms of the four sets of determining variables, the dynamics of the system are such that competitive performance has important influences on these variables. Thus, successful international performance provides the finance and incentives for upgrading the sources of competitive advantage (it may also engender complacency), promotes the development of related and supporting industries, raises the affluence and expectations of domestic customers, and promotes rivalry by encouraging new entry.

The result is a theory which is gloriously rich but hopelessly intractable. The strength of the theory is its cogency in explaining the international success of particular industries, such as the German printing-press industry, the American patient-monitoring equipment industry, the Italian ceramic tile industry, and the Japanese robotics industry. The key weakness of the theory is in its predictive power. Ambiguity over the signs of relationships, the complexity of interactions, and dual causation render the model unproductive in generating clear predictions. Porter's prescriptions in the form of 'national agendas' are symptomatic of this predictive weakness. Porter establishes imperatives for each country, most of which relate to the removal of impediments to the process of upgrading. But there is little prediction of how each country's industry pattern of competitive advantage is likely to evolve in terms of the industry clusters which will prosper, which will lose out to international competition, and what the implications of structural change and differential rates of upgrading will be for national rates of economic growth.

7.6 Policy recommendations

The differences between Porter's theory of national competitive advantage and the existing theory of international trade and investment are highlighted by their respective public policy implications. From an initial premise that government's aim is to maximize the level and growth of the nation's living standard, Porter defines the primary policy goal as:

> ... to *deploy a nation's resources (labor and capital) with high and rising levels of productivity.* ... To achieve productivity growth, an economy must be continually upgrading. This requires relentless improvement and innovation in existing industries and the capacity to compete successfully in *new* industries. (Porter 1990a: 617)

The appropriate role for government is to contribute to the conditions which are most conducive to the upgrading of competitive advantage, working through each of the four corners of the national diamond and taking actions which improve the interaction between these influences. In some instances, the government can act directly to augment the conditions for upgrading national competitive advantage – for example, through investing in education, training, and infrastructure; fiscal measures which encourage private investment; and encouraging the creation and dissemination of information. In general, however, government's influence is indirect, partial, and is only observable after a substantial lapse of time. The policy prescriptions which derive from Porter's analysis diverge from conventional ideas about government policies to promote national prosperity. Porter's view of the appropriate role of government is at odds with the role envisaged by most proponents of a more active industrial policy:

> Many see government as a helper or supporter of industry. Yet many of the ways in which government tries to 'help' can actually hurt a nation's firms in the long run. ... Government's proper role is as a *pusher and challenger*. There is a vital role

for pressure and even adversity in the process of creating national competitive advantage. (Porter 1990*a*: 681)

As a result, Porter suggested that policies directed toward enhancing national competitiveness often have effects which are the opposite of those intended. Table 7.2 contrasts some policy implications arising from Porter's analysis of national competitive advantage with those of conventional wisdom.

7.7 Contribution to competitive strategy theory

The primary contribution of *The Competitive Advantage of Nations* is to the analysis of international trade and investment, and, by implication, to the economic development of nations. At the same time, the book contributes to business strategy analysis in two main areas. First, Porter's integration of the theory of competitive strategy with theory of international trade and comparative advantage extends the analysis of strategy formulation to an international environment. Second, his emphasis upon innovation and 'upgrading' as central to the creation and sustaining of competitive advantage helps reformulate the strategy model within a dynamic context.

Strategy is a quest for superior performance through establishing a competitive advantage over rivals. Competitive advantage is conventionally analyzed in terms of the selection of a strategy which matches a firm's resource strengths to the requirements for success in the market environment ('key success factors'). In a domestic industry, firms face a common environment, and competitive advantage is primarily concerned with exploiting superior resources and capabilities. Internationalization of the strategy model has hitherto assumed that firms are faced with a common global market environment, and the key strategic issues are exploitation of global-scale economies (Levitt 1983), international cross-subsidization to squeeze domestically based competitors (Hamel and Prahalad 1985), and organization in order to reconcile the benefits of globalization with those of national differentiation (Bartlett and Ghoshal 1989).

In Porter's view, the globalization of markets does not simply transpose firms from a national to an international environment. Even in the most globally competitive and homogeneous markets, the national environment – as represented by the four corners of the national diamond – continues to influence a firm's potential for competitive advantage and, hence, its strategy formulation because of the influence of the proximate environment both on resource availability and on key success factors within its market environment. Two of Porter's national-level variables – factor conditions and the presence of successful related and supporting industries – are influential in

Table 7.2. Government policy and national competitiveness: examples of differences between Porter and conventional wisdom

Policy measure	Traditional thinking	Porter model
Devaluation	Improves the competitiveness of domestic industries by giving them a cost advantage over overseas competitors	Devaluation is detrimental to the upgrading process: it encourages dependence upon price competition and a concentration upon price-sensitive industries and segments. It discourages investment in innovation and automation.
Policy toward R&D	Government investment in R&D stimulates innovation within the country. Defense-based research offers commercial spin-offs. Cooperative research pools efforts and avoids wasteful duplication.	Importance of *diffusion* of technology means that research within universities is more effective than research within government laboratories. Government should support research into commercially relevant technologies in preference to defense-related research. Government should support research institutions focused upon industry clusters or cross-cutting technologies. Cooperative research is of limited value since it may blunt rivalry.
Government procurement	Provides secure home demand for domestic firms, hence encourages investment and economies of learning and scale. Defense procurement, in particular, provides an early market for technically sophisticated products.	While government can act as an early, sophisticated buyer, procurement can easily act to protect weak national champions from international and domestic rivalry, and distort product development from global market needs.
Regulation of product and process standards	Stringent regulations impose costs which hamper competitiveness in home and overseas markets.	Stringent performance, safety, and environmental standards can pressure firms to improve quality, upgrade technology, and provide superior product features. Particularly beneficial are regulations which anticipate standards which will spread internationally.
Antitrust policy and regulation of competition	The presence of international competition means that domestic monopolies and mergers are ineffective in creating and exercising market power. The interests of global competitiveness may require the relaxation of antitrust constraints in order to encourage strategic alliances and the development of world-class competitors.	Antitrust policy plays an important role in maintaining the strength of domestic rivalry, but must not act as a barrier to vertical collaboration between suppliers and buyers, which is integral to innovation. Regulation of competition, on the other hand, is likely to be detrimental to rivalry and new enterprise creation: deregulation of competition and privatization of domestic monopolies usually spurs national advantage.

determining a firm's resource strengths, while the other two – rivalry and home demand conditions – have their primary influence upon conditions for success within the immediate market.

A consequence of Porter's introduction of the national environment into the strategy framework is increased emphasis on the role of resources and capabilities as determinants of competitive advantage. Porter's prior contributions to strategy analysis concentrated upon the role of the industry environment in determining strategy (*Competitive Strategy*) and the use of the value chain as a vehicle for analyzing opportunities for competitive advantage and for configuring a firm's system of activities (*Competitive Advantage*). By establishing a pivotal role for resources and capabilities as sources of competitive advantage, he implicitly endorses the resource-based approach to strategy analysis represented by the work of Barney (1986a), Dierickx and Cool (1989), and Rumelt (1984). Porter's primary contribution to the analysis of the role of resources in the determination of competitive advantage and the formulation of strategy is to recognize that the firm's resource base is not simply a function of its own past investments but is also determined by the conditions of resource supply and resource creation within its environment. Although this idea is hardly novel (Kogut 1985), Porter's model is interesting because of the interaction which occurs between firm-level and country-level sources of competitive advantage.

An even more significant departure of the strategy analysis in *The Competitive Advantage of Nations* from that of Porter's prior work is the shift from a static to a dynamic analysis of competitive advantage. The greatest weakness of Porter's prior strategy analysis was the steady-state concept of competitive advantage inherent in his description of positions of cost and differentiation advantage. This static analysis of competitive analysis reflects a static concept of competition derived from the 'structure–conduct–performance' model of IO economics (Barney 1986b). In *The Competitive Advantage of Nations*, Porter dispenses with this concept of competition as a static variable whose strength depends upon market structure, in favor of a Schumpeterian concept of competition – a process of dynamic change in which innovative and imitative behavior is constantly creating and destroying positions of competitive advantage. The result is an analysis of competitive advantage at the firm level which is dynamic in the sense that competitive advantage is a consequence of change.

Change may be exogenous through the emergence of new technologies, changing buyer needs, new industry segments, shifting input supply conditions, or changes in government regulations. In such cases, competitive advantage accrues to firms which move early in exploiting the emerging opportunities. Alternatively, change may be endogenous through innovation by firms. Once created, competitive advantage is subject to erosion. A firm's ability to sustain its competitive advantage depends upon the ease with which competitors can duplicate the competitive advantage, the number of distinct sources of advantage the firm possesses, and the firm's ability to continually upgrade its sources of competitive advantage.

Porter's dynamic approach to competitive advantage contains little that is new. Most of these ideas about the creation and sustaining of competitive advantage have been previously put forward by Dierickx and Cool (1989), Ghemawat (1986), Rumelt (1984, 1987), and others. Porter's contribution to this analysis is primarily in exploring the conditions which are conducive to innovation and the speedy exploitation of environmental changes. In addition to the national factors which promote innovation and upgrading – factors such as domestic demand conditions and strong national rivalry – he also points to specific managerial actions at the level of the individual firm. Most of these recommendations deal with two sets of influences upon dynamic competitive advantage: information and motivation. By maximizing interchange with buyers, suppliers, and firms in related industries, a firm can maximize the information and knowledge available within its national cluster. By targeting customers which are the most sophisticated, demanding, and which have the most difficult needs, a firm can help establish leadership in quality and innovation. By establishing performance norms on the basis of the toughest regulatory standards and the performance levels of the most successful competitors, opportunism and pressure for innovation can be maintained.

A striking feature of these recommendations is that many of them directly contradict prescriptions arising from the static analysis in Porter's *Competitive Advantage*. Within the static industrial organization model, strategy is a quest for monopoly rents which are achieved through locating within industries and segments where competition is weak, and by initiating changes in industry structure which moderate competitive pressures. However, such conditions are also likely to blunt the incentives for dynamic competitive advantage. Porter acknowledges the revisionism of his new doctrine:

> These prescriptions may seem counterintuitive. The ideal would seem to be the stability growing out of obedient customers, captive and dependent suppliers, and sleepy competitors. Such a search for a quiet life, an understandable instinct, has led many companies to buy direct competitors or form alliances with them. In a closed, static world, monopoly would indeed be the most comfortable and profitable solution for companies.
>
> In reality, however, competition is dynamic. Firms will lose to other firms who come from a more dynamic environment. Good managers are always running a little scared. They respect and study competitors. An attitude of meeting challenges is part of organizational norms. An organization that values stability and lacks self-perceived competition, in contrast, breeds inertia and creates vulnerabilities. Some

companies maintain only the myth that they believe in competition. Success grows out of making the myth a reality. . . . The aim in seeking pressure and challenge is to create the conditions in which competitive advantage can be preserved. Short-term pressure leads to long-term sustainability.

In global competition, the pressures of demanding local buyers, capable suppliers, and aggressive domestic rivalry are even more valuable and necessary for long-term profitability. These drive the firm to a faster rate of progress and upgrading than international rivals, and lead to sustained competitive advantage and superior long-term profitability. (Porter 1990a: 586–7)

7.8 Conclusions

Porter's *The Competitive Advantage of Nations* addresses the central theme in the development of the world economy: internationalization. At the corporate level, growth in the volume of international transactions has transformed the competitive environment of firms: management faces greater risks, opportunities, and pressure for efficiency and flexibility. At the industry level, internationalization has accelerated technical change, compressed product life cycles, and increased the geographical concentration of industries. At the national level, internationalization has greatly increased disparities between nations in their rates of economic development. Among the major industrialized nations, Japan and Germany achieved more rapid productivity progress than the United States, Canada, and Britain during the greater part of the period 1950–90. Even more startling are the disparities in growth rates between, on the one hand, Korea, Taiwan, Singapore, Hong Kong, and more recently, mainland China, and, on the other hand, those achieved by countries which appeared during the 1950s to be the most promising candidates for future development (such as Argentina, New Zealand, and the Philippines).

Our understanding of these phenomena has been limited by the widening gulf between economic science, which has retreated into irrelevant theoretical rigor, and the superficiality of most policy prescriptions. The achievement of *The Competitive Advantages of Nations* is not just in entering this gap, but in doing so with an analysis of international competitive performance of unprecedented scope. A single analytical framework provides a cogent explanation of competitive advantage within industries which range from chocolate to auctioneering, and among countries as different as Sweden and Singapore. Moreover, a critical strength of Porter's analysis is its ability to span three levels of aggregation: the firm, the industry, and the nation.

At all three levels, Porter offers new insights into the determinants of competitive advantage, but it is at the intermediate level where his analysis offers the most striking advance over prevailing knowledge. His theory of how national factors influence competitive advantage within individual industries extends well beyond current theories of competitive advantage based upon resource endowments, and integrates and broadens contributions to trade theory based upon industrial organization and the product life cycle. Most important, however, is Porter's emphasis upon dynamic determinants of competitive advantage, particularly through innovation and investment in more complex factors of production.

At the level of the firm, Porter's main contribution is in integrating Schumpeterian approaches to competition and resource-based approaches to strategy within his analysis of competitive advantage. The resulting framework suggests an emerging consensus within the strategic management field. The hostility of some strategic management researchers to Porter's earlier work may be due not so much to opposition to economic concepts and theories *per se*, as to opposition to an equilibrium framework which is incapable of addressing competition as a process of dynamic rivalry.

Least successful is Porter's analysis of economic development at the national level. The problem here seems to be that the further he departs from the micro-foundations of his theory, the more difficulty he experiences in explaining relationships between economic aggregates. Hence, despite the novelty and the appeal of many of his recommendations for government policy, the persuasiveness of his prescriptions is limited by doubts as to whether his analysis is adequate in explaining economic development at the national level.

More generally, the ambitious scope of the book inevitably means shortcomings both in theory, exposition, and empirical analysis. The versatility and richness of Porter's theory is achieved partly through concepts whose definitions are adjusted to suit the needs of different parts of the analysis, and theoretical relationships which are indeterminate and sometimes inconsistent. In terms of exposition, Porter has a tendency to reinforce his ideas by repeating them in differentiated forms, and at the empirical level the theory is applied selectively and qualitatively without resort to rigorous testing of its predictive validity.

But these shortcomings are trivial when compared to the achievement of *The Competitive Advantage of Nations*. The major analytical contribution of the book is in offering new insights into the development of industries and nations within their international contexts, and in extending the theory of international trade and investment to address these issues. Yet it also has great significance for the study of strategic management. This is partly due to reformulation of the competitive strategy framework within an international, nationally differentiated environment, and the recasting of the analysis of competitive advantage within a dynamic context. Even more important is a broadening of the horizons of strategic management by extending its concepts and theories from the level of the firm to the level of the nation, and a lowering of the barriers which separate strategic management from economics.

Acknowledgments

This is an updated and revised version of Grant, R. M. (1991). 'Porter's "Competitive Advantage of Nations": An assessment', *Strategic Management Journal*, 12(7), 535–48. I would like to thank Wiley for permission to reproduce parts of this article.

8

Domestic demand, learning, and
The Competitive Advantage of Nations:
a review of the empirical evidence

Jan Fagerberg

8.1 Introduction

Why do some countries maintain higher levels of competitiveness than other countries? What are the crucial factors behind such differences? Which policies can governments pursue to improve the relative performance of their economies? Questions such as these motivate concerns regarding the competitiveness of countries. Although the concept of country competitiveness has proven to be controversial, the importance of the underlying challenges makes it unlikely that this issue will lose the attention of policymakers soon.[1]

The competitiveness term may be applied at several levels. It may relate to a country, a sector (or industry) within a country, or a single firm. When applied to a country it usually takes on a double meaning, relating to both the economic well-being of its citizens, normally measured through GDP per capita, and the trade performance of the country.[2] When applied to a sector or industry, however, competitiveness is normally defined as export specialization. Hence, a country is said to be competitive in a particular sector if its share in world trade (of products from that industry) is above that of the average for the country. As discussed in greater length by Michael Porter in his book *The Competitive Advantage of Nations* (1990a), competitiveness on different levels of aggregation may be related. For example, firm- and/or sector-level features may affect competitiveness at the national level and vice versa.

Traditionally, textbook explanations of specialization patterns in international trade have focused on differences in supply conditions. Countries, it is argued, tend to specialize in areas of production that make intensive use of factors of production with which the country is relatively well equipped. However, empirical research has shown that the explanatory power of this type of theory is limited. This initiated an active search for alternative approaches from the early 1960s onward. Many of the new theories which were developed (often labeled 'neo-technological' theories[3]) came to focus on differences in technological capabilities across countries and sectors as the main explanatory factor behind the observed differences in patterns of export specialization. This focus is now widely shared, among many 'mainstream' economists also, and is supported by a large amount of empirical research. However, what causes technological capabilities to differ often remains unexplained.

The publication of *The Competitive Advantage of Nations* by Porter in 1990 led to increasing attention being given to the favorable impact that the domestic market, through 'advanced domestic users', may have on the international competitiveness of a country. It was argued that *interaction between users and producers of technology* acts as a major impetus to technological change. Interaction, however, involves costs. These reflect, among other things, the stability of the user–producer relationship and the degree of 'proximity', defined to include factors such as language, the legal system, the education system, and so on. Hence, most stable user–producer relationships are of a national character. The above, together with the assumption that a country's comparative advantage in the long run will be in areas where its rates of learning and innovation are high (compared to other countries), suggests that countries in the long run tend to develop comparative advantages in areas where, by a comparative standard, there are many advanced domestic users.

The idea that the domestic market may affect competitiveness positively is by no means a new one: it dates back at least to List (1841). However, neoclassical trade theorists have normally regarded it as 'theoretically unsound' and as a cover for protectionism. This chapter presents a critical appraisal of the theoretical and empirical evidence based on the hypothesis of a positive impact of domestic market, through 'advanced domestic users', on the international competitiveness of a country.

8.2 Why should 'advanced domestic users' matter?

Most attempts to explain the specialization patterns of countries in international trade have focused on supply conditions. According to the standard neoclassical theory of international trade, countries ought to specialize in areas of production that make intensive use of factors of production with which the country is relatively well equipped. In spite of the dominant role played by traditional neoclassical theory in this area, there has always been a strand of thought that has emphasized learning as a potential source of comparative advantage. This tradition points to the potential effects of relations between firms or sectors, within the domestic economy, on innovation and learning, and the impact of this on the international competitiveness of the country and its specialization pattern in international trade.

The idea that the structure of the domestic economy, or links between firms from different sectors of the economy, may have a bearing on competitiveness has a long tradition in economics. List (1841) in his famous defense for protectionism pointed to the positive impact that such relations may have in the process of industrialization. Perroux (1955), combining a Schumpeterian and 'structuralist' perspective, arrived at similar conclusions in his analysis of industrial development ('growth-poles'). Hirschman (1958) made 'linkages' one of the most influential concepts in development economics. Linder (1961), to whom we will return below, discussed the implications of such relations for trade theory. Mistral (1982), working in the French structuralist–institutionalist tradition, coined the concept 'structural competitiveness' to cover the positive impact that relations between different sectors of the economy have on national export performance.

The precise nature of the assumed relationship between 'structure' and competitiveness is of course not the same in all these contributions. Nor is it always clear why some links have a greater positive impact than others. An interesting interpretation is presented by Linder (1961). His argument runs as follows. First, a need that cannot be sufficiently satisfied by existing products arises on the demand side. Since entrepreneurs for various reasons (culture, language, proximity) tend to be better informed about developments in the home market than in markets elsewhere, they will usually be the first to react to the demand for new or improved products arising in the domestic market. The outcome of this activity – the innovation – then enters a period of testing and revision in which the home market is assumed to play a critical role.

> Whether it is a question of 'critical revision' of an invention or a product development work in general, it must be carried out in close contact with the market . . . If, for some odd reason, an entrepreneur decided to cater for a demand which did not exist at home, he would probably be unsuccessful as he would not have easy access to crucial information which must be funnelled back and forth between producer and consumers. The trial-and-error period which a new product must almost inevitably go through on the market will be the more embarrassing costwise, the less intimate knowledge the producer has of the conditions under which his product will have to be used. And, if there is no home demand, the producer will be completely unfamiliar with such conditions. (Linder 1961: 89)

Linder assumes that the introduction of the product in the export market will have to wait for this testing in the home market to be completed. However, if the product is successful at home it will probably be a success on the export market too (Linder 1961: 88). The evolutionary flavor of the argument is quite obvious: entrepreneurs strive to solve problems that arise in their environments (domestic market); learn as possible solutions (innovations) are proposed, tested, and improved; and eventually – on the basis of accumulated experience – penetrate foreign markets as well.

Linder has also pointed out that the importance of 'the home market', as discussed above, varies across countries, sectors, and products. For instance, he did not expect this to be very important in developing (or semi-industrialized) countries, nor did he expect it to contribute much to the explanation of differences in trade performance in standardized (or, more generally, 'non-innovative') products (Linder 1961: 90). In these cases he expected other factors to be more important. Thus, what is discussed here is not a general theory of export specialization, but a partial one that may (and should) be combined with other approaches.

Porter (1990a) presented an evolutionary scheme of economic development based on similar ideas. Echoing Linder, he argues that traditional supply factors, although important in the earlier stages of development, are not among the prime determinants of 'competitive advantage' in more advanced countries, where growth is assumed to be innovation-driven. The most competitive industries in an advanced country, he argues, tend to be highly integrated ('clustered'), both vertically and horizontally, with favorable consequences for learning, innovation, and 'competitive advantage'. In Porter's scheme, this typically starts with integration between customers in traditional industries and suppliers of machinery and other types of advanced equipment, then widens through spillovers and feedbacks to and from related and supporting industries (Porter 1990a: 554–5).

Porter, along the lines of Linder, contends that a high degree of integration between customers and suppliers (or users and producers) affects international competitiveness positively. This hypothesis is intuitively appealing, and there is a large amount of descriptive evidence that can be used in its defense (see Porter 1990a). However, in spite of the growing popularity of this approach, many still probably feel that it is a phenomenon in search of a theory.

It is assumed that the development of new technology in many cases requires close communication and interaction between the users and producers of technology (Lundvall 1985, 1988). To achieve this end, a channel – and a common code – of communication must exist. The establishment of channels and codes of communication involves fixed costs, and this implies that in a stable user–producer relationship, the cost per transaction is decreasing. This is clearly an argument for keeping relationships stable. Furthermore, lower transaction costs are likely to lead to a higher volume of transactions. Hence, a higher rate of innovation might be expected in a market characterized by enduring user–producer relationships, compared to a more 'atomistic' market structure. To the extent that the parties of a stable user–producer relationship can prevent the (immediate) diffusion to others of the innovations they make, as seems likely, they may (for some time at least) keep the benefits for themselves.[4] Indeed, the fact that the relationship is of an enduring character, and is recognized as such by both parties, may significantly increase the probability of appropriating the benefits. Thus, a stable user–producer relationship may be interpreted as an institution that reduces the costs – and increases the pace – of innovation and learning, while at the same time making it easier to appropriate the economic benefits.[5] As a result, the competitive position of participating firms is likely to improve. To some extent, this holds for both users and producers. This assumption has much in common with the approach of the 'national system of innovation' (Lundvall 1992*a*, Edquist 1997), stressing the importance of 'user–producer relationships' (Lundvall 1992*b*) and 'networks' (Håkansson 1987; Gelsing 1992).

However, the importance of stable relationships may vary across industries. It should be expected to be of special importance in industries characterized by complex and user-specific technology. In these cases, the need for close communications and interaction between users and producers of technology is likely to be large, and the costs of establishing new relationships of this kind high. In other cases, products and technologies may be highly standardized: both transaction costs and the need for enduring user–producer relationships will be low.

To the extent that this type of interaction takes place mainly *within country borders*, this should be expected to affect patterns of export specialization (or comparative advantage) across countries as well. Since, as pointed out by both Linder and Porter, the costs associated with communication and interaction increase with distance and differences in culture, language, institutional settings, and so on, this may be a reasonable assumption to make. Porter even holds that the importance of the domestic market for competitive advantage is growing.

> While globalization of competition might appear to make the nation less important, instead it seems to make it more so. With fewer impediments to trade to shelter uncompetitive domestic firms and industries, the home nation takes on growing significance because it is the source of the skills and technology that underpin competitive advantage. (Porter 1990*a*: 19)

However, it may also be argued that the increasing role of multinationals in world production has reduced the costs of communication and interaction significantly, and that the Linder–Porter hypothesis therefore was more relevant in the past than it is now. The empirical evidence presented in this chapter may shed some light on this controversy.

Furthermore, not all 'user–producer relationships' promote innovation to the same extent. Lundvall suggests that: 'Being closely linked to conservative users having a weak technical competence might be a disadvantage for a producer, and vice-versa' (Lundvall 1988: 355–6). Thus, the mere existence of a home market for a particular product or technology is not enough to generate the necessary innovations and, hence, comparative advantage. A necessary condition is that domestic users are both sophisticated and demanding.

Another issue raised by Porter is the extent to which a competitive market structure is a necessary condition for the positive impact of user–producer interaction on competitiveness. He argues that: 'Favorable demand conditions...will not lead to competitive advantage unless the state of rivalry is sufficient to cause firms to respond to them' (Porter 1990a: 72). Porter seems to be most concerned with competition among producers (suppliers) of technology.[6] However, a similar argument holds for the user side: users that are under continuous pressure to improve their performance are more likely than others to demand improvements from their suppliers. As Porter points out:

> One competitive industry helps to create another in a mutually reinforcing process. Such an industry is often the most sophisticated buyer of the products and services it depends on. Its presence in a nation becomes important to developing competitive advantage in supplier industries. (Porter 1990a: 149)

8.3 Empirical methods and evidence

In this section we will discuss the available evidence and problems related to empirical testing. First, it may be noted that 'the home market hypothesis' (or the Linder–Porter hypothesis) commands considerable empirical support at a descriptive level. Andersen et al. (1981a) provide a good illustration of this point by showing that in the case of Denmark, which is a large exporter of agricultural products, the three engineering products with the highest specialization index (called 'revealed comparative advantage index'; Balassa 1965) all belong to the group 'agricultural machinery'. Similar examples can be found for other countries. For instance, Sweden has been shown to be specialized in both pulp and paper and machinery for that sector, and Norway in both shipping/fishing, shipbuilding, and so on. (Andersen et al. 1981a). In *The Competitive Advantage of Nations* (1990a), Porter presents a large amount of historical evidence and descriptive statistics on export specialization that can be interpreted in support of the Linder–Porter hypothesis. These descriptive case studies are often interesting and perceptive, but it is of course difficult to know how representative they are.

In spite of the large amount of descriptive evidence available, there has been a dearth of statistical work done to test the hypothesis. This is not surprising, given the complexities involved. To test the hypothesis, a relatively large number of exporting sectors, as well as domestic users of the products from these sectors, must be identified and defined. While this may be easy in theory, it is more difficult in practice, since the available statistics are not collected for this purpose: most 'advanced' products are not classified according to users, and even when this is the case it is not always easy to find internationally comparable data for users on a sufficiently disaggregated level. Furthermore, assuming that these problems can be solved, we have to establish what we mean by an 'advanced user sector', and decide how this can be distinguished empirically from a less advanced one. To the best of our knowledge, there are only a few empirical studies that manage to overcome these complexities, to which we will now turn: Andersen et al. (1981*a*), Fagerberg (1995), and Beise-Zee and Rammer (2006).

The hypothesis tested by Andersen et al. is as follows: If internationally competitive producers exist in one sector of the economy, and these producers buy their technology from another sector of the economy, the latter sector should also be expected to be internationally competitive as well. For instance, if a country specializes in exporting agricultural products, it should be expected to specialize in exporting agricultural machinery too. Thus, in the interpretation of Andersen et al., 'advanced user sectors' are identified as sectors in which the country has a comparative advantage. This interpretation has the advantage of enabling us to use the same data source, trade statistics, and the same index of revealed comparative advantage (Balassa 1965) to measure the strength of both *'producer' (export) sectors* and *'user' (home market) sectors*. The problem, of which Andersen et al. were well aware, is that this interpretation introduces a bias toward products where the trade statistics allow a link to be made. For 'producer' sectors (or products), this implies that most of them belong to the group 'specialized machinery', where users in most cases are relatively well specified. On the user side, the consequence is that users in the non-trading sectors of the economy (or in other sectors not covered by the international trade statistics) are excluded from the investigation. For instance, the link between technology producers and public-sector users cannot be taken into account.

Let X denote exports, i the exporting country, and j the export product. The index of revealed comparative advantage (S) for country i in product j can be presented as follows:

$$S_{ij} = \frac{X_{ij}/\sum_n X_{nj}}{\sum_m X_{im}/\sum_n \sum_m X_{nm}} \tag{1}$$

where $n=1, \ldots i, \ldots, N$, and $m=1, \ldots j, \ldots M$. Then the model considered by Andersen et al. may be presented as follows:

$$S_{ij}^t = f(S_{ik}^t) \tag{2}$$

where k denotes the home market for product j and t denotes year.

The exact form of the functional relationship (equation 2) was not specified by Andersen et al. They chose instead to use the Spearman rank correlation coefficient to test the hypothesis of a positive correlation between export specialization (measured by equation 1) in selected engineering products and their associated 'user' sectors. The data set consisted of data for thirteen pairs of producer–user sectors for nine to eleven OECD countries and for selected years 1954–72. In general, a positive correlation was found to exist between the two rankings, but the level of significance was in most cases rather low. Of the thirteen pairs included in the main test presented by Andersen et al., only three exhibited significant correlations following traditional statistical criteria: aircraft engines/aircraft, agricultural machinery/food, and textile machinery/textiles.

Thus, the results presented by Andersen et al., although not inconsistent with the tested hypothesis, cannot be interpreted as being very supportive. One reason for this somewhat disappointing result may be that some explanatory variables have been omitted. If, as argued earlier, the home-market hypothesis is only a partial theory of comparative advantage, the rank correlation test used by Andersen et al. may be misleading, since the rankings may also be affected by other variables not included in the test. In this case, a more appropriate method would be to use a multivariate test where the Linder–Porter hypothesis is included together with other variables assumed to affect export specialization.

Another problem, also discussed by Andersen et al., is the possibility of a significant time lag between the interactive learning process and its impact on comparative advantage. For instance, the original stimulus to a high degree of specialization in textile machinery may have come from a domestic textile industry that later disappeared. In other cases both sectors continue to be strong. It is only in this latter case that a regression between the comparative advantages of the producer and user sectors (and other relevant variables) *at a particular point of time* is the appropriate method. Thus, this method is likely to underestimate the total, long-run impact of 'the home market' on comparative advantage.

Fagerberg (1995) goes to greater lengths to resolve these issues, using a new and larger data set consisting of data for twenty-three pairs of products, sixteen OECD countries, and three selected years (1965, 1973, and 1987). Generally, the methodology is the one proposed by Andersen et al. An attempt is made to render the definition of the home-market sector more precise by the use of more disaggregated statistics. To measure competitiveness, Fagerberg uses the index of revealed comparative advantage. In addition, three new 'home market indexes' are introduced to account for three of the most important service sectors of the economy: health care, telecommunications, and shipping. Telecommunications and health services, until recently at least, were not traded on the world market to the same extent as the majority of manufactured goods. For telecommunications, the number of per capita telephone lines in the country was used as proxy for their quality; for health services, quality was equated with the amount of per capita economic resources devoted to this purpose. When divided by an average across selected OECD countries, a value larger than one implies that the 'quality' of these services in the country is higher than the OECD average. As for shipping, the merchant fleet registered in the country (measured in tons) was divided by the country's exports of goods and services to arrive at the indicator of competitiveness. Again, when divided by the OECD average, a value greater than one shows the country's comparative advantage in the sector. The resulting sample is larger than that of Andersen et al. (twenty-three compared to thirteen), but still has a strong bias toward the group 'specialized machinery' which accounts for around two-thirds of the 'export products' included in the test. By comparison, there is only one chemical product included in the sample (pharmaceuticals).

Since, according to Linder, the theory does not hold for developing or semi-industrialized countries, the industrially less developed OECD countries at the time were excluded from the sample: Greece, Iceland, Portugal, Turkey, and Yugoslavia. Australia and New Zealand were excluded due to lack of data for the earlier years. 1965 was chosen as the first year (this was the first year with data for Japan and Finland). In addition, one year from the early 1970s (1973) and the last year available (1987) were included.

The specification of the model adopted by Fagerberg (1995) is as follows:

$$\log(S_{ij} + 0.1) = C_i + a\log(S_{ik} + 0.1) \tag{3}$$

This model includes two independent variables: the home-market index S_{ik} and a country-specific dummy variable C_i. The inclusion of the latter reflects the possibility that there may exist additional, country-specific factors that affect comparative advantage, and which should be taken into account to avoid biased results.[7] For instance, a country with a comparative advantage in natural-resource-based products will by definition not have a comparative advantage for manufactured products. Since the dependent variable in all twenty-three cases belongs to the manufactured group, this implies that the dependent variable may be biased against countries specializing in

139

natural-resource-based products. The inclusion of a country-specific constant term may correct for this type of bias. The logarithmic form of the model was chosen to obtain a better approximation to the assumption of normally distributed variables.[8] Since there were zeros in the data matrix, a small positive number (0.1) was added to all observations to allow the transformation to be made.

The questions Fagerberg (1995) asked are as follows:

1. Is there a positive relationship between the two specialization indexes, as argued by Linder and Porter; that is, is the coefficient a positive?
2. Does the impact of the home-market variable (S_{ik}) decline over time?
3. To what extent does the introduction of a time lag for the home-market variable (S_{ik}) improve the explanatory power of the model?
4. Are there significant differences across countries, or home markets, in the impact of the home-market variable (S_{ik})?

To answer the first two questions, equation 3 was tested on data for 1965, 1973, and 1987, with and without the country-specific dummy variable C_i. The results are reported in Table 8.1. In all cases, the coefficient a was significantly larger than zero at the 1 percent level, as the Linder–Porter hypothesis would predict. The numerical estimate of a was remarkably stable across both time and differences in specification (the estimate varied between 0.43 and 0.49). Furthermore, there was no tendency toward a decrease in the numerical value of the estimate for a or its significance. The only notable

Table 8.1. The hypothesis tested

1965

$$S_{ij} = -0.37 + 0.43 S_{ik}$$
$$(7.54)^* \quad (8.14)^*$$
$R^2 = 0.15(0.15)$ \qquad (1.1)
SER = 0.90

$$S_{ij} = C_i + 0.43 S_{ik}$$
$$(9.00)^*$$
$R^2 = 0.39(0.36)$ \qquad (1.2)
SER = 0.78

1973

$$S_{ij} = -0.26 + 0.47 S_{ik}$$
$$(5.69)^* \quad (8.62)^*$$
$R^2 = 0.17(0.17)$ \qquad (1.3)
SER = 0.85

$$S_{ij} = C_i + 0.49 S_{ik}$$
$$(9.58)^*$$
$R^2 = 0.36(0.33)$ \qquad (1.4)
SER = 0.76

1987

$$S_{ij} = -0.21 + 0.45 S_{ik}$$
$$(4.76)^* \quad (8.15)^*$$
$R^2 = 0.15(0.15)$ \qquad (1.5)
SER = 0.81

$$S_{ij} = C_i + 0.49 S_{ik}$$
$$(9.19)^*$$
$R^2 = 0.33(0.30)$ \qquad (1.6)
SER = 0.74

$N = 368$

Notes: OLS is used as method of estimation. Absolute t-values are in brackets. R^2 in brackets is adjusted for degrees of freedom. An asterisk (*) denotes significance at 1 percent level.

Source: Fagerberg (1995).

difference between the tests reported in Table 8.1 relates to the impact of the country-specific dummy variable C_i. In all cases the inclusion of this variable significantly increased the explanatory power of the model, but less so in 1987 than for earlier years, indicating that the importance of the country-specific factors may be reduced somewhat during this period.

Patterns of comparative advantage may be viewed as the result of a long-term historical process. Thus, there may be rather long lags present in the impact of user–producer interaction on comparative advantages. To shed some light on this issue, a number of tests were conducted by including a lagged independent variable. Table 8.2 shows the results. Given that patterns of comparative advantage change only slowly, the home-market variables should be expected to be strongly correlated across years, which was indeed the case. To avoid multicollinearity in cases where two annual observations of S_{ik} were to be included, their first differences were taken (as can be seen in (2.2) and (2.4) in Table 8.2).

The results of the tests with lagged variables in Table 8.2 should be compared to the result without lags in (1.6) of Table 8.1. It then becomes clear that the explanatory power of the instantaneous relationship ((1.6) of Table 8.1) is not inferior to any of the lagged relationships, when adjustments for differences in degrees of freedoms are made. Thus, surprisingly perhaps, there is not strong support in the data for long lags. This is also confirmed by the low weights given to the lagged independent variables in (2.2) and (2.4) of Table 8.2.[9]

Furthermore, Fagerberg (1995) goes on to examine potential cross-country variations in the impact of the home market. In the tests reported above, it is assumed that all countries are identical except for the country-specific dummy variable C_i. Although there is no prior information that leads us to believe that the impact of the home-market variable on comparative advantage differs substantially across countries, this possibility cannot be excluded *a priori*.

Table 8.2. Testing for lags (1987)

$S_{ij87} = C_i + 0.39 S_{ik65}$ $\quad\quad (8.46)^*$	$R^2 = 0.31(0.28)$ SER = 0.75	(2.1)
$S_{ij87} = C_i + 0.50 S_{ik65} + 0.34(S_{ik87} - S_{ik65})$ $\quad\quad (9.37)^* \quad\quad (3.85)^*$	$R^2 = 0.34(0.30)$ SER = 0.74	(2.2)
$S_{ij87} = C_i + 0.43 S_{ik73}$ $\quad\quad (8.64)^*$	$R^2 = 0.31(0.28)$ SER = 0.75	(2.3)
$S_{ij87} = C_i + 0.49 S_{ik73} + 0.39(S_{ik87} - S_{ik73})$ $\quad\quad (9.20)^* \quad\quad (2.97)^*$	$R^2 = 0.33(0.30)$ SER = 0.74	(2.4)
$N = 368$		

Notes: OLS is used as method of estimation. Absolute *t*-values are in brackets. R^2 in brackets is adjusted for degrees of freedom. An asterisk (*) denotes significance at 1 percent level.

Source: Fagerberg (1995).

To account for this possibility, a test of the restriction that $a_1 = a_2 = \ldots = a_i = \ldots = a_N = a$ was undertaken. The results are ambiguous. In no case can the hypothesis of a common coefficient a for all countries be rejected at the 1 percent level. However, for 1965 and 1973 – but not for 1987 – the tests indicate that the hypothesis can be rejected if the weaker criterion of a 5 percent significance level is adopted.

The model written as equation 3 is further tested for each country in the sample. An examination of the unrestricted (country-specific) estimates for the coefficient a suggests that the sample countries may be divided roughly into four groups, depending on the strength of the relationship between S_{ik} and S_{ij}. For five countries (Japan, Denmark, Finland, Norway, and Switzerland), the estimates of the coefficient a are positive, significant at the 1 percent level, for all three years. Clearly, for these countries there is strong support for the hypothesis of a positive relationship between the two indices. Then follows a group of seven countries where there is some support, although weaker (positive, significant at the 10 percent level, for at least two years): Canada, the United States, Germany, Italy, the Netherlands, Spain, and Sweden. For Belgium and Austria too, a positive relationship is reported, though significant for one year only (at the 5 and 10 percent level, respectively). However, for France and the United Kingdom, the results give no support at all for the hypothesis of a positive relationship between the two indices. Taking this information into account, the above test of the restriction is repeated (a common value of a for all countries) on the sample but excluding Austria, France, and the United Kingdom this time. For this sample it was not possible to reject the restriction for any year.

The fact that the hypothesis is not supported empirically for some countries deserves an explanation. First, it cannot be excluded that this – at least to some extent – is the result of imperfect data or methods. It can be shown that there is a positive relationship between the statistical significance of the estimate a and the variance of the dependent variable; that is, those countries with a 'flat' structure of export specialization (low variance) generally have poor results. Low variance is a common problem in small samples, and it is possible that the results would have improved if the number of 'pairs' included in the test had been larger. This was not possible with the available data. The problem of a 'flat' structure of export specialization was especially pronounced for Belgium and France, and it is possible that the poor results for these countries may be explained by data limitations. This explanation is less probable for the United Kingdom and Austria, where the reported variances do not differ much from that of the sample as a whole. In general, the reported results show no clear relation to variables commonly used in cross-country analyses of specialization patterns, such as – for instance – country size or income level (past or present). Arguably, a much more detailed analysis of economic, institutional, and cultural factors seems to be required. For instance, significant cross-country differences are found in the degree of inter-firm collaboration (for example, Tylecote 1993).

The possibility of differences across home markets – in their impact on the competitiveness of suppliers – is perhaps more interesting. Porter (1990a) presents a well-argued case for assuming that home markets exposed to international competition are more conducive than others to fostering internationally competitive suppliers. Fagerberg (1995) presents some evidence that there may be significant differences between different types of home market. Generally speaking, the relationship between the two indices appears to be much stronger for home-market sectors exposed to international competition (traditional manufacturing, production of transport equipment and shipping) than for more 'sheltered' sectors (agriculture and public-sector services). For public-sector services these results may be affected by the problem of finding reliable indicators. Still, the results lend clear support to Porter's view on the importance of competition.

Both Andersen et al. (1981a) and Fagerberg (1995) tested the Linder–Porter hypothesis at a macro level, using international trade statistics available for a sample of countries. More recently, Beise-Zee and Rammer (2006) took a different approach with a dataset obtained from an innovation survey of 4,786 firms in manufacturing and service industries in Germany. The approach taken by Beise-Zee and Rammer is distinct from the previous two studies in two ways. First, Andersen et al. and Fagerberg examined pairs of 'producer' and 'user' sectors where trade statistics allowed a link to be made. As they were aware, this forced them to exclude from their investigation those relationships which trade statistics were not disaggregated enough to reveal. For instance, some equipment industries (including some well-known high-tech industries such as computer manufacturing) could not be included, as their products are used in many sectors. Beise-Zee and Rammer overcome this limitation by using data from a survey in which firms were asked to identify the sources of their innovations. In the survey, these sources include customers, competitors, suppliers, and research institutions. Firms that introduced product innovations were also asked to name the industries that had provided the most important innovation impulses and whether the innovation-triggering customers came from domestic or foreign sources. This detailed data set allows Beise-Zee and Rammer to cover a greater number of pairs of 'producer–user' sectors and to analyze their relationships more accurately than their two predecessors. They show that virtually all product innovators that specified users (or market demand) as sources answered that they interacted with domestic users.[10]

A second departure point for Beise-Zee and Rammer (2006) from their predecessors is their inclusion of variables other than export specialization when characterizing the advanced nature of user sectors. As discussed earlier, an issue when testing the Linder–Porter hypothesis is how an 'advanced user sector' is defined and distinguished empirically from a less advanced one. Andersen et al. (1981a, 1981b) and Fagerberg (1995) used trade specialization as an indicator of competitiveness and applied it to a user sector as well as a producer sector. However, there may be other aspects of a user sector that impact upon the trade specialization of a producer sector.[11] Beise-Zee and Rammer deal with this issue by including a set of explanatory variables representing the sectoral characteristics of a user sector. The variables include the quality of demand, the degree of competition, and the degree of outward foreign direct investment, as well as the degree of export orientation as a substitute for the revealed comparative advantage.[12] The quality of demand is measured by a sector's share of total demand in a country (which is Germany in the case of the Beise-Zee and Rammer study) divided by the sector's average share in total demand in OECD countries. The degree of competition is measured by the price level in a sector in OECD countries divided by the price level in the particular sector in a country. The degree of outward foreign direct investment is measured by the ratio of outward foreign direct investment by a sector in a country to the total domestic gross fixed investment of this sector in the country, divided by the OECD average ratio of the sector. Finally, the degree of export orientation is measured by the export share of total turnover for a sector in a country, divided by the OECD average ratio for the sector.

The model tested by Beise-Zee and Rammer may be written as follows:

$$E_i = \alpha S_{i(j)} + \beta Z_i + \gamma I_i + u_i \qquad (4)$$

where E_i is the ratio of exports to turnover made by firm i in industry j, S is a vector for industry characteristics that have a direct effect on exports made by firm i, Z is a vector for general characteristics of firm i, and I is a vector for firm i's innovation-specific activities including the sources from which firm i receives innovation impulses.

For the purpose of this chapter we focus primarily on whether the sectoral characteristics of a user sector are found to have any impact upon the trade performance of firms in a producer sector. In both manufacturing and service industries, Beise-Zee and Rammer find that firms introducing product innovations export a greater share of their turnover as they receive innovation impulses from a user sector with a high degree of export orientation. This is consistent with the finding of Andersen et al. and Fagerberg that an 'advanced user sector' (showing a strong export performance) induces a strong export performance on the part of a producer sector. By contrast, the other variables added by Beise-Zee and Rammer reflecting various user-sector's characteristics do not show any significant impact upon the export performance of firms in a producer sector. Hence, the tests conducted by Beise-Zee and Rammer (2006) lend support to the findings reported by Andersen et al. (1981*a*, 1981*b*) and Fagerberg (1994, 1995).

8.4 Conclusion

The view that the home market may have a positive impact on the competitiveness of domestic producers is by no means a new one. Indeed, it has been widely held for at least a century. In spite of this, most empirical work in this area has been of a descriptive character. Against this background, this chapter reviews the evidence presented by three econometric studies. In general, their findings are consistent with the predictions made by Linder (1961) and Porter (1990*a*). Of the three studies, Fagerberg (1995) addressed a set of five questions. The main empirical findings were:

1. There is strong support in the data for the hypothesis of a positive impact of advanced domestic users on competitiveness.
2. There is no evidence of a weakening of this relationship during the period 1965–87.
3. The time lag between the initial stimulus (from the domestic market) and the impact on competitiveness appears to be relatively short.
4. For most countries there is some support for the hypothesis. The most notable exceptions are France and the United Kingdom.
5. The relationship appears to be stronger in cases where the home market is exposed to international competition.

More recently, Beise-Zee and Rammer (2006) approach the first question addressed by Fagerberg (1995) by using survey data from firms in Germany. Their results are consistent with the earlier findings of Fagerberg and Andersen et al.

Hence, the evidence presented in this chapter indicates that interaction between domestic users and producers of technology may have a positive impact on both technological progress and international competitiveness. This is especially so if these relationships develop in a competitive environment; that is, that the positions of both users and producers may be contested. Thus, contrary to popular belief, this approach does not favor protectionism. However, policies that encourage stronger interaction between different actors in the innovation system, such as users and producers of technology, may be a very good idea.

Acknowledgments

I would like to thank the editors of this volume for help and advice in revising this chapter for publication, and Oxford University Press for permission to reproduce parts of the following article: Fagerberg, J. (1995) 'User–producer interaction, learning and comparative advantage', *Cambridge Journal of Economics*, 19(1), 243–56.

Notes

1. For a critique of the concept and its use, see, for example, Krugman (1994*a*). For an extended discussion, see Fagerberg (1996).
2. There are many definitions, most of which reflect this 'double meaning' in one way or another. A typical example is the following: competitiveness is 'the degree to which, under open market conditions, a country can produce goods and services that meet the test of foreign competition, while simultaneously maintaining and expanding domestic real income' (see OECD 1992: 237).
3. For an overview, see Dosi and Soete (1988).
4. Several factors may contribute to this. New knowledge may be very specific and difficult to transfer ('tacit knowledge'). Secrecy and legal procedures (patents and trademarks) are other means.
5. This way of looking at things shows some similarity with parts of the 'new growth' literature (see Verspagen 1992 for an overview). However, this literature (Romer 1986, and others), as well as the older literature in this area (Arrow 1962; Kaldor and Mirrlees 1962), discusses externalities of activities *internal to firms* (investment and/or production). This chapter focuses on the effects of *interaction between different firms*.
6. Porter especially emphasizes the importance of domestic rivalry, but acknowledges that, for small open economics, foreign competitors may serve a similar function (1990*a*: 121).
7. This is the so-called 'least-squares dummy variables method' (LSDV), which is developed for use in pooled datasets. For details, see Johnston (1984).
8. The index of revealed comparative advantage (S) has a skew distribution, with a long tail to the right. This creates problems in regression analysis, because it violates the assumption of normality. A logarithmic transformation of the data reduced this problem significantly.
9. In (2.2) of Table 8.2, the implicit weight is 0.16 for S_{ik65} and 0.34 for S_{ik87}, while in (2.4) the implicit weight is 0.10 for S_{ik73} and 0.39 for S_{ik87}.
10. Of 4,786 responses obtained in the survey, 57.6 percent introduced at least one product innovation during three years prior to the survey, and 65.2 percent of those innovating firms stated that they responded to impulses from single customers or market demand. Of those firms that received innovation impulses from users (either specific users or general market), 43.9 percent stated that the

users were solely from Germany, and 55.3 percent stated that they were both from Germany and abroad, leaving only 0.8 percent interacting with users from abroad. Furthermore, follow-up interviews revealed that for those who interacted with users both from Germany and abroad, the vast majority of demand-driven innovation was attributable to Germany.

11. The inclusion of the country-specific dummy variable C_i in Fagerberg (1995) (equation 3) to some extent compensates for this, as the dummy might reflect cross-country differences in such aspects of an 'advanced user sector'.

12. The specification of the model tested in the study includes the same set of variables (except for export orientation due to an issue of endogeneity in econometric estimation) for a producer sector as well. See equation 4.

9

The growth and competitiveness of nations: Porter's contribution

Brian Snowdon

9.1 Introduction

Why are some countries rich and others poor? This is perhaps the most important question facing social scientists. Within economics it has certainly motivated some of the most influential and enduring contributions to the literature – most notably Adam Smith's *The Wealth of Nations* (1976, original 1776). Since sustained economic growth is *the* most important determinant of living standards, there is no more important issue challenging the research efforts of economists than to understand the causes of economic growth. Recently, issues relating to catch-up and convergence, endogenous growth, the impact of globalization, the quality of governance, political and economic barriers to development, the relative importance of the role of geography versus institutions, and global environmental issues, have dominated discussions of economic growth and development. Increasingly, in order to unravel the 'mystery' of economic growth, economists have also begun to appreciate the value of economic history and the previous research carried out by economic historians (Helpman 2004).

Against this background, Michael Porter's *The Competitive Advantage of Nations* (1990a), while emerging from the interface between strategic management and microeconomics, can also be viewed as addressing this central concern of economists and economic historians. In his attempt to bridge the gap between the micro-oriented strategic management literature and the economics literature relating to economic growth, development, and trade, Porter's analysis of the competitiveness of nations has proved to be an important and stimulating, if controversial, contribution. In particular, he has ignited debate on the meaning and measurement of 'competitiveness' in the context of nations and regions rather than at the micro-level of firms, where the use of this terminology is widespread and has a more precise meaning. Porter's leadership and research contribution to the production of the World Economic Forum's (WEF) annual *Global Competitiveness Report* (*GCR*) has highlighted the importance of a nation's microeconomic fundamentals in providing the sound foundations necessary to foster sustained economic development and growth.

Within mainstream economics, explanations of poor economic growth performance have often emphasized macroeconomic factors such as low saving and investment rates, high and volatile inflation, excess government indebtedness, and aggregate instability. Porter's contributions have been important in redressing the balance by reminding economists that while macroeconomic stability is certainly necessary for improved economic performance, sustained improvements in productivity are rooted firmly in the microeconomic fundamentals and innovative capacity of any economy (Furman et al. 2002).

The *GCR*, published since 1979, is the WEF's 'flagship' publication and aims to provide a comprehensive quantitative and qualitative assessment of the strengths and weaknesses of the majority of the world's economies. Porter's involvement dates back to the late 1990s, and he has recently acted as Editor and Co-Director of the GCR. In this chapter, his contribution to the analysis of the growth, development, and competitiveness of nations is assessed.

9.2 The importance of economic growth

The importance of economic growth as a basis for improvements in human welfare cannot be overstated, and is confirmed by the experience of history and numerous contemporary empirical studies. In *The Wealth of Nations*, Adam Smith recognized and highlighted the importance of growth of output per worker rather than aggregate production as *the* key indicator of economic development for the 'progressive state'. Here we find a strong link between the work of Adam Smith and Michael Porter, for as Porter (1990a: 6) notes: 'Productivity is the prime determinant in the long-run of a nation's standard of living, for it is the root cause of national per capita income' (see also Cho and Moon 2000).

Angus Maddison's comprehensive data (2007) confirm that even small inter-country differences in growth rates of per capita income, if sustained over long periods of time, lead to *significant* differences in relative living standards between nations. The importance and effect of compound growth on material living standards is clearly illustrated in Table 9.1, which provides data on the impact on GDP per capita of the differential comparative growth

Table 9.1. GDP per capita, selected East Asian and African countries, 1950–2003 (Gheary-Khamis international dollars)

Country	1950	1960	1970	1980	1990	2003
Botswana	349	403	647	1,765	3,306	4,937
Ghana	1,122	1,378	1,424	1,157	1,063	1,306
Kenya	651	726	915	1,051	1,117	998
Nigeria	753	854	1,192	1,424	1,214	1,349
Somalia	1,057	1,277	1,138	1,037	1,083	877
Uganda	687	713	869	577	598	850
Zaire	570	748	768	598	510	212
57 African countries	**890**	**1,063**	**1,355**	**1,538**	**1,449**	**1,549**
China	448	662	778	1,061	1,871	4,803
Hong Kong	2,218	3,134	5,695	10,053	17,541	24,098
Malaysia	1,559	1,530	2,079	3,657	5,132	8,468
Singapore	2,219	2,310	4,439	9,058	14,220	21,530
South Korea	854	1,226	2,167	4,114	8,704	15,732
Taiwan	924	1,492	2,980	5,869	9,886	17,284
Thailand	817	1,078	1,694	2,554	4,633	7,195

Source: Adapted from Maddison (2007).

experiences of the 'miracle' East Asia economies and the majority of sub-Saharan African economies (Snowdon 2007; Blanke and Sala-i-Martin 2009).

The recent *Growth Report* from the Commission on Growth and Development (CGDR) (2008) provides a reflective assessment on how developing countries can achieve a sustained acceleration in economic growth. The Commission was given the task to 'take stock of the state of theoretical and empirical knowledge on economic growth with a view to drawing implications for policy for the current and next generation of policymakers'. An accumulation of empirical evidence, combined with new theoretical insights, have made it increasingly clear that the divergent growth experience across the world's economies cannot be explained by variations in the rate of factor accumulation alone (Porter 2001*a*, 2004). A good policy environment, sound institutions, and enlightened leadership are key factors influencing growth outcomes. Many mathematical growth models that focus on the proximate determinants of growth remain institution and policy-free zones.

With this in mind the *Growth Report* focuses on the economic performance of thirteen 'successful' (measured by per capita GDP growth) developing countries: Botswana, Brazil, China, Hong Kong, Indonesia, Japan, South Korea, Malaysia, Malta, Oman, Singapore, Taiwan, and Thailand. Remarkably, these countries have managed to sustain at least 7 percent per capita income growth for twenty-five years or more, and, according to the *CGDR*, they share the following five policy ingredients:

1. They have all engaged with the global economy through trade, FDI, ideas, and regional integration.

2. Each country has maintained *relative* macroeconomic stability.

3. They have all benefited from high rates of saving and investment financed predominantly from domestic sources (investment rates of at least 25 percent of GDP).

4. They have each benefited from political leadership that has been 'committed, credible, inclusive and pragmatic'.

5. Each of the successful economies has given a high priority to the market allocation of resources within an inclusive, competitive environment, where the role of government, focused on development, has allowed public sector activity to complement private sector activity.

While Porter endorses (1)–(4) above, it is with respect to (5) that he has laid great emphasis in his work on national 'competitiveness'. In common with Adam Smith, a key element unifying all of Porter's research is the need to 'establish a deep and sophisticated understanding of the nature of competition in individual markets' (Snowdon and Stonehouse 2006: 164). Porter presents a dynamic Schumpeterian vision of competition as a major factor contributing to the rate of innovation and the quality of the business environment. This theme has recently been emphasized by other economists interested in the determinants of the wealth and poverty of nations (Baumol 2002; Lewis 2004; Parente and Prescott 2006) as well as the World Bank (2008).

9.3 What is competitiveness?: Comparative versus competitive advantage

The idea of competitiveness when applied in the context of firms or industries is relatively straightforward. Increasingly the notion of competitiveness has been applied to countries and regions, especially after the publication in 1990 of Porter's *The Competitive Advantage of Nations* (Huggins 2003; Porter and Ketels 2003; Huggins and Davies 2006; Huggins and Izushi 2008; Huggins et al. 2008; IMD 2009). However, when it comes to discussing nations rather than firms there is much confusion and debate relating to the meaning of the word 'competitiveness'. The use of this terminology has been described as 'ill-defined', 'dangerous', 'obsessive', 'elusive', and 'meaningless' (Reinert 1995; Aiginger 2006a; Siggel, 2006). Robert Reich, in his review of Porter (1990a), argues that 'National competitiveness is one of those rare terms of public discourse to have gone directly from obscurity to meaninglessness without any intervening period of coherence' (quoted in Reinert 1995: 25). In the words of the 2008 Nobel Laureate in Economics, Paul Krugman, the rhetoric of 'Pop Internationalism' emphasizes competition between nations rather than the potential for mutual gains from trade (Cohen 1994; Krugman,

1994*a*, 1994*b*, 1996*a*, 1996*b*; Prestowitz 1994; Scharping 1994; Steil 1994; Thurow 1994).

Given this neo-mercantilist perception, non-economists are always likely to see winners and losers emerging from international trade. But national economies are not like giant corporations, and hence the 'ground-level view of businessmen is often deeply uninformative about the inherently general equilibrium issues of international trade' (Krugman 1994*c*: 23–4). It is hardly surprising then that, according to Krugman (1996*b*: 24), 'Economists in general do not use the word "competitiveness". Not one of the textbooks in international economics I have on my shelves contains the word in the index'. In contrast, the terminology of international competitiveness is widespread in textbooks on international business.

In orthodox neoclassical trade theory, economists have devoted much time and research to identifying the gains from trade and also explaining the pattern of world trade. What makes a particular country 'competitive' in certain products and services, and not others? The theory of comparative advantage attempts to answer this question.

9.4 Comparative advantage

The birth of modern economics with the publication of the Adam Smith's *The Wealth of Nations* is closely associated with the rejection of mercantilist ideas on trade. The classical economists presented what Jagdish Bhagwati refers to as a 'benign impact' story of the mutual gains from trade (Snowdon 2001). While it was Adam Smith who first provided a coherent intellectual and practical challenge to the mercantilist doctrines of protectionism, it was David Ricardo who in 1817 first clearly (and rigorously) demonstrated the mutual gains from trade by developing his most lasting contribution to economics: 'the law of comparative advantage' (Krugman and Obstfeld 2009). Ricardo showed how, by specializing and removing barriers to foreign trade, countries are able to use their resources more efficiently, thus allowing an expansion of their feasible set of consumption possibilities through mutually beneficial trade. This argument stands even when some countries are more efficient (have an absolute advantage) at producing almost everything than other countries. What is important for mutual gain is that by definition each country possesses a *comparative advantage* in the production of some goods. Therefore, countries should specialize in the production of those goods in which they are relatively, not absolutely, more efficient.

The classical economist's story of trade is predominantly one of optimism because the theory of comparative advantage implies that all countries are 'competitive' in the production of something. Thus, according to Krugman

(1987a: 131), the idea of comparative advantage remains a simple but powerful idea, but one that 'conflicts with both popular stubborn prejudices and powerful interests'. More specifically, Krugman (1996a: 9, 10, 40, 84) writes:

> International trade is not a zero sum game.... To a trained economist, the idea that international trade is a competition that bears any serious resemblance to military rivalry sounds very strange...countries do not compete with each other the way corporations do...competitiveness is a meaningless word when applied to national economies...The conflict among nations that so many policy intellectuals imagine prevails is an illusion; but it is an illusion that can destroy the reality of mutual gains from trade.

Ever since Ricardo's simple but remarkable insight, the economic benefit that countries can potentially derive from free trade is one issue that the overwhelming majority of economists agree upon. In Ricardo's theory the source of comparative advantage lies in exogenous technological (productivity) differences between countries. But his model does not explain satisfactorily either the source of technological gaps between nations or what patterns of trade are likely to emerge between countries (Porter 1990a; Krugman and Obstfeld 2009).

Subsequent work by Eli Heckscher (1919), and the 1977 and 1970 Nobel Laureates in Economics, Bertil Ohlin (1933) and Paul Samuelson (1948, 1949; also Stolper and Samuelson 1941), focused on relative factor endowments as the main source of comparative advantage (see Baldwin 2008; Krugman and Obstfeld 2009). Unlike Ricardo's analysis, the Heckscher–Ohlin–Samuelson (H–O–S) factor proportions theory of trade assumes that all countries have access to the same technology thereby ruling out different relative labor productivities as the reason why nations gain from specialization and trade. In effect, for each industry, all countries have access to the same production function. In the H–O–S model, the mutual gains from trade arise because different countries have different factor endowments (intensities) and hence relative factor prices will vary across countries. The relative price of labor will be cheap in labor-abundant economies, whereas in capital-abundant countries the relative price of capital will be low. Therefore, labor-abundant economies will tend to specialize in labor-intensive commodities (such as agricultural products, textiles) and capital-abundant economies will tend to produce capital-intensive commodities (such as high-tech manufactured goods).

In a major survey of the empirical evidence, Leamer and Levinsohn (1994: 34) conclude that 'there appears to be a substantial effect of relative factor abundance on the commodity composition of trade'. More recently, Justin Lin (2009), Chief Economist at the World Bank, argues that China's reform strategy since 1979 has followed a 'comparative advantage following strategy' compared to the capital-intensive, heavy industry, 'comparative advantage defying strategy', characteristic of the period 1949–79 (Adams et al. 2006; Lin and Wang 2008). Thus, the conclusion of the two workhorse models in neoclassical trade theory – the Ricardian and H–O–S models – is that trade is a positive-sum game. For both capital-abundant and labor-abundant regions, the post-trade situation is superior to the autarky situation.

9.5 Increasing returns and new trade theory

Not surprisingly, neither the Ricardian nor H–O–S models provide a completely satisfactory description of global trade data. In both the Ricardian and H–O–S neoclassical models of *inter-industry* trade, the source of comparative advantage is based on initial endowments of either technology or factor proportions, and both models assume constant returns to scale. During the first age of globalization (1800–1914), the vast bulk of trade, in line with the H–O–S theory of comparative advantage, consisted of 'dissimilar goods' being exchanged between 'dissimilar countries' (Krugman 2009a). However, it soon became clear to economists via empirical research that many features of international trade did not fit the Ricardian and H–O–S stories (Grubel and Lloyd 1975).

Increasingly, during the second age of globalization, post-1950, trade involved the exchange of similar (differentiated) manufactured goods between countries with similar factor endowments. As Porter (1990a: 12) highlights, such *intra-industry trade* cannot be explained by orthodox comparative advantage theories which are based on countries making the most of their differences. This gave rise to what Paul Krugman (2009a) calls the 'similar–similar' problem: that is, the significant role played in global trade by 'exchanges of similar products between similar countries'. The 'New Trade Theory', inspired by Krugman's seminal paper (1979), is based on non-comparative advantage trade, and focuses on the influence of increasing returns and imperfect competition. Economies of scale, both internal and external to the firm, by lowering unit costs, along with the preferences of consumers for variety, are a prime motivation for countries to specialize and trade (Krugman and Obstfeld 2009).

Porter (1990a: 13) also argues that 'the assumptions underlying comparative advantage were more persuasive in the eighteenth and nineteenth centuries', but are an incomplete explanation of trade patterns in a world characterized by scale economies, imperfect competition, differentiated products, and globalized industries where firms have become decoupled 'from the factor endowments of a single nation'.

The 'new' trade theories supplemented, rather than replaced, the traditional comparative cost models, and helped to solve the puzzle of similar–similar trade. However, the new models failed to predict which countries would produce which differentiated product. It is precisely here that *The Competitive Advantage of Nations* makes an innovative contribution. The new trade theories are incomplete because they fail to explain which firms, in which industries, in which nations, will reap the gains from scale economies (Porter 1990*a*: 16). Recognizing that the Ricardian and H–O–S theories 'have grown inadequate for the task', Porter (1990*a*: 2) sets out to explain 'the role played by a nation's economic environment, institutions, and policies in the competitive success of its firms in particular industries'. As Grant indicates in chapter 7 of this volume, the main innovative contribution of Porter's analysis is 'in extending the theories of international trade and international direct investment to explain more effectively observed patterns of trade and investment between developed countries'.

9.6 Competitive advantage

As noted above, the notion of national competitiveness is a slippery concept, since according to the theory of comparative advantage, all nations can be competitive in the production of something. Given the inherent vagueness of the concept there have been numerous attempts to define the 'Holy Grail' of national competitiveness more precisely.

It is important at the outset to distinguish between notions of competitiveness in the short run and long run. In the short run, international competitiveness can be defined as 'the level of real exchange rate which, in conjunction with appropriate domestic policies, ensured internal and (broadly defined) external balance' (Boltho 1996: 2). Given this macroeconomic definition, a 'lack of competitiveness would mean that a country, at full employment, was running a persistent (and unwelcome) balance of payments deficit' (Boltho 1996: 2). Therefore, 'the country would suffer from an inappropriate level of the real exchange rate' (Boltho 1996: 2). However, as Boltho notes, since the measurement of the real exchange rate is 'fraught with difficulties', several indicators have been used as proxies – in particular, relative unit labor costs expressed in a common currency (Fagerberg 1988; Muellbauer 1991; Eltis and Higham 1995; Llewellyn 1996; Barrell et al. 2005).

In the longer run, since it is assumed that the real exchange rate will converge to its equilibrium value, the definition of competitiveness focuses on productivity, innovation, and living standards (Boltho 1996; Fagerberg 1996). For example, the 1995 UK White Paper, *Competitiveness: Forging Ahead*, defines competitiveness as 'the degree to which a country can, under free and fair market conditions, produce goods and services which meet the test of international markets, while simultaneously maintaining and expanding the real incomes of its people over the long term' (DTI 1995; Eltis and Higham 1995: 71). Similarly, the European Commission's definition (2003*a*) is that 'competitiveness is understood to mean high and rising standards of living of a nation (or group of nations) with the lowest possible level of unemployment, on a sustainable basis' (Grilo and Koopman 2006).

In *The Competitive Advantage of Nations*, Porter (1990*a*: 3–11) notes that it is 'far from clear what the term competitiveness means when referring to a nation' and that we 'must abandon the whole notion of a "competitive nation" as a term having much meaning for economic prosperity'. He rejects definitions based on exchange rates, 'cheap and abundant labor', availability of 'bountiful natural resources', global market share of exports, low unit labor costs, government policy, management practices, and labor–management relations. Instead, he turns his attention to the principle economic goal of society – to 'produce a high and rising standard of living for its citizens'. Since material living standards are equated to output per capita, driven by the productivity of a nation's labor and capital resources, Porter (1990*a*: 6) argues that:

> The only meaningful concept of competitiveness at the national level is national productivity. A rising standard of living depends on the capacity of a nation's firms to achieve high levels of productivity and to increase productivity over time.

Thus, Porter's concept of competitiveness focuses on value-generating activities that 'create' prosperity. In a similar vein, Aiginger (2006*b*: 162) argues that 'competitiveness should be defined as the ability to create welfare'. Furthermore, any application of this concept must include an '*outcome assessment*' and a '*process assessment*'. Productivity is clearly a core element in outcome competitiveness while the WEF's annual *GCRs* attempt to identify the process by which nations become more competitive (Llewellyn 1996).

9.7 The determinants of national competitive advantage

The publication in 1990 of *The Competitive Advantage of Nations* is generally viewed as an heroic attempt to build a bridge between the fields of strategic management and international economics. Initially, it created much more of a stir in the management literature than in the economics literature where it created hardly a ripple (Grant 1991; Pressman 1991; Davies and Ellis 2000). However, as is discussed below, Porter's analysis has certainly had a major influence on the eminent growth economist, Xavier Sala-i-Martin, the architect of the recent Global Competitiveness Index (GCI), published annually by the WEF (Snowdon 2006).

Porter's aim in *The Competitive Advantage of Nations* is to show how competitive advantage is 'created and sustained through a highly localized process' where successful 'companies achieve competitive advantage through acts of innovation' (Porter 1990*b*: 74). One of the main contributions of his analysis is to provide a framework for thinking about the major influences that can shape a nation's competitive advantage. Unlike the H–O–S model, which focuses on inherited factor endowments, Porter (1990*b*: 74) emphasizes that the 'factors most important to competitive advantage in most industries, especially the industries most vital to productivity growth in advanced economies, are not inherited but are created within a nation'. Inherited 'basic factors', such as abundant unskilled labor, can provide an initial source of comparative advantage, while 'advanced factors', such as sophisticated skills and R&D facilities, are much more important for competitive advantage and can be created by firms and governments. As Porter argues, 'Nations succeed in industries where they are particularly good at factor creation. Competitive advantage results from the presence of world class institutions that first create specialized factors and then continually work to upgrade them' (Porter 1990*b*: 78).

In *The Competitive Advantage of Nations*, Porter (1990*a*: 71–3) argues that national environments have a significant influence on the performance of firms and industries, and the drivers of national advantage can be found in four broad domestic determinants: (*a*) factor input conditions; (*b*) demand conditions; (*c*) firm strategy, structure, and rivalry; and (*d*) related and supporting industries. These four broad components make up Porter's '*diamond*' framework which he describes as 'a mutually reinforcing system'. Moreover, because 'almost everything matters for competitiveness', improving competitiveness will be 'a marathon not a sprint' (Porter 2004). The following presents a brief interpretation of these components in addition to those provided by Grant in chapter 7:

- *Demand conditions*: The supply-side H–O–S model ignores the influence of demand, and conventional wisdom also seems to suggest that the globalization of markets should reduce the importance of domestic demand conditions on the performance of firms. However, in Porter's analysis, home demand plays a key role in the determination of competitiveness. Moreover, 'the size of home demand is less significant than the character of home demand', in particular the 'sophistication' of finicky home consumers who pressure companies to meet 'high standards', 'to innovate and upgrade', and to 'respond to tough challenges' (Porter 1990*b*: 79). It is also important that domestic demand 'anticipates' international needs.

- *Firm strategy, structure, and rivalry*: In each nation there are systematic differences in the structure and characteristics of industries, and the national economic environment also influences the creation, management, and organization of firms. Particularly important is the vigor of domestic rivalry between firms which, by creating competitive pressure, encourages firms to lower costs, improve quality and service, and continuously innovate and upgrade their activities. As is evident from Porter's publications, the importance of competition as a driver of dynamic improvement is a central theme running throughout the whole body of his work (Porter 1980a, 1994; Porter and van der Linde 1995a; Porter and Takeuchi 1999; Porter et al. 2000; Sakakibara and Porter 2001; Porter and Sakakibara 2004; Porter and Teisberg 2006a).

- *Related and supporting industries*: A major finding in Porter's case study work is that there appears to be a tendency for successful industries to form 'clusters' within each country. These clusters of related and supporting industries form a sophisticated network of suppliers and customers that are an essential component for competitive dynamism within a nation. Here the work of Porter can be linked to the classic work of Alfred Marshall (1890), who developed the idea of external economies, and Albert Hirschman (1958), who emphasized the importance of forward, horizontal, and backward linkages in the development process. It also connects to the more recent work on external economies, agglomeration economies, and the 'new' geography of trade literature associated with Paul Krugman, Anthony Venables, and Edward Glaeser (Krugman 1991; Fujita et al. 1999; Glaeser and Gottlieb 2009; Glaeser 2010; also see chapters 10–12 in this volume). During the 1990s, both Porter and Krugman appear to have rediscovered the Marshallian notions of 'knowledge spillovers', 'labor market pooling', and 'specialized suppliers' (Krugman 2009a).

- *Chance and the role of government*: In addition to the four corners of the diamond, Porter also notes how competitive advantage is influenced by the role of government and by luck. He rejects both the laissez-faire and dirigiste schools of thought with respect to the role of government. For Porter, the government should act as a catalyst and 'Government policies that succeed are those that create an environment in which companies can gain competitive advantage rather than those that involve government directly in the process. It is an indirect rather than direct role' (Porter 1990b: 86). The key role of government is to maintain a competitive environment, provide macroeconomic stability, and establish a stable social, legal, and political institutional environment within which firms can succeed. It is not the role of government to operate a highly interventionist industrial policy that attempts to 'pick winners' (Porter 1998a; Ketels 2006; Snowdon and Stonehouse 2006).

In many cases, chance historical events, by influencing the four components of the diamond, can be very important in creating discontinuities and path dependency that affect a nation's competitive position (Porter 1990*a*: 124–5). Chance events include major technological breakthroughs, energy shocks, political and environmental shocks, and surges of world or regional demand. However, nations with 'the most favorable diamond will be most likely to convert chance events into competitive advantage' (Porter 1990*a*: 125).

9.8 The global economic landscape: flat or lumpy?

During recent years, several authors have argued that one major impact of globalization has been the 'death of distance' (Cairncross 1997), and as a consequence 'the world is flat' (Friedman 2005). The Cairncross–Friedman hypothesis is that distance no longer matters much for economic relationships because technological progress, including the ICT revolution, has increasingly eroded the importance of particular geographical locations as centers of economic activity. Thomas Friedman's book in particular has stirred up considerable controversy (Leamer 2007; Christopherson et al. 2008). However, gravity models, which model trade between countries as a positive function of GDP levels, population size, and *distance*, 'have produced some of the clearest and most robust empirical findings in economics' (Leamer and Levinsohn 1994: 34). Thus, 'distance matters and it matters a lot!... The world is not getting dramatically smaller', and the increase in observed trade in the post-1950 period can be 'almost fully' explained by the growth of European and Asian nations rather than by the death of distance (Leamer and Levinsohn 1994: 34).

Critics of the Caincross–Friedman hypothesis also point to the important dynamic forces of spatial agglomeration, including the emergence of mega city-regions. With falling transport costs, increasing international economic integration is quite consistent with the concentration in geographical space of many economic activities (Leamer and Levinsohn 1994; Crafts 2005). Indeed, as Porter (1998*a*: 11) notes: 'Economic geography in an era of globalization involves a paradox' because 'the enduring competitive advantages in a global economy are often heavily local'. Globalization has certainly reduced many of the traditional advantages of specific locations since 'capital and other inputs can be efficiently sourced in global markets'. However, in Porter's analysis, global sourcing is 'a second best solution compared to a cluster'. Therefore, Porter (1998*b*: 90) argues against the 'world is flat' vision:

> In a global economy – which boasts rapid transportation, high-speed communication, and accessible markets – one would expect location to diminish in importance. But the opposite is true. The enduring competitive advantages in a global economy are often heavily local, arising from concentrations of highly

specialized skills and knowledge, institutions, rivals, related businesses, and sophisticated customers.

In *The Competitive Advantage of Nations*, Porter highlights the importance of spatial agglomerations of economic activity, driven by centripetal forces, arguing that these clusters of firms and industries are an important source of competitive advantage (Venables 1996). Indeed, Porter (1998*b*) reminds us that while economic geography 'has been all but absent from economic models' in recent decades, it was an important element in Adam Smith's analysis in *The Wealth of Nations* as well as Marshall's *Principles of Economics* (1890), which contains 'a fascinating chapter on the externalities of specialized industrial locations' (Snowdon and Stonehouse 2006).

The location of firms and industries influences competitiveness via its effect on productivity and the growth of productivity. Porter argues that the impact of location on competitiveness is mainly determined by the four main components of the diamond, and that productivity is greatest where there are clusters of economic activity. Consequently, during the last twenty years, Porter has given special attention to the crucial role played within the diamond framework of the formation of 'clusters' (Porter 1995, 1996*a*, 1998*a*, 1998*b*, 2000*c*, 2001*a*, 2003; Porter and Sölvell 1998; Martin and Sunley 2003; Bristow 2005; Ketels 2006; Motoyama 2008).

Porter defines clusters as 'geographical concentrations of interconnected companies and institutions in a particular field' (Porter 1998*b*). According to him, cluster development improves competitiveness by (*a*) reducing transaction costs and increasing the flow of information; (*b*) allowing firms easier access to specialized suppliers, employees, and information; (*c*) increasing firms' capacity for innovation and productivity growth; and (*d*) stimulating the formation of new businesses that expand the cluster. Excellent examples of cluster development include: information technology in Silicon Valley, California; financial services in Wall Street, New York, and the City of London; wine production in Burgundy; biotechnology in Boston; aircraft in Seattle; auto production in Detroit; and the numerous tourism clusters throughout the Mediterranean and elsewhere.

While technological progress during the twentieth century has dramatically reduced transportation and communication costs, in Porter's analysis, particular locations remain attractive because of the benefits of agglomeration and the clustering of economic activities. As Crafts (2005) has argued, a more correct interpretation of the 'death of distance' is the significant increase in international trade in services it permits, rather than making all locations equally attractive.

9.9 Measuring and analyzing global competitiveness

In 1971 Professor Klaus Schwab founded the WEF as a non-governmental organization committed to improving the state of the world. For the last twenty-five years the flagship publication of the WEF has been the annual *GCR*, the objective of which is to provide a detailed assessment of the 'competitiveness' of a large sample of nations. Previously, the *GCR* analyzed the competitiveness of nations using two alternative but complementary approaches (Snowdon 2007). The first approach to measuring competitiveness utilized the Business Competitiveness Index (BCI) developed by Michael Porter, which first appeared in the *GCR 2000* (prior to the *GCR 2004–5*, the BCI was known as the 'Microeconomic Competitiveness Index'). The BCI combined hard data with information gleaned from the Executive Opinion Survey of leading business executives and entrepreneurs from more than 100 countries. This survey is conducted during the first five months of each year by the WEF in cooperation with an extensive network of partner institutes (Blanke and Loades 2004). The second approach used the medium to long-term macroeconomic-oriented Growth Competitiveness Index, developed by John McArthur and Jeffrey Sachs (2001).

In addition to the Growth Competitiveness Index and BCI, the *GCR 2004–5* introduced the Global Competitiveness Index (GCI) – a new index developed by Xavier Sala-i-Martin and Elsa Artadi (2004). The underlying rationale for developing the GCI is to 'consolidate the WEF's work into a single index' that reflects the growing need to take into account a more comprehensive set of factors that significantly influence a country's growth performance (Snowdon 2006). Further work on the GCI by Porter et al. (2008) has now been completed and the WEF's *GCR 2009–10* contains just one index of national competitiveness, the GCI. However, important methodological and theoretical elements of the Growth Competitiveness Index, Porter's BCI, and the Artadi and Sala-i-Martin GCI, have been absorbed within the new GCI.

9.10 Porter's recent analysis of competitiveness

Porter's most recent analysis of the determinants of competitiveness is shown in Figure 9.1, which illustrates his basic general framework for thinking about the determinants of productivity and productivity growth (Porter et al. 2008). The central purpose of the new GCI is to identify the underlying causes of a nation's productivity, the broadest measure of which is GDP per capita adjusted for Purchasing Power Parity (PPP). According to Porter et al. (2008), GDP per capita is 'the best single, summary measure of competitiveness performance available

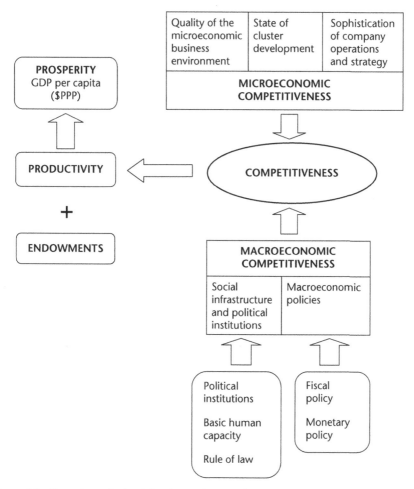

Figure 9.1. Porter's analysis of the determinants of competitiveness

across countries'. Endowments in the form of natural resources, climate, and geographical location will also influence productivity either positively or negatively (Snowdon 2007).

There is wide agreement among economists that the political, legal, and social institutions of an economy, combined with macroeconomic stability, create an environment conducive to economic success (Snowdon and Vane 2005). However, for that potential success to be realized also requires improvements in the microeconomic business environment (World Bank 2008). Microeconomic determinants of competitiveness include the sophistication of company operations and strategy, and the influence of the various factors included in Porter's diamond analysis, including the important role of cluster development.

A significant contribution of Porter's competitiveness analysis is to distinguish between the competitiveness challenges that exist at different levels of a nation's development. Porter (1990a, 2004) distinguishes three types of economy, each of which is characterized by a distinctive stage of competitive development: (a) low stage of development, *factor-driven economies*, where low-cost labor and/or unprocessed natural resources provide the dominant source of competitive advantage; (b) middle stage of development, *investment-driven economies*, where efficiency improvements dominate competitive advantage; and (c) high stage of development, *innovation-driven economies*, where competitive advantage depends on 'the ability to produce innovative products and services at the global technology frontier'. As Porter (2004: 31) argues, 'companies must shift from competing on endowments or comparative advantages (low-cost labor or natural resources) to competing on competitive advantages arising from superior or distinctive products and processes'. Rather than use GDP per capita, Porter et al. (2008) recommend and make use of an index of Social Infrastructure and Political Institutions (SIPI) as a proxy for a nation's stage of development.

9.11 The current Global Competitiveness Index

As noted by Porter et al. (2008), the *GCR 2004–5* represented a transition period because it was decided that subsequent reports would make use of a new single GCI that consolidates and extends the current dual-track approach involving the construction of the macroeconomic-oriented Growth Competitiveness Index and the microeconomic-oriented BCI. In the initial construction of the new 'flagship' GCI, Sala-i-Martin and Artadi (2004: 51) take as their starting point a productivity-based definition of competitiveness similar to Porter's:

> Competitiveness is defined as the set of institutions, policies, and factors that determine the level of productivity. The level of productivity in turn, sets the sustainable *level* of prosperity that can be earned by an economy [and]...a more competitive economy is one that is likely to grow at larger rates over the medium to long run.

In other words, productivity as a measure of competitiveness has both static and dynamic elements. However, because the 2003 rank correlation between the Growth Competitiveness Index and BCI was 95.4 percent, Sala-i-Martin and Artadi (2004) argue that the macroeconomic and microeconomic determinants of competitiveness cannot and should not be separated. Because there are numerous and complex determinants of competitiveness, Sala-i-Martin and Artadi (2004) and Sala-i-Martin et al. (2009) base the GCI on three basic principles:

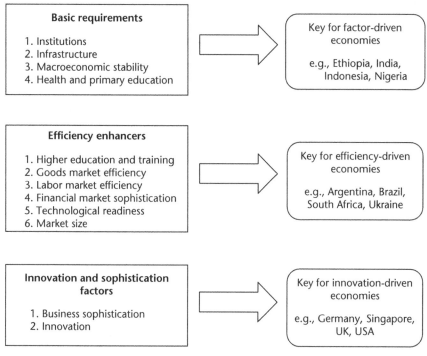

Figure 9.2. The stages of development framework
Source: Adapted from Sala-i-Martin et al. (2009)

- *Principle 1*: While extensive research indicates that the determinants of productivity are complex, the main influences can be encompassed within twelve complementary *'pillars of competitiveness'*: (*a*) institutions, (*b*) infrastructure, (*c*) macroeconomic stability, (*d*) personal security, (*e*) basic human capital, (*f*) advanced human capital, goods market efficiency, (*g*) labor market efficiency, (*h*) financial market efficiency, (*i*) technological readiness, (*j*) openness/market size, (*k*) business sophistication, and (*l*) innovation.

Table 9.2. The weights attached to each sub-index

Sub-index	Factor-driven economy (%)	Efficiency-driven economy (%)	Innovation-driven economy (%)
Basic requirements	$a_1 = 60$	$a_2 = 40$	$a_3 = 20$
Efficiency enhancers	$a_1 = 35$	$a_2 = 50$	$a_3 = 50$
Innovation and sophistication factors	$a_1 = 5$	$a_2 = 10$	$a_1 = 30$

Source: Adapted from Sala-i-Martin et al. (2009).

While each pillar is an important contributor to growth in all circumstances, the *relative* importance of their role depends on the stage of development of a country. Sala-i-Martin et al. (2009) adapt Porter's theory (1990*a*) of stages of development; that is, economies can be classified as *factor-driven*, *efficiency-driven*, or *innovation-driven*.

Taking this into account, the GCI organizes the twelve pillars into three sub-indexes: 'Basic Requirements' (BR), 'Efficiency Enhancers' (EE), and 'Innovation and Sophistication Factors' (IF). Figure 9.2 indicates which of the pillars are key in each stage of an economy's development.

- *Principle 2*: While basic requirements, efficiency enhancers, and innovation and sophistication factors play a role in all economies, following Porter (1990*a*; Porter et al. 2008), they are given different weights in the construction of the GCI depending on a country's stage of development. Table 9.2 shows the assignment of weights used, and the GCI 2009–10 is therefore constructed as a weighted composite index comprising these three elements as follows:

$$\mathrm{GCI} = \alpha_1 \mathrm{BR} + \alpha_2 \mathrm{EE} + \alpha_3 \mathrm{IF}, \text{where } \alpha_1 + \alpha_2 + \alpha_3 = 1$$

- *Principle 3*: In the GCI 2009–10 framework, the classification of countries, according to stage of development, is based on two criteria, namely GDP per capita ($) and the percentage of total exports in the form of primary commodities. The income thresholds used to classify countries according to the stage of development are shown in Table 9.3. As economies develop, they move smoothly from one stage to the next. Therefore, there are also two additional groups of *transition economies* and the weights of the sub-indexes 'change smoothly as a country develops'. This overall framework provides Global Competitiveness rankings for 133 countries representing each of the five country groupings. Table 9.4 provides data on selected 2009–10 rankings for thirty countries.

Table 9.3. Stages of development: the income thresholds

Stage of development	GDP per capita ($ US)
Stage 1: Factor-driven (S1)	<2,000
Transition from Stage 1 to Stage 2 (T1–2)	2,000–3,000
Stage 2: Efficiency-driven (S2)	3,000–9,000
Transition from Stage 2 to Stage 3 (T2–3)	9,000–17,000
Stage 3: Innovation-driven (S3)	>17,000

Source: Adapted from Sala-i-Martin et al. (2009).

Perhaps the most significant feature of the 2009–10 rankings is that the United States, after being ranked first for several years, has slipped into second place behind Switzerland. The main reason for this has been the growing macroeconomic instability relating to fiscal and trade imbalances, as well as the well-documented crisis in the financial sector. However, the *GCR* remains optimistic about the long-term economic prospects of the United States because of its 'excellent' university system, 'highly sophisticated and innovative companies', flexible labor market, and 'sheer size' of the domestic market. Controversially, the *GCR 2009–10* (Sala-i-Martin et al. 2009: 41) is critical of those, such as Nobel Laureates Joseph Stiglitz (2009) and Paul Krugman (2009*b*), who see the financial crisis of the late 2000s as evidence of serious market failure and the need for increased regulation of the financial sector.

Table 9.4. The Global Competitiveness Index 2009–10: selected rankings

Country	GCI 2009–10 rank	GCI 2008–9 rank	Basic requirements rank	Efficiency enhancers rank	Innovation and sophistication factors rank
Switzerland (S3)	1	2	3	3	3
The United States (S3)	2	1	28	1	1
Singapore (S3)	3	5	2	2	10
Germany (S3)	7	7	8	14	5
Japan (S3)	8	9	27	11	2
United Kingdom (S3)	13	12	26	8	14
Australia (S3)	15	18	14	9	21
France (S3)	16	16	15	16	15
Korean Rep. (S3)	19	13	23	20	16
Saudi Arabia (T1–2)	28	27	30	38	33
China (S2)	29	30	36	32	29
Chile (T2–3)	30	28	32	33	43
Czech Rep. (S3)	31	33	45	24	26
South Africa (S2)	45	45	77	39	39
Italy (S3)	48	49	67	46	34
India (S1)	49	50	79	35	28
Indonesia (T1–2)	54	55	70	50	40
Brazil (S2)	56	64	91	42	38
Russian Fed. (T2–3)	63	51	64	52	73
Egypt (T1–2)	70	81	78	80	71
Ukraine (S2)	82	72	94	68	80
Argentina (S2)	85	88	84	84	76
Libya (T1–2)	88	91	68	110	111
Nigeria (S1)	99	94	118	77	70
Pakistan (S1)	101	101	114	92	84
Bangladesh (S1)	106	111	108	97	114
Venezuela (T1–2)	113	105	104	108	130
Ethiopia (S1)	118	121	111	120	115
Zimbabwe (S1)	132	133	132	130	124
Burundi (S1)	133	132	133	133	133

Source: Adapted from Sala-i-Martin et al. (2009).

At the other end of the rankings, while there are some strong area-specific performances (Botswana, Mauritius, South Africa, Tunisia), the generally poor showing of the majority of countries in sub-Saharan Africa remains a major concern (Blanke and Sala-i-Martin 2009).

9.12 Conclusion

During the twenty years since the publication of *The Competitive Advantage of Nations*, a systematic, if imperfect, applied framework has been developed to assess the complex phenomenon of the competitiveness of nations and regions. It is unfortunate, but understandable, that Porter, building on his earlier research in the fields of strategic management, chose to use the word 'competitive' in the title of his famous book because, unless very carefully defined, it immediately conjures up images of a zero-sum world of winners and losers. As Krugman (1994*a*) has so clearly articulated, the idea that nations are in competition, like Pepsi and Coke, when engaging in international trade is nonsense. However, 'competitive images are exciting' and appeal to the business community, the media, and also publishers! Although Porter attempts to circumvent this problem by clearly analyzing the competitiveness of a nation in terms of factors which influence its longer-term productivity, this is unlikely to prevent the media, business leaders, and politicians continuing to engage in the zero-sum rhetoric of 'Pop Internationalism' (Krugman 1996*a*). However, notwithstanding this caveat, *The Competitive Advantage of Nations* should be recognized as an heroic attempt to build a dynamic framework of analysis that helps to bridge the gap between the fields of competitive strategy and international economics.

As the world's leading business academic, Porter's tome inevitably created considerable interest and could not have been published at a more opportune time, given that it coincided with the breakdown of the communist centrally planned economies and the consequent spread of globalization to more than twenty additional nations. During the last decade there has evolved a congruence between the research of Porter and mainstream growth theorists, in that there is growing recognition of the importance of microeconomic fundamentals if an environment conducive to sustainable growth is to be created (Baumol 2002; OECD 2004; Commission on Growth and Development 2008). In the 2005 *World Development Report*, the World Bank emphasizes the conditions that are necessary to create a good investment climate, echoing one of Porter's central ideas when it notes that:

Private firms are at the heart of the development process. Driven by the quest for profits, they invest in new ideas and new facilities that strengthen the foundations of economic growth and prosperity. (World Bank 2004: 1)

However, to many commentators Porter's 'theory' is too ambitious and lacks precision and determinacy. The result is an end product that Grant describes in chapter 7 as 'gloriously rich but hopelessly intractable'. Davies and Ellis (2000) provide a more negative assessment, arguing that Porter's analysis is 'hopelessly rich but gloriously intractable', and that all the major assertions in the book have been refuted. The majority of economists also continue to neglect *The Competitive Advantage of Nations* and remain skeptical of overambitious attempts to quantify the competitiveness of nations (Lall 2001). Porter's wide-ranging qualitative case study approach and verbal reasoning, lacking in predictive power, have little appeal to those committed to a traditional positivist research methodology. Consequently, textbooks in international economics tend to remain a Porter-free zone (Krugman and Obstfeld 2009).

To others, Porter's research program on the competitiveness of nations 'is fully grounded in economic principles', and offers new insights and a breadth of vision, supported by case studies, that is so often lacking in the narrow mathematically formulated models that typically characterize the economics literature (Ketels 2006). That one of the world's most eminent neoclassical growth theorists, Columbia University's Xavier Sala-i-Martin, has been one of the main architects of the current GCI, speaks volumes. Finally, there is no question that Porter's work has contributed to the revival of interest in regional science and economic geography (see chapters 10–12 in this volume). Porter's plea (1994: 38) for a renaissance in the study of agglomeration and external economies, and the need for economic geography to move 'from the periphery to the mainstream', has certainly been answered (Krugman 2009*a*).

Section 3
Clusters and Regions

10

Clusters and competitiveness: Porter's contribution

Christian H.M. Ketels

10.1 Introduction

Clusters have been known to exist at least since the days of Marshall. But Michael Porter's work, first in *The Competitive Advantage of Nations* (Porter 1990*a*) and then in *On Competition* (originally published in 1998 (Porter 1998*c*); updated and expanded edition in Porter 2008*b*), has undoubtedly had a singular role in raising the profile of these ideas to a wider audience, especially many practitioners in business and government. Cluster initiatives, one of the ways in which practitioners have responded to Porter's cluster ideas, have multiplied in number in the last few years. An Internet search for cluster initiatives in 2005 identified 1,400 such initiatives. Since then, these initiatives have become much more numerous (Ketels et al. 2006). Cluster-policy programs, too, have been multiplying. A review for the European Commission in 2007 indicated that all EU member countries had some types of cluster-policy program in place (Oxford Research 2008).

Critics have argued that such popularity itself is no proof of profoundness (Martin and Sunley 2003; for a different perspective, see Benneworth and Henry 2004).[1] While this is true, so is the opposite: popularity is clearly not a sign of conceptual weakness. At the minimum, it is a strong signal of relevance. And given that interest in these ideas has remained strong, if not grown over the last two decades, popularity is an indication of the robustness of Porter's ideas. He clearly struck a chord, most definitely with practitioners. Understanding why this has been the case is relevant not only for policy practice but also for academic research that aims to be relevant.

This chapter first looks at the origins of Porter's interest in clusters. Rather than representing a break relative to his earlier work on companies, clusters and the broader notion of competitiveness turn out to be natural extensions of his prior thinking. The second section of the chapter identifies the key characteristics of Porter's conceptual thinking on clusters. The discussion explores the particular perspective that Porter has taken, often as a result of his specific background and prior research interests. It contrasts these ideas to the work in related academic fields and finds differences but few, if any, fundamental incompatibilities. The third section turns to extensions of these core concepts in Porter's more recent work. A central focus of this work has been the creation of broad-based empirical datasets that allow the testing and further development of the original cluster framework. The fourth section then explores the policy implications to be drawn from Porter's work on clusters. Porter develops recommendations on how to leverage clusters as a tool in economic development. While many current cluster programs are broadly consistent with these ideas, some policy practice and much of the academic criticism of policies inspired by Porter's cluster work have taken a different direction, looking instead into ways of creating clusters. The fifth section discusses why Porter's work in this field has had such a profound impact, especially on practitioners. A central reason is that he addresses the very specific needs of different practitioner constituencies, providing a framework and actionable ideas to which they could easily relate. The final section turns to a number of open issues that will determine whether Porter's long-term impact on the practice and thinking in this field will reach its full potential.

10.2 Origins

Porter's interest in clusters developed almost accidentally. Having been called into President Ronald Reagan's Commission on Industrial Competitiveness in 1985, he went out to use his perspective as an industrial economist and business strategy researcher to better understand the competition the United States was facing. Given his professional background, he wanted to understand the firm-level reasons as to why the United States seemed to be falling behind some of its international peers – in particular, Japan. Porter quickly noted that each of the countries with which the United States competed seemed to have strengths in specific industries rather than across the board. He assembled an international team of researchers to take a closer look at the leading industries across these countries to understand the drivers of their success. This work – which as earlier chapters in this book illustrate, culminated in *The Competitive Advantage of Nations* (Porter 1990*a*) – very quickly revealed that in many industries the most successful companies happen to be co-located in a relatively small number of locations.

This observation could not be easily explained by Porter's existing research. His work on competitive advantages had focused on drivers internal to firms as the key explanation of their success. Unless one would be willing to believe that the executives making the right strategic choices to build such advantages were accidentally co-located in a few places, this approach did not solve the puzzle. His work on market attractiveness could explain how companies from a given industry could capture varying levels of economic returns depending on the market structures they faced locally. But the motivation for Reagan's Commission had been that foreign companies started to out-compete their US rivals on their own markets, where everyone was exposed to the same market structure conditions.

Porter needed to develop a concept to systematically capture how the external environment at a company's home base influenced its capacity for value creation and innovation. This would extend his previous work in two respects. It would add a second pillar to his work on value chains, which had provided the basis to understand how activities within the firm contribute to value creation. And it would add perspective to his work on market structures, which had identified five forces to understand how value was captured among suppliers, producers, and consumers.

The Diamond of business environment qualities – the new framework that Porter developed – provided an integrated perspective on the many different factors that influence how productive a company can be in a given location (Porter 1990a). Compared to the existing literature, this new approach provided three critical innovations. First, it opened the way for viewing the systemic interactions among different external conditions in affecting the value-creation potential of a company. Access to better skilled employees or infrastructure, for example, becomes much more of an asset when market conditions create an incentive for companies to use these capabilities. This insight moved beyond much of the existing literature that had looked for individual factors to explain differences in country performance, neglecting the interactions between them. And it provided a new way of overcoming the sterile ideological debate about whether open markets (less government) or better factor inputs (more government) are the critical drivers of a location's prosperity.[2]

Second, it introduced demand conditions as a critical influence on the value generation capabilities within a location. Economists had thought about the impact of local demand basically in terms of its overall quantity, if at all. Porter, heavily influenced by his work with companies, provided a very different perspective. For companies, demand is clearly crucial; it is regularly the number one item that managers worry about, much ahead of factor input conditions and often even ahead of rivals. Porter's framework highlights the nature of demand that pushes companies to develop new and better products and services. Exposure to more sophisticated customers can enable companies to develop distinct advantages relative to their rivals, increasing the value they are able to generate.

Third, it explicitly acknowledged the role of related and supporting industries and introduced the notion of clusters. Related and supporting industries contribute to the productive capability of a firm by giving it ready access to specialized inputs and services without having to face the different types of transaction costs associated with sourcing from other locations. Clusters extend this notion further, pointing out the role of competitors, specialized research and standard-setting institutions, government agencies, and other public and private bodies that facilitate linkages and common action. Clusters enable and push companies to leverage the opportunities of a given business environment.

Overall, Porter's work on clusters has logically emerged from his earlier work on company strategy. For Porter, competition is the unifying phenomena, and his work looks at how it affects companies, clusters, and locations, and what they can do to succeed in an environment where competition is a critical organizing principle.[3] Porter's work on clusters is an important element of his broader analysis of how location affects prosperity and company performance. Clusters exist because they provide real economic benefits to the companies that co-locate. But clusters as agglomerations are not the sole driver of performance; they emerge because of specific business environment conditions and enable companies to leverage these conditions more effectively.[4] Clusters are not a substitute for weak business environment conditions. In fact, under such conditions they are very unlikely to emerge naturally in response to market signals. To fully understand their dynamics and avoid policy mistakes, clusters have to been seen within the context of the overall competitiveness framework.

10.3 Key elements of Porter's cluster concept

Porter (2008b: 215) defines clusters as 'a geographically proximate group of interconnected companies and associated institutions in a particular field, linked by commonalities and complementarities'. His work is driven by his interest in their role in enabling companies to reach higher levels of productivity. While the general categories Porter uses to describe clusters are not fundamentally different from the broader related literature, his background in business and market analysis provides his work with a unique perspective. Two dimensions are particularly important.

First, geographic proximity within the cluster is the defining element that enables cluster dynamics to develop. Porter's background in business strategy analysis gave his perspective on proximity a particular flavor. Deep interactions with local partners are sources of sustainable competitive advantages. While working with the best global research center located somewhere else might provide clear benefits, it is something that competitors from any location in the world in principal can copy. A close relationship with a local partner, however, is something that in its depth is only achievable for companies located there. Working with leading suppliers and research centers around the world is conversely, a necessity to enter competition at the most advanced level. But it does not provide the type of sustainable competitive advantages which engagement in a strong local cluster can deliver. Few other analytical approaches to clusters contain such a clear notion of the different and complementary role of local and global linkages (see also Bathelt et al. 2004; Wolfe and Gertler 2004). For Porter, it was a natural complement to his work on global strategy (Porter 1986a).

Second, value-creation proximity – that is, the strengths of relations between different activities in creating value for customers – within a cluster is a necessary condition for co-location to be relevant. Only if activities affect each other's value creation, does geographic proximity between them matter. This perspective leads to a view of clusters as entities that cut across narrowly defined industries and often also across broad economic sectors such as manufacturing or services. Porter's earlier work on value chains clearly indicates that such categories were of little use to understand the range of activities that had to be combined in order to produce a competitive product or service. This perspective also opens the view for including specialized government agencies, business associations, and other organizations into the cluster if their activities have a significant impact on the companies' value creation. Porter argues that organized collaboration can significantly enhance the impact of co-location on performance. But he also notes that many of the cluster dynamics play out even in the absence of such organized joint efforts as an automatic consequence of proximity.

Overall, Porter's approach to defining clusters is driven by revealed economic outcomes, that is, evidence that being close to one another matters for economic performance, and not by generic definitions such as the use of a common technology (a central consideration for the definition of industries in official statistics) or by a specific type of linkage (common labor market, common factor inputs, knowledge or other non-pecuniary spillovers). All of the above could underpin the presence of a cluster; but what matters to Porter is the overall impact revealed through cluster dynamism, not the specific mechanism through which it is achieved. This approach has been criticized as 'fuzzy' (Martin and Sunley 2003), making it impossible to truly test the cluster approach empirically. Section 3 below shows that this principles-based definition can be translated into testable empirical definitions, a process that was under way but had not been published when the criticism was voiced.

There is no fundamental conflict between the core elements of Porter's work on clusters and other schools of thought in this area. They are all grounded in related prior work by Marshall, Jacobs, and others. Porter discusses these connections explicitly in a chapter on clusters in *On Competition* (Porter 1998*d*). But while there is a lot of common ground, there are also, not surprisingly, differences in their respective foci, methods, and policy conclusions.[5]

The literature on Industrial Districts (such as Becattini 1990) concentrates on the particular type of clusters present in Northern Italy, focused strongly on the social embeddedness of clusters (Porter and Ketels 2009). The new economic geography literature (such as Fujita et al. 1999) uses mathematical models to analyze the impact of differences in trade costs between regions on agglomeration patterns under conditions of forward and backward linkages and spillovers. These models abstract from business environment conditions that in Porter's framework are the foundation of cluster emergence and economic performance. In the new economic geography and the related urbanization literature (for example, Jacobs 1969; Scott 2006; Glaeser 2008), the focus tends to be on economy-wide linkages, not on linkages within more narrowly defined clusters. The literature on innovation systems (such as Nelson 1993; Cooke and Morgan 1998) focuses on the dynamics of knowledge flows, localized learning, and innovation, often with a bias toward science-driven innovation. This is one of the central dynamics within clusters that Porter analyzes in his work, but not the only one.

As in the broader literature on regional studies, the focus in the innovation systems literature is on public policy and the science system, not primarily on the role of companies in related industries. The literature on value chain analysis (such as Humphrey and Schmitz 2000; Gereffi et al. 2001) concentrates on how the position of companies and clusters in developing economies within global value chains affects economic development. The focus of this work is often on the power relations within global value chains and how this might hinder or help economic development. There is also a large empirically driven literature on the geography of innovation, mostly focusing on advanced economies (such as Saxenian 1994; Audretsch and Feldman 2003). The work on creative regions (Florida 2002) concentrates on identifying factors that enable regions to attract and retain a 'creative class', seen as a necessary asset for economic development and especially regions' ability to be hotbeds of new ideas.

Despite the many linkages and complementarities between these different strands of work, there is a sense that they have largely developed in parallel to each other and especially to Porter's work. The use of different methods in particular seems to have been a barrier to the flow of ideas. The focus on different dynamics or issues leads to different or even opposing conclusions:

the new economic geography literature points out how economic integration can increase the divergence between central and peripheral regions (World Bank 2009a), while the cluster literature argues that economic integration creates opportunities for all regions to attract clusters. The literature on creative regions identifies characteristics to which all regions should aspire, while the cluster literature identifies the need to develop a unique profile of capabilities that is different across each region. A sense of competing for the attention of the same decision-makers might have also added to an unwillingness to fully engage.

Whatever the reason, the lack of productive dialogue is problematic. There are no fundamental incompatibilities across the different approaches. Where deeper differences in perspective exist, they tend to reflect the focus on one particular dynamic rather than another. The opposing views of the new economic geography and cluster literature on the impact of integration on especially peripheral regions are a good example. In practice, both dynamics are at work, and what is needed is a conceptual approach that identifies the conditions under which one or the other empirically dominates.[6] This is only one example of where the lack of an effective dialogue between the different approaches has limited progress in the field.

10.4 Empirical tests of Porter's cluster concept: cluster mapping

In the first decade after the publication of *The Competitive Advantage of Nations*, Porter's work was focused on case studies and further developments of the conceptual framework. He worked with a number of countries and regions that had taken an interest in his ideas, from the Basque Country in Spain to New Zealand, Portugal, Colombia, the countries of Central America, the state of Massachusetts in the United States, and many others. Cluster mobilization was often a central part of these projects. The 1998 *Harvard Business Review* article 'Clusters and the new economics of competition' (Porter 1998b) summarized many of the key findings from this work, establishing the central role of clusters in his overall thinking on competitiveness.

Over time, the focus of Porter's work began to include large-scale quantitative efforts on data generation and analysis. Already *The Competitive Advantage of Nations* had used trade data to gain insights into the cluster specialization of countries, and into their competitive positions in global markets. But these first efforts were not sufficient to test the impact of cluster presence on economic outcomes, a core hypothesis of Porter's conceptual thinking. In the late 1990s he started an initiative to derive a quantitative mapping of clusters to conduct such tests. He sought to identify clusters from the revealed locational patterns of economic activity across the United

States. Based on the existing data structure in terms of regions (states and economic areas in the case of the United States) and industries (4- and 5-level SIC-codes), he looked at the locational patterns of employment within narrow industries and regions. In a first step, this led to a separation of industries where employment was significantly concentrated across regions (Porter calls them traded cluster industries) from industries where employment was evenly spread across space (Porter calls them local industries). For the first group of industries, the co-location of employment across industries was then a main determinant to identify forty-one cluster categories, that is, groups of industries that tended to co-locate (see Porter 2003 for more details of the approach).

This mapping of industries into clusters resulted in a data set covering the entire US economy that indicated employment numbers per cluster for each region. The data set also included average wages, job creation, establishments, and patenting by regional cluster.[7] In 'The economic performance of regions', Porter uses this data to test key hypotheses derived from his conceptual framework (Porter 2003). This analysis provides a more nuanced understanding of the role of clusters for regional prosperity. At the national level, the traded cluster sector accounts for about one-third of US employment and registers higher wages, higher productivity, and higher productivity growth than the economy overall. The traded cluster sector also accounts for the vast majority of patenting in the United States. At the regional level, higher wages in a region's clusters are highly correlated with wages in the local industries and with a region's overall wage level. Employment mix across clusters or between clusters and local industries is not a dominant driver of average regional wages. However, increasing employment specialization in clusters is associated with higher wage growth, and a higher share of employment in strong clusters – that is, regional clusters with a location quotient above a cut-off point – is associated with a higher average regional wage and higher regional patenting intensity (Delgado et al. 2007).

At the cluster level, higher specialization within a regional cluster, measured by standard location quotients, is correlated with higher relative wages compared to the national wage in the cluster category. Higher specialization seems to have a stronger impact, if it is not only driven by high employment in a narrow industry but reflects strong employment positions across several industries within a cluster. While these findings on the positive relationship between cluster presence and economic performance are quite consistent with the related literature, especially from economic geography studies, they are for the first time derived within a consistent cluster framework. More recent analysis distinguishes between simultaneous cluster (agglomeration) and catch-up (dispersion) effects. Higher initial employment within a narrow industry reduces future employment growth within that industry, but increases job growth in related industries within a cluster (Delgado et al. 2007).

Porter's initial results for the United States were found to hold also for Canadian (Institute for Competitiveness and Prosperity 2002) and European datasets (European Commission 2007; Sölvell et al. 2008). Overall, these studies indicate that US regions receive more meaningful economic benefits from their higher levels of specialization compared to their European peers. Medium-sized European regions in particular are much less specialized in their employment portfolios around clusters than are their US counterparts. Comparisons within the European Union also highlight the importance of general business environment conditions alongside cluster specialization. Across all twenty-seven EU member countries – a heterogeneous group of economies at different levels of economic development and overall competitiveness – there is no statistical relationship between cluster presence and regional performance. But as soon as subgroups of countries at similar overall levels of competitiveness are created, the relationship is significant within the subgroup of the old EU members in Western Europe (EU-15) as well as the subgroup of newer members in Central Europe (EU-8).

The empirical findings inspired new conceptual thinking on the role of cluster linkages. One dimension of these linkages is geographic: the data revealed that regions and regional clusters register higher performance if neighboring regions are specialized in the same fields. This may suggest the misalignment of administrative regions used for statistics with the functional economic regions companies operate within. But it is also consistent with possible synergies between neighboring regions, an observation that influenced Porter's work on collaboration between neighboring regions[8] and synergies between metropolitan and rural regions (Porter et al. 2004).

Another dimension of these linkages is related to the value-creation process. The cluster-mapping exercise revealed that cluster categories were not isolated islands, but often connected through industries that had significant ties to more than one cluster. Porter exploited this observation to systematically track which clusters were linked to one another through a significant number of 'shared' industries (Delgado et al. 2007). In the regional analysis, it turns out that regions that have strong clusters in related fields are doing better than regions that have strong clusters without such connections. This observation influenced Porter's thinking on the evolution of regional economies and the diversification of a country's export portfolio. For regions, growth is likely to occur in related fields, not completely new fields without any relation to existing activities.[9] Similarly for exports, growth is most likely to occur through strengthening positions within existing clusters[10] and through diversification into related clusters.[11]

10.5 Policy implications of Porter's work

Porter's conceptual work and the supporting empirical tests indicate that strong clusters go hand in hand with strong economies. The lessons drawn by practitioners from this observation have, however, in some cases been quite different from Porter's own reasoning and advice. This section first presents Porter's own view about the policy implications of the cluster framework, and then contrasts these ideas with some of the applications seen in practice.

Clusters are the appropriate level for government and companies to engage in efforts to improve competitiveness. This is at the heart of many of Porter's discussion of the policy implications from the cluster approach (Porter 1998b). He sees clusters as a powerful tool for policy diagnostics, design, and delivery, not as something that government policy ought to create. Based on this general view, he identifies five broad roles for public policy (Porter 1998b). First, include an analysis of the cluster portfolio and individual clusters in your assessment of the local economy. Second, ensure that overall economic policies strengthen the general business environment to support the natural emergence of clusters. Third, remove policies that actively work against the emergence of clusters, for example, by opposing tendencies for regional specialization. Fourth, leverage clusters as a delivery channel and object of economic policies to upgrade the relevant business environment conditions and thus competitiveness. Fifth, encourage the emergence of cluster organizations that can strengthen the linkages and spillovers within clusters.

The two last roles are most visibly different from traditional approaches. On organizing policies around clusters, Porter sees, for example, cluster-based workforce development efforts or foreign direct investment attraction as being more effective than efforts organized by individual companies or broad sectors of the economy (see Porter in Mills et al. 2008). Targeting individual companies has a strong impact on these particular firms, but is highly distortive across the markets in which they operate. General programs for large swaths of the economy avoid much of the distortive effect, but are also known to be not very effective in using public resources. Clusters provide a better trade-off between these two concerns. Distortions are reduced, because by definition the linkages transmitting such possible distortions are strong within the cluster but weak outside. Impact is increased, because the policy reaches a receptive group of companies, and the cluster dynamics enhance the policies' direct impact.

Porter suggests organizing policies toward clusters not only because this makes them more effective but also because it allows these policies to be more informed. At a fundamental level, a cluster focus helps, especially regional government, to obtain a more nuanced sense of the economy.[12] But moving beyond this diagnostic phase, clusters also offer an effective platform to then engage the private sector in a dialogue about policy design. One of the key challenges for policymakers is to identify how scarce resources should be used in order to have the optimal impact on the competitiveness of companies and the overall economy. In making these trade-offs – say, spending on a new university instead of giving an R&D tax credit – governments need to understand how companies will react to these policies and whether they address any binding constraints they face. Many countries have established policy dialogues between the public and the private sector at the level of the entire economy. But these discussions have a tendency to focus on the few issues relevant for all companies, such as taxes and general bureaucracy. A dialogue at the level of a cluster can go much deeper, addressing the many more technical issues that are together hugely important for competitiveness.

On mobilizing cluster initiatives, Porter is as much concerned with enhancing the level of positive spillovers within the cluster as with identifying specific efforts to improve the underlying business environment. In a static sense, cluster initiatives (Porter sees them as a particular type of what he calls 'Institutions for Collaboration') can enable higher levels of interactions between companies within a given business environment. Porter mentions his own work with the medical device cluster in Massachusetts, where prior to the creation of MassMEDIC many of the companies did not realize the breadth of related companies nearby (Porter 1998*b*). In a dynamic sense, cluster initiatives can be platforms for joint action between companies, or between the private and the public sector, to improve the underlying competitiveness of the cluster. Porter argues strongly for private-sector leadership in cluster initiatives. This might be influenced by his experiences in the United States, where the private sector tends to be willing to take the initiative. In Europe, behavior is often different, and governments play a more important role in launching cluster efforts. The emerging empirical literature finds such public-sector leadership consistent with effective cluster mobilization, as long as the private sector assumes responsibility for the action agenda of the initiative (Sölvell et al. 2003).

The actual practice of cluster policies and cluster initiatives is highly heterogeneous, depending on the economic context and also on the economic policy orientation of governments. In advanced economies, cluster policy has become a relatively widely used policy tool, especially in innovation policy and also in regional and small- and medium-sized enterprises (SME) policies. Cluster policy is in most of these cases designed as an additional pillar alongside existing programs, usually with a modest share of overall funding. In the United States, the federal government has traditionally not had a cluster policy, but both the Economic Development Administration (EDA) and the Small Business Administration (SBA) are now funding cluster-based efforts. US cluster activity has traditionally been driven by private-sector leaders, but some US states also have active cluster programs. There is some degree of 'me-too' cluster initiatives found across all states – for example, in life sciences – but this is not typical. In Europe, as well as in Canada and Japan, government plays a significantly more important role as the initiator of cluster efforts. Many of the more recent cluster programs (such as those in France, Germany, and Sweden) award funding based on open competitions. A few countries and regions have used the cluster framework as a more fundamental basis of their economic and innovation policy (such as Finland, see Ylä-Anttila and Palmberg 2007, and the Basque Country). Local and regional governments have found a new role in the mobilization of cluster efforts, often using co-financing available through the EU structural funds. National governments and the European Union remain largely focused on financing, limiting the public–private dialogue on national/EU-level policies affecting clusters.

In developing and emerging economies, cluster efforts are hampered by the generally weaker clusters and general business environment conditions. In Latin America, organizations like the Inter-American Development Bank and the Corporación Andina de Fomento (CAF), but also national entities like Fundacion Chile, are engaged in cluster programs, some with many years of experience. In Africa and developing economies in Asia, the World Bank, UNIDO, USAID, and others make use of cluster initiatives. While these efforts have had local success, in particular in upgrading the export abilities of some regional clusters, they still account for a relatively small fraction of overall economic development activities. In general, clusters have not become a tool in driving competitiveness upgrading at a broader level. In the emerging economies of Asia and the Middle East, governments are much more willing to actively engage in the creation of clusters. These programs target specific industries rather than clusters, often through dedicated investments or incentives. In many cases, this has led to a proliferation of virtually identical cluster efforts across neighboring regions with little relation to their existing capabilities and economic base. Some of these efforts have been successful, usually if the selected industries leverage existing strengths and the policies used impose high levels of competition alongside government support. But the failures are numerous, with little positive impact on either the wider economy or overall competitiveness.

The notion of government 'creating clusters' finds no support in Porter's own work,[13] and characterizes only a segment of actual government cluster policies. The evolution of clusters is a complex, market-driven process that government influences but cannot effectively control.[14] Nevertheless, the suspicion that cluster creation is the essence of cluster policy underpins much of the academic criticism of Porter's influence on government policies. Interestingly, the creation of clusters is a much more natural policy in other conceptual approaches than in Porter's framework. In models of the new economic geography literature, for example, agglomeration is the key mechanism, and cluster policy is understood to mean the artificial creation of agglomeration (Baldwin et al. 2003; Duranton 2009). Many of the authors from this field are rightly critical of such policies (Martin et al. 2008a) that rely on little if any empirical evidence to support their effectiveness. But these policies are also diametrically opposed to what Porter's work suggests cluster policy should be.[15]

The issue that concerns policymakers significantly more is how to generate more impact from existing cluster programs and initiatives (High Level Advisory Group on Clusters 2008). While there are significant data on how the presence of clusters relates to economic outcomes, there is no comparably systematic data on the impact of cluster initiatives or programs. The available case studies and individual program evaluations point toward a positive impact on the companies involved and on generally improved public–private cooperation at the regional level, but do not quantify the economic returns achieved (Ketels 2009a). The benefits accruing to the wider regional or national economy are often small. These observations suggest that current cluster-policy practice is concentrated on mobilizing existing clusters to achieve higher levels of performance. But there is little evidence of cluster policy being used to strengthen cluster portfolios or to upgrade general business environment quality.

10.6 Drivers of success: how did Porter's cluster concept become so influential?

Porter's work on clusters and competitiveness has had an exceptional influence compared to alternative approaches in the literature. And its impact has proven to be remarkably robust over time: over the last few years a whole new wave of cluster efforts were launched, more than a decade after *The Competitive Advantage of Nations* was published (Davies 2006).

Reviewing the discussion so far, the depth of this impact is somewhat surprising. Porter's conceptual framework has many unique features. But it also shares key notions with most of the other work in this area. There is an emerging consensus on the empirical benefits of clusters. And there is widespread agreement that clusters are a useful analytical tool to inform policymaking. But whether cluster programs and initiatives driven by government are sufficiently powerful or even a good investment from a societal point of view remains in dispute. From a conceptual perspective, the lack of consensus on what cluster policy is and how it should be implemented remains acute. Part of this is the result of an insufficient engagement with Porter's work on the issue. But part of it may also reflect a lack of specificity in his writing on the specifics of cluster policy. From an empirical perspective there are many practitioners who find Porter's approach a very powerful inspiration for their work. But the experience with the first wave of cluster efforts in the 1990s also suggested a need to significantly systematize the advice on specific tools and structures (den Hertog and Remøe 2001; European Commission 2002, 2003b).

Why has Porter's work on clusters achieved such a significant, long-lasting impact on policy thinking, despite the skepticism of other academics and the heterogeneous ways in which policymakers have translated his thinking into practice?

Porter's work has a number of features that distinguish it from alternative approaches. Maybe most importantly, he is willing to address the big policy questions that ultimately motivate practitioners. Where many other researchers focus on dealing with narrow questions within a given conceptual framework, Porter puts the key policy question first, and then draws elements from different research approaches and methods to identify an appropriate response. A key strength of his work is the ability to develop conceptual frameworks that integrate different, narrower ideas into a coherent overall framework. A second key principle for Porter is an orientation toward action. He aims to create models that help practitioners understand reality in ways that enable them to make better decisions in a specific context. He is less interested in description for its own sake or in the identification of general principles that work 'on average' but provide little help in making more informed decisions in a specific situation.

These general characteristics of Porter's work on clusters (as of his work on business strategy and industry analysis) go some way toward explaining the impact he has been able to generate. An important additional aspect is the attractiveness of his work on clusters for three specific target groups: business executives, policymakers, and cluster practitioners.

Business executives are an audience that other schools of thought in this field have generally failed to excite with their ideas. Porter's work has been unique in capturing their imagination. Partly this is a function of the reputation he built with this group through his previous work on strategy and industry analysis. But it is also driven by the fact that he connects his findings on clusters and competitiveness with key issues that business executives face. And it is helped by making his arguments in a language that relates to business executives' need for practical solutions:

- Globalization and economic reforms have increased competitive pressure in many markets, often dramatically. Companies have responded by increasing efficiency, a process that can to some degree occur within firms. But it often also requires shifting the boundaries of the firm (outsourcing of non-core activities) and systemic changes across the industry value chain. For both, the cluster framework provides an essential tool to organize individual choices within companies and joint action across clusters (Best 2001; Ketels 2007; Porter 2008*b*: ch. 7).

- Globalization has also changed the relevance of location for competition by exposing companies – directly or through the rivals they face – to a much broader set of different business environments. Companies have responded by reorganizing the geographic footprint of their value chains (Baldwin 2006; Berger 2006). The cluster framework provides them with a tool to think about these choices and evaluate potential locations. Porter's work on global strategy (Porter 1986*b*) created a natural platform to explore clusters as the local sources of competitive advantages exploited in global markets (Enright 2000; Porter 2000*a*; 2008*b*: ch. 8).

- Innovation has become an increasingly important driver of competition and seems ever harder to achieve within companies alone. The cluster framework provides a natural context in which to think about how to engage with open systems of innovation (Chesbrough 2003). Locally, clusters are a structure in which collaboration with partners can be organized (Best 2001). Globally, clusters are the concentrations of innovative activity that companies can analyze and, if appropriate, tap into to connect with emerging sources of new ideas. Clusters play an important role in the innovative capacity of locations (Furman et al. 2002).

- The pressure on companies to contribute to solving the broader challenges facing the communities in which they are operating is increasing. Companies cannot ignore this pressure for fear of the negative effects on their bottom line, particularly if NGOs brandish their failure to behave in socially responsible ways. But companies also face the interests of their shareholders that ask for returns on all of the company's activities contributing to the bottom line. The cluster framework provide a means to organize collaboration with the public sector to improve the external context in a modern way, and to structure companies' efforts to address social issues in ways that are aligned with long-term competitiveness (Porter and Kramer 2006).

Policymakers are the more traditional target group for the work of academic researchers. But even with them Porter is able to target a specific need that had not been addressed well in previous work. Policymakers at the national and regional level, and also in international organizations like the OECD, UNIDO, and the World Bank, are looking for growth-policy concepts that moved beyond the traditional mix of sound macroeconomic policies, market openings, and investments in long-term knowledge assets (OECD 1999, 2003; den Hertog and Remøe 2001; Pietrobelli and Rabellotti 2004; Zeng 2008).

The cluster framework, especially if seen in the context of the wider competitiveness approach of which it is part, outlines a policy development method whereby government can play an active role without committing the costly mistakes of traditional industrial policy (Porter 2008b: ch. 7). For a number of functional policy areas struggling with concerns about their impact, like regional policy, innovation policy, policies for small- and medium-sized companies (SMEs), workforce development, investment attraction, and poverty alleviation, the cluster framework provides new tools and approaches (Porter 1996a; Landabaso 2001; UNIDO 2001; Nadvi and Barrientos 2004; Porter et al. 2004; Ketels 2005; European Commission 2008; World Bank 2009b). For subnational regions, a level of government often ignored in the traditional macroeconomic policy discussions, the cluster framework defines an important role in economic policy (Rosenfeld 2002; Porter et al. 2005; OECD 2007) and provides conceptual guidance on how to effectively organize the decentralization of economic policy responsibilities.

For some policymakers, however, the motivation for using cluster policies might have been different. Some seemed to hope that cluster policies would provide a way to achieve growth while avoiding the hard work of improving the business environment. It is often easier to find support for a program that encourages collaboration within a cluster, than taking on the power of entrenched interest groups that are holding back competitiveness upgrading. Others truly believed that cluster policies could 'create' clusters, bypassing the arduous path of economic development in which clusters gradually emerge in response to improving business environment conditions.

Economic development practitioners that are in day-to-day contact with businesses, either as consultants or as employees of public or public–private entities with an economic development mission, are a third important target group. For them, the cluster framework provided a clear job description in terms of their own role and of the tools and approaches they could use (Waits 2000).[16] And it is much more accessible and implementation-oriented than the related academic literature.

10.7 Where to go from here

There is overwhelming evidence of the major impact Porter's work on clusters has had over the last two decades. But this success – especially the huge wave of government-initiated cluster-policy programs launched in the last few years – also creates high expectations for the economic outcomes to be achieved. The jury is still out as to whether or not these expectations will be met, despite the success of many individual cluster efforts and policies. There are a number of factors that will be important for this to happen – and for Porter's work in this area to reach its full potential impact.

For academic research, the future legacy of Porter's work on clusters will depend on whether his ideas will be reconnected to the related approaches in the field. Despite the large number of citations, Porter's work has not been fully incorporated into the traditional academic discourse. Younger scholars interested in studying clusters in Porter's tradition find it hard to establish themselves in the available academic career paths. As discussed above, there are no fundamental incompatibilities between the more standard work in economic geography, regional studies, and other related fields and Porter's conceptual framework. The differences that exist are in perspective and method, not more. Porter's more recent analysis of cluster-mapping data brings him closer to the mainstream discourse, especially in terms of methods. There is significant potential for using this data in more systematic evaluations of cluster-policy interventions and their impact. This is an issue where disagreement currently remains high and little relevant data is available. Porter's work has more insights to provide to other academic research, as much as his own thinking could integrate more comprehensively the work of others.

For practitioners, the future legacy of Porter's work will depend on whether the activities being implemented in this spirit will be able to achieve impact. Despite the significant case-based indications that cluster programs can deliver positive results, there is no large-scale quantitative data about their effectiveness. And where impact has been visible, it has often tended to be localized within the cluster rather than achieving a meaningful impact on an entire regional or national economy. Both of these issues can be addressed. There needs to be an effort similar to the cluster-mapping project, but this time tracking the many cluster policies and programs around the world to evaluate their impact.[17] The evaluations of individual cluster programs regularly conducted by public funding agencies do not deliver this type of comparable data. The evaluation of companies that participate in cluster-type programs is useful, but does not capture the impact on business environment conditions (Martin et al. 2008*b*). In addition, there needs to be more conceptual work to provide policymakers with the tools to ensure that cluster policies deliver broader benefits to the economy than is typical today (Ketels 2009*a*). Porter's thinking provides the foundations for this work, but in his writings these issues have not been dealt with explicitly.

Most importantly, perhaps, the confusion that still exists about the policy conclusions to be drawn from Porter's work on clusters need to be addressed. Many policies are called cluster policies but have little or no relation to the action recommendations that can be drawn from Porter's work. And many cluster policies are launched to reach objectives that they are ill-equipped to achieve. Any of the failures occurring because of these mistakes will inevitably create a backlash against cluster policies. And they fuel a discussion in the academic literature that has little to do with Porter's original ideas, provides little practical guidance on the real implementation issues practitioners face, and fails to reflect the insights that these ideas can provide for future research. A stronger focus on the research, and conceptual thinking underlying Porter's thinking on cluster policy, rather than on clusters as a diagnostic tool, may be part of the answer to overcoming the misperceptions among practitioners. A more explicit engagement of the research undertaken in the Porter tradition with the related academic literature might be another. But it will also require a greater willingness in the broader research community to fully engage with Porter's ideas, despite the different language he uses. Twenty years after *The Competitive Advantage of Nations* and ten years after 'Clusters and the new economics of competition', Porter's cluster framework continues to have significant potential as a rich source of new research and ideas.

Notes

1. See Motoyama (2008) for a broader discussion of the critique.
2. On both accounts, there are interesting similarities between Porter's thinking and some of the arguments made by Rodrik (2007) and Hausmann et al. (2005).
3. See Porter's new introduction to *On Competition*, updated and expanded edition (2008*b*).
4. See Porter et al. (2008) and Furman et al. (2002) on the integration of the cluster dimension into broader assessments of competitiveness and innovative capacity.
5. See Cortright (2006) for a discussion of the different strands of literature.
6. See Brülhart (2009) as an interesting example of such a discussion.
7. The data is accessible at http://data.isc.hbs.edu/isc/.
8. Porter has worked extensively with Central America through CLADCS, a research center at INCAE Business School. See Ketels (2009*b*) for an application to the Baltic Sea region.
9. Neffke et al. (2009) provide evidence on the evolution of specialization patterns across Swedish regions that confirm this view.
10. This is consistent with recent empirical findings (Newfarmer et al. 2009) that indicate significant export potential for developing economies in areas of existing export categories.
11. Hausmann and Klinger (2007) independently proposed a related approach. They identify proximity between product groups based on the income level of countries that export them, not by underlying cluster linkages revealed through co-location of economic activity. They do not discuss the potential for improving exports in existing products, and suggest the use of more traditional industrial policy tools to implement their approach.

12. See Porter's presentation to the National Governors Association in the United States, based on Porter et al. (2005).
13. See the interview with Michael Porter in Svenska Dagbladet, 28 January 2008. See also several of Porter's presentations in the Middle East on this point, which are available at http://www.isc.hbs.edu.
14. See the case studies and discussions in Braunerhjelm and Feldman (2006) and Bresnahan and Gambardella (2004); see also Sölvell (2008) and Konakayama and Chen (2007).
15. See Ketels (2009a) for a further discussion of these misperceptions.
16. The Competitiveness Institute (http://www.tci-network.org) was created by a number of these practitioners in 1998 to promote and develop the use of the cluster concept in regional economic development. TCI has grown to a network of 1,700 members in almost 100 countries.
17. Sölvell et al. (2003) take a small step in this direction for the narrow field of cluster initiatives.

11

On diamonds, clusters, and regional development

Edward J. Malecki

11.1 Introduction

Unusually for a business scholar, Michael Porter has made important contributions to local and regional development. Porter's 'diamond model' and 'clusters' have been applied in localities, regions, and countries throughout the world. In several respects, the two concepts are inextricably interrelated; both the diamond and the cluster rely on links to other industries, institutions, infrastructures, and policies. As Christian Ketels highlights in the previous chapter, although both the diamond model and the cluster have been misunderstood and misapplied, both concepts are central to how regions and localities understand their potential within an economic, social, political, and institutional framework. This chapter begins by tracing the roots of Porter's cluster concept, beginning with *Competitive Strategy*, followed by *Competitive Advantage* and *The Competitive Advantage of Nations*.

The cluster concept is most fully elaborated in *On Competition*, although few adherents or critics appear to have read this fuller account of clusters. The chapter then presents the advantages of a fully conceived account of clusters. This fuller account bears more similarity to the influential model of regional innovation systems than criticisms of clusters as a chaotic concept suggest. Regional innovation systems embody an array of linkages (traded interdependencies) among firms in a region as well as untraded interdependencies and interactions between firms and other institutions and organizations. As territorial innovation models, both Porter's concept of clusters and the innovation systems approach are subject to the issue of scale. Also, the degree to which they are dependent on their national and sectoral contexts is under-explored.

In exploring these issues, the chapter finds on balance more that is useful in the cluster concept for understanding regional and local competitiveness.

The field of regional development is concerned with the economic (and political–economic) processes that affect places and their residents differently. The outcomes of these processes are manifested in tremendous variations in wealth and poverty, in innovativeness, and in competitiveness (Malecki 1997). Technological change is among the central processes that influence regional development, particularly through the emergence of new products, services, firms, and industries (Thomas 1975; Malecki 1991). Indeed, in the 1970s it seemed that only two sets of factors determined economic growth – albeit growth of different kinds. Places that offered low costs, especially from low wages and also from low taxes, were beginning to threaten the post-war prosperity of Western economies (Fröbel et al. 1980). At the same time, high-tech growth in a few areas – notably northern California's Silicon Valley and Boston's Route 128 – gave rise to an alternative and more attractive development path based on technology and entrepreneurship.

Understanding regional competition required new ideas beyond economists' simple production functions in which only capital and labor are the factors of production. Two prominent ideas were already on the table. First, an unexplained 'residual' in growth was believed to be a result of technological change (Solow 1956). That is, knowledge could be considered as an input to economic activity (Romer 1986). Second, the product life cycle addressed the international division of labor and highlighted the distinction between new and mature products. Both topics had led to new explorations of variations in the economic geography and the varying development prospects of places. Porter (1980a) included both topics prominently in *Competitive Strategy*, but from the perspective of firms and industries rather than of places.

As earlier chapters have highlighted, one of Porter's principal contributions in *Competitive Strategy* was the 'three generic strategies': overall cost leadership, differentiation, and focus. These were presented in the context of five forces driving industry competition, illustrated in a 'diamond' (but not called a diamond) that included suppliers and buyers (or linked firms), existing competitors, and threats from new technologies and from new entrants. Porter's competitive framework meshed nicely with the emerging focus of geographers and regional scientists on inter-firm linkages and technological change.

In *Competitive Strategy*, Porter also devoted attention to the product (and industry) life cycle, which had received attention previously from Abernathy and Utterback (1978), Krumme and Hayter (1975), Thomas (1975), and Norton and Rees (1979). The product life cycle had been propounded by Vernon (1966) and elaborated by Wells (1972), and this model has remained influential in such texts as *Global Shift* (Dicken 2007) because it shows clearly that all production is not identical. It is more valuable for a firm and for its workers to produce new products, with few competitors, than mature products, for which low prices predominate.

The value of *Competitive Strategy* (Porter 1980a) to the social sciences was noted by some in the mid-1980s. For example, Malecki (1984) cited it in support of the distinction between a focus on new products and a primary concern with low-cost, standardized production. This distinction is key to understanding the difference between non-routine and routine activities (see also Malecki and Varaiya 1986). New products, not yet produced in large volumes, remain somewhat experimental, thereby demanding workers with greater skills, including scientists and engineers to tweak the product and enable mass production. Because people with skills are not to be found everywhere, the innovativeness and creativity associated with new products and services endow the places where they are common with advantages over other places.

Overall cost leadership can easily become a 'low road' strategy based on competition on the basis of low cost and high volume, which makes it impossible to innovate (Harrison 1994; Steinfeld 2004). Innovation (through 'differentiation') can result not only in growth but also in development of the capacity to learn, adapt, and be prepared for the unexpected (Lundvall and Johnson 1994; Rutten and Boekema 2007). Importantly, 'high road' strategies reinforce the virtuous circle of learning, growth of knowledge, and innovation (Cooke 1995; Malecki 2004), without which regional failure is likely (Enright 1996).

As this chapter will show, Porter's ideas have been applied among the social sciences. They have also had broad application within two cottage industries that owe much to Porter: competitiveness as a policy concern, and the regional development industry, broadly conceived. While both had antecedents, it is fair to say that Porter has been a catalyst for wider awareness.

11.2 From strategy to advantage

In 1985, in *Competitive Advantage*, Porter (1985a) shifted from a focus on industries to firms and their linkages within a *value chain*. Building on the three generic competitive strategies, Porter expanded his framework to embrace the linkages with other firms and businesses. The value chain concept, which encompasses the activities that a firm performs to design, produce, market, deliver, and support a product, was highly influential. It provided one of the first attempts to see a firm holistically – both its internal operations and its linkages with other firms. The five forces that drive industry competition were now labeled 'competitive forces that determine industry profitability' (Porter 1985a: Figure 1-1) and elements of industry structure (Porter 1985a: Figure 1-2), elaborated with lists of 'determinants' of each of the forces and entry barriers. The three generic strategies became (more or less) four, with a focus strategy split into cost focus and differentiation focus.

Although Porter was not cited in the first edition of *Global Shift* (Dicken 1986), both *Competitive Advantage* (Porter 1985*a*) and *The Competitive Advantage of Nations* (Porter 1990*a*) were cited in the second edition (Dicken 1992) and in Malecki (1991). This brought Porter's work to the attention of scholars of economic geography and regional development. Porter's work (1985*a*) was used to discuss 'generic' competitive strategies (Dicken 1992: 142–3). However, Dicken relied most on the introductory comments in *Competition in Global Industries* (Porter 1986*a*), and the conceptual framework for the edited collection (Porter 1986*b*) to explain the types of international competitive strategy which a multinational might pursue (Dicken 1992: 143–4, 194–5).

Porter (1985*a*) recognized the significance of location, but primarily as 'a separate cost driver' or a source of variation in costs. 'Location has some influence...on the cost of almost every value activity. Firms do not always understand the impact of location beyond obvious differences such as wage rates and taxes, however' (Porter 1985*a*: 83). The varied sophistication – specifically, technological sophistication – of buyers was also acknowledged to differ from country to country. This recognition that sophisticated buyers can stimulate product differentiation is only hinted at, however, awaiting a fuller analysis in *The Competitive Advantage of Nations* (Porter 1990*a*). It should be noted that *Competitive Advantage* (Porter 1985*a*) included a much more detailed view of the role of technology, which had scarcely figured in *Competitive Strategy*.

11.3 The competitive advantage of places

When *The Competitive Advantage of Nations* (Porter 1990*a*) was published in 1990, it had a larger impact than either of Porter's earlier books. Its greater impact was justified for several reasons. First, it was a book that bridged the divide between business scholars – the principal audience of both *Competitive Strategy* and *Competitive Advantage* – and the broader audiences of social scientists and policy-makers. Second, it was a much more ambitious work, totaling 855 pages, nearly as long as the two previous books combined (which were 396 and 557 pages, respectively). Third, the 1990 book was a much more scholarly endeavor. For example, it included 311 references, compared with only 60 in *Competitive Strategy* and 56 in *Competitive Advantage*.

The Competitive Advantage of Nations also marked a major shift for Porter, from a scholar focused on competing firms to a scholar of competing places. The 'threat' from Japanese firms during the 1980s had given rise to a cottage industry which tried to understand just how Western companies were failing to be competitive. It was obviously a result of more than culture. Early attempts to understand the new international competition included the collection edited by Teece (1987), which included a contribution by Porter (1987b).

The principal contribution of *The Competitive Advantage of Nations* was the 'diamond' model of the determinants of national advantage (see Figure 1.3 in chapter 1 of this volume). At first presented simply, it was elaborated into a 'complete system' incorporating the roles of government and of chance. It is clear that the 'diamond' was the intended focus of *The Competitive Advantage of Nations*. In chapter 4, Porter (1990a: 131) identifies two elements – domestic rivalry and geographic industry concentration – that 'have especially great power to transform the "diamond" into a system'. Domestic rivalry promotes upgrading of an entire national 'diamond', while geographic concentration elevates and magnifies the interactions within the 'diamond'. 'Constant improvement and upgrading' is the most important reason why competitive advantage is sustained – more important than low costs or investment (Porter 1990a: 51). Parallel to that is a model of national competitive development, with three stages of advancement: factor-driven, investment-driven, and innovation-driven (Porter 1990a: 546, Figure 10-1).

A second contribution – clusters – happened to be identifiable in many of the ten countries on which the book focused. Porter had discovered economic geography and the importance of geographic concentration. Elaborating on this in chapter 4, Porter cites a few classic works in location theory and the French concept of *filières*. This chapter, 'The Dynamics of National Advantage', alternates between determinants at the national scale and those that are an outcome of a cluster. Clusters were particularly significant in Italy, where earlier research also had identified many industrial districts (for example, Piore and Sabel 1984), and in Germany, led by the Baden-Württemberg region (Cooke and Morgan 1994).

Porter discovered that national economies are not uniformly distributed: 'Competitors in many internationally successful industries, and often entire clusters of industries, are often located in a single town or region within a nation' (Porter 1990a: 154). He also learned that there are untraded interdependencies among firms, universities, suppliers, and sophisticated customers. Moreover: 'Geographic concentration of an industry acts as a strong magnet to attract talented people and other factors to it' (Porter 1990a: 157). But Porter maintains at first a distinction between his concept of a cluster, as an interlinked set of firms and institutions, from a geographically proximate group of firms and institutions: 'The process of clustering, and the interchange among industries within the cluster, also works best when the industries involved are geographically concentrated' (Porter 1990a: 157); while he also goes on to suggest that: 'The cluster itself, particularly if it is geographically concentrated, may contain the seeds of its own demise' (Porter 1990a: 171).

A brief subsection on 'The Competitive Advantage of Cities and Regions' appears on pages 157–9, in which Porter (1990a: 158) reminds the reader: 'But nations are still important. . . . Yet it is the combination of national and intensely local conditions that fosters competitive advantage'. Porter learned about economic geography during the 1990s, at first at the national scale as he saw the wider environment of public- and private-sector actions (or the national innovation system) and, later, as an outcome of agglomeration. Porter saw technological learning as the key process in dynamic agglomeration economies, as sophisticated buyers and suppliers reinforce one another in innovation.

Among institutional support within a cluster, Porter (1990a: 134) describes special programs in local schools and universities, government-supported technical institutes and training centers, specialized apprenticeship programs, and specialized university research. In effect, Porter is acknowledging implicitly the importance of the national innovation system as well as of regional innovation systems. Porter (1998d) cites Nelson (1993) as well as Lundvall's early work on interactive learning, but seems unaware of the wealth of research it spawned (for example, Lundvall 1992a; Morgan 1997; Oinas and Malecki 2002; Cooke et al. 2004).

During the 1990s Porter further developed the concept of clusters, communicating far beyond his original market of business scholars.[1] In Porter (1996a), commenting on Markusen (1996a), he addresses several issues of spatial structure. First, he asserts that agglomeration economies operate at the scale of the cluster and need not be associated with large cities. Second, he asserts that the 'most important agglomeration economies are dynamic rather than static efficiencies and revolve around the rate of learning and the capacity for innovation' (p. 87). Cumulative causation takes place as firms based elsewhere 'gravitate to favorable cluster locations' in their field. Porter, far more here than elsewhere, shows a growing awareness of the contributions of geographers. Third, he sees a focus on high-tech industry as too restrictive, identifying highly productive, wealth creation in agriculture, shoes, and other industries perceived as low-tech. Fourth, he advises against industry targeting and 'picking winners' among new industries, and against regional policies that subsidize firms to locate or operate in uncompetitive locations.

Perhaps prompted by delving into regional economies and by this exchange with Markusen, Porter (1998b, 1998d) elaborated the concept of clusters beyond what had appeared as an appendage to the national context in Porter (1990a). Indeed, a decade earlier, regions were seen as little more than representations for variations in cost and demand for different product characteristics (Porter 1985a: 246–7). Porter's 1998 book, *On Competition*, has attracted less attention than his earlier books, perhaps mainly because of its thirteen chapters, eleven of which had been published previously in the *Harvard Business Review* between 1979 and 1996.[2] In the longest original chapter in the book, at 91 pages, he laid out his theory of clusters in detail (Porter 1998*d*). Always highly cited by business and management scholars, Porter began to address new audiences. He packaged the diamond and the cluster for economic geographers (Porter 2000*a*), for local economic development practitioners and scholars (Porter 2000*b*), and for regional development experts (Porter 2003). Along with this subnational focus, the diamond model morphed into sources of locational – not merely national – competitive advantage (Porter 1998*d*: 211, Figure 7.4; Porter 2000*a*: 258, Figure 13.1).

11.4 Clusters

Porter's initial definition (1990*a*) of clusters was that they consist 'of industries related by links of various kinds' (p. 131). It is apparent that clusters were not in the original plan for the research, but were discovered as national economies were unwrapped. It is noteworthy that clusters were defined initially in aspatial terms – as linked industries – with geographic proximity added later. As Malmberg and Power (2006: 54–5) observe, there was a 'gradual slide in the definition of the cluster concept' from *clusters as functionally related industries* to *clusters defined by geographical proximity*. This has contributed to a 'conceptual mess'. Porter had changed the definition to center on the geographical identity of clusters:

> A cluster is a geographically proximate group of interconnected companies and associated institutions in a particular field, linked by commonalities and complementarities. (Porter 1998*d*: 199)

A second cottage industry had grown out of Porter (1990*a*) and grew worldwide during the 1990s: the regional development industry based on clusters, as Porter's influence diffused to policymakers in many nations, regions, and localities worldwide (Lagendijk and Cornford 2000). Lagendijk and Cornford (2000) note that clusters were 'nowhere properly defined' and that they performed 'a largely supportive role in the articulation of the central "diamond" concept'. However, by building a strong link between clusters and the notion of 'competitiveness', and by presenting graphic cluster maps, Porter (1990*a*) had launched 'clusters' as a regional development concept. His book thus contributed to building the 'fact of clusters' (Lagendijk and Cornford 2000: 214). Several assessments have appeared, including Asheim et al. (2006*a*), Martin and Sunley (2003), and Steiner (1998*a*). The flaw of nearly all research on clusters has been to ignore the phrase 'and associated institutions'. Input–output data do not include institutions, of course, as they are not part of the web of transactions of sales and purchases that define inter-firm linkages. Instead, the role of institutions in a cluster is much like that of *untraded interdependencies* and 'knowledge spillovers' in a locality: they are critically important but nearly impossible to measure (Storper 1995, 1997).

In all places, the popular cluster concept has been widely misapplied as merely the collection of sectors that have traded interaction, indicated by input–output linkages. Not measured in input–output matrices are the links between firms and organizations and institutions (Porter 1998*b*; Austrian 2000). These links and other intangible, untraded interdependencies among firms are often more important than input–output relations (Chesnais 1986; Storper 1997; Peneder 2001). In addition, other essential elements of a *learning region* – R&D, strong but flexible institutions, a culture of trust and networking – are impossible to measure from available data in most places. Steiner (2006) extends the cognitive metaphor to ask 'Do clusters think?' He concludes that they do, but only to the degree that knowledge sharing is a central process.

Specific cases, such as the California wine cluster, mentioned only briefly in Porter (1990*a*) but elaborated and illustrated prominently in Porter (1998*b*, 1998*d*), had an impact. As Feser (1998*a*: 298) notes, 'Compelling case-study-oriented contributions in economic geography and industrial organization motivate and inform policy to a much greater degree than the formal models and tests of externalities and agglomeration economies in urban economics and regional science'. In fact, it is only by combining the linkages among local firms – which requires a degree of input–output accounting – with qualitative investigation that one can identify clusters of the sort that Porter has identified (Austrian 2000).

Obviously, identification of these non-firm actors and of untraded linkages requires talking with many local actors. This raises the possibility that the different perspectives of scholars and non-scholars will matter. For example, scholars demand airtight definitions, so that a cluster in one place is more or less the same as a cluster in another place. People who work in business and government are likely to be far less concerned with strict definitions, but they do not have an identical view. Perhaps surprisingly, the public sector consistently has a more positive outlook, perhaps because private-sector actors have an international perspective (Teigland and Lindqvist 2007: 779). We could conclude that it is policymakers – more than the business community – who are enthralled with clusters.

11.5 Are all clusters 'clusters'?

Clearly, Porter was not the first to 'discover' clusters. Steiner (1998*b*) provides a concise overview of precursors to clusters – mainly studies of industrial agglomeration – to highlight the paradox that Porter's (1990*a*) 'contribution was taken as the starting point, offering a holistic framework to show how interdependence affects innovation and growth. This led to notions and concepts such as embeddedness, social networks, untraded interdependencies, and led to a new emphasis on economies of scale in a geographical context' (Steiner 1998*b*: 3). Because Porter did not invent the term 'cluster', a minor academic industry has grown around the labels used to describe geographic agglomerations of firms. These include Asheim (1996), Cooke (2002), Enright (1996), Feser (1998*b*), Feser and Sweeney (2002), Giuliani (2005), Lagendijk (2006), Moulaert and Sekia (2003), O'Gorman and Kautonen (2004), and Rosenfeld (1997).

A second geographic interpretation of 'clusters' emerged almost simultaneously from the work of Krugman (1991) and others who were attempting to develop new models to explain geographic concentration.[3] In this work, of which Ellison and Glaeser (1997) is among the most cited, they emphasize the input–output linkages between an industry and its important upstream suppliers as well as its important downstream customers. This focus on 'coagglomeration of related industries' ignores non-firm actors, reinforcing the preference of economists to concentrate on economic actors (firms) and to ignore institutions. The tendency is to use a top-down approach, defining inter-firm relationships with national-level, rather than local-level, data – specifically input–output data.

Feser and Bergman (2000: 12) justify this practice: 'Although the conduits of interdependence between firms extend well beyond supplier linkages, input–output flows provide the single best uniform means of identifying which firms and industries are most likely to interact through a myriad of interrelated formal and informal channels'. This is an heroic assumption, because in an industry of highly differentiated firms, it is not at all clear that input–output connections, or the upstream and downstream linkages among sectors, will characterize the firms in any one location. Hendry et al. (2000), for example, find that clusters of firms in the optoelectronics industry, which have global customers and global suppliers, have few if any local interactions.

Researchers of industrial districts have been most reluctant to adopt Porter's cluster concept. This is in large part a result of the fact that industrial districts had been identified by Italian scholars long before Porter 'rediscovered' them. Porter (1998*d*: 269, note 5) attempts to pull them – 'Industrial districts are a special case of clusters' – as well as technopoles and science cities (ibid., note 6), under the cluster umbrella. In the case of industrial districts, at least, Italian scholars have insisted on using the original term, despite Porter's inclusion of a lengthy list of Italian 'clusters'. Belussi (2006: 77) provides a fine comparison of the two concepts, and defines industrial districts as '"socio-economic systems" joining together a community of people with common values or culture'. Maskell (2001: 922–3, note 3) notes that the term 'industrial district' is typically used 'when wishing explicitly to emphasize the values and norms shared by co-localized firms' (see also Harrison 1992). However, even Belussi (2006) acknowledges a blending or overlap of the terms, including work by Italian authors.

The division between the two concepts is seen in the attempt by Paniccia (2006) to create a typology of industrial districts (see also Markusen 1996b and Park 1996). Porter, on the other hand, eschews the scholarly delineation of differences and offers clusters as an all-embracing concept. In fact, a typology helps policymakers to know that not all clusters are alike, and that local conditions must be taken into account. Clusters differ, critically, in their knowledge bases (Asheim and Coenen 2005; Gertler and Wolfe 2006). Knowledge does not figure in Porter's diamond or his clusters. In effect, the flood of research on knowledge (such as Nonaka and Takeuchi 1995; Cooke 2002; Bathelt et al. 2004; Malecki and Hospers 2007), the absorptive capacity of firms (Cohen and Levinthal 1990; Rush et al. 2007), and regions (Foss 1996d; Mahroum et al. 2008) has grown beyond clusters. Giuliani's taxonomy (2005) of cluster absorptive capacity (Table 11.1) remains a more useful framework for scholars, if not for policymakers. Absorptive capacity remains a key process for understanding the economic capability of regions (Mahroum et al. 2008).

Innovative milieus are a second ideal type, in which 'soft' processes – learning and interaction – are central, while also difficult to measure and difficult for policy to create (Maillat 1995). Innovation, learning, and know-how are the most important competitive advantages. Networks, competition, and rules of cooperation, as well as relational capital, facilitate these. Yet they occur differently within each territory, because economic development processes take place in a specific space and time context (Crevoisier 2004). McCann (2001: 62) identifies the key point of Porter's cluster model: that proximity enables firms to observe the competitive developments of one another, and this visibility itself acts as a spur to all firms to continue to improve their individual competitiveness. The result of this process of intense localized competition is to increase the competitiveness of the cluster as a whole as well as the firms within it. Proximity or co-location is relatively easy to measure but is a shallow definition of a cluster. Even input–output links are far less meaningful than explicit collaboration and informal knowledge spillovers. The problem, once again, is that the latter are harder to measure and must be done from the bottom-up, locally within each cluster.

In particular, the process of *collective learning* is central. As noted above, Porter nods in this direction but leaves the process among the black-box processes that take place within clusters. Within regional development research, by contrast, collective learning is recognized as a 'high road' process, found only in the highest-performing regional economies (Capello 1999; Keeble and Wilkinson 1999; Lawson and Lorenz 1999). The concept of the 'learning region' is an attempt to capture the various dynamics of learning

Table 11.1. A taxonomy of the absorptive capacity of clusters

Cluster absorptive capacity	Knowledge base of the firms	Intra-cluster knowledge system	Extra-cluster knowledge system
Basic	Firms have weak knowledge bases, low-skilled human resources, and limited in-house knowledge generation. Firms' knowledge bases are far from best practice	The cluster is characterized by very limited and weak knowledge linkages between firms	The cluster has no links with sources of knowledge outside the cluster, and no firm plays the role of technological gatekeeper
Intermediate	Firms are varied in their knowledge bases. Some firms have in-house R&D, but most effort is toward adaptation rather than the creation of knowledge	The cluster has a somewhat connected intra-cluster knowledge system, but some firms are cognitively isolated	The cluster has some connection with extra-cluster knowledge sources. A few firms play the role of technological gatekeeper
Advanced	Firms have very strong knowledge bases and operate at the technological frontier. Human resources are highly skilled, and firms perform innovative R&D	The cluster has a dense intra-cluster knowledge system	The cluster is well connected with extra-cluster sources of knowledge, and many firms are technological gatekeepers

Source: Adapted from Giuliani (2005: 281, Table 2).

within regions (Morgan 1997; Rutten and Boekema 2007). However, Lagendijk and Cornford (2000: 217) see the learning region as 'more of a "black box" . . . than has been the case with clusters'.

At the same time that Porter (1990*a*) appeared, the European Commission assessed regional competitiveness, identifying several factors as most important to regional economies: proximity to markets, the communication system, financial institutions, and product life-cycle stage (Nam et al. 1990). Although Porter included an array of institutions as major actors in a cluster, he stopped short of elaborating the processes by which clusters maintain and renew their innovativeness. This is accomplished much more fully – but without Porter's easily grasped diagrams – by the group of researchers who study innovative milieux (the GREMI – *Groupe de Recherche Européen sur les Milieux Innovateurs* – such as Aydalot and Keeble 1988; Camagni 1991; Bramanti and Ratti 1997). As Giuliani (2005: 271) notes, in contrast to the GREMI research, 'social and cultural aspects were less emphasized in Porter's definition of cluster'.

Regional competitiveness includes not only productive capital but also a number of other 'softer' dimensions of a regional socioeconomy, including human capital, socioinstitutional capital, knowledge/creative capital, infrastructural capital, and cultural capital (Kitson et al. 2004). The sum of these various attributes gives rise to region-specific knowledge and competence, and to institutions, which will be distinct from those in other regions. Because they have grown out of the regional setting and are part of both its stability and its dynamics, learning can occur (Maskell et al. 1998; Boschma 2004). This is the essence of Porter's belief that productivity and innovation – not low wages, low taxes, nor a devalued currency – are the definition of competitiveness (Porter 2000b: 30). This is a high-road, rather than a low-road, approach to local development, and one of the benefits of both Porter's diamond and cluster models is that they stress high-road policies.

Simmie (2006) prefers to use the concept of innovation systems (which can be called local or regional; see Cooke et al. 2004). He criticizes Porter for suggesting that clusters cause innovation. Instead, 'competitive clusters are an effect of the interactions of a functioning innovation system and not a cause' (Simmie 2006: 183). Proximity is no guarantee of interaction either among firms or between firms and local universities (D'Este and Patel 2007). Few of these assertions have been tested empirically, but Gordon and McCann (2005) examine in detail firms in London, and conclude that 'innovating businesses appear to derive benefits from a London location in a diffuse and flexible manner implied by models of pure agglomeration applied at the wider regional level, rather than through the more specific and stable links highlighted in the social network model' (p. 541). In general, an interdisciplinary, multifaceted, and multilevel approach is needed to unravel the intricacies of regional development (Lagendijk 2006).

Porter has continued to use the diamond and the cluster as the core of his research for the past two decades. Empirically, he has gone beyond the case studies in Porter (1990a) and, as Ketels outlines in the preceding chapter, he has assembled several datasets to bolster, if not exactly test, his theories. The idea of clusters grew into a large effort within the United States (Porter and van Opstal 2001; Porter 2003). Further, he has revised the diamond model in the context of international competitiveness for the annual *Global Competitiveness Report*. Arguably, clusters – simpler to grasp and more malleable for local variation – are the greatest legacy of *The Competitive Advantage of Nations*.

11.6 Clusters as policy

Steiner (1998b) identifies three elements in common among the various definitions of clusters – Porter's as well as others: specialization, proximity, and cooperation among actors, which lead to spillovers and synergies. 'Hence the demand for policy intervention: clusters a good thing, policy should therefore create, develop, and support such clusters' (Steiner 1998b: 4). For policymakers the cluster concept has presented an innovative approach, allied with the appeal of 'competitiveness' and with the advantage of low implementation costs. The cluster concept has also appealed to regional scientists and planners because 'it rekindled thinking about linkages between economically related activities in spatial agglomerations' and, in addition, 'could be absorbed within regional development agendas characterised by an increased emphasis on "soft" development factors, notably collaboration and partnerships between business and development agencies'. Clusters had further appeal when 'invoking the success stories of Silicon Valley, Emilia Romagna, Baden-Württemberg, and others' (Lagendijk and Cornford 2000: 214).

Among the largest efforts to track cluster initiatives are the cluster surveys by a trio of Swedish researchers.[4] In 2003 they identified 509 cluster initiatives, mainly in Europe. Responses were obtained from clusters in thirty-one countries (Sölvell et al. 2003). A 2006 survey identified over 1,400 cluster initiatives among developing and transition economies (Ketels et al. 2006). This 'industry', based largely in Sweden, is closely connected with Porter. Moreover, it displays an awareness and provides a link to the academic literature, including Malmberg et al. (1996), and the various antecedents and variations on agglomeration and clustering. It remains the case, however, as Ketels (chapter 10 in this volume), Enright (1996), and Pike et al. (2006: 112) note, that 'critical evaluation of the actual impacts of cluster policy on local and regional development has been limited'.

Knowledge sharing and learning do not take place in every cluster. Not all clusters of plants in a given industry are the same. McCann and Arita (2006) point out that some clusters, which they call 'industrial complex' clusters, are intended to keep knowledge from flowing out, and therefore are very different from 'new industrial clusters' where knowledge flows (both in and out) are considered positive. Cullen (1998) defines five types of cluster in which organizational learning can take place, two of which are 'Porterian'.

As Asheim (1996: 384) notes: 'Porter's book *The Competitive Advantage of Nations* reflects a change in the understanding of the strategic factors which promote innovation and economic growth. Porter's main argument for the importance of clusters is that they represent the material basis for an innovation-based economy'. In none of his work does Porter grapple explicitly with learning as a collective inter-firm process. Indeed, whether or not encased in a 'cluster initiative', the existence of learning is critical – and it is impossible to document with secondary data. This is a normal practice in research on regional innovation systems, and Tödtling and Trippl (2004) provide an excellent example in Austria, detailing local and non-local sources of knowledge. By focusing on *local* links, Porter generally fails to acknowledge the importance of non-local connections (for example, Oinas and Malecki 2002; Simmie 2004; Malmberg and Power 2006).

Some believe that Porter was 'vague' about the spatial scale and the geographic distance over which clustering processes, such as inter-firm linkages, knowledge spillovers, business and social networks, and rivalry, operate (Martin and Sunley 2003). In fact, Porter (1998*d*: 256) was not vague, but rather all-inclusive. He suggests that clusters apply to cities and towns, metropolitan areas, states or provinces, nations, and groups of neighboring countries. It is little wonder, then, that cluster research has been equally broad in scope. Clusters have been defined at the national scale (Feser and Bergman 2000) and at the scale of the metropolitan region (Feser and Sweeney 2002; Funderberg and Boarnet 2008). In fact, van der Linde (2002) identifies seven distinct scales or boundaries of clusters in his meta-study of 833 clusters. Porter generalizes on the dynamics of clusters: 'The boundaries of clusters continually evolve as new firms and industries emerge, established industries shrink and decline, and local institutions develop and change' (Porter 1990*a*: 204). This is a less problematic statement when clusters are defined only as linked industries rather than as geographical units.

Why has Porter's cluster been so influential? The cluster concept turns out to be 'a nice little backyard capitalism, which is small enough to stay under control, but big enough to ensure regional dynamics' (Steiner 2002: 209). Feser and Luger (2003: 12) suggest that:

> Perhaps one reason the story of clustering in Porter's *Competitive Advantage of Nations* resonates so strongly with policy-makers even as it echoes much of the literature that preceded it is that it is couched in the more accessible verbal language of business strategy rather than in the mathematically refined vernacular of urban and regional economics.

In short, Porter's 'brand' of clusters is a result of its accessibility of language, its flexibility of interpretation, and the authority he is able to exert as a Harvard-based expert on business strategy and, by extension, to virtually any other economic domain. 'Cluster' is a term to be preferred, for example, over regional production systems or innovative milieux. However, Porter's 'brand' of clusters continues to draw criticism for its elastic and flexible definition, which is difficult to implement and replicate from place to place. At worst, such flexibility dooms clusters to the status of a 'chaotic concept' (Martin and Sunley 2003). But policy-makers are rarely interested in 'scientific' definitions. They are interested in success – what works elsewhere or what might work here. Porter (2005) makes this easy; he includes as an appendix 'a how-to guide' for assessing regional economic competitiveness and innovative capacity.

As a mode of inquiry, rather than as a technical methodology, cluster analysis and its flexibility can be appropriate (Feser and Luger 2003). The cluster remains a popular vehicle for policy (for example, den Hertog and

Remøe 2001; DATAR and Ministère de l'Economie, des Finances et de l'Industrie 2005; Rosenfeld 2007). However: 'The danger of a cluster-based approach to policy is that it detracts from the need to take a more holistic view of regional development' (Martin and Sunley 2003: 28). Benneworth and Henry (2004) believe that Martin and Sunley are too harsh in their criticism of Porter's 'brand' of clusters. The concept should instead be taken to embrace a number of theoretical threads written for a number of audiences, with there being a 'multiplicity of cluster debates', not all of which involve Porter (Benneworth and Henry 2004: 1017). Research which combines several perspectives, such as Keeble and Nachum (2002), can provide a deeper and more holistic understanding of what is driving a cluster.

Feldman and Francis (2004, 2006) and Feldman et al. (2005) suggest that entrepreneurship is most frequently the missing piece in accounts of clusters. How can entrepreneurship begin in a locality or cluster? This requires, first, information (to reduce uncertainty and ambiguity), and second, networks, which are the means for sharing information. However, only when the local firms are innovative is there the possibility for what Julien (2007) calls 'a dynamic regional fabric'.

Lawson (1999) puts it simply: some regional systems of interaction are better than others. Porter and Sölvell (1998) acknowledge that clusters have an affinity with innovative milieus in the fluidity of knowledge exchange. In the end, however, 'the social dimensions of cluster formation and cluster dynamics remain something of a black box in Porter's work' (Martin and Sunley 2003: 16). This is the essence of Motoyama's critique (2008: 353), by which 'the current theory is more focused on describing how a cluster is organized today rather than how a cluster emerged'. Research has tended to affirm Porter's generalizations. High rates of entry by new firms, or local levels of entrepreneurship, dense networks of personal contacts with other firms, and a fluid local labor market with movement of people from firm to firm, all promote a 'learning region' (May et al. 2001; Malmberg and Power 2006).

Clusters should not be inward-looking. Cappellin (1998) suggests that regional and municipal governments should develop a 'foreign policy'. Malecki (2007) suggests that policy-makers undertake regular benchmarking efforts in order to be aware of situations elsewhere. Technology foresight programs and technology-scanning activities embody the ongoing absorptive capacity of a region (Foss 1996d; Koschatzky 2005; Roveda and Vecchiato 2008). The cluster analysis approach as a mode of inquiry – as opposed to a methodology – 'begins with a good faith and well-documented effort to describe trends and patterns of business location, industrial interdependence (regional and interregional), and the supporting local infrastructure of institutions and programmes. It includes an explicit accounting of the labour, infrastructure, and knowledge input needs of a region's industrial base, and it

considers the ability of the region to respond to those needs (its "capacity")'
(Feser and Luger 2003: 23).

11.7 Back to national competitiveness

Porter's diamond model of clusters joined the policy debate as globalization had
begun to be felt at several scales. The success of Japanese firms and those in the
Four Tigers (Hong Kong, Korea, Singapore, and Taiwan) needed understanding.
How had these places succeeded in besting US and European firms? Porter did
not invent the concept of international competitiveness. The *Global Competitiveness Report* (*GCR*) of the World Economic Forum first appeared in 1979. Porter
has been involved in the *GCR* since 1998, and he has contributed a substantive
chapter to the report annually, initially called the Microeconomic Competitiveness Index and, since 2003, relabeled the Business Competitiveness Index.
These indices were created parallel to those of the Global Competitiveness
Index (GCI). Beginning in 2009, the new GCI combines macroeconomic competitiveness indicators, including social infrastructure and political institutions,
with microeconomic competitiveness (Porter et al. 2008).

Although the 'diamond' model receives additional visibility in the *GCR*
(Figure 11.1), Porter admits: 'The main reason why I am involved with the
Global Competitiveness Report is not so much that I am interested in the actual
rankings of countries; rather, I am interested in the data' (Snowdon and Stonehouse 2006: 170). With such data, Porter has been able to study the determinants of national innovative capacity (Porter and Stern 2001; Furman et al.
2002), and these studies have figured in editions of the *GCR*. The diamond
model remains a centerpiece, but data and analysis have begun to take prece-
dence. The new GCI is the product of a large-scale analytical exercise, combining principal components and regression analyses (Porter et al. 2008).

11.8 Conclusion

Porter, like Krugman, is accused of reinventing the wheel (Martin and Sunley
1996, 2003). Various theories of agglomeration of firms are well known to
have benefits for regional economic performance, such as employment, wage
levels, and productivity gains. Yet Porter (2003: 571) is able to assert, unaware
of its lack of novelty to readers of *Regional Studies*, that 'Our findings suggest
that regional analysis must become far more central to research and policy
formulation in competitiveness and economic development. Our results
reveal the need for much of economic policy to be decentralized to the
regional level'. 'Constructing advantage' is possible, as Cooke (2007) has

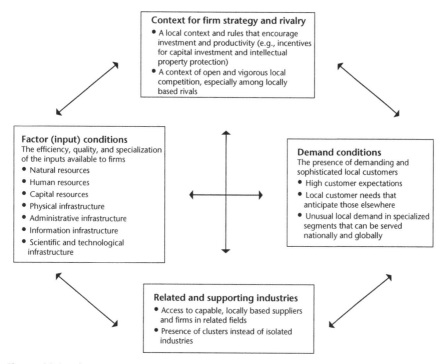

Figure 11.1. The microeconomic business environment

Source: Based on Porter et al. (2008: 55, Figure 4)

shown. However, the distinction drawn by Fromhold-Eisebith and Eisebith (2005) between planned, purposeful explicit top-down and unplanned, implicit bottom-up cluster promotion is important. A great deal of what passes for 'policy' is unintentional and 'just happens' as time passes. However, the created clusters that seem to have the greatest longevity and local control are those that have sprung 'bottom-up'. Creating clusters is not easy, however, if only because the dynamic, ongoing processes that are central to the innovative milieux are missing.

As territorial innovation models, both Porter's concept of clusters and the innovation systems approach are subject to the issue of scale. Innovation is the central element in economic development, and clusters are but one part of the development process (Malecki 1997). The local, regional, national, and global scales must be understood, as well as their interconnections, and these have been more deeply assessed for innovation systems (Bunnell and Coe 2001; Oinas and Malecki 2002). Porter's conception of geography is minimal – a criticism that could be made of most business scholars. Nations are seen as spatial units, but all subnational scales are treated as more or less identical, without an awareness of spatial subtleties such as flows and, even more, untraded interdependencies.

Competitiveness attained by creating local synergies among local actors, and integrating external connections into the local relational web, exploits spillovers and increasing returns that are at the foundation of economic development in its positive-sum, *generative* sense (Camagni 2002a: 89). This is what policy-makers, regional development scholars, and Porter himself want to generate. Cluster policies gave rise to the illusion that the process is quick, rather than one that typically takes a long period of time.

Notes

1. Enright is acknowledged by Porter (1990a: xvi) as the overall project coordinator of *The Competitive Advantage of Nations*. Enright (1996) makes clearer the distinction between industrial clusters and regional clusters, and Enright (1998) synthesizes the literature on firm strategy and resources with that on regional clusters, little of which was evident in Porter (1990a).
2. An updated and expanded edition of *On Competition* was published in October 2008. The three key chapters in the section 'The Competitiveness of Locations' remain in the new edition: 'The Competitive Advantage of Nations'; 'Clusters and Competition: New Agendas for Companies, Governments, and Institutions'; and 'Competing Across Locations: Enhancing Competitive Advantage through a Global Strategy'.
3. Porter cites Krugman (1991) in support of dynamic agglomeration economies. However, there is nothing dynamic in Krugman's model of 'industry localization'. Agglomeration happens by chance and without knowledge spillovers.
4. The Center for Strategy and Competitiveness at the Stockholm School of Economics has been a proponent of clusters.

12

Regional competitiveness: clusters or dynamic comparative advantage?

Ron Martin and Peter Sunley

12.1 The rise and spread of competitiveness talk

Even a casual observer cannot fail to notice how social science is swept along by a succession of new buzzwords and new jargon. Business economics and management studies in particular have a reputation for being prone to fads and fashions in terminology and concepts. Most often these fads are short-lived and (thankfully) have little impact outside business and management studies themselves. But from time to time certain buzzwords and concepts developed in those disciplines find their way into other academic fields, and even into public policy circles. The notion of 'competitiveness' is a prime example. Although economics has long been concerned with competition as a key driving force of capitalist growth and development, the concept of 'competitiveness' has not traditionally been part of the standard economics lexicon.[1] It was only in the mid- to late 1980s that the term 'competitiveness' suddenly burst onto the scene, primarily through the writings not of mainstream economists but those of certain business school gurus.

While initially developed to explain the economic performance of individual firms, the concept of competitiveness soon became invoked to account for national differences in economic success. As such the notion readily appealed to policy-makers, and it quickly became a prominent topic of public policy discourse. Policy experts and consultants the world over have elevated 'competitiveness' to the status of a 'natural law' of the modern capitalist economy, and assessing a nation's competitiveness and devising policies to enhance it have become officially institutionalized tasks across numerous countries.[2] The rhetoric of national competitiveness is now universal.

An intriguing feature of this rise of 'competitiveness talk' is that it has not been confined to national economic policy, but has spread to policy debates and interventions at the regional, urban, and local levels. One manifestation of this has been that central governments have expressed increasing interest in the 'regional foundations' of national competitiveness, and with developing new forms of regionally-based policy initiatives to help improve the 'competitiveness' of regions and cities and thence the performance of the national economy as a whole (see OECD 2007). This has been a prominent theme in the United Kingdom, for example, where the competitiveness of the country's regions and cities was a central plank in New Labour's national growth and productivity agenda (HM Treasury 2001, 2003, 2004; ODPM 2003, 2004; DTI 2005).[3]

In France, officially designated local 'pôles de compétitivité' are a key component of the national industrial policy introduced there in 2004 (www. compétitivité.gouv.fr). And in EU policy discourse, regional 'competitiveness' has assumed particular prominence. The European Commission sees the improvement of 'regional competitiveness' as one of three key spatial policy objectives – along with regional cohesion and regional cooperation – needed to secure the Lisbon Agenda goal of making the European Union the 'world's most productive and innovative economy', to help underpin the stability of the European single currency, and to reduce regional economic disparities across the Union (European Commission 2003a, 2004).

At the same time, individual city and regional authorities in many countries have themselves taken up the issue of 'competitiveness' as part of their own economic development agendas: 'competitiveness' has come to be regarded as critical for understanding and promoting local economic performance. Like their national counterparts, regional and city policy-makers have become preoccupied with knowing the relative 'competitive standing' of their local economies compared with others, not just other regions and cities within their own national jurisdiction, but with areas elsewhere across the globe. Devising local strategies to improve the 'competitiveness' of their locality is now regarded as a primary task by many regional and city policy-makers.

Three sets of influences might be identified as explaining why the idea of 'regional competitiveness' has recently assumed such importance in policy circles. The first has to do with the general discourse around globalization. The argument, propounded by governments, policy-makers, and academics of all political and ideological persuasions, is that globalization brings with it not only expanding trade but also increasingly intense 'competition' between firms, between nations, and between regions and cities over shares of new and existing markets. The image – and the rhetoric – is one of mounting competition from new players in the global economy – the 'threat' from the BRIC group (Brazil, Russia, India, and China) being frequently invoked in this context.[4] These economies are typically portrayed as seriously challenging the economies of the old advanced nations, not only in traditional export markets but also as prospective competitors in an increasing array of high-value and high-technology activities. No nation, no region, no city, it is argued, is immune from the implications of the 'new global competition'.

A second factor has been the growth of regions and cities themselves as arenas of economic policy intervention and economic governance. The policy emphasis on the supply-side over the past two decades or so has led states to argue that many economic supply-side frictions, inflexibilities, and barriers to national growth originate at the local level and are therefore best addressed at that scale. So, states have been busy decentralizing, even devolving, various policies relating to the labor market, small firms, entrepreneurship, innova-tion, and even venture capital, down to regional authorities and agencies, though often within nationally set guidelines and targets. Within this new governance environment, and charged to become more competitive, regional and city authorities also have cast their own local development strategies around this objective. There has been a demand, therefore, for expert knowl-edge on how to measure and promote local competitiveness. One inevitable trend this has spawned is the compilation of regional competitiveness indexes, league tables, and the desire for benchmarking.

Third, if the rise of regional competitiveness talk in policy circles has been bound up with the discourse around globalization, it has been equally influ-enced by the writings of key academics. Despite the fact that there has been, and continues to be, academic debate about what, precisely, is meant by the notion of 'regional competitiveness' (see Kitson et al. 2004; Bristow 2005), within policy circles, if there is a dominant view on this concept it is Porter's cluster model, and the particular interpretation and explanation of local and regional competitiveness he uses that model to promote. Over the past two decades, Porter more than anyone else has championed a whole new policy and consultancy industry concerned with measuring and promoting 'compet-itive advantage'. Government after government has bought in to a competi-tiveness agenda by virtue of securing his advice and analysis. Although his early work was concerned with the competitiveness of firms and industries, he soon argued that his basic national model – the so-called 'competitiveness diamond' – was equally applicable to regions, cities, and even localities. Just as Porter has argued that 'every country must try to understand and master competition' (Porter 1998c: 1), so he has promulgated the idea that every region must likewise try to understand and master competition.

What Porter (2001b) argues is that a 'new economics of competition' is emerging that is associated with six transitions: from macroeconomic policies to microeconomic policies that recognize that the 'drivers' of prosperity are based at the subnational level; from a concern with current productivity to emphasizing innovation, as the basis of sustained productivity growth; from the economy as a whole as the unit of analysis to a focus on 'clusters' (groups of interlinked specialized activities, typically geographically localized); from internal to external sources of company success, recognizing that the location of a company can affect the capabilities it can draw upon; from separate to integrated economic and social policy; and from national to regional and local levels as the locus of analysis and policy intervention. Indeed, according to Porter, regions, cities, and clusters assume a pivotal role in understanding this 'new competition':

> The more that one thinks in terms of microeconomics, innovation, clusters and integrating economic and social policy, the more the city-region emerges as an important unit. Issues or policies that span nations or are common to many nations will be increasingly neutralized, and no longer sources of competitive advantage. However, it is not a matter of one unit of geography supplanting another.... The task is to integrate the city-region with other economic units, and to adopt a more textured view of the sources of prosperity and economic policy that encompasses multiple levels of geography. (Porter 2001*b*: 141)

Porter's notion of the cluster is central to his view about the nature and drivers of competitiveness. In fact, the two concepts are inextricably interlinked in his work and policy advice: it is the geographical clustering of related firms that creates various localized external increasing-returns effects that in turn improve the competitiveness of the firms concerned compared to their non-clustered counterparts. Clustering is thus claimed to be a key source of competitive advantage both for the firms involved and for the region where the cluster is located: clusters and their promotion are key to regional competitiveness.

Our aim in this chapter is to examine the conceptual and empirical foundations for this argument. To begin, we outline the key elements in Porter's theory of 'clusters as drivers of competitiveness'. We then move on to the question of whether the empirical evidence supports the model: are firms inside clusters more competitive than their counterparts outside clusters? This discussion then moves us on to consider how the cluster model differs from modern reinterpretations of comparative advantage. We argue that the cluster approach can be subsumed within a more general dynamic comparative advantage perspective on regional competitiveness. Some implications for cluster-based regional policies rounds off the chapter.

12.2 Porter's cluster model of competitiveness

There is little doubt about the formative influence Michael Porter has exerted over our thinking about the notions of competition, competitiveness, and competitive advantage. These notions are not unproblematic, as we shall discuss later, but more than any other writer, Porter has sought to construct an integrated framework for linking the competitive advantage of firms, industries, nations, regions, and localities. A key element in his framework has been to emphasize the role that location – whether at the large geographical scale of the nation or the smaller geographical scale of the region or locality – plays in competition and competitive advantage. In contrast to most treatments of competitiveness, which concentrate either on macroeconomic policies or on comparative advantages, Porter takes a different approach, arguing that the 'competitiveness of locations' is primarily rooted in the nature of the business environment they offer firms. 'Access to labor, capital and natural resources', he argues, 'does not determine prosperity, because these have become widely accessible' (Porter 1998c: 7). Rather, 'competitiveness arises from the productivity with which firms in a location can use inputs to produce valuable goods and services' (Porter 1998c: 7).

Porter seeks to capture the effect of location on the productivity of firms in terms of his well-known 'diamond model', made up of four primary facets: factor conditions (the nation's position in factors of production necessary to compete in a given industry); demand conditions (the nature of home demand for the industry's product or service); related and supporting industries (the presence or absence in the nation of supplier industries and related industries that are internationally competitive); and firm strategy, structure, and rivalry (the conditions in the nation governing how companies are created, organized, and managed, and the nature of domestic rivalry). And he goes on to stress how the cluster – 'one of the most important ideas in my [sic] overall competitiveness theory' (Porter 1998c: 7) – intensifies the interactions between these four sources of firm competitive advantage. Thus, the diamond as a diagnostic tool of business context is transformed into a prescriptive and normative model of agglomeration. Clusters – as geographical concentrations of interconnected companies, associated industries, and specialized institutions (Porter 1998d; see also Porter 1998a) – are regarded as a spatial manifestation of the diamond's interactions, and the advantages and external economies to be gained by clustering are held to affect competition in three broad ways:

> . . . first by increasing the productivity of constituent firms or industries; second by increasing their capacity for innovation and thus for productivity growth; and third, by stimulating new business formation that supports innovation and expands the cluster. Many cluster advantages rest on external economies or spillovers across firms and industries of various sorts. . . . A cluster may thus be defined as a system of interconnected firms and institutions whose value as a whole is greater than the sum of its parts. (Porter 1998d: 213)

Clusters promote the competitive advantage of the firms concerned, then, by raising their productivity and promoting productivity growth (Figure 12.1). This focus on productivity is at the heart of Porter's theory, for in his view, when we talk about competitiveness or competitive advantage (he uses the two terms interchangeably), what we are really talking about is productivity:

> To understand competitiveness, the starting point must be the sources of a nation's prosperity. A nation's standard of living is determined by the productivity of its economy, which is measured by the value of its goods and services produced per unit of the nation's human, capital and natural resources. Productivity depends both on the value of a nation's products and services, measured by the prices they can command in open markets, and the efficiency with which they can be produced. *True competitiveness, then, is measured by productivity.* Productivity allows a nation to support high wages, a strong currency and attractive returns to capital,

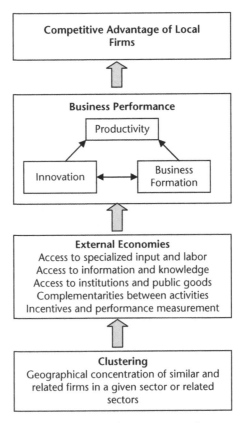

Figure 12.1. Porter's model of clusters and competitive advantage

and with them a high standard of living. (Porter and Ketels 2003: 7, italics added for emphasis)

Competitiveness, then, is productivity, and the productivity of an economy – local, regional, or national – will be determined by the productivity of all of the firms making up that economy. By enhancing the business environment for firms, clustering confers advantages that allegedly raise the productivity (or competitiveness) of the firms located in the cluster. Cluster firms should, according to the theory, be more productive – more competitive – than they would be if they were not co-located in clusters. By implication, therefore, the presence of clusters in a region will raise the overall productivity and hence the competitiveness of that region or locality in the global economy (Porter 2000b). Moreover, Porter also argues that a region with overlapping strong clusters – that is, clusters of related or interlinked industries or services – will perform better than a region with strong but non-overlapping clusters.

Given that regions are not self-sufficient economically, of particular importance for a region is the presence or otherwise of strong export-orientated clusters, and it is these that are accorded special attention in Porter's writings. Export-orientated clusters are those comprising industries that compete outside the region, whether with similar industries in other domestic regions or with industries and regions in other countries. In this respect they are key sources of regional wealth and employment, and generate the income with which to pay for the goods and services that have to be imported from elsewhere. Such clusters figure prominently in Porter's discussion of the concept and the empirical examples which he uses to illustrate it.

This model raises several issues. There are numerous questions, for example, that attach to the very notion of the cluster itself – such as how clusters are defined and conceptualized, and whether clusters do in fact enhance the interactions and spillovers between firms. These are not the direct focus of our attention here, however (for a detailed critical discussion of these issues, see Martin and Sunley 2003). Rather, our concern is with two other matters. First, the model implies that firms in a cluster should, other things being equal, be more competitive – that is, have higher productivity and be more innovative – than similar firms that are not located in a cluster. Is it the case, however, that within a particular sector of activity, firms inside clusters outperform their non-clustered counterparts? Is clustering necessary for a firm to be competitive in its field in global markets? Second, is the cluster model the only way of thinking about regional competitiveness? Porter explicitly contrasts his approach with more traditional interpretations, such as comparative advantage, arguing that the latter is both static in orientation and no longer of relevance in today's globalized world. But is his idea of competitive advantage through clustering really that different from modern versions of comparative advantage? Both of these issues are not only important in their own right, from an academic point of view; they are obviously also of considerable potential policy relevance.

12.3 Does clustering raise the competitive performance of firms?

The underlying assumption of Porter's cluster model is that clustering enhances innovation, innovation enhances productivity, and higher productivity improves firm performance. Few attempts have been made to put these assumptions to the test by comparing the economic performance of firms located inside clusters with those located outside clusters. Throughout Porter's discussions of clusters, the competitive advantages they are alleged to confer on firms are rarely demonstrated or verified empirically. It is as though the logic of the argument is so self-evident that its empirical interrogation is not required. Nor is this reticence to put the theory to the test confined to Porter's work; the same presumption about the alleged benefits to firms of clustering permeates the study of clusters in other disciplines, including economic geography, where the cluster concept has met with considerable enthusiasm. Thus, as Malmberg and Maskell put it:

> Whereas economic geographers and others have devoted considerable efforts in documenting the existence of spatial clustering not many attempts have been made in terms of showing differences in firm performance between those located inside and outside localized clusters. (Malmberg and Maskell 2002: 435)

Cluster studies have tended to focus on case studies of innovative regional clusters, typically, highly successful ones. While such studies sometimes compare the performance of one such cluster with another, such as Silicon Valley and Route 128 (Saxenian 1994), they rarely compare firms in these clusters with similar unclustered firms, nor whether significant variations in competitive performance exist across firms within the same cluster. Further, the relevance of anecdotal evidence from these specific, typically self-contained, and rather distinctive clusters for a general discussion on the importance of local and regional conditions for the competitiveness of firms can be questioned (Lundquist and Olander 1999).

Several years ago, in our assessment of the cluster notion, we observed that the evidence for the beneficial effects of clustering on firm performance was patchy, mixed, and inconsistent (Martin and Sunley 2003). Despite the increasing diffusion of cluster ideas and the proliferation of cluster strategies, the growing research into clusters and firm performance has confirmed rather than undermined this observation. Research has produced a variable and mixed set of findings about whether innovation, productivity, and growth tend to be higher within, as against outside, clusters. While a number of cases of particular clusters have tended to be broadly supportive of the effects envisaged by Porter (see, for example, Visser 1999), more extensive comparative work has found little strong support for the claim that clustering demonstrably raises firm performance.

McDonald et al. (2007), for example, examine whether the depth of UK clusters, as measured by the extent of their local supply chains, is correlated with employment growth and international significance in terms of their share of national exports. They find that established local supply chains are linked to employment growth, especially in manufacturing, but are not significant for international export success. Instead, they find stronger evidence that cluster performance is more strongly related to industrial sector, which is at odds with Porter's claim that the performance of clusters is not determined by the sectors in which their firms specialize.

A similar skeptical conclusion emerges from Eriksson and Lindgren's (2009) thorough analysis of the relationships between labor productivity and workplace location in Sweden. After controlling for various firm characteristics, they report that localized concentrations of similar and related firms do not explain any substantial part of variations in firm competitiveness. Local labor market mobility does have a positive effect on productivity, but this effect is marginal compared to the importance of firm-level internal economies of scale. In their words, 'spatial proximity and co-location alone do not tell us much about the competitiveness of firms' (Eriksson and Lindgren 2009: 48). Similarly, Hendry and Brown (2006) report that clustering is not a significant determinant of firm performance (as measured by sales and employment) in the UK optoelectronics sector; market positioning and firm life cycle are far more important. There are probably several reasons underlying this lack of correlation between clusters, on the one hand, and firm performance and competitiveness, on the other.

One reason is that clusters can suffer from adverse location selection as leading firms try to avoid unwanted knowledge spillovers and other outward leakages. Shaver and Flyer's (2000) study of foreign 'greenfield' investment in the United States, for instance, finds that firms possessing superior technologies, human capital, and suppliers have an incentive to locate away from other firms so that their knowledge advantages and awareness of opportunities do not leak out to neighboring firms. This, they argue, explains their finding that clustered foreign entrants actually have lower survival rates. McCann and Arita's (2006) examination of clusters in the global semiconductor industry suggests that leading multinational firms tend to co-locate their high-technology establishments close to each other, but they do so in order to maintain tight organizational and informational control and avoid outward knowledge spillovers to other firms. Hence spatial concentration is not *prima facie* evidence that clustering necessarily confers productivity advantages to firms.

Similarly, evidence that clustering leads to higher rates of innovation is far from unequivocal. On the one hand, Folta et al. (2006) find that clustered biotechnology companies have higher rates of patenting (see also Baptista and Swann 1998). But on the other hand, Beaudry and Breschi (2003) use patent records to compare the innovation records of UK and Italian firms inside and outside of clusters, and reject the view that clustering increases their propensity to innovate. Clustering has no significant effect and, moreover, their results point to some negative externalities arising from clustering. They conclude that it is the type of co-located firms and not clustering or cluster size *per se* that matter. Firm innovative performance is only positively affected when firms co-locate with other innovative firms within the same industry, whereas a strong local co-presence of non-innovative firms produces negative externalities. Such a finding lends support to the view that such innovative high-technology clusters are primarily a product of successful broader regional innovation systems, and that clustering is not of itself a fundamental cause of their innovative performance (Simmie 2006).

The lack of association between clustering and innovation may be explained by the fact that geographical proximity and intense local rivalry can in some instances decrease firms' commitment to R&D investment, because of the way in which local knowledge spillovers may lead to 'free-riding' (Beal and Gimeno 2001). Lee (2009) uses an extensive multi-industry nine-country dataset on the relations between location and R&D intensity and finds again that, after controlling for other factors, clustering *per se* has a negative affect on firms' propensity to invest in R&D. The underlying reasons are that clustered firms with high technological competences are more likely to suffer from detrimental knowledge spillovers, which may reduce their incentive to invest in R&D. Also, clustered firms that are exclusively reliant on local, rather than global networks, may well be more likely to suffer from technological convergence and lock-in.

Another important cause of the absence of a clear universal relationship between clusters, firm performance, and innovation is that the consequences of clusters are not static but alter as the clusters and their constituent firms, industries, and institutions evolve. It is now widely recognized that while clustering may reinforce growth in the early stages of an industry, it can conversely lead to and reinforce decline during the mature and later stages of an industry's development, due to congestion and competition effects (Braunerhjlem and Carlsson 1999). Saturation and density effects may mean that firm formation rates are lower in clusters than in non-clustered locations, as industries develop toward maturity. So, while there is some support for the view that high-technology clusters will raise entrepreneurship and start-up rates in the early phases of industry development (Cooper and Folta 2000), there is little conclusive evidence of whether this effect is apparent in other types of industry, or how far it continues over the entire cluster life cycle. Hence, Rocha's comprehensive review of the relations between clustering and entrepreneurship cautiously concludes that it is difficult to generalize: 'In effect, both positive results and caveats are found at different levels of analysis and at different stages of development of a cluster' (Rocha 2004: 391).

Our argument is not that clustering is never beneficial for firm performance and competitiveness. The existing literature includes several examples where clustering produces beneficial effects, especially for young firms and new entrants in knowledge-intensive industries and producer services (Wennberg and Lindqvist 2010).[5] Most notably, Folta et al. (2006) report that economies of agglomeration benefit American biotechnology firms' ability to innovate through supporting patenting and by helping them to attract alliance and private equity partners. They also find, however, that these benefits decline as clusters become larger, and that even in a young industry, such as biotechnology, diseconomies of agglomeration play an important role once clusters exceed about sixty-five firms. Furthermore, it is also worth noting that there is still little consensus on the causes of these benefits. Gilbert et al. (2008) find that clustering boosts the innovation performance of weaker young firms, specifically IPO-based new ventures, but they claim that technological knowledge spillovers alone are not an important cause of this effect.

Thus, while there is some evidence that clustering provides benefits for firm performance in some knowledge-intensive industries, other evidence indicates that the assumed positive relationship between clustering and firm competitiveness is neither necessary nor sufficient. In the first place, there has been increasing recognition that clusters typically contain heterogeneous firms, some of which are more able to benefit from co-location than others (ter Wal and Boschma 2007). Some argue that it is those firms with a larger accumulation of knowledge capabilities which tend to be better able to benefit from local knowledge externalities. Firms that lack absorptive capacity may not be able to absorb local knowledge spillovers, so that location in a cluster may not yield a substantial impact on their productivity. For example, Giuliani's (2007) examination of wine clusters finds that the diffusion of knowledge is not pervasive and shaped by geographical proximity alone, but instead is responsive to the asymmetric distribution of firm knowledge bases. Firms with stronger knowledge bases are more likely to exchange innovation-related knowledge. Thus, when a cluster is dominated by firms with weak knowledge bases, with poor capabilities to transfer and absorb knowledge, leading firms will tend to look elsewhere for partners and collaborators, and Porterian cluster benefits are unlikely to operate. McCann and Folta's (2011) recent research into the probability of patenting by US biotechnology companies claims that it is both firms with higher knowledge stocks and younger firms with higher uncertainty which benefit from clustering. The key point is that the relationship between clustering and outcomes is mediated and moderated by firm characteristics, so we need to be wary of stylized claims about universal cluster benefits for firm performance.

Secondly, there is also a considerable body of work which shows that clustering is insufficient for high firm performance. In particular, it has been widely documented that innovative and high-productivity companies typically have significant non-local and international connections and linkages, and not just local intra-cluster relationships. Not surprisingly, firms with both intra- and inter-regional ties with buyers and suppliers have been found to outperform others (Oerlemans and Meeus 2005; Frideres 2010). Indeed, it has been widely argued that national and international knowledge flows are absolutely essential for innovative and competitive dynamism (Simmie 2004). Clearly, 'local buzz' and 'global pipelines' are not alternatives, and both can feed and reinforce each other; but their balance is likely to vary from industry to industry, and in many cases it now appears that the importance of local knowledge spillovers has been exaggerated (Wolfe and Gertler 2004).

Ultimately, of course, the source of a firm's competitive advantage lies in its dynamic capabilities or organizational processes that create, integrate, recombine, and release resources (Eisenhardt and Martin 2000; Ambrosini and Bowman 2009). Without such capabilities, firms are likely to enjoy only a short-term competitive advantage and will fail to respond to their constantly changing environments. Such capabilities are typically shaped both by internal processes, such as path-dependent learning, management practice, cognition, and strategy, and by external factors, such as the business environment and the degree of uncertainty (Ambrosini and Bowman 2009). Clusters are, in effect, one dimension of this external environment which may shape and moderate dynamic capabilities.

In some circumstances there are grounds for arguing that local clustering acts as a key source and enabler of a firm's dynamic capabilities, but this is unlikely to be universally true. More often, we believe, clustering will be one factor among many, and its effects are frequently indeterminate and offset by other processes and conditions. Given the limited evidence base, it is wisest to conclude that the question as to the strength of connection between clustering and the operation and strength of firm dynamic processes remains a largely open and unanswered question. A great deal more research is required before we can be confident that local spillovers and externalities are genuinely strong determinants of the dynamic capabilities of firms and their competitive success over the long term.

On reflection, there are several possible responses to the weakness and ambivalence of evidence on the competitive effects of clustering. The first,

of course, is to argue that it stems from the multiple and contrasting definitions of clusters and research designs utilized, the consequent measurement
problems, and the widespread divergence between the conceptual definition
of clusters and their empirical identification (Rocha 2004). There is still little
consensus on how clusters should be distinguished from other types of
agglomeration, and different units and scales of analysis are often confused
(Martin and Sunley 2003). Negative results can be dismissed as indicative of a
failure to identify a 'true' cluster with proper institutional support and tacit
knowledge exchanges. Moreover, as we have seen, most studies are based on
only certain sectors and are unable to ascertain the generalizability of their
conclusions. A further response is to argue that researchers have focused on
different dimensions of firm performance, and that these have been assessed
mainly through proxies such as patenting or employment growth. There are
clearly problems with the interpretation of these statistics.

While these caveats undoubtedly have some force, the basic point remains,
namely, that there is as much empirical evidence to question the claim that
clustering enhances the competitiveness of firms, and hence regions, as there
is evidence to support it. Clearly, firms co-locate because certain benefits are
perceived from doing so, and the local clustering of similar and related firms
may well facilitate labor hiring, access to specialist supporting firms, and
perhaps even certain types of knowledge spillover and technological learning.
But clustering by itself does not guarantee that such processes will necessarily
occur, or, even if they do, that they will necessarily have the alleged beneficial
impacts on firm performance. As research has made clear, much will depend
on the type of industry, the capabilities of the firms involved, historical
circumstances, the stage of development of the cluster, and a host of other
contextual and conjunctural factors. In short, the evidence is mixed, and
caution should therefore be exercised when invoking the cluster model to
explain or define regional competitiveness. Further, the cluster model perhaps
assigns too much importance to the *local* business context, to local interactions and externalities.

What is of equal, if not greater, importance is the wider context within which
local firms operate – not only the wider regional and national environment,
but of course the international or global market in which such firms increasingly compete. As Porter (1986c: 26) himself had argued, and contrary to his
later work on clusters, 'many forms of competitive advantage for the global
competitor derive less from *where* the firm performs its activities than from *how*
it performs them on a worldwide basis: economies of scale, proprietary
learning, and differentiation with multinational buyers are not tied to
countries but to the configuration and co-ordination of the firm's worldwide
system'. It is the ability of firms to learn from, adapt to, and anticipate changing
global markets and global competitors that is key to their remaining

competitive, in the sense of pursuing constant upgrading and innovation, and achieving sustained sales and profitability. And as part of these processes, firms may even collaborate with overseas rivals in order to remain competitive.

Even though he stresses the importance of global competition and global markets throughout his work, Porter's cluster model nevertheless prioritizes the local over the global as the key arena shaping the competitiveness of firms. For a number of reasons, therefore, we are led to question whether the cluster model *per se* can really provide an adequate model for thinking about the 'competitiveness of locations'. At the very least, whether and to what extent it provides a superior alternative account to other perspectives remains an open question. It is this issue that we now explore.

12.4 The competitiveness of regions: clusters or comparative advantage?

Our previous discussion about the evidence on firm performance suggests that clusters may be neither necessary nor sufficient for regional competitiveness. A region's firms may be highly productive, and may enjoy a competitive advantage in their respective industries and markets even though they do not exhibit clustering. On the other hand, a region may have several clusters, but these need not (or need no longer) be competitive, so that the regional economy may suffer from an inferior growth rate or standard of living. In such cases, the cluster model would seem an incomplete conceptualization of regional competitiveness. Another, and more general, way of conceptualizing regional competitiveness is provided by the concept of comparative advantage that originally derives from international trade.

Trade is a key aspect when measuring competitiveness. Although the definition of national competitiveness has attracted debate and division (for example, Reich 1990), one theme nevertheless tends to recur, namely some reference to a nation's ability to produce goods and services that meet the test of international markets, while at the same time maintaining high and sustainable levels of income and employment (Cellini and Soci 2002; see also the list of definitions in Aiginger 2006*b*). Krugman, despite his critical stance of the notion of competitiveness, admits that national competitiveness is approximately defined as 'the combination of favorable trade balance and something else' (1996*a*: 7). Trade performance, in other words, is often seen to be a key indicator, an *output* or *revealed measure* to be more precise, of a nation's competitiveness. Trade performance is thus important for the discussion of regional competitiveness. A region's wealth creation and employment will in most instances depend on the ability of the region's firms to export goods and services to markets in other regions and/or other countries.

As noted above, Porter also emphasizes that it is export-orientated clusters that play a particularly important role in determining the competitiveness of locations and regions. Further, he argues that it is not the particular sectors in which a location or region specializes that matters: it is not what a region produces, but how well it produces it, which is where clustering is assumed to play a highly positive role since, the argument goes, clustering improves the efficiency with which a region produces its goods and services.

Porter's viewpoint would seem to stand in direct contrast to traditional comparative advantage theory, which would argue that it is how efficiently a region can produce certain goods compared to other goods that determines what the region specializes in. According to standard Ricardian comparative advantage theory, nations, and by extension regions, will tend to specialize in those activities in the production of which they are more efficient compared to all the other activities that could be produced. A nation (or region) need not have an absolute efficiency advantage in producing any product over all countries (regions); it need only be relatively more efficient in producing some products than others in order to benefit from trade. The question is what determines comparative advantage: why is a nation or region more efficient in certain sectors of activity compared with the relative efficiency of these sectors in other nations or regions? In traditional comparative advantage theory, a nation's (and a region's) pattern of specialization and exports is shaped by its endowments of the classic production factors of land, labor, and capital.

It is this theory that Porter criticizes and sets his cluster theory against. According to Porter, comparative advantage theory is both unrealistic and outmoded as a definition and explanation of 'competitiveness' and trade. He criticizes the theory on various grounds: its static nature; its neglect of economies of scale; its assumptions that technologies are identical everywhere; products are undifferentiated; intra-industry trade is unaccounted for; the pool of national (or regional) factor endowments is pre-given and fixed; and there is no reference to firm strategy. In his view:

> All these assumptions bear little relation, in most industries, to actual competition. At best, factor comparative advantage theory is . . . useful primarily for explaining broad tendencies in the patterns of trade (for example, its average labor or capital intensity) rather than whether a nation exports or imports in individual industries. (Porter 1990a: 12)

He goes further by suggesting that Ricardian factor comparative advantage has long been an incomplete explanation for trade, especially in those industries and segments of industries involving sophisticated technology and highly skilled employees – precisely, he says, the sectors that are now most important to national productivity. As more and more industries have become knowledge-intensive, he argues, so the role of factor costs has weakened even further. Yet 'while the insufficiency of factor advantage in explaining trade is widely accepted, what should replace or supplement it is far from clear' (Porter 1990*a*: 16). In his view, while the alternative theories that have been proposed – economies of scale theories, technology-gap theories, product-cycle accounts, and multinational enterprise theories – all make some valuable points, ultimately they leave the key question unanswered: why do firms based in particular nations and regions achieve international success in distinct segments and industries? It is this question that his cluster-based productivity theory of competitiveness is intended to answer. Productivity is key to regional economic success.[6] However, the roots of regional productivity ('competitiveness') lie not in local factor endowments, but rather in the localized increasing returns that derive from the geographical clustering of similar and interrelated firms, and especially from local knowledge spillovers.

What we appear to have then is, on the one hand, a comparative advantage theory of regional competitiveness which draws on Ricardian-type factor endowments, and on the other, Porter's cluster theory which has strong links to Smithian- and Marshallian-type increasing returns. But does Porter's 'alternative' cluster theory actually run counter to notions of comparative advantage? Is it really that different? Much depends on how comparative advantage is interpreted and conceptualized in a regional context. Porter's portrayal of comparative advantage theory is the traditional, static 'fixed factor endowments' view; and that is not difficult to criticize. But comparative advantage theory has in fact moved on from the standard Ricardian model that Porter attacks. In recent years, scholars have begun to rethink the traditional theory in several main respects (see, for example, Courant and Deardorff 1992; Hunt and Morgan 1995; Nelson 1995, 1996; Maneschi 1998, 2000; Redding 1999; Krugman 2009*c*).

One major development concerns the recognition that the conventional notion of 'endowments' or 'resources' in the theory needs to be updated and redefined. Some commentators argue that in terms of what is relevant to the competitiveness of the individual firm, what matters is not just labor, capital, and land, but a host of other resources – some internal to the firm, others external. Thus, recognition is given to the influence that political institutions, regulatory arrangements, cultural forms, infrastructures, and other such exogenous resources and constraints can exert on a firm's productivity or competitive advantage. All these are resources or factors that differentiate one national economy from another. Even more crucially, however, a central role is now accorded to past technological change as manifested in the endogenous cumulated stock of knowledge, skills, and technical assets, both within and outside the individual firm.

The potential for productivity growth in an economy depends, in part at least, on differences in the scope for 'learning' across different firms, sectors, and economies (regional and national). Learning effects are a key source of technical advance, and hence of productivity growth. If the potential for such learning effects differs across sectors, then different patterns of specialization will produce different time paths of productivity growth in the economy and hence of comparative advantage. Thus, technological upgrading, innovation, and spillovers of knowledge figure just as importantly in modern comparative advantage theory as they do in cluster theory (see Maneschi 1998; Redding 1999). If learning effects and inter-firm knowledge spillovers are localized, then productivity rises faster in the region (cluster) that first develops an industry or specialism. Such a competitive lead is likely to be self-reinforcing, and as Krugman graphically describes it:

> Like a river that digs its own bed deeper, a pattern of specialization, once established, will induce relative productivity changes that strengthen the forces preserving that pattern. Clearly, history matters here even for the long run...Comparative advantage is created over time by the dynamics of learning, rather than arising from underlying national characteristics. (Krugman 1987*b*: 47)

As Hunt and Morgan (1995) argue, such a rethinking of comparative advantage provides it with a direct link to competence theories of the firm. For these authors, rather than being a theory of national specialization, trade, and competitiveness, the new 'comparative advantage of competition' is seen as having micro-foundations, in the sense that what matters is not only the resources available to a firm but how that firm uses and deploys those resources strategically to gain a competitive advantage over other rival firms. Indeed, they use the term 'resource advantage theory of competition' to distance their view of comparative advantage from the traditional model (Hunt and Morgan 1997). Since each firm in an industry is a unique entity in time and space, firms will differ in the resources available to them, the way these resources are deployed, and hence their competitive advantage. Furthermore, this conception of comparative advantage is necessarily dynamic:[7]

> Competition, then, consists of the constant struggle among firms for a comparative advantage in resources that will yield a superior marketplace position of competitive advantage, and thereby superior financial performance. Once a firm's comparative advantage in resources enables it to achieve superior performance through a position of competitive advantage in some market segments or segments, competitors attempt to neutralize ands/or leapfrog the advantaged firm through acquisition, imitation, substitution or major innovation. The comparative advantage theory of competition is, therefore, inherently dynamic. (Hunt and Morgan 1995: 8)

Since some of the resources that firms utilize strategically to construct their dynamic competitive advantage are external to the firm, and because knowledge and other such spillovers are often held to be localized, the cluster concept and the dynamic comparative advantage theory summarized above are not necessarily opposing theories of regional competitiveness. Indeed, Krugman (2009c) has recently argued that comparative advantage and localized increasing returns are not alternative ways of thinking about international trade and national competitiveness, but complementary approaches. Patterns of comparative advantage – export specialization and trade – *between* nations, both historical and current-day, he argues, are closely associated with the localization of those specialisms *within* nations.[8] In other words, the increasing-returns effects arising from industrial localization within a nation give that nation a comparative advantage in the industry concerned. As an extension of this thinking to a regional context, Krugman has placed considerable emphasis on these externalities as a driver of what he now acknowledges as regional competitiveness: 'An industry or cluster of industries generates spillovers, which reinforces that industry's local advantage, or in some cases spillovers to other industries, which are thereby encouraged to locate in a particular region' (Krugman 2005: 39). Clearly, clusters are one form that such industrial localization may take.

Krugman goes further in this direction by arguing that another key cause of regional competitiveness, apart from local externalities, relates to what he calls a region's 'fundamentals' – local characteristics external to firms which have to do with region-specific cultural, social, institutional, environmental, and governance structures and resources, which serve to differentiate one region from another. As examples of fundamentals he cites a well-educated population; a local culture of entrepreneurship; sustained public-policy differences, such as differences in tax rates; and the quality of social and physical infrastructures. Such fundamentals, unlike labor and capital, are relatively immobile between regions, and constitute key resources on which local firms can directly or indirectly draw as sources of competitive advantage. Of course, such regional fundamentals may not necessarily act to promote comparative advantage: poor fundamentals (such as an inferior local education system, lack of a local business culture, a confrontational or inflexible local industrial relations culture, poor infrastructure, and so on) may lower the competitive advantage of a region's firms.

But Krugman's (2005) interpretation of regional competitiveness does not stop there. Conventional comparative advantage theory, as applied to national economies, assumes zero factor mobility. As Krugman argues, while this may be reasonable for national economies – capital movements between nations rarely account for more than a fifth of investment, and labor mobility is low – for regions this assumption is much less valid. Inter-regional movements of capital (firms and investment finance) and labor (workers and entrepreneurs) within a country can be substantial; which means that it is unrealistic to think of these two standard factor endowments as being fixed or pre-given in a regional context. Movements of labor and capital will not only be sensitive to regional differences in comparative advantage, economic growth, and productivity, but will also tend to accentuate those differences.

Unlike the cross-regional convergence taking place under the assumption of identical technologies everywhere, a significant difference in technologies (and their slow diffusion) between two regions would lead to sustained movements of labor and capital out of the less productive region into the more productive region: investment capital and venture capital would be expected to move to more productive regions where opportunities and returns are higher; and higher wages in such regions would draw in skilled and enterprising workers from elsewhere. Such movements would tend to reinforce the productivity of firms in the more prosperous region relative to firms in the less prosperous. Krugman (2005) suggests that factor mobility makes inter-regional differentials in growth rates much more sensitive than international differentials in growth rates to differences in productivity (efficiency), so that regional competitiveness also concerns the relative attractiveness of regions to labor and capital:

> Success for a regional economy, then, would mean providing sufficiently attractive wages and/or employment prospects and return on capital to draw in labor and capital from other regions. It makes sense to talk about 'competitiveness' for regions in a way one would not talk about it for larger [national] units. (Krugman 2005: 37)

The inter-regional mobility of capital and labor adds another element to the dynamic nature of the resources available to a region's firms, the competitive advantage of those firms, and hence a region's comparative advantage. But it also has implications for inter-regional development: the competitive growth of one region may well hold back the competitiveness and growth of another; and one region's inflow of skilled and productive workers may well be another region's loss. According to Camagni (2002b), inter-regional factor mobility can in fact mean that if a region falls behind in its productivity compared to other regions it can become locked into a vicious spiral of decline: capital and labor move out to other regions; productivity falls further behind, leading to further exodus of capital, labor, and ideas, and thence to even further falling behind in productivity; and so on.

It is undoubtedly true that we observe regions which, having lost comparative advantage in their key sector(s) or specialism(s), have gone into relative decline. But regions rarely go into absolute decline. In fact, there are many instances of regions reinventing themselves economically, either by re-establishing comparative advantage in their existing industries, through the application by local firms of new technologies, methods, or materials, or through the emergence and creation of new specialisms, new clusters, and new patterns of comparative advantage. This reinvention is often a result of local firms converting or building on particular technical or material strengths, skills, or other resources inherited from the region's declining sectors or still present in the region's fundamentals.

The basic point is that if a wider view is taken of endowments or resources, and learning, technology, and a region's externalities and fundamentals are included in those resources, the idea of comparative advantage takes on renewed relevance in discussions of regional competitiveness. Furthermore, it becomes a dynamic concept.[9] In his cluster theory Porter puts great store on innovation and upgrading as key to maintaining the competitiveness of firms, of clusters, and thus of regions, over time. A dynamic, resource-based notion of comparative advantage has a similar emphasis. What is essential to dynamic regional comparative advantage is *adaptation* to constantly changing markets, competition, and technology. How well firms adapt to the ever-shifting threats and opportunities that arise in the global economy determines whether they remain competitive in their respective industries. In terms of a regional economy as a whole, adaptation takes on a further dimension, not only in relation to the ability of its firms, clusters, and industries to adapt to changing market conditions and opportunities, so as to maintain their competitiveness, but also in relation to how well the economy is able to develop new productive industries, sectors, and technologies of activity over time; that is, how well it adapts its economic structure. Comparative advantage is an evolving feature of a regional economy, and adaptation is the key to its maintenance over the long term.

What all this suggests is a more general conception of regional competitiveness than that provided by the cluster model – possibly of the sort illustrated in Figure 12.2. A region's resources (externalities and fundamentals, to use Krugman's terms) afford location-specific comparative advantage (or disadvantage) to a region's firms. How firms draw on and deploy these resources, in combination with their own internal resources, influences their competencies and capabilities, and thence their productivity, innovation, and competitive advantage in the markets and export sectors for which they produce and in which they compete. Since market conditions are constantly evolving, the competitive advantage of a region's firms will also depend on how well they adapt to these shifting conditions.

At the regional scale, the outcome will be a particular pattern of inter-firm and inter-sectoral competitive advantage that represents the comparative advantage of the region relative to other regions. This particular pattern is not static, however, but evolves over time as the competitive advantage and adaptability of its firms change. Further, the region's resources and the changing competitive fortunes of the region's firms together influence the scope and

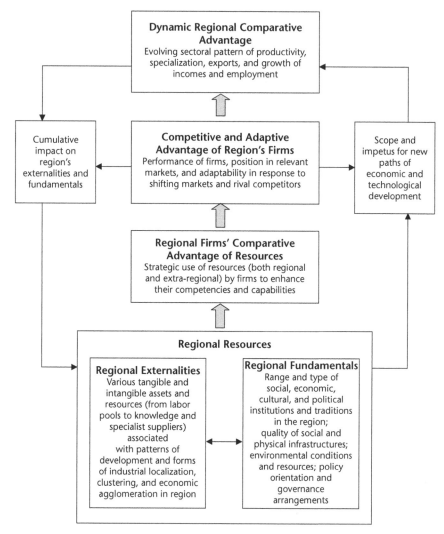

Figure 12.2. A more general model of regional competitiveness

impetus for the emergence of new paths of industrial and technological development which may form the basis of new forms of regional comparative advantage. At the same time, the region-wide pattern of economic development, specialization, and comparative advantage can be expected to feed back on the region's resources (both externalities and fundamentals): either to reinforce existing resources, characteristics, and assets, or to reshape them. Regional competitiveness, then, is a dynamic, co-evolutionary process, involving both elements of continuity (and path dependence) and elements of change and adaptation.

Where do clusters fit into such a conception? The model in Figure 12.2 does not depend on the presence of clusters, as other forms of economic agglomeration and spatial organization can also give rise to favorable externalities on which a region's firms can draw. And a region's fundamentals may be more important than its externalities for the competitiveness of local firms. But neither does this conception rule out clusters nor deny that they may play a key role in shaping a region's comparative advantage. Ultimately, the issue of what role clusters play in shaping the competitiveness of a region's firms is a matter for empirical enquiry, not theoretical presumption.

12.5 Conclusions and implications

Our aim in this chapter has been to revisit Michael Porter's cluster model of regional competitiveness and to assess its empirical validity (in terms of whether cluster firms in an industry outperform their non-clustered counterparts), as well as its claimed superiority over the idea of comparative advantage. We have argued that the evidence on the first of these issues raises some doubts about whether clustering is in fact necessary or sufficient for firms to be highly productive and competitive. On the second issue, our discussion suggests that there are three possible positions one might take on the question of the cluster model of competitive advantage versus a model based on comparative advantage.

One could adhere to the traditional notion of comparative advantage, interpreted in terms of a region's pre-given and fixed 'endowments' of land (and climate), labor (skills), and capital. It is then easy to criticize this conception as static, outmoded, and devoid of any consideration of innovation and other strategies that firms use to compete in the market place. On this basis, Porter's cluster theory of competitive advantage does indeed appear to be a more relevant way of thinking about the competitiveness of firms, industries, and regions, though still not without its problems and limitations. A second option, however, and one we have tried to argue for here, is to acknowledge that the idea of comparative advantage has in fact undergone revision and revival of late, to take into account the fact that a firm's comparative advantage depends not just on the sorts of endowments stressed in the traditional version of comparative advantage theory, but on a host of other tangible and intangible factors and resources that shape a firm's competences, capabilities, and innovativeness.

In its modern guise, comparative advantage theory is dynamic, not static. It recognizes that firms are constantly having to upgrade and reconfigure their competitive advantage in the face of changing market and competitive conditions. How this is achieved, and the extent to which is accomplished, will vary from firm to firm, even in the same industry, and is shaped by the external resources available to firms in the region in which they are located: geography matters. To our way of thinking, the idea of regional dynamic comparative advantage is more general than Porter's cluster model, and subsumes the latter.

A third option, following authors such as Tavoletti and te Velde (2008), might be to argue that comparative advantage and competitive advantage are complementary, that they move through a sequence of cycles, or what these writers call a 'helix process', whereby a region's or cluster's initial basic comparative advantage becomes undermined by the rise of competitors which have a greater comparative advantage, which then puts pressure on the original region's firms to recreate comparative advantage in their industry by exploiting competitive advantages based on innovation and collective learning. This option is not far removed from the model of dynamic regional comparative advantage developed here.

We began by noting how Porter's vision of cluster-based competitiveness has become highly influential in policy circles, so it is fitting to conclude by considering some of the policy implications of our discussion. There is little doubt that Porter's emphasis on the need to understand the specific characteristics of regional and local economies, and then to design policies that address the health of the micro-business environment and raise firm productivity, has had beneficial consequences. The effort to create regional policies that foster highly competitive micro-environments and address weaknesses in the local supply-side and in the quality of demand has been of undoubted value. Such competitive advantage strategies are clearly preferable to non-interventionist, fixed-factor comparative advantage approaches to regional restructuring (Thomas et al. 2008). Nevertheless, it is clear that cluster approaches to regional competitiveness have encountered a series of obstacles and problems (Martin and Sunley 2003; Asheim et al. 2006*b*).

The first obstacle, of course, has been the basic difficulty in identifying clusters and their constituent firms. Despite all the cluster documents, guides, handbooks, and prescriptions, the definitions used by cluster policies continue to be arbitrary and highly variable. Although Porter recognizes that not all clusters are alike, the way he defines and differentiates them is discursive and superficial. Thus, they are asserted to 'vary in size, breadth, and state of development. Some clusters consist of small- and medium-sized firms... Other clusters involve both large and small firms' (Porter 1998*d*: 204). We are left wondering at the lack of critical reflection involved in such observations, and even more so at the absence of skepticism from the eager policy clients of such a simplistic prospectus.

The second key and related problem is the ambiguity surrounding the selectivity implied by cluster-based policies. Cluster policy has been criticized for being a disguised form of industrial policy which continues to be based on 'picking winners' – in effect, substituting clusters for industrial sectors. In this view it is inevitable that cluster initiatives will support some industries and not others (Hospers et al. 2009). Porter and his associates have, of course, strongly denied this and argued that cluster policies should support *all* clusters: 'In cluster theory, all clusters can improve productivity and deserve attention' (Porter 1998*a*: 12). Porter insists that policy should not seek to build and construct clusters in a top-down fashion. Ketels (this volume) adds that the selection of clusters should be pragmatic and respond to those clusters that want to engage with public authorities. But in the absence of clear definitions of when a spatial collection of firms has sufficient critical mass, proximity, and interrelatedness to represent a cluster, the exhortation to support those clusters that are seeking policy help seems to be an inconclusive and risky policy recommendation.

The third key ambiguity shown by cluster policy concerns the degree to which clusters in a regional economy are an end in themselves or a means to raising the productivity and competitiveness of firms. In some instances it appears that Porter sees clusters as primarily a means of encouraging collaboration and dialogue between firms and local public agencies. This collective dialogue should, he argues, focus on how to upgrade and leverage the advantages of clusters. At the same time, however, he argues that all clusters are valuable, and that what is important is not the industrial characteristics of particular clusters but rather their size and critical mass. As he says, 'My argument is that, in the global economy, so long as you have the clusters – the critical mass – a particular field of business activity can be extremely efficient and productive' (Snowdon and Stonehouse 2006: 166; also Ketels 2006: 129). The danger of this view, of course, is that it exaggerates the benefits of fostering critical mass *per se*, and does not recognize the need to weigh the balance of congestion costs and to more closely scrutinize the types of feedbacks typical of different forms of clusters.

For all its insights then, we would conclude that policies to promote, foster, and support regional competitiveness should be embedded in a broader appreciation of regional dynamic advantage if they are to be successful and effective. Such a perspective is important for several reasons. First, it implies that all forms of knowledge spillover may be highly important to regional competitiveness and it does not prioritize knowledge spillovers generated by clusters. The key here is to recognize that, in addition to clusters, other spatial structures and distributions of firms in a regional economy (such as several large but dispersed plants or a diversified conurbation) may well exhibit high productivity and lead to positive feedback in terms of external resources, and may thus represent key drivers of regional dynamic advantage.

Second, while Porter is correct to highlight that some clusters are powerful sources of knowledge spillovers, it is important to note that these might be diffused throughout the regional economy and not just circulated among particular cluster-based groupings. This implies that a critical aim of regional policies should be to support innovation diffusion and knowledge transfer much more broadly than through narrowly defined, cluster-based collaborations.

Third, while cluster policy emphasizes the advantages of high levels of cluster specialization within a regional economy, a broader adaptive approach would seek to encourage spillovers and the transfer of competences between related sectors: arguably, what matters for regional competitiveness is neither sectoral variety nor sectoral specialization, but related variety (Frenken et al. 2007). The dangers of fine specialization in a global economy are well known, and a comprehensive regional policy should seek to construct dynamic advantage through facilitating spillovers and entrepreneurial transfers to related sectors (see Asheim et al. 2009). Without such 'platform-based' policies, encouraging cluster specialization could well heighten regional instability.

Furthermore, a regional dynamic advantage interpretation questions the focus on critical mass (based on the notion of increasing returns to scale in knowledge spillovers) and instead emphasizes the need to take a more discriminating approach to clusters. The importance of comparative advantage means that any decision to support a cluster must take into account several key issues, including whether the cluster is based on the use of resources that the region in question can provide efficiently, whether the cluster can adapt and compensate by exploiting other resources, and how the development of the cluster will alter those resources through feedback effects. Moreover, this assessment should include an analysis of how the particular cluster stands relative to other similar clusters elsewhere, and with which its firms are in competition, and indeed whether the cluster can feasibly attract mobile capital and labor. Where clustered firms are not highly productive and losing market share, contributing strong negative feedbacks on their regional economies, then it is obvious that policy support for those firms may be the wrong strategy. Policymakers have no option but to evaluate whether these weaknesses are remediable or not and, if not, create incentives that nudge actors into related fields with better prospects.

In our view, then, clusters are at best only one element of policies intended to promote and enhance regional competitiveness. As we have noted, the implication of the interpretation of regional competitiveness we have adopted here is that any targeted measures designed to foster clusters should be set in the context of measures designed to strengthen regional externalities and fundamentals. There are many forms of external dynamic advantage that do not depend on the presence of clusters, and there are no grounds for attaching lower priority to these. Equally, regional fundamentals have a critical role in shaping economic development. What this means is that cluster initiatives by themselves are unlikely to provide a comprehensive means of improving the institutional and organizational contexts for regional competitiveness. The importance of regional fundamentals and externalities in dynamic comparative advantage means that regional policy has to seek more comprehensive and holistic measures that shape the business and knowledge environment for the whole regional economy and not just for those firms recognized as being located in clusters. And above all, given that regional competitiveness is a dynamic process, not a static state of affairs, the regional policy task is essentially about promoting, enhancing, and fostering adaptation.

Notes

1. Reinert (1995) suggests that while the term 'competitiveness' may only recently have entered economic parlance, similar notions have long been implicit in economic writings, as far back as the Classical theorists, if not earlier.
2. The United States led the way in the early 1990s by setting up a governmental Competitiveness Policy Council to report regularly on and promote the competitiveness of the American economy. Soon after, the European Commission established a European Council of Competitiveness, and undertook to produce a regular Competitiveness Report on the performance of the EU economy. Since then, measuring and promoting competitiveness have become key activities of almost all of the OECD nations. The United Kingdom has even had a Minister for Competitiveness.
3. To this end it produces regular reports on the 'state of the regions', based on a variety of 'competitiveness indicators'.
4. In the 1990s it was Japan that was considered to be the leading global 'threat' to the economies of the United States and Europe – a view promoted particularly by Lester Thurow in his alarmist 1992 tome *Head to Head: The Coming Economic Battle Among Japan, Europe and America.*
5. Another set of literature reports the somewhat unsurprising benefits of market-based clustering in industries such as hotels and tourism (see Canina et al. 2005). And an obvious case can be made that the clustering of banks, investment houses, and the myriad of supporting specialist institutions, in London and New York, confers undoubted competitive advantage on these cities as leading global financial centers.
6. One important qualification of this view is that high productivity does not always translate into high economic welfare, as its delivery may, in some circumstances, compromise social and environmental goods (Aiginger 2006b).
7. The notion of 'dynamic comparative advantage' had in fact been invoked in the new trade theory some years earlier (see Krugman 1987b; Grossman and Helpman 1991).
8. Krugman believes that though once regarded as a thing of the past, comparative advantage has reasserted itself in the world economy in recent decades: 'Over the past century world trade has gone through a great arc. At the beginning of the century

trade was primarily between countries with very different resources exporting very different goods, so that it seemed to be a comparative advantage world. By the 1980s trade was largely between countries with similar resources exporting similar goods, so that economists turned to increasing-returns models to make sense of what they say. But today, with the rise of China and other low-wage economies, we seem once again to be in a comparative advantage world, in which countries with very different resources export very different goods' (Krugman 2009*c*: 12).

9. On the continuing relevance of the concept of comparative advantage in the new trade theory, and the richer connotations this concept has acquired, see Maneschi (1998, 2000) and Redding (1999).

13

Conclusion: Porter's perspective

Robert Huggins and Hiro Izushi

13.1 Introduction

In this concluding chapter we not only provide an interpretation of the key perspectives and debates concerning Michael Porter's contributions across the range of fields and disciplines into which he has delved, but also his own views on his career, contributions, and his critics. To this end, we draw on comments made by Porter in an interview he undertook with us at Harvard Business School in July 2009. This interview provides a fascinating insight into the nature of his thinking, especially in terms of seeking to connect the various strands that have contributed to his remarkable career.

Throughout all his work, Porter's sustained mantra is *competition*, and he has consistently and emphatically used the competition metaphor to argue and promote its importance as the underlying driver of economic and business success. As he states: 'Competition is one of society's most powerful forces for making things better in many fields of human endeavor.... Competition is pervasive, whether it involves companies contesting markets, countries coping with globalization, or social organizations responding to societal needs' (Porter 2008*b*: xi).

Porter does not consider such pervasiveness to be merely restricted to the traditional corporate sector, but also extending to the arts, education, the environment, health care, and philanthropy, which he argues increasingly require competition in order to efficiently manage growing needs within a context of increasingly scarce resources (Porter 2008*b*). As Cho and Moon (2000) argue, whereas Adam Smith considers wealth to be created by endowments, Porter's thesis is that wealth is created by choices.

For Porter, competition not only underlies economic success but more broadly the success of society, and issues relating to activities such as corporate social responsibility have become important factors in his socioeconomic competition equation. Increasingly, he has promoted the integration of economic and social policy, arguing that 'there is no conflict between a healthy economy and a just and fair society' (Porter 2001*b*: 154). He considers his key role in achieving this to be that of changing the practices of decision-makers across both the private and public sectors by communicating with them in a 'language' they understand:

> I am very slow with my work. Part of it is the desire to have a rich empirical understanding of the phenomenon. Part of it is the process of working things out until I feel that it is completely clear and there is no jargon, ambiguity, or confusion. However, to get to that point in the writing, one's mind has to get to a certain clarity in its thinking. This is why it typically takes me five years to complete a book.... Typically, in the first instance my work is best appreciated by practitioners, and the scholars often scratch their heads and say 'what is this?', because it is a different way of cutting into things. (Porter, interview with authors)

As Porter is keen to point out, the intellectual environment at Harvard Business School has clearly been crucial in supporting his journey, particularly in the early years, and while this environment was often highly challenging of his ideas, it greatly helped to refine his thinking:

> It [Harvard Business School] has been a very supporting environment, but there was a big fight about generalization. Because of my acculturation at Harvard Business School, all of my work has to be holistic, in the sense that it tries to encapsulate the full richness of the topic, but in a way that is actually manageable. Roland Christensen was a phenomenal mentor, and continually urged me to be holistic in my approach. (Porter, interview with authors)

13.2 *Competitive Strategy* and *Competitive Advantage*

At the outset, a key aspect of Porter's original challenge was to move beyond the rather stylized theories laid out by economists regarding how and why industries are structured and organized as they are:

> The problem I had was that economics work was very stylized. For example, the Joe Bain work identified three or four main entry barrier categories, but it was clear there was more to it than that in real industries. I came to this insight of the Five Forces, and one had to see these Forces collectively. But in order to get from the IO view of industry structure to the Five Forces view, much work had to be done and I wrote a whole bunch of papers, flushing out various issues, such as the paper Richard Caves and I wrote on switching costs and barriers to exit. That was an idea critical to a rich view of industry competition, but which was absent in the economics literature. (Porter, interview with authors)

For Porter, his use of the industrial organization theory of Joe Bain and others is much more enriched than the form originally developed in the 1950s and 1960s:

> When I started out there was some work on industry structure in the field of industrial economics. The framing of that work was on how to limit firm profitability and create allocative efficiency in the economy. I quickly realized that there were some IO ideas, like the work of Joe Bain on entry barriers and others, that could be mobilized not only to address that question, but they could also be turned on their head and mobilized to actually help firms understand their industry environment. (Porter, interview with authors)

As Porter makes clear, his seminal *Competitive Strategy* (Porter 1980*a*) did not emerge overnight, but was the result of numerous iterations and drafts whereby he honed and refined his ideas:

> In retrospect, the first version of *Competitive Strategy* was clumsy and too heavily dependent on the IO view of industries. I discarded the first draft completely and started over. There was another three or four years of work in which I worked out a lot of the nuances in the concepts in order to build up the Five Forces. At the time I was teaching case study after case study and reading article after article, so I developed an increasingly deep understanding of industries. I had to build out many pieces of the Five Forces, rather than take what was already in the economics literature and go with it, because the economics literature did not capture many of the realities and nuances of competition. (Porter, interview with authors)

The success of his Five Forces and generic strategy models brought Porter center stage in the strategic management field and cemented his influence upon both scholars of strategic management and business practitioners:

> As an afterthought, in the last six months before *Competitive Strategy* was locked up, I decided I needed to say something about positioning, because it was clear that companies in the same industry have very different levels of performance. That is when the notion of generic strategies was developed, which started laying out the most basic and fundamental variables in thinking rigorously about positioning. This thinking turned into a little chapter completed at the last minute, but it got more attention than I would have ever imagined. I am very proud of that, obviously, and extremely stunned about how powerful and enduring the original ideas in *Competitive Strategy* have been. I was fortunate to be in the right place and time to bring a new paradigm into the field.
>
> What I was able to do [with the Five Forces] is pack a lot of theoretical horsepower into a framework that, at least at the first level, is extremely intuitive. Each of the Five Forces explodes in complexity. If I had gone with twenty forces it would have been a complete failure, and if had only two it would have been a complete failure. Coming up with the final Five Forces was a process of exploration and

testing applicability in industry after industry. Over the whole period of my doctoral work, MBA training, and time as a younger faculty member, I looked at hundreds of industries. This allowed me to discover aspects of industry competition I had not thought of or incorporated, so I added them in. (Porter, interview with authors)

For Porter a key outcome of the *Competitive Strategy* project was the subsequent influence of his work in the field of business economics and the widening of research on competition:

Partly as result of publishing the Five Forces, some areas of economics research got a lot richer. All of a sudden there was a whole generation of game theoretic research on industry competition, for example, and I feel proud that on some level my work helped shape this. I was still very much an economist in those days and those were the people I spent time with. I was fortunate to get to know and interact with many microeconomic thought leaders, and get them interested in strategy. (Porter, interview with authors)

However, acknowledgment of this influence did not come easy, and even within Harvard it took some time to win over colleagues:

By the time I was up for full professor all this [*Competitive Strategy*] had happened and everybody was applauding. However, when I came up for Associate Professor, I had only written a paper called *Note on the Structural Analysis of Industries*. Although I did get promoted, the review of the note suggested it was a 'noble experiment that failed'. There was a very strong view here [Harvard Business School] among some business policy faculty that you cannot generalize about strategy. Therefore, any effort to create a general framework in strategy was doomed. This view changed just a couple of years later. (Porter, interview with authors)

Porter followed up *Competitive Strategy* with *Competitive Advantage* (Porter 1985a). The breadth alone of *Competitive Advantage* is to be admired, with Porter highlighting his view that it is difficult to disconnect the internal from the external factors driving competitive advantage:

Following *Competitive Strategy* and the Five Forces, the next big challenge was the value chain and the notion of competitive advantage. In a way, this was harder because there was no preexisting structure. The existing work about the firm was very diffuse. There was operations research, which was about optimization within constraints. There was the production function concept in economics, but this is very stylized. In business, there was the idea of the McKinsey business system, but this was not a general framework. In general, the value chain was very much a critique of economics. In a sense, I was trying to create a theory of the firm that reflected the choices firms actually make. Firms do not think about production functions; firms think about changing the way they conduct their activities. The value chain had to be operational and something which firms could use at a granulated level. (Porter, interview with authors)

Interestingly, in *Competitive Advantage*, Porter already begins to consider, albeit in an embryonic manner, some of the key issues that will later concern him in much greater detail when developing his notion of clusters. For instance, he discusses issues concerning learning and spillovers, as well as the spatial and geographic scope of industries. Also, the 'value system' concept, consisting of the connections of firms with their buyers and suppliers, resembles the connections apparent in clusters.

13.3 Porter versus the resource-based view

As *Competitive Advantage* makes clear, for Porter it is activities and the value chain, rather than resources, which make strategy operational. Porter (1991) views resources as intermediate factors lying between activities and the creation of competitive advantage, but argues that the resource-based argument is potentially a circular one, which does not make transparent the types of unique resources that facilitate competitive advantage:

> I think the value chain continues to be very a powerful metaphor for managers examining their choices and sources of advantage. Underneath the value chain are often some 'assets' or resources that enable activities, such as skills or relationships. The trouble with the resource-based view is that resources are poorly defined, and tangled up in cause and effect. It is very hard to avoid the circularity argument, i.e. a factor is a resource because it led to success. I believe that few resources are truly exogenous, and even fewer are valuable independent of the strategy or positioning in which they are employed. Wal-Mart's locations are valuable because of Wal-Mart's strategy, for example, and are not valuable to many other retailers. 'Resources' are attractive to economists who look at external constraints around which choices are optimized. In actual companies, there are countless opportunities to relax constraints and find new ways to compete. The key is to make choices and tradeoffs, rather than rest on a particular resource. (Porter, interview with authors)

According to Porter the vagueness of the resource-based view (RBV) has led to its implosion, with many researchers increasingly questioning the applicability of this view (Stonehouse and Snowdon 2007). For Porter, the RBV cannot stand on its own as a theory of competitive advantage. As J.-C. Spender and Jeroen Kraaijenbrink conclude in their chapter in this volume, the continuing dominance of the RBV may warrant some concern and rethinking.

Nevertheless, an increased preoccupation by strategic management researchers on the internal environment of the firm has served to marginalize Porter's efforts in this discipline. In recent years it is the resource-based perspective that has become the dominant paradigm in strategic management research. Porter may in part be losing the battle to the RBV due to his focus on industries at a time when there are arguments to suggest that previously distinct industry boundaries are becoming blurred (Teece 2007), possibly resulting in the homogenization – rather than the distinction which is key to Porter's approach – of industrial organization. This has been coupled with an on-going debate on the extent to which industry effects actually impinge on firm performance. While Porter (McGahan and Porter 1997) has produced evidence suggesting that these effects are of clear significance, others remain more skeptical (Rumelt 1991). More recently, Porter has suggested that while industry effects may not be as dramatic as firm effects, they are usually more enduring (Stonehouse and Snowdon 2007).

As the RBV has come to be firmly placed at the 'cutting edge' of strategic management research, Porter's Five Forces has become more the standard methodological framework adopted by those preparing an MBA dissertation. Our view is that it is the wrong approach to increasingly polarize the RBV and Porter's Five Forces and Value Chain/activities frameworks, and we suggest that more considered theory building should be undertaken to further integrate these perspectives in a complementary and holistic fashion. However, the theoretical waters have become further muddied with scholars becoming increasingly attracted to concepts such as dynamic capabilities, which seek to account for the evolutionary nature of the resources and sources of knowledge underpinning firm success.

Within the dynamic capabilities framework, Teece (2007) describes the external environment within which firms are situated as a business 'ecosystem' consisting of organizations, institutions, and individuals that impact on the firm and its customers and suppliers, including complementors, suppliers, regulatory authorities, standard-setting bodies, and educational and research institutions. In some respects, Teece's business ecosystems sound remarkably similar to Porter's concept of clusters, yet Teece (2007) makes no reference to it, sticking to a critique of Porter's work that largely goes no further than the Five Forces. If nothing else, this indicates the extent to which Porter's cluster research, discussed later, is divorced from the theoretical advances being made in contemporary strategic management research, with the cluster concept in many ways failing to permeate the discipline he is most recognized as shaping.

This failure to make a clear connection between clusters – and the linkages and networks upon which they are founded – and more contemporary management concepts, such as those concerning complementarity and the growth of open innovation models (Chesbrough 2003), has meant that many in management research continue to focus only on Porter's earlier work, which is often critical of the roles of alliances, particularly those related to innovation. This situation is hardly new, and the disciplinary positioning of their work is something that most academics have to consider at certain points in their career. In Porter's case it is probable that the placing of his cluster research outside the mainstream management outlets is at least partly due to the fact that this research is attempting to impact on the decisions of public policymakers, rather than corporate managers.

Although there are a number of articles published in leading management journals (such as Tallman et al. 2004) that draw on Porter's cluster concept, these remain exceptions to the general rule. Our view is that the constructs underlying the notion of clusters still falls short of a fully fledged 'theory' that will be accepted by the management discipline. However, such a theory is possible, particularly if it were to draw upon and integrate with other state-of-the-art developments in the management field. This need not include concepts such as Teece's dynamic capabilities (2007), which we consider to be highly abstract, but should certainly incorporate the growing literature around open models of innovation.

13.4 Static or dynamic frameworks?

A key criticism of Porter's work in relation to the RBV and dynamic capabilities is that it suffers from an innate static nature that fails to account for the dynamic environments within which many firms operate. In particular, a key criticism relates to Porter's dependence (1980a) on the structure–conduct–performance paradigm emerging from industrial economics (Teece 2007). In this paradigm, industry structure is considered exogenous, with firms reacting to it. Teece (2007) argues that industry structure is in fact endogenous, emerging for the learning and innovation undertaken by firms. We have some sympathy with both perspectives, and suggest that in reality the relationship between firms/entrepreneurs and the industry structure is in fact symbiotic (Kamien and Schwartz 1982; Geroski and Pomroy 1990; Geroski 1991). The claim that his frameworks are in someway static is one which Porter strongly counters:

> I am puzzled by criticism that my work is somehow static. This is something I have never quite understood. I think my work is invariant of time and provides a way to understand the significance of whatever changes are underway. A lot of work in management is really about trends. My work is not about trends; it is about what is invariant of trends, so you will never see a variable in one of my frameworks that is a trend. It will always be something that is an underlying fundamental. It will be about something like the switching cost, and not, for example, an IT variable, which is necessarily going to be dependent on the state of IT. (Porter, interview with authors)

Despite claims that Porter's frameworks are in some way static, he was in fact discussing the evolution of industries as far back as *Competitive Strategy* in

1980. In *The Competitive Advantage of Nations* (Porter 1990*a*), Porter presents an evolutionary framework of the processes underlying national competitive development, consisting of factor-driven, investment-driven, innovation-driven, and wealth-driven stages of development. Drawing on analogies from evolutionary biology, he highlights how clusters may become over-insular and locked into outdated and uncompetitive practices. In his chapter, Robert Grant supports the view that in *The Competitive Advantage of Nations* Porters adopts a far more dynamic view of competition from that he previously employed. According to Porter:

> All of my work tries to be independent of any given moment of time, and any particular technology, taste or circumstance. I aspire to work on the fundamental underlying economic principles. Of course, as time progresses the opportunities and ultimately the manifestation of these principles will evolve. Even though I had not heard of the Internet when we did the Five Forces, it was very easy to use the Five Forces to look at the Internet, because the unit of analysis was not the technology but the underlying drivers of competition. (Porter, interview with authors)

13.5 *The Competitive Advantage of Nations*

Following *Competitive Advantage*, Porter subsequently expanded the sphere of his operation and influence by diversifying into other academic disciplines – especially the economic development of nations, urban and regional planning, and more recently, health care services. By the time of this diversification he was no longer a newcomer with little influence but a well-known figure with strong brand recognitions. He made full use of his brand, and this was evident in *The Competitive Advantage of Nations* (Porter 1990*a*). Porter went to great lengths to address policy-makers, rather than competing directly with incumbents in the field, especially other academics researching economic development:

> In *The Competitive Advantage of Nations* the concern is not with the firm, but with the location and the collective prosperity of the location, whereas *Competitive Advantage* is focused on the firm's ability to maximize sustained profitability, which then results in shareholder value. A lot of things can be ported back and forth but there are nuances because there are different units of analysis. (Porter, interview with authors)

While economists researching economic development relied increasingly upon technically sophisticated but harder-to-understand econometrics, policy-makers as the 'buyers' of ideas saw less relevance in the approach taken by many economists. Porter seized this opportunity and positioned his ideas under a 'package' different from more traditional theories of economic development. His targeting of policy-makers was reinforced by his involvement in the World Economic Forum and the publication of *Global Competitiveness Reports*, coupled with the introduction of the 'Diamond' framework:

> It [policy] is an infinitely complex problem. There are hundreds of policy areas that lie underneath the Diamond. There is this gigantic mountain of detailed policies. The Diamond provides a template for understanding how all these policies fit together. It helps understand the heart of the problem, which is what is driving the productivity of any region or location. (Porter, interview with authors)

While the tone Porter uses in *Competitive Strategy* in 1980 is often quite confrontational – for example, warfare, battleground, fighting brands, attacks, punish, and so on – echoing that associated with Sun Tzu's *The Art of War* (Krause 1996), in *The Competitive Advantage of Nations* Porter begins to seriously address the issue of cooperation, coupled with an attempt to forge a tighter connection with his early work on company strategy. Rather than the confrontational view of competition presented in *Competitive Strategy*, his later work emphasizes the coexistence of competition and cooperation through which peer firms stimulate improved efficiency and innovation (Porter 2008*b*). Generally, it is through the cluster paradigm that Porter has sought to integrate his earlier work on industry and competitive analysis with his more recent work on national and regional level economic analysis:

> Clusters go back for centuries and centuries, but the way in which collaboration occurs in clusters and the nature of that collaboration keeps evolving with the capacity for new forms of such collaboration. For instance, there has been a lot of innovation in terms of the vehicles for collaboration across firms, and technology has enabled some of these. (Porter, interview with authors)

The evolution in Porter's thinking has occurred partly as a result of the opportunities – in particular, *The Competitive Advantage of Nations* project – which opened to him to pursue avenues that were becoming fundamental to economic (development) policymakers. In many ways, these opportunities have allowed him to shape policy-making agendas across the globe. Through a fusing of his academic writings and consultancy research, Porter influenced and stamped his mark on these agendas from the 1990s onwards:

> The more I got into it, the more I discovered that we lacked a clear definition or accepted framework for competitiveness. Some people thought it was export market shares and others thought it was unit labor costs, or driven by the value of currency. There were lots of different views. I set out to work on the question, which was a long project because there are a myriad of things that make nations successful. I had to assemble extraordinary evidence to take on Ricardo and others. That is why we decided to undertake this ten-nation study [in *The Competitive Advantage of Nations*] and look deeply at these countries and their successful industries. (Porter, interview with authors)

Importantly, Porter is always keen to make clear that the firm-level competitiveness and national/locational-level competitiveness remain distinct concepts, with conflation resulting in confusion (Snowdon and Stonehouse 2006):

> Industry is very important to the firm because it has a big impact on profitability. The industry level is critical to understanding firm profitability, but less fundamental to understanding firm productivity, because productivity is affected by externalities across related industries (clusters). The firm's goal is sustained profitability for itself. This is not exactly the same goal as that of a location, which is to maximize the collective productivity of the firms operating in that location. These are subtle but important differences. (Porter, interview with authors)

From a policy perspective, some macroeconomists are skeptical of the type of microeconomic interventions that Porter recommends in *The Competitive Advantage of Nations* (see, for instance, Minford 2006), which is perhaps unsurprising given that his ideas can often be viewed as orthogonal to the economic mainstream:

> I see all my work as micro. In competitiveness there is a role for what might more classically be considered macroeconomic policy, but we focus on the microeconomic underpinnings of competitiveness. The competitiveness research focuses on the way in which the business environment surrounding firms affects the way they compete and their productivity. The firm, cluster, region, and nation can be thought of as a nested set of layers. (Porter, interview with authors)

As Brian Snowdon highlights in his chapter, Porter's microeconomic perspectives have been important in redressing the balance in explaining that the sources of economic growth are as much, if not more, related to firm and industry level innovation as they are to monetary and fiscal policy. According to Porter:

> Whereas economists are much more comfortable with tying to create the right tax incentives and develop human capital, and then just assume that all the other stuff within firms will take place, my work aims to get inside the black box at the micro-level. Economists tend to focus on the broad inputs and leave the details of what firms do to the invisible hand. (Porter, interview with authors)

13.6 Clusters

In his earlier work Porter is skeptical of collaboration and cooperation, especially in the form of strategic alliances, which he appears to consider as being a precursor to merger or acquisition, or otherwise destined to fail. In his eyes, these forms of collaboration are often anticompetitive forms of collusion. In this case, he doubts that such alliances result in efficiencies in undertaking innovation (Porter 1990a).

In his later work on clusters, cooperation and collaboration through informal and social networking across firms is very much considered to be a positive benefit of operating within a cluster environment. His cluster-view of cooperation is quite different from his earlier view that cooperation, especially between rivals, 'usually undermines competitive advantage in the long run. It reduces incentives and saps rivalry, ultimately slowing progress' (Porter 1990a: 667). However, in a change from his previous skepticism of inter-firm alliances and collaboration, Porter (2008b) argues that successful cluster upgrading will depend on paying significant and explicit attention to relationship building, which he considers to be a vital characteristic of cluster-development initiatives:

> There's a body of work on networks and collaboration that is highly useful in thinking about how to make clusters operational and improve the way they actually function. My work on clusters highlights how various forms affect productivity at the regional or national level. Cluster collaboration takes many forms, but bears little resemblance to conventional strategic alliances or cartels. What I personally do all the time is try to help clusters organize themselves better for collaboration, so in practice I do a lot of this. (Porter, interview with authors)

Porter's increasing preoccupation with the local environment, and the development of cluster models, has resulted in his work becoming of significant interest to a band of researchers in fields such economic geography and industrial dynamics. This has necessarily taken him into new scholarly areas outside the management field:

> The antecedent of my thinking on clusters is the work of Alfred Marshall, which started to recognize the importance of externalities. Marshall's work is very provocative but it did not offer a comprehensive framework for thinking about these externalities. There is also the Italian work on Industrial Districts, particularly the research of Professor Giacomo Becattini. However, the overwhelming thrust of the economics literature on competitiveness was really much more top-down and macro-driven. (Porter, interview with authors)

Porter (2008b) argues that policy should seek to upgrade all clusters in economy. A problem here is that such a proposition may result in cluster policies being situated within a very difficult position between industrial policy and more generic economy-wide polices that simply offers support to all firms and industries. Due to the inherent difficulties in implementing cluster policies, not least their identification, cluster initiatives have tended to lean toward one of the other forms, mainly traditional industrial policies that seek to pick winners.

In his chapter, Christian Ketels – a colleague of Porter – argues that any idea that government should seek to create clusters is not supported by Porter. Porter (2008b) seeks to make clear that cluster-based policy approaches are fundamentally different from traditional industrial policy approaches, which he considers are based on seeking to pick winners in the form of desirable industries. Fundamentally, however, this appears to have failed to come across to policy-makers, who have used policies labeled as cluster initiatives to support and subsidize those particular industrial sectors which they consider offer a basis for future economic growth.

As Edward Malecki indicates in his chapter, the cluster concept has often been misapplied as referring to a collection of trading sectors. In a pure Porterian sense, many 'cluster' policies are not in fact cluster initiatives but industry-level policy, and as Porter (2008b: 265) states, 'focusing policy at the industry level presumes that some industries are better than others and runs grave risks of distorting or limiting competition.'

Although Porterian-based policymaking has often led to identikit and off-the-shelf strategies being developed by governments and their agencies around the world (Martin and Sunley 2003), Porter's overall impact has been positive. It has resulted in the adoption of more analytical and sophisticated approaches to policy and strategy building, incorporating a broader perspective of the external and global environment within which firms, nations, regions, and cities exist and increasingly function. This has proved prescient as economies and firms shift to more open and globalized market structures. For Porter, the continuation of such globalization heightens the relevance of clusters:

> What has happened is the globalization of more activities and industries. The technological constraints and opportunities have shifted, and the Internet has opened up, for example, services competitiveness in fields that used to be local rather than traded. Now we are going through a funny reversal because of the rising costs of energy and the carbon issue. It is taking us backward in a way, so we are probably going to see less dispersed value chains. We are also seeing the increased specialization of clusters in different locations, and because it is less efficient to ship goods around all parts of the world we are probably going to see a re-deepening of clusters. (Porter, interview with authors)

Interestingly, although Porter's work has for many years discussed the globalization of competition, it has continually been focused on the practices of large multinationals, and has given short shrift to the internationalization practices and propensities of many SMEs that are often key actors within clusters.

13.7 Regions and clusters

In recent years Porter has expended considerable effort in seeking to 'prove' that clusters exist on-the-ground, and that firms operating within them achieve superior performance (Porter 2003; Delgado et al. 2007, 2010). Although he still appears to feel he has some way to go in convincing his desired audience, Porter may also want to increase the time spent in further developing the theory behind clusters – especially a theory that is transferable to management audiences. Importantly, despite his own resistance to economic modeling, he is now seriously engaged in the use of such techniques to measure cluster effects and performance:

> We have now developed a methodology for identifying clusters and the boundaries of clusters based on a very simple but very powerful idea; that is, if you find industries co-located over and over again, it is a pretty good sign there are externalities. My more recent research with Mercedes Delgado and Scott Stern finds that clusters are fundamental at both the industry and the regional level; they affect employment and patenting. We also find that a region with a series of strong clusters that are overlapping performs better than a region with strong clusters that do not overlap. Similarly, clusters in neighboring and adjacent regions also matter. For example, if you have a strong auto cluster in your location, also having a strong auto cluster next door, has an even greater positive impact on performance. So, there is the pure cluster effect, the cluster overlap effect, and the neighbor effect. (Porter, interview with authors)

According to Porter (2008b: 252), 'anything that can be efficiently sourced from a distance . . . has been essentially nullified as a competitive advantage in advanced economies.' To our minds, this overlooks the fact that knowledge sourced from a distance is not necessarily readily available to all knowledge seekers. Indeed, the capability to identify and source knowledge efficiently at a distance may be highly varied depending on the location within which a firm is situated. Therefore, although we partly agree with Porter (2008b: 253) that 'the enduring competitive advantages in a global economy are often heavily local, arising from concentrations of highly specialized skills and knowledge', he overlooks the fact that the capability to access knowledge from global sources is in fact highly related to these local advantages. In fact, this capability remains a very important competitive advantage restricted to a relatively small band of regions with the existing stock of knowledge, networks, and absorptive capacity to efficiently identify, access, and utilize such global sources (Huggins and Izushi 2007; Huggins 2008).

While it is all well and good for more 'lucky' regions (Storper 1997) to establish clusters that are able to simultaneously circulate knowledge from both localized and globalized sources, an initial prerequisite for less lucky regions is to develop mechanisms to access the type of knowledge required to stimulate economic development which lies outside their borders. A limitation of the cluster approach is the emphasis that it places on local- and regional-level networks to access knowledge, as opposed to access through networks that are geographically wider.

It is our consideration that linking more explicitly the concept of the value system, which Porter previewed in *Competitive Advantage* (Porter 1985a), and clusters, would provide a more satisfactory theoretical understanding of the nature of geographically defined linkages across firms and other actors. Porter (2008*b*) does go some way to addressing this when he states that clusters consist of upstream suppliers and downstream channels and customers, alongside more horizontal links with institutions such as universities and training providers. However, he never goes as far as mapping the flows of value, which is understandable given the complex data and methodological constraints, although he nonetheless has a strong view on the causes of performance differences across locations:

> There is a big literature on what causes regional performance. There is the Jacobs effect – which concerns the diversity and heterogeneity of regional economies – and the specialization effect. These two have been pitted against each other. We believe this is the wrong formulation. It is not whether you are specialized in a particular industry versus whether you have a diverse urban economy, but the configuration of clusters of related industries. (Porter, interview with authors)

A key point made by Christian Ketels in his chapter is that the future academic legacy of Porter's cluster concept will rely on reconnecting his ideas with related scholarly approaches. For Porter, such connection will be strongly influenced by his ability to provide quantifiable evidence to other scholars of the impact of clusters on locational performance:

> A meta question regarding my competitiveness work relates to the measurement frontier, and further statistical analysis. This is going to be the key to taking this work to the next level of acceptance and impact. A lot of economists want to see empirical testing. We have been focused on measuring competitiveness and clusters, and looking at their impacts statistically using the best available methodologies and techniques. (Porter, interview with authors)

A more conceptual problem raised by Ron Martin and Peter Sunley in their chapter is that Porter's cluster model and views on regional competitive advantage do not assign due justice to already advanced thinking in the field. Similar to Martin and Sunley's view that Porter takes a rather primitive view of theories of comparative advantage, others argue that his view of international trade is similarly outdated (Davies and Ellis 2000). While it is possible to dispute both assertions, these criticisms are interesting when considering more closely the evolution of Porter's thinking. For instance, Porter's development (1990*a*) of the Diamond framework in *The Competitive Advantages of Nations* led to a wave of criticism from researchers of international business, who argued that the Diamond model lacks applicability in nations that rely heavily on their multinationals, the activities of which are necessarily undertaken beyond national boundaries.

The key protagonist in this debate was Alan Rugman (1991, 1992), who suggested the idea of double-diamond models that cross international borders, particularly to account for Foreign Direct Investment. Interestingly, and importantly, twenty years after the publication of *The Competitive Advantage of Nations*, Porter has become increasingly concerned with the nature and role of cross-border connectivity:

> The Diamond was absolutely relevant to multinational corporations, because it referred to the attributes of location in whatever nations a multinational operates in. Weaknesses in the home Diamond may cause a multinational to lose global competitiveness. Increasingly, multinationals relocate business unit headquarters to other countries as a means of seeking out the best Diamond. In my more recent work we have examined cross-national economic integration with neighboring countries, and the extent to which the business environment in a given nation can be affected by coordination with neighboring nations. For example, if you have a road system that goes to a border and then stops it is not as productive as if there were a road on the other side of that border that connects to other population centers. Therefore, there is a need, for example, for power grids and logistical networks to be coordinated across neighboring nations, in order to maximize the productivity of a particular location. In other words, there is a unit of analysis we can call 'the neighborhood' across which economic coordination occurs. (Porter, interview with authors)

13.8 Countering the critics

Building on, rather than departing from, his earlier work is crucial to Porter, and each of his three key books (Porter 1980a; 1985a; 1990a) open with a presentation of the main frameworks, beginning with the Five Forces. In their chapter, Omar Aktouf and colleagues argue that Porter's methodological approach in relation to the Five Forces framework has innate inadequacies that render the prescriptive power of his tools to be at best weak. While we understand the reasoning behind this view, we have considerable sympathy with Porter's argument that his research has built upon an in-depth understanding of the studied industries:

> Everything I do embodies a normative framework. There is always a pretty clear performance objective, whether it is productivity or profitability. I very much believe in economics, but I do not believe in being tied to a particular methodology in addressing complicated problems. I am not against models, rigor, and statistical testing at all, but I do think that methodology should be the tail not the dog. It has been a little uncomfortable for me over the years, taking the incoming missiles on that dimension, but what is greatly heartening is acceptance by actors in the real world. Whenever I meet someone who tells how the insights from one of my books or articles made them wealthy because they achieved this incredible competitive edge, it makes my day. (Porter, interview with authors)

As Stonehouse and Snowdon (2007) indicate, Porter is often criticized by scholars of organizational behavior, even though the key fundamentals of his work do not seek to contribute to or comment on this field of study. As Robert Hoskisson and colleagues indicate in their chapter, Porter's aims largely lie beyond organizational behavior concerns.

Such criticism is common across most of Porter's work, whereby one school of thought seeks to criticize him in relation to one particular aspect of his thinking. The complexity of the phenomena he is seeking to understand has necessarily resulted in the eclectic nature of his thinking and writing, which has often compounded the level of criticism. In his chapter, Nicolai Foss suggests that a downside of such eclecticism is that taken as a whole Porter's writings and tools can be seen as lacking a degree of consistency, especially with regard to their theoretical roots and underpinnings. The generic strategy framework, for instance, came in for particular criticism, especially with evidence from Japan suggesting that some firms are able to successfully combine both differentiation and low cost (Stonehouse and Snowdon 2007):

> When I came back into the strategy field after *The Competitive Advantage of Nations* I was motivated by the critique of the generic strategies concept. The dominant critique at the time was the possibility that a firm can be low cost and differentiated at the same time. That was a puzzle and led me to the notion of operational effectiveness versus strategic positioning. In the process of thinking about this I started focusing on the question of the underlying roots of strategy itself. The article 'What is strategy?' (Porter 1996b) is really the start of the third major generation in my work. (Porter, interview with authors)

Porter (1991) is continuously careful to avoid referring to his theoretical constructs – such as the Five Forces, the Value Chain, and the Diamond – as models, instead preferring the term 'frameworks'. This approach appears to allow him the flexibility to add new variables to these frameworks, which he categorizes as sub-factors underlying his core factors or forces. This has led to criticisms that rather than building theory and analysis, Porter is responsible for creating exhaustive, and not always original, laundry lists, and then passing them off as an explanation (Davies and Ellis 2000; *The Economist*, 8 October 1994, cited in Cho and Moon 2000: 98). Conversely, he is critical of attempts by some economists to build economic models that are divorced from the experiences of managers:

> Where economists often go wrong when undertaking work similar to mine is to select variables as key drivers in their model that are orthogonal to the experiences of managers. For instance, concepts like externalities and institutions are completely meaningless to practitioners. (Porter, interview with authors)

Porter is himself also somewhat critical of competing perspectives on firm-level strategy, in addition to those relating to the RBV. For instance, he is skeptical of the recent work on *Blue Ocean Strategy*, and the notion of uncontested market space, developed by Kim and Mauborgne (2005):

> I think the *Blue Ocean Strategy* idea has added little to our understanding at the theory level. It is about positioning, and leaves out industry structure. It basically says that firms need to compete in different ways from their competitors. Of course, this is what we have been saying for a long time, at least back to generic strategies. Business people like Blue Ocean because it is intuitively understandable. My work can get a bit dry and geeky. (Porter, interview with authors)

Our view is that while a number of the criticisms of Porter's work are valid, they are almost an inevitable outcome for a scholar who has sought to build bridges across wide disciplinary valleys. His efforts have provided others with a toolbox of frameworks to explore in more depth the nature of competition and competitive advantage from a range of challenging yet accessible vantage points:

> In management there are different genres of books, and I have always been on the more complicated, difficult, and elaborate end of the spectrum, whilst still trying to be accessible. The challenge I always face is how to cut into problems in a way that allows me to be general. The Five Forces is meant to be a general theory of industry structure that applies to any industry. We know, however, that any industry has tens of thousands of differences, so how do we cut into this in a way that practitioners can get their arms around, but which is also complete and does not result in key omissions. I try to keep my ideas accessible, but there is other work that reduces these complicated things to fairly simple concepts such as core competencies and builds entire articles around one idea. My work is orthogonal to these approaches. (Porter, interview with authors)

13.9 Current and future challenges

In many ways, Porter's overarching thesis is quite simple: competition promotes upgrading, or what in later years he more commonly refers to as innovation. According to Porter, competition and innovation, rather than the shifting of costs, lie at the heart of addressing fundamental societal and environmental problems. For instance, on health care he states that competition should weed low-value providers from the system; on the natural environment he argues that pro-innovation forms of regulation are needed to stimulate environmental improvement; on inner-city regeneration he proposes that economic policies based on catalyzing competition, rather than social investment, are the answer.

Porter sees the aim of competition to be the delivery of value. Furthermore, for him, only the right type of competition will prove effective. For instance, in recent years he has argued that only the creation of positive-sum competition will foster the type of innovation required to manage the environment and rectify the ills of the US health care system, which he views as being riddled with the 'wrong type of competition' (Porter 2008b). With respect to health care in the United States, he argues that bad competition is manifested by the active players dividing up value, resulting in a zero-sum game, instead of creating it (Porter and Teisberg 2006a, 2006b).

He is particularly critical of hospitals that have created closed networks inhibiting good competition and not rewarding the best providers (Porter and Teisberg 2006a, 2006b). It could be argued that these networks, which are usually localized in their geographic scope, are in fact an example of clusters, albeit ones that are apparently malfunctioning. Porter calls for changes in health-care strategies as a means of inducing the ingredients for change. However, a number of the recommendations which he makes, such as simplified billing, accessible information, and transparent pricing, appear to relate more to the operational effectiveness of the health-care system rather than a new strategic direction (Porter and Teisberg 2006a, 2006b).

Some of the outstanding challenges and questions with which Porter's work leaves us include those relating to the changing nature of industrial structure and the shift in focus to smaller and more fluid firms producing goods and services with increasingly shorter life cycles in niche markets and industries. Also, as the external environment becomes ever more global in its reach and speed of change, the ability of firms and governments to actually strategically manage within this environment becomes more complex and resource-intensive. Extensions of Porter's existing frameworks will be required to more precisely address where and how strategy and policy-making can make a difference. More widely, one of the outstanding issues resulting from Porter's work is the need for much greater consideration concerning the integration of micro- and macro-level theories of competitiveness. As Porter acknowledges, this is no easy task:

> The problem with measuring competitiveness, if you believe my world-view, is that it is impossibly complicated. There are so many things to measure. For measuring the output of competitiveness, we believe productivity is the ultimate coming together of all the influences, and will be highly correlated with per capita income. To measure the causes of competitiveness there is an impossibly broad set of factors for which there is often little objective data. This is why I got involved in the *Global Competitiveness Report*, because with its executive survey we had the ability to measure some of those factors for which there are usually no objective metrics. (Porter, interview with authors)

In the past, many of those who have sought to criticize Porter have used the Nobel Prize-winning economist Paul Krugman's argument (1994a) that the 'competitiveness' of nations has become a 'dangerous obsession', lacking both theoretical and empirical justification. Therefore, debates have often set Porter and Krugman against each other. In reality, the relationship between the two men appears to be far more respectful, with Krugman having spent some time with Porter at Harvard. Furthermore, Krugman openly acknowledges Porter as a key influence on his own work – particularly in relation to his key theory concerning the economic geography of location choice and increasing returns:

> Michael Porter had given me a manuscript copy of his book on *The Competitive Advantage of Nations*, probably late 1989. I was much taken by the stuff on clusters, and started trying to make a model – I was on a lecture tour, I recall, and worked on it evenings, I started out with complicated models with intermediate goods and all that, but after a few days I realized that these weren't necessary ingredients, that my home market stuff basically provide the necessary. I got stumped for a while by the analytics, and tried numerical examples on a spreadsheet to figure them out. It all came together in a hotel in Honolulu. . . . (Paul Krugman, cited in Brakman et al. 2009: 504)

One outstanding question is whether or not Porter's work is also considered to be of sufficient relevance and quality to be awarded the Nobel Prize for Economics. Although some may consider the majority of his work to be outside the traditional economics rubric, and more aligned with the 'newer' schools of business management, it should be noted that Porter has already been awarded (in 1997) the Adam Smith Prize by the National Association of Business Economists (Stonehouse and Snowdon 2007).

Such are the demands on Porter's time, and such is the wide-ranging nature of his curiosity, he is inevitably juggling a number of quite disparate balls. At the time of writing there is talk of a new strategic management text, but this remains to be published. We would hope that this text attempts to complete the task Porter set himself in his *Strategic Management Journal* article of 1991 (Porter 1991) in seeking to integrate – and adapt as necessary – the key strands of his work. It is debatable as to whether or not he accomplishes this in 1991, and the article reads as two, if not three, distinct parts. As others in this book have alluded to, from an underlying theoretical perspective such integration will require the reconciling of his initial dependence on the industrial organization theory of Bain and Mason with his more recent allegiance to evolutionary theories stemming from the work of Schumpeter (de Man 1994). This return to the mainstream strategy field is clearly a task he is keen to achieve:

> There is another phase of strategy research which has not seen the light of day yet because of other distractions. This phase looks at the interface between strategy and organization, and seeks to understand why so many companies do not have a clear strategy. These are issues we have recognized in the field for many years but

have not done much about. I have taken another rather large detour into the area of health-care delivery, but it is deeply informed by everything that came before. Also, I am learning things about strategy and competition from the health care work that I did not know. So hopefully we will have another chapter in the strategy work. (Porter, interview with authors)

References

Abernathy, W. J. and Utterback, J. M. (1978) 'Patterns of industrial innovation', *Technology Review*, 80(7), 40–7.

Adams, F. G., Gangnes, B., and Shachmurove, Y. (2006) 'Why is China so competitive? Measuring and explaining China's competitiveness', *World Economy*, 29(2), 95–122.

Aghion, P. and Howitt, P. (1992) 'A model of growth through creative destruction', *Econometrica*, 60(2), 323–51.

Aguayo, R. (1990) *Dr. Deming: The American Who Taught the Japanese About Quality*, Secaucus, NJ: Carol Publishing Group.

Aiginger, K. (2006*a*) 'Revisiting an evasive concept: Introduction to the special issue on competitiveness', *Journal of Industry, Competition and Trade*, 6(2), 63–6.

—— (2006*b*) 'Competitiveness: From a dangerous obsession to a welfare creating ability with positive externalities', *Journal of Industry, Competition and Trade*, 6(2), 161–77.

Ambrosini, V. and Bowman, C. (2009) 'What are dynamic capabilities and are they a useful construct in strategic management?', *International Journal of Management Reviews*, 11(1), 29–49.

Amit, R. and Zott, C. (2001) 'Value creation in e-business', *Strategic Management Journal*, 22(6/7), 493–520.

Andersen, E. S. (1994) *Evolutionary Economics: Post-Schumpeterian Contributions*, London: Pinter Publishers.

—— Dalum, B., and Villumsen, G. (1981*a*) *International Specialization and the Home Market*, Aalborg: Aalborg University Press.

—— —— —— (1981*b*) 'The importance of the home market for technological development and the export specialization of manufacturing industry', in Freeman, C. (ed.) *Technological Innovation and National Economic Performance*, Aalborg: Aalborg University Press, pp. 53–102.

Andrews, K. (1971) *The Concepts of Corporate Strategy*, Homewood, IL: Dow Jones-Irwin.

Ansoff, H. I. (1965) *Corporate Strategy: An Analytic Approach to Business Policy for Growth and Expansion*, New York, NY: McGraw-Hill.

Argyres, N. and McGahan, A. M. (2002*a*) 'Introduction: Michael Porter's *Competitive Strategy*', *Academy of Management Executive*, 16(2), 41–2.

—— —— (2002*b*) 'An interview with Michael Porter', *Academy of Management Executive*, 16(2), 43–52.

Arrow, K. (1962) 'The economic implications of learning by doing', *Review of Economic Studies*, 29(3), 155–73.

Asheim, B. T. (1996) 'Industrial districts as "learning regions": A condition for prosperity', *European Planning Studies*, 4(4), 379–400.

—— and Coenen, L. (2005) 'Knowledge bases and regional innovation systems: Comparing Nordic clusters', *Research Policy*, 34(8), 1173–90.

—— Boschma, R., and Cooke, P. (2009) 'Constructing regional advantage: Platform policies based on related variety and differentiated knowledge bases', Utrecht University Papers in Evolutionary Economic Geography 07.09.

—— Cooke, P., and Martin, R. (eds.) (2006a) *Clusters and Regional Development: Critical Reflections and Explorations*, London: Routledge.

—— —— —— (2006b) 'The rise of the cluster concept', in Asheim, B., Cooke, P., and Martin, R. L. (eds.) *Clusters and Regional Development*, London: Routledge, pp. 1–29.

Audretsch, D. and Feldman, M. (2003) 'Knowledge spillovers and the geography of innovation', in Henderson, V. and Thisse, J. F. (eds.) *Handbook of Regional and Urban Economics*, Amsterdam: Elsevier Publishing, pp. 2713–39.

Austrian, Z. (2000) 'Cluster case studies: The marriage of quantitative and qualitative information for action', *Economic Development Quarterly*, 14(1), 97–110.

Aydalot, P. and Keeble, D. (eds.) (1988) *High Technology Industry and Innovative Environments: The European Experience*, London: Routledge.

Bain, J. S. (1956) *Barriers to New Competition, Their Character and Consequences in Manufacturing Industries*, Cambridge, MA: Harvard University Press.

—— (1959) *Industrial Organization*, New York, NY: Wiley.

—— (1968) *Industrial Organization* (2nd edition), New York, NY: Wiley.

Balassa, B. (1965) 'Trade liberalization and revealed comparative advantage', *The Manchester School*, 33(2), 99–123.

Baldwin, R. (2006) 'Globalisation: The Great Unbundling(s)', Paper prepared for the Finnish EU Presidency, Prime Minister's Office, Helsinki.

Baldwin, R. E. (2008) *The Development and Testing of the Heckscher-Ohlin Models: A Review*, Cambridge, MA: MIT Press.

Baldwin, R., Forslid, R., Martin, P., Ottaviano, G., and Robert-Nicoud, F. (2003) *Economic Geography and Public Policy*, Princeton, NJ: Princeton University Press.

Baptista, R. and Swann, P. (1998) 'Do firms in clusters innovate more?', *Research Policy*, 27(5), 525–40.

Barnard, C. I. (1938) *The Functions of the Executive*, Cambridge, MA: Harvard University Press.

—— (1968) *The Functions of the Executive* (30th anniversary edition), Cambridge, MA: Harvard University Press.

Barnett, W. P. and Burgelman, R. A. (1996) 'Evolutionary perspectives on strategy', *Strategic Management Journal*, 17(Summer Special Issue), 5–19.

Barney, J. B. (1986a) 'Strategic factor markets: Expectations, luck and business strategy', *Management Science*, 32(10), 1231–41.

—— (1986b) 'Types of competition and the theory of strategy: Toward an integrative framework', *Academy of Management Review*, 11(4), 791–800.

—— (1991) 'Firm resources and sustained competitive advantage', *Journal of Management*, 17(1), 99–120.

—— (2001) 'Resource-based theories of competitive advantage: A ten-year retrospective on the resource-based view', *Journal of Management*, 27(6), 643–50.

—— (2002*a*) *Gaining and Sustaining Competitive Advantage* (2nd edition), Englewood Cliffs, NJ: Prentice-Hall.

—— (2002*b*) 'Strategic management: From informed conversation to academic discipline', *Academy of Management Executive*, 16(2), 53–7.

—— and Hoskisson, R. E. (1990) 'Strategic groups: Untested assertions and research proposals', *Managerial and Decision Economics*, 11(3), 187–98.

Barrell, R., Choy, A., Holland, D., and Riley, R. (2005) 'The sterling effective exchange rate and other measures of UK competitiveness', *National Institute Economic Review*, 191(1), 54–63.

Bartlett, C. A. and Ghoshal, S. (1989) *Managing across Borders: The Transnational Solution*, Boston, MA: Harvard Business School Press.

—— —— (2002) 'Strategic advantage', *Executive Excellence*, 19(7), 7–8.

Bathelt, H., Malmberg, A., and Maskell, P. (2004) 'Clusters and knowledge: Local buzz, global pipelines and the process of knowledge creation', *Progress in Human Geography*, 28(1), 31–56.

Baum, J. A. C. and Korn, H. J. (1996) 'Competitive dynamics of interfirm rivalry', *Academy of Management Journal*, 39(2), 255–91.

Baumol, W. J. (2002) *The Free Market Innovation Machine: Analyzing the Growth Miracle of Capitalism*, Princeton, NJ: Princeton University Press.

Beal, B. D. and Gimeno, J. (2001) 'Geographic agglomeration, knowledge spillovers, and competitive evolution', INSEAD Working Paper 2001/26/SM.

Beaudry, C. and Breschi, S. (2003) 'Are firms in clusters really more innovative?', *Economics of Innovation and New Technology*, 12(4), 325–42.

Becattini, G. (1990) 'The Marshallian district as a socio-economic notion', in Pyke, F. S., Becattini, G., and Sengenberger, W. (eds.) *Industrial Districts and Inter-firm Co-operation in Italy*, Geneva: International Institute for Labor Studies, pp. 37–51.

Beise-Zee, R. and Rammer, C. (2006) 'Local user-producer interaction in innovation and export performance of firms', *Small Business Economics*, 27(2–3), 207–22.

Belussi, F. (2006) 'In search of a useful theory of spatial clustering: Agglomeration versus active clustering', in Asheim, B., Cooke, P., and Martin, R. (eds.) *Clusters and Regional Development: Critical Reflections and Explorations*, London: Routledge, pp. 69–89.

Benneworth, P. and Henry, N. (2004) 'Where is the value added in the cluster approach? Hermeneutic theorising, economic geography and clusters as a multi-perspectival approach', *Urban Studies*, 41(5/6), 1011–23.

Bennis, W. and O'Toole, J. (2005) 'How business schools lost their way', *Harvard Business Review*, 83(5), 96–104.

Berger, S. (2006) *How We Compete: What Companies Around the World are Doing to Make it in Today's Global Economy*, New York, NY: Currency Doubleday.

Berle, A. A. and Means, G. C. (1932) *The Modern Corporation and Private Property*, New York, NY: Macmillan.

Bernheim, D. and Whinston, M. D. (1990) 'Multimarket contact and collusive behavior', *RAND Journal of Economics*, 21(1), 1–26.

Best, M. H. (2001) *The New Competitive Advantage: The Renewal of American Industry*, Oxford: Oxford University Press.

Bettis, R. A. and Hitt, M. A. (1995) 'The new competitive landscape', *Strategic Management Journal*, 16(Summer Special Issue), 7–19.

Biggadike, E. R. (1981) 'The contributions of marketing to strategic management', *Academy of Management Review*, 6(4), 621–32.

Blanke, J and Loades, E. (2004) 'Capturing the state of country competitiveness with the executive opinion survey', In Porter, M. E., Schwab, K., Sala-i-Martin, X., and Lopez-Claros, A. (eds.) *The Global Competitiveness Report 2004–05*, New York, NY: Palgrave Macmillan, pp. 199–208.

—— and Sala-i-Martin, X. (2009) 'Examining Africa's competitiveness', in World Economic Forum (ed.) *The Africa Competitiveness Report 2009*, New York, NY: Palgrave Macmillan, pp. 3–29.

Boeker, W., Goodstein, J., Stephan, J., and Murmann, J. P. (1997) 'Competition in a multimarket environment: The case of market exit', *Organization Science*, 8(2), 126–42.

Boltho, A. (1996) 'The assessment: International competitiveness', *Oxford Review of Economic Policy*, 12(3), 1–16.

Boschma, R. (2004) 'Competitiveness of regions from an evolutionary perspective', *Regional Studies*, 38(9), 1001–14.

Bower, J. L. (1982) 'Business policy in the 1980s', *Academy of Management Review*, 7(4), 630–8.

Bowman, E. H. (1981) 'Competitive strategy: Techniques for analyzing industries and competitors (Review)', *Sloan Management Review*, 22(3), 65–8.

—— Singh, H., and Thomas, H. (2002) 'The domain of strategic management: History and evolution', in Pettigrew, A., Thomas, H., and Whittington, R. (eds.) *Handbook of Strategy and Management*, London: Sage, pp. 31–51.

Boyd, H. W. (1981) '*Competitive Strategy* (Review)', *Journal of Business Strategy*, 1(3), 85–6.

Brakman, S., Garretsen, H., and van Marrewijk, C. (2009) *The New Introduction to Geographical Economics*, Cambridge, MA: Cambridge University Press.

Bramanti, A. and Ratti, R. (1997) 'The multi-faced dimensions of local development', in Ratti, R., Bramanti, A., and Gordon, R. (eds.) *The Dynamics of Innovative Regions: The GREMI Approach*, Aldershot: Ashgate, pp. 3–44.

Brandenburger, A. (2002) 'Porter's added value: High indeed!', *Academy of Management Executive*, 16(2), 58–60.

—— and Nalebuff, B. (1996) *Co-opetition*, New York, NY: Doubleday.

Brander, J. (1981) 'Intra-industry trade in identical commodities', *Journal of International Economics*, 11(1), 1–14.

—— and Eaton, J. (1984) 'Product line rivalry', *American Economic Review*, 74(3), 323–34.

Braunerhjelm, P. and Carlsson, B. (1999) 'Industry clusters in Ohio and Sweden, 1975–1995', *Small Business Economics*, 12(4), 279–93.

—— and Feldman, M. P. (eds.) (2006) *Cluster Genesis: Technology-Based Industrial Development*, Oxford: Oxford University Press.

Bresnahan, T. and Gambardella, A. (eds.) (2004) *Building High-Tech Clusters: Silicon Valley and Beyond*, Cambridge, MA: Cambridge University Press.

——— and Schmalensee, R. (1987) 'The empirical renaissance in industrial economics: An overview', *The Journal of Industrial Economics*, 35(4), 371–8.

Bristow, G. (2005) 'Everyone's a "winner": Problematising the discourse of regional competitiveness', *Journal of Economic Geography*, 5(3), 285–304.

Brülhart, M. (2009) 'Is the new economic geography passé?', 7 January, available at http://www.voxeu.org/index.php?q=node/2759.

Bulow, J. I., Geanakoplos, J. D., and Klemperer, P. D. (1985) 'Multimarket oligopoly: Strategic substitutes and complements', *Journal of Political Economy*, 93(3), 488–511.

Bunnell, T. G. and Coe, N. M. (2001) 'Spaces and scales of innovation', *Progress in Human Geography*, 25(4), 569–89.

Cairncross, F. (1997) *The Death of Distance: How the Communication Revolution Will Change Our Lives*, Boston, MA: Harvard Business School Press.

Camagni, R. (2002*a*) 'Territorial competitiveness, globalisation and local milieux', *European Spatial Research and Policy*, 9(2), 63–90.

——— (2002*b*) 'On the concept of territorial competitiveness: Sound or misleading?', *Urban Studies*, 39(13), 2395–411.

——— (ed.) (1991) *Innovation Networks: Spatial Perspectives*, London: Belhaven Press.

Camerer, C. and Weigelt, K. (1988) 'Experimental tests of a sequential equilibrium reputation model', *Econometrica*, 56(1), 1–36.

Canina, L., Enz, C. A., and Harrison, J. S. (2005) 'Agglomeration effects and strategic orientations: Evidence from the U.S. lodging industry', *Academy of Management Journal*, 48(4), 565–81.

Cannella, Jr., A. A. and Hambrick, D. C. (1993) 'Effects of executive departures on the performance of acquired firms', *Strategic Management Journal*, 14 (Summer Special Issue), 137–52.

Capello, R. (1999) 'Spatial transfer of knowledge in high technology milieux: Learning versus collective learning processes', *Regional Studies*, 33(4), 353–65.

Cappellin, R. (1998) 'The transformation of local production systems: International networking and territorial competitiveness', in Steiner, M. (ed.) *Clusters and Regional Specialisation: On Geography, Technology and Networks*, London: Pion, pp. 57–80.

Caves, R. E. (1984) 'Industrial organization, corporate strategy and structure', in Lamb, R. B. (ed.) *Competitive Strategic Management*, Englewood Cliffs, NJ: Prentice-Hall Inc., pp. 134–70.

——— and Porter, M. E. (1976) 'Barriers to exit', in Masson, R. T. and Qualls, P. D. (eds.) *Essays on Industrial Organization in Honor of Joe S. Bain*, Cambridge, MA: Ballinger, pp. 36–69.

——— ——— (1977) 'From entry barriers to mobility barriers: Conjectural decisions and contrived deterrence to new competition', *Quarterly Journal of Economics*, 91(2), 241–61.

——— ——— (1978) 'Market structure, oligopoly, and stability of market shares', *Journal of Industrial Economics*, 26(4), 289–313.

——— ——— (1980) 'The dynamics of changing seller concentration', *Journal of Industrial Economics*, 29(1), 1–15.

——— Khalilzadeh-Shirazi, J., and Porter, M. E. (1975) 'Scale economies in statistical analyses of market power', *Review of Economics and Statistics*, 57(2), 133–40.

—— Gale, B. T., and Porter, M. E. (1977) 'Interfirm profitability differences: Comment', *Quarterly Journal of Economics*, 91(4), 667–75.

——— Porter, M. E., and Spence, A. M. (1980) *Competition in the Open Economy: A Model Applied to Canada*, Cambridge, MA: Harvard University Press.

Cellini, R. and Soci, A. (2002) 'Pop competitiveness', *Banca Nazionale del Lavoro Quarterly Review*, 55(220), 71–101.

Chakravarthy, B., Mueller-Stewens, G., Lorange, P., and Lechner, C. (eds.) (2003) *Strategy Process: Shaping the Contours of the Field*, Oxford: Blackwell Publishing.

Chamberlin, E. H. (ed.) (1954) *Monopoly and Competition and their Regulation: Papers and Proceedings of a Conference Held by the International Economic Association*, London: Macmillan.

Chandler, A. D. (1962) *Strategy and Structure: Chapters in the History of the Industrial Enterprise*, Cambridge, MA: MIT Press.

Chen, M.-J. (1996) 'Competitor analysis and interfirm rivalry: Toward a theoretical integration', *Academy of Management Review*, 21(1), 100–34.

Chesbrough, H. (2003) *Open Innovation: The New Imperative for Creating and Profiting from Technology*, Boston, MA: Harvard Business School Press.

Chesnais, F. (1986) 'Science, technology and competitiveness', *STI Review*, (1), 85–129.

Cho, D.-S. and Moon, H.-C. (2000) *From Adam Smith to Michael Porter: Evolution of Competitiveness Theory*, London: World Scientific.

Christopherson, S., Garretson, H., and Martin, R. (2008) 'The world is not flat: Putting globalization in its place', *Cambridge Journal of Regions Economy and Society*, 1(3), 343–9.

Coase, R. H. (1937) 'The nature of the firm', *Economica*, 4(16), 386–405.

Cohen, S. S. (1994) 'Speaking freely', *Foreign Affairs*, 73(4), 194–7.

Cohen, W. M. and Levinthal, D. A. (1990) 'Absorptive capacity: A new perspective on learning and innovation', *Administrative Science Quarterly*, 35(1), 128–52.

Collier, D. (1981) '*Competitive Strategy* (Book Review)', *Journal of Business Strategy*, 1(4), 85–8.

Commission on Growth and Development (2008) *The Growth Report: Strategies for Sustained Growth and Inclusive Development*, Washington, DC: World Bank.

Commons, J. R. (1924) *Legal Foundations of Capitalism*, New York, NY: Macmillan.

Conner, K. R. (1991) 'A historical comparison of resource-based theory and five schools of thought within industrial organization economics: Do we have a new theory of the firm?', *Journal of Management*, 17(1), 121–54.

Cooke, P. (1995) 'Keeping to the high road: Learning, reflexivity and associative governance in regional economic development', in Cooke, P. (ed.) *The Rise of the Rustbelt: Revitalizing Older Industrial Regions*, London: UCL Press, pp. 231–45.

—— (2002) *Knowledge Economies: Clusters, Learning and Cooperative Advantage*, London: Routledge.

—— (2007) 'To construct regional advantage from innovation systems first build policy platforms', *European Planning Studies*, 15(2), 179–94.

—— and Morgan, K. (1994) 'The regional innovation system in Baden-Württemberg', *International Journal of Technology Management*, 9(3/4), 394–429.

——— (1998) *The Associational Economy: Firms, Regions, and Innovation*, Oxford: Oxford University Press.

—— Heidenreich, M., and Braczyk, H.-J. (eds.) (2004) *Regional Innovation Systems: The Role of Governance in a Globalized World* (2nd edition), London: Routledge.

Cool, K. O. and Schendel, D. (1987) 'Strategic group formation and performance: The case of the U.S. pharmaceutical industry, 1963–1982', *Management Science*, 33(9), 1102–24.

Cooper, A. C. and Folta, T. B. (2000) 'Entrepreneurship and high-technology clusters', in Sexton, D. L. and Landstrom, H. (eds.) *The Blackwell Handbook of Entrepreneurship*, Oxford: Blackwell Publishers, pp. 349–67.

Cortright, J. (2006) 'Making sense of clusters: Regional competitiveness and economic development', Discussion paper prepared for the Brookings Institution Metropolitan Policy Program, Washington, DC: Brookings Institution.

Courant, P. N. and Deardorff, A. V. (1992) 'International trade with lumpy countries', *Journal of Political Economy*, 100(1), 198–210.

Crafts, N. (2005) 'The "death of distance": What does it mean for economic development?', *World Economics*, 6(3), 1–14.

Crevoisier, O. (2004) 'The innovative milieus approach: Toward a territorialized understanding of the economy?', *Economic Geography*, 80(4), 367–79.

Cullen, J. (1998) 'Promoting competitiveness for small business clusters through collaborative learning: Policy consequences from a European perspective', in Steiner, M. (ed.) *Clusters and Regional Specialisation: On Geography, Technology and Networks*, London: Pion, pp. 238–53.

Cyert, R. M. and March, J. G. (1963) *A Behavioral Theory of the Firm*, Englewood Cliffs, NJ: Prentice-Hall.

D'Aveni, R. A. (1994) *Hypercompetition: Managing the Dynamics of Strategic Maneuvering*, New York, NY: Free Press.

D'Este, P. and Patel, P. (2007) 'University-industry linkages in the UK: What are the factors underlying the variety of interactions with industry?', *Research Policy*, 36(9), 1295–313.

Dahmén, E. (1970) *Entrepreneurial Activity and the Development of Swedish Industry 1919–1939*, Homewood, IL: American Economic Association Translation Series.

Daily, C. M., Dalton, D. R., and Rajagopalan, N. (2003) 'Governance through ownership: Centuries of practice, decades of research', *Academy of Management Journal*, 46 (2), 151–8.

DATAR and Ministère de l'Economie, des Finances et de l'Industrie (2005) '71 clusters', Available at http://www.competitivite.gouv.fr/spip.php?rubrique36&lang=en

Davies, A. (2006) 'A review of national cluster policies: Why are they popular – again?', GOV/TDPC, 12, Paris: OECD.

Davies, H. and Ellis, P. (2000) 'Porter's *Competitive Advantage of Nations*: Time for the final judgement?', *Journal of Management Studies*, 37(8), 1189–213.

Davis, J. H., Schoorman, F. D., and Donaldson, L. (1997) 'Toward a stewardship theory of management', *Academy of Management Review*, 22(1), 20–47.

de Jong, H. W. and Shepherd, W. G. (eds.) (2007) *Pioneers of Industrial Organization: How the Economics of Competition and Monopoly Took Shape*, Cheltenham: Edward Elgar.

de Man, A.-P. (1994) '1980, 1985, 1990: A Porter exegesis', *Scandinavian Journal of Management*, 10(4), 437–50.

Dean, T. J., Brown, R. L., and Bamford, C. E. (1998) 'Differences in large and small firm responses to environmental context: Strategic implications from a comparative analysis of business formations', *Strategic Management Journal*, 19(8), 709–28.

Delanty, G. (1997) *Social Science: Beyond Constructivism and Realism*, Minneapolis, MN: University of Minnesota Press.

Delgado, M., Porter, M. E., and Stern, S. (2007) 'Clusters, convergence, and economic performance', Cambridge, MA: NBER, manuscript.

—— —— —— (2010) 'Clusters and entrepreneurship', *Journal of Economic Geography*, 10(4), 495–518.

Deming, W. E. (1986) *Out of the Crisis: Quality, Productivity and Competitive Position*, Cambridge, MA: Cambridge University Press.

Demsetz, H. (1973) 'Industry structure, market rivalry, and public policy', *Journal of Law and Economics*, 16(1), 1–9.

den Hertog, P. and Remøe, S. (eds.) (2001) *Innovative Clusters: Drivers of National Innovation Systems*, Paris: OECD.

Dicken, P. (1986) *Global Shift: Industrial Change in a Turbulent World*, New York, NY: Harper & Row.

—— (1992) *Global Shift: The Internationalization of Economic Activity* (2nd edition), New York, NY: Guilford Press.

—— (2007) *Global Shift: Mapping the Changing Contours of the World Economy* (5th edition), New York, NY: Guilford Press.

Dierickx, I. and Cool, K. (1989) 'Asset stock accumulation and sustainability of competitive advantage', *Management Science*, 35(12), 1504–11.

Dosi, G. (2000) *Innovation, Organization and Economic Dynamics: Selected Essays*, Cheltenham: Edward Elgar.

—— and Soete, L. (1988) 'Technical change and international trade', in Dosi, G., Freeman, C., Nelson, R., Silverberg, G., and Soete, L. (eds.) *Technical Change and Economic Theory*, London: Pinter, pp. 401–31.

—— Freeman, C., Nelson, R. R., Silverberg, G., and Soete, L. (eds.) (1988) *Technical Change and Economic Theory*, London: Pinter Publishers.

DTI (1995) *Competitiveness: Forging Ahead*, Cm 2867, London: HMSO.

—— (2005) *Regional Competitiveness and the State of the Regions*, London: Department of Trade and Industry, available at http://www.dti.gov.uk/sd/rci

Duranton, G. (2009) 'California dreamin: The feeble case for cluster policies', Working paper, Toronto: University of Toronto.

Dutton, J. E., Fahey, L., and Narayanan, V. K. (1983) 'Toward understanding strategic issue diagnosis', *Strategic Management Journal*, 4(4), 307–23.

Dyer, J. H. and Singh, H. (1998) 'The relational view: Cooperative strategy and sources of interorganizational competitive advantage', *Academy of Management Review*, 23(4), 660–79.

Edquist, C. (ed.) (1997) *Systems of Innovation: Technologies, Institutions and Organizations*, London: Pinter.

Edwards, C. D. (1955) 'Conglomerate bigness as a source of power', in Universities-National Bureau Committee for Economic Research (ed.) *Business Concentration and Price Policy: A conference of the Universities-National Committee for Economic Research*, Princeton, NJ: Princeton University Press, pp. 331–52.

Eisenhardt, K. M. (1989) 'Agency theory: An assessment and review', *Academy of Management Review*, 14(1), 57–74.

—— and Martin, J. A. (2000) 'Dynamic capabilities: What are they?', *Strategic Management Journal*, 21(10/11), 1105–21.

Eliashberg, J. and Chatterjee, R. (1985) 'Analytical models of competition with implications for marketing: Issues, findings, and outlook', *Journal of Marketing Research*, 22(3), 237–61.

Ellison, G. and Glaeser, E. L. (1997) 'Geographic concentration in U.S. manufacturing industries: A dartboard approach', *Journal of Political Economy*, 105(5), 889–927.

Eltis, W. and Higham, D. (1995) 'Closing the UK competitiveness gap', *National Institute Economic Review*, 154, 71–83.

Ely, R. T. (1903) *Studies in the Evolution of Industrial Society*, New York, NY: Macmillan.

Enright, M. J. (1996) 'Regional clusters and economic development: A research agenda', in Staber, U. H., Schaefer, N. V., and Sharma, B. (eds.) *Business Networks: Prospects for Regional Development*, Berlin: Walter de Gruyter, pp. 190–213.

—— (1998) 'Regional clusters and firm strategy', in Chandler, A. D., Hagström, P., and Sölvell, Ö. (eds.) *The Dynamic Firm: The Role of Technology, Strategy, Organization, and Regions*, Oxford: Oxford University Press, pp. 315–42.

—— (2000) 'The globalization of competition and the localization of competitive advantage: Policies towards regional clustering', in Hood, N. and Young, S. (eds.) *The Globalization of Multinational Enterprise Activity and Economic Development*, New York, NY: St. Martin's Press, pp. 303–31.

Enz, C. A. (1986) 'Strategy textbooks: A case of consistently inconsistent evaluations', *Academy of Management Review*, 11(1), 226–37.

Eriksson, R. and Lindgren, U. (2009) 'Localized mobility clusters: Impacts of labour market externalities on firm performance', *Journal of Economic Geography*, 9(1), 33–53.

Etzioni, A. (1961) *A Comparative Analysis of Complex Organizations: On Power, Involvement, and their Correlates*, New York, NY: Free Press.

European Commission (2002) *Regional Clusters in Europe*, Observatory of European SMEs 2002, No. 3, Luxembourg: Office for Official Publications of the European Communities.

—— (2003a) *European Competitiveness Report 2003*, Brussels: European Communities.

—— (2003b) *Final Report of the Expert Group on Enterprise Clusters and Networks*, Brussels: European Commission.

—— (2004) *A New Partnership for Cohesion: Convergence, Competitiveness and Cooperation*, Brussels: European Commission.

—— (2007) *Innovation Clusters in Europe: A Statistical Analysis and Overview of Current Policy Support*, DG Enterprise and Industry Report, Brussels: European Commission.

—— (2008) 'The concept of clusters and cluster policies and their role for competitiveness and innovation: Main statistical results and lessons learned', Europe INNOVA/PRO INNO Europe Paper, No. 9, Commission Staff Working Document SEC (2008) 2637, Brussels: European Commission.

Fagerberg, J. (1988) 'International competitiveness', *Economic Journal*, 98(391), 355–74.

—— (1992) 'The "home-market hypothesis" reexamined', in Lundvall, B.-Å. (ed.) *National Systems of Innovation – Towards a Theory of Innovation and Interactive Learning*, London: Pinter, pp. 226–41.

—— (1994) 'Domestic demand, learning and comparative advantage', in Johansson, B., Karlsson, C., and Westin, L. (eds.) *Patterns of a Network Economy*, Berlin-Heidelberg: Springer.

—— (1995) 'User-producer interaction, learning and comparative advantage', *Cambridge Journal of Economics*, 19(1), 243–56.

—— (1996) 'Technology and competitiveness', *Oxford Review of Economic Policy*, 12(3), 39–51.

Fama, E. F. (1980) 'Agency problems and the theory of the firm', *Journal of Political Economy*, 88, 288–307.

Farjoun, M. (1994) 'Beyond industry boundaries: Human expertise, diversification and resource-related industry groups', *Organization Science*, 5(2), 185–99.

Fayol, H. (1949) *General and Industrial Management*, New York, NY: Pitman.

Feldman, M. P. and Francis, J. L. (2004) 'Homegrown solutions: Fostering cluster formation', *Economic Development Quarterly*, 18(2), 127–37.

—— —— (2006) 'Entrepreneurs as agents in the formation of industrial clusters', in Asheim, B., Cooke, P., and Martin, R. (eds.) *Clusters and Regional Development: Critical Reflections and Explorations*, London: Routledge, pp. 115–36.

—— —— and Bercovitz, J. (2005) 'Creating a cluster while building a firm: Entrepreneurs and the formation of industrial clusters', *Regional Studies*, 39(1), 129–41.

Feser, E. J. (1998*a*) 'Enterprises, external economies, and economic development', *Journal of Planning Literature*, 12(3), 283–302.

—— (1998*b*) 'Old and new theories of industry clusters', in Steiner, M. (ed.) *Clusters and Regional Specialisation: On Geography, Technology and Networks*, London: Pion, pp. 18–40.

—— and Bergman, E. M. (2000) 'National industry cluster templates: A framework for applied regional cluster analysis', *Regional Studies*, 34(1), 1–19.

—— and Luger, M. I. (2003) 'Cluster analysis as a mode of inquiry: Its use in science and technology policymaking in North Carolina', *European Planning Studies*, 11(1), 11–24.

—— and Sweeney, S. H. (2002) 'Theory, methods and a cross-metropolitan comparison of business clustering', in McCann, P. (ed.) *Industrial Location Economics*, Cheltenham: Edward Elgar, pp. 222–59.

Fiegenbaum, A. and Thomas, H. (1995) 'Strategic groups as reference groups: Theory, modeling and empirical examination of industry and competitive strategy', *Strategic Management Journal*, 16(6), 461–76.

Finkelstein, S. and Hambrick, D. C. (1996) *Strategic Leadership: Top Executives and Their Effects on Organizations*, St. Paul, MN: West Publishing.

Florida, R. (2002) *The Rise of the Creative Class: And How It's Transforming Work, Leisure, Community and Everyday Life*, New York, NY: Basic Books.

Floyd, S., Roos, J., Jacobs, C., and Kellermanns, F. (eds.) (2004) *Innovating Strategy Process*, Oxford: Blackwell Publishing.

Folta, T. B., Cooper, A. C., and Baik, Y.-S. (2006) 'Geographic cluster size and firm performance', *Journal of Business Venturing*, 21(2), 217–42.

Foss, N. J. (1996*a*) 'More critical comments on knowledge-based theories of the firm', *Organization Science*, 7(5), 519–23.

—— (1996*b*) 'Research in strategy, economics, and Michael Porter', *Journal of Management Studies*, 33(1), 1–24.

—— (1996c) 'Whither the competitive perspective?', in Foss, N. J. and Knudsen, C. (eds.) *Towards a Competence Theory of the Firm*, London:Routledge, pp. 175–200.

—— (1996d) 'Higher-order industrial capabilities and competitive advantage', *Journal of Industry Studies*, 3(1), 1–20.

—— (1998) 'The resource-based perspective: An assessment and diagnosis of problems', *Scandinavian Journal of Management*, 14(3), 133–49.

—— (1999) 'Edith Penrose, economics and strategic management', *Contributions to Political Economy*, 18(1), 87–104.

—— (2000) 'Equilibrium vs. evolution in the resource-based perspective: The conflicting legacies of Demsetz and Penrose', in Foss, N. J. and Robertson, P. L. (eds.) *Resources, Technology, and Strategy: Explorations in the Resource-based Perspective*, London: Routledge, pp. 11–30.

—— and Eriksen, B. (1995) 'Competitive advantage and industry capabilities', in Montgomery, C. A. (ed.) *Resource-Based and Evolutionary Theories of the Firm: Towards a Synthesis*, Boston, MA: Kluwer Academic Publishers, pp. 43–69.

—— and Ishikawa, I. (2007) 'Towards a dynamics resource-based view: Insights from Austrian capital and entrepreneurship theory', *Organization Studies*, 28(5), 749–72.

—— Knudsen, C., and Montgomery, C. A. (1995) 'An exploration of common ground: Integrating evolutionary and strategic theories of the firm', in Montgomery, C. A. (ed.) *Resource-Based and Evolutionary Theories of the Firm: Towards a Synthesis*, Boston, MA: Kluwer Academic Publishers, pp. 1–17.

Foster, L., Haltiwanger, J., and Syverson, C. (2008) 'Reallocation, firm turnover, and efficiency: Selection on productivity or profitability?', *American Economic Review*, 98(1), 394–425.

Fox, H. W. (1982) '*Competitive Strategy* – Book Review', *Journal of Marketing*, 46(3), 124.

Frenken, K., Van Oort, F., and Verburg, T. (2007) 'Related variety, unrelated variety and regional economic growth', *Regional Studies*, 41(5), 685–97.

Frideres, L. (2010) 'Clusters and the competitiveness of firms: A case study of software clusters in the Luxembourg Greater Region', Unpublished PhD thesis, Department of Geography, University of Cambridge.

Fried, V. H. and Oviatt, B. M. (1989) 'Michael Porter's missing chapter: The risk of antitrust violations', *Academy of Management Executive*, 3(1), 49–56.

Friedman, M. (1953) *Essays in Positive Economics*, Chicago, IL: University of Chicago Press.

Friedman, T. L. (2005) *The World is Flat: A Brief History of the Twenty-First Century*, New York, NY: Farrar, Straus, and Giroux.

Fröbel, F., Heinrichs, J., and Kreye, O. (1980) *The New International Division of Labour: Structural Unemployment in Industrialised Countries and Industrialisation in Developing Countries*, Cambridge, MA: Cambridge University Press.

Fromhold-Eisebith, M. and Eisebith, G. (2005) 'How to institutionalize innovative clusters? Comparing explicit top-down and implicit bottom-up approaches', *Research Policy*, 34(8), 1250–68.

Fujita, M., Krugman, P., and Venables, A. (1999) *The Spatial Economy: Cities, Regions, and International Trade*, Cambridge, MA: MIT Press.

Funderberg, R. G. and Boarnet, M. G. (2008) 'Agglomeration potential: The spatial scale of industry linkages in the Southern California economy', *Growth and Change*, 39(1), 24–57.

Furman, J. L., Porter, M. E., and Stern, S. (2002) 'The determinants of national innovative capacity', *Research Policy*, 31(6), 899–933.

Furrer, O., Thomas, H., and Goussevskaia, A. (2008) 'The structure and evolution of the strategic management field: A content analysis of 26 years of strategic management research', *International Journal of Management Reviews*, 10(1), 1–23.

Galbraith, J. K. (1967) *The New Industrial State*, Boston, MA: Houghton Mifflin.

Ganley, W. T. (2004) 'The theory of business enterprise and Veblen's neglected theory of corporation finance', *Journal of Economic Issues*, 38(2), 397–403.

Gartner, W. B. (1985) 'Review: [untitled]', *Academy of Management Review*, 10(4), 873–5.

Gavetti, G. and Levinthal, D. A. (2004) 'The strategy field from the perspective of management science: Divergent strands and possible integration', *Management Science*, 50(10), 1309–18.

Gelsing, L. (1992) 'Innovation and the development of industrial networks', in Lundvall, B.-Å. (ed.) *National Systems of Innovation: Towards a Theory of Innovation and Interactive Learning*, London: Pinter, pp. 116–28.

Gereffi, G., Humphrey, J., Kaplinsky, R., and Sturgeon, T. J. (2001) 'Introduction: Globalisation, value chains and development', *IDS Bulletin*, Special Issue, 32(3), 1–8.

Geroski, P. A. (1991) *Market Dynamics and Entry*, Oxford: Basil Blackwell.

—— and Pomroy, R. (1990) 'Innovation and the evolution of market structure', *Journal of Industrial Economics*, 38(3), 299–314.

Gertler, M. A. and Wolfe, D. A. (2006) 'Spaces of knowledge flows: Clusters in a global context', in Asheim, B., Cooke, P., and Martin, R. (eds.) *Clusters and Regional Development: Critical Reflections and Explorations*, London: Routledge, pp. 218–35.

Ghemawat, P. (1986) 'Sustainable advantage', *Harvard Business Review*, 64(5), 53–8.

—— (1991) 'Resources and strategy: An IO perspective', Mimeo, Harvard Business School.

—— (1997) *Games Businesses Play: Cases and Models*, Cambridge, MA: MIT Press.

—— (2002) 'Competition and business strategy in historical perspective', *Business History Review*, 76(1), 37–74.

Ghoshal, S. (2005) 'Bad management theories are destroying good management practices', *Academy of Management Learning & Education*, 4(1), 75–91.

Gilbert, B. A., McDougall, P. P., and Audretsch, D. B. (2008) 'Clusters, knowledge spillovers and new venture performance: An empirical examination', *Journal of Business Venturing*, 23(4), 405–22.

Gimeno, J. (1994) 'Multipoint competition, market rivalry and firm performance: A test of the mutual forbearance hypothesis in the United States airline industry, 1984–1988', Unpublished PhD dissertation, Purdue University.

—— (2004) 'Competition within and between networks: The contingent effect of competitive embeddedness on alliance formation', *Academy of Management Journal*, 47(6), 820–42.

—— and Woo, C. Y. (1996) 'Hypercompetition in a multimarket environment: The role of strategic similarity and multimarket contact in competitive de-escalation', *Organization Science*, 7(3), 322–41.

Ginsberg, A. and Venkatraman, N. (1985) 'Contingency perspectives of organizational strategy: A critical review of the empirical research', *Academy of Management Review*, 10(3), 421–34.

Giuliani, E. (2005) 'Cluster absorptive capacity: Why do some clusters forge ahead and others lag behind?', *European Urban and Regional Studies*, 12(3), 269–88.

—— (2007) 'The selective nature of knowledge networks in clusters: Evidence from the wine industry', *Journal of Economic Geography*, 7(2), 139–68.

Glaeser, E. L. (2008) *Cities, Agglomeration, and Spatial Equilibrium*, Oxford: Oxford University Press.

—— (2010) *Agglomeration Economics*, Chicago, IL: University of Chicago Press.

—— and Gottlieb, J. D. (2009) 'The wealth of cities: Agglomeration economies and spatial equilibrium in the United States', *Journal of Economic Literature*, 47(4), 983–1028.

Gordon, I. R. and McCann, P. (2005) 'Innovation, agglomeration, and regional development', *Journal of Economic Geography*, 5(5), 523–43.

Grant, R. M. (1991) 'Porter's "Competitive Advantage of Nations": An assessment', *Strategic Management Journal*, 12(7), 535–48.

Greening, T. (1980) 'Diversification, strategic groups and the structure-conduct-performance relationship: A synthesis', *Review of Economics and Statistics*, 62(3), 475–7.

Greer, D. F. and Rhoades, S. A. (1976) 'Concentration and productivity changes in the long and short run', *Southern Economic Journal*, 43(2), 1031–44.

Grilo, I. and Koopman, G. J. (2006) 'Productivity and microeconomic reforms: Strengthening EU competitiveness', *Journal of Industry, Competition and Trade*, 6(2), 67–84.

Grimm, C. M. and Smith, K. G. (1997) *Strategy as Action: Industry Rivalry and Coordination*, Cincinnati, OH: South-Western College Publishing.

Grossman, G. M. and Helpman, E. (1991) *Innovation and Growth in the Global Economy*, Cambridge, MA: MIT Press.

Grubel, H. G. (1967) 'Intra-industry specialization and the pattern of trade', *Canadian Journal of Economics and Political Science*, 33(2), 374–88.

—— and Lloyd, P. J. (1975) *Intra-industry Trade: The Theory and Measurement of International Trade in Differentiated Products*, London: Macmillan.

Gulati, R. and Singh, H. (1998) 'The architecture of cooperation: Managing coordination costs and appropriation concerns in strategic alliances', *Administrative Science Quarterly*, 43(4), 781–814.

HM Treasury (2001) *Productivity in the UK: 3 – The Regional Dimension*, London: HM Treasury.

—— (2003) *Productivity in the UK: 4 – The Local Dimension*, London, HM Treasury.

—— (2004) *Devolving Decision Making: Meeting the Regional Economic Challenge – Increasing Regional and Local Flexibility*, London: HM Treasury.

Habermas, J. (1990) *Moral Consciousness and Communicative Action*, Cambridge, MA: MIT Press.

Håkansson, H. (ed.) (1987) *Industrial Technology Development – A Network Approach*, London: Croom Helm.

Haleblian, J. and Finkelstein, S. (1993) 'Top management team size, CEO dominance, and firm performance: The moderating roles of environmental turbulence and discretion', *Academy of Management Journal*, 36(4), 844–63.

Hambrick, D. C. (1994) '1993 Presidential address: What if the Academy actually mattered', *Academy of Management Review*, 19(1), 11–16.

—— and Cannella, Jr., A. A. (2004) 'CEOs who have COOs: Contingency analysis of an unexplored structural form', *Strategic Management Journal*, 25(10), 959–79.

—— and Mason, P. A. (1984) 'Upper echelons: The organization as a reflection of its top managers', *Academy of Management Review*, 9(2), 193–206.

Hamel, G. and Prahalad, C. K. (1985) 'Do you really have a global strategy?', *Harvard Business Review*, 63(4), 139–48.

Hamermesh, R. G. (1983) 'Introduction', in Hamermesh, R. G. (ed.) *Strategic Management*, New York, NY: John Wiley & Sons, pp. 1–9.

Hands, D. W. (1988) 'Ad hocness in economics and the Popperian tradition', in de Marchi, N. (ed.) *The Popperian Legacy in Economics: Papers Presented at a Symposium in Amsterdam, December 1985*, Cambridge, MA: Cambridge University Press, pp. 121–37.

Harrigan, K. R. and Porter, M. E. (1983) 'End-game strategies for declining industries', *Harvard Business Review*, 61(4), 111–20.

Harrison, B. (1992) 'Industrial districts: Old wine in new bottles?', *Regional Studies*, 26 (5), 469–83.

—— (1994) *Lean and Mean: The Changing Landscape of Corporate Power in the Age of Flexibility*, New York, NY: Basic Books.

Hatten, K. J. (1974) 'Strategic models in the brewing industry', Unpublished PhD dissertation, Purdue University.

—— and Hatten, M. L. (1987) 'Strategic groups, asymmetrical mobility barriers and contestability', *Strategic Management Journal*, 8(4), 329–42.

—— and Schendel, D. E. (1977) 'Heterogeneity within an industry: Firm conduct in the U.S. brewing industry, 1952–71', *Journal of Industrial Economics*, 26(2), 97–113.

—— —— and Cooper, A. C. (1978) 'A strategic model of the U.S. brewing industry: 1952–1971', *Academy of Management Journal*, 21(4), 592–610.

Hausmann, R. and Klinger, B. (2007) 'The structure of the product space and the evolution of comparative advantage', CID Working Paper No. 146, Cambridge, MA: Center for International Development, Harvard University.

—— Rodrik, D., and Velasco, A. (2005) 'Growth diagnostics', Working paper, Cambridge, MA: John F. Kennedy School of Government, Harvard University.

Heckscher, E. (1919) 'The effects of foreign trade on the distribution of income', *Ekonomisk Tidskrift*, 21, 497–512. (A complete translation is available in Flam, H. and Flanders, M. J. (eds.) (1991) *Heckscher-Ohlin Trade Theory*, Cambridge, MA: MIT Press, pp. 39–69).

Helfat, C. E. and Peteraf, M. A. (2003) 'The dynamic resource-based view: Capability lifecycles', *Strategic Management Journal*, 24(10), 997–1010.

Helpman, E. (2004) *The Mystery of Economic Growth*, Cambridge, MA: Harvard University Press.

—— and Krugman, P. R. (1989) *Trade Policy and Market Structure*, Cambridge, MA: MIT Press.

Henderson, B. D. (1981) '*Competitive Strategy* (Book Review)', *Journal of Business Strategy*, 1(4), 84–5.

Hendry, C. and Brown, J. (2006) 'Dynamics of clustering and performance in the UK opto-electronics industry', *Regional Studies*, 40(7), 707–25.

—— —— and DeFillippi, R. (2000) 'Regional clustering of high technology-based firms: Opto-electronics in three countries', *Regional Studies*, 34(2), 129–44.

Hendry, J. (1990) 'The problem with Porter's generic strategies', *European Management Journal*, 8(4), 443–50.

Hertz, D. B. (1981) '*Competitive Strategy* (Review)', *Journal of Business Strategy*, 1(3), 86–8.

High Level Advisory Group on Clusters (2008) *The European Cluster Memorandum*, Brussels: European Commission.

Hirschman, A. O. (1958) *The Strategy of Economic Development*, New Haven, CT: Yale University Press.

Hitt, M. A. (1998) 'Twenty-first century organizations: Business firms, business schools, and the academy', *Academy of Management Review*, 23(2), 218–24.

—— Keats, B. W., and DeMarie, S. M. (1998) 'Navigating in the new competitive landscape: Building strategic flexibility and competitive advantage in the 21st century', *Academy of Management Executive*, 12(4), 22–42.

—— Ireland, R. D., Camp, S. M., and Sexton, D. L. (2001) 'Strategic entrepreneurship: Entrepreneurial strategies for creating wealth', *Strategic Management Journal*, 22(6/7), 479–91.

—— —— —— —— (eds.) (2002) *Strategic Entrepreneurship: Creating a New Mindset*, Oxford: Blackwell Publishing.

Hofer, C. W. and Schendel, D. (1978) *Strategy Formulation: Analytical Concepts*, St. Paul, MN: West Publishing.

Horovitz, J. (1984) 'New perspectives on strategic management', *Journal of Business Strategy*, 4(3), 19–33.

Hoskisson, R. E. and Turk, T. A. (1990) 'Corporate restructuring: Governance and control limits of the internal capital market', *Academy of Management Review*, 15(3), 459–77.

—— Hill, C. W. L., and Kim, H. (1993) 'The multidivisional structure: Organizational fossil or source of value?', *Journal of Management*, 19(2), 269–98.

—— Hitt, M. A., Wan, W. P., and Yiu, D. (1999) 'Theory and research in strategic management: Swings of a pendulum', *Journal of Management*, 25(3), 417–56.

—— —— Johnson, R. A., and Grossman, W. (2002) 'Conflicting voices: The effects of institutional ownership heterogeneity and internal governance on corporate innovation strategies', *Academy of Management Journal*, 45(4), 697–716.

Hospers, G.-J., Desrochers, P., and Sautet, F. (2009) 'The next Silicon Valley? On the relationship between geographical clustering and public policy', *International Entrepreneurship Management Journal*, 5(3), 285–99.

Hout, T., Porter, M. E., and Rudden, E. (1982) 'How global companies win out', *Harvard Business Review*, 60(5), 98–108.

Huggins, R. (2003) 'Creating a UK Competitiveness Index: Regional and local benchmarking', *Regional Studies*, 37(1), 89–96.

—— (2008) 'The evolution of knowledge clusters: Progress and policy', *Economic Development Quarterly*, 22(4), 277–89.

—— and Davies, W. (2006) *European Competitiveness Index 2006–07*, Pontypridd: Robert Huggins Associates.

—— and Izushi, H. (2007) *Competing for Knowledge: Creating, Connecting, and Growing*, London: Routledge.

—— —— (2008) *UK Competitiveness Index 2008*, Cardiff: Centre for International Competitiveness, University of Wales Institute, Cardiff.

—— —— Davies, W., and Shougui, L. (2008) *World Knowledge Competitiveness Index 2008*, Cardiff: Centre for International Competitiveness, Cardiff, University of Wales Institute, Cardiff.

Humphrey, J. and Schmitz, H. (2000) 'Governance and upgrading: Linking industrial cluster and value chain research', IDS Working Paper No. 120, Brighton: Institute of Development Studies, University of Sussex.

Hunt, M. S. (1972) 'Competition in the major home appliance industry, 1960–1970', Unpublished PhD dissertation, Harvard University.

Hunt, S. D. and Morgan, R. M. (1995) 'The comparative advantage theory of competition', *Journal of Marketing*, 59(2), 1–15.

—— —— (1997) 'Resource-advantage theory: A snake swallowing its tail or a general theory of competition?', *Journal of Marketing*, 61(4), 74–82.

IMD (2009) *World Competitiveness Yearbook 2009*, Lausanne: International Institute for Management Development.

Institute for Competitiveness and Prosperity (2002) 'A view of Ontario: Ontario's clusters of innovation', Working Paper No. 1, Toronto: Institute for Competitiveness and Prosperity.

Ireland, R. D., Hitt, M. A., and Vaidyanath, D. (2002) 'Alliance management as a source of competitive advantage', *Journal of Management*, 28(3), 413–46.

Jacobs, J. (1969) *The Economy of Cities*, New York, NY: Random House.

Jacobson, R. (1992) 'The "Austrian" school of strategy', *Academy of Management Review*, 17(4), 782–807.

Jemison, D. B. (1981*a*) 'The contributions of administrative behavior to strategic management', *Academy of Management Review*, 6(4), 633–42.

—— (1981*b*) 'The importance of an integrative approach to strategic management research', *Academy of Management Review*, 6(4), 601–8.

Jensen, M. C. and Meckling, W. H. (1976) 'Theory of the firm: Managerial behavior, agency costs and ownership structure', *Journal of Financial Economics*, 3(4), 305–60.

Johnston, J. (1984) *Econometric Methods*, New York, NY: McGraw-Hill.

Julien, P.-A. (2007) *A Theory of Local Entrepreneurship in the Knowledge Economy*, Cheltenham: Edward Elgar.

Kaldor, N. and Mirrlees, J. A. (1962) 'A new model of economic growth', *Review of Economic Studies*, 29(3), 174–92.

Kamien, M. I. and Schwartz, N. (1982) *Market Structure and Innovation*, Cambridge: Cambridge University Press.

Kaplan, S. and Norton, D. (1996) *The Balanced Scorecard: Translating Strategy into Action*, Boston, MA: Harvard Business School Press.

Karnani, A. and Wernerfelt, B. (1985) 'Multiple point competition', *Strategic Management Journal*, 6(1), 87–96.

Keeble, D. and Nachum, L. (2002) 'Why do business service firms cluster? Small consultancies, clustering and decentralization in London and Southern England', *Transactions of the Institute of British Geographers*, New Series, 27(1), 67–90.

—— and Wilkinson, F. (1999) 'Collective learning and knowledge development in the evolution of regional clusters of high technology SMEs in Europe', *Regional Studies*, 33 (4), 295–303.

Kesner, I. F. and Sebora, T. C. (1994) 'Executive succession: Past, present, & future', *Journal of Management*, 20(2), 327–72.

Ketels, C. (2005) 'Finding the right match', in Passow, S. and Runnbeck, M. (eds.) *What's Next? Strategic Views on Foreign Direct Investment*, Stockholm: Invest in Sweden Agency, pp. 104–15.

—— (2006) 'Michael Porter's competitiveness framework – Recent learnings and new research priorities', *Journal of Industry, Competition and Trade*, 6(2), 115–36.

—— (2007) *The Role of Clusters in the Chemical Industry*, Report made available at the 41st Annual Meeting of the European Petrochemical Association, Brussels: European Petrochemical Association.

—— (2009a) *Clusters, Cluster Policy, and Swedish Competitiveness*, Expert Report No. 30, Stockholm: Swedish Globalization Council.

—— (2009b) *State of the Region Report 2009: Boosting the Top of Europe*, Report prepared for the Baltic Development Forum in collaboration with the Nordic Council of Ministers and the Nordic Investment Bank, Copenhagen: Baltic Development Forum.

—— Lindqvist, G., and Sölvell, Ö. (2006) *Cluster Initiatives in Developing and Transition Economies*, Stockholm: Center for Strategy and Competitiveness, Stockholm School of Economics.

Khurana, R. (2007) *From Higher Aims to Hired Hands: The Social Transformation of American Business Schools and the Unfulfilled Promise of Management as a Profession*, Princeton, NJ: Princeton University Press.

Kiechel III, W. (1981) 'Three (or four, or more) ways to win', *Fortune*, 104(8, October 19), 181–8.

Kim, W. C. and Mauborgne, R. (2005) *Blue Ocean Strategy: How to Create Uncontested Market Space and Make the Competition Irrelevant*, Boston, MA: Harvard Business School Press.

Kirzner, I. M. (1973) *Competition and Entrepreneurship*, Chicago, IL: University of Chicago Press.

Kitson, M., Martin, R. L., and Tyler, P. (2004) 'Regional competitiveness: An elusive yet key concept?', *Regional Studies*, 38(9), 991–9.

Klein, J. (2001) 'A critique of *Competitive Advantage*', Paper presented at Critical Management Studies Conference, July 11–13, Manchester.

Kogut, B. (1985) 'Designing global strategies: Comparative and competitive value-added chains', *Sloan Management Review*, 26(4), 15–38.

—— (1988) 'Joint ventures: Theoretical and empirical perspectives', *Strategic Management Journal*, 9(4), 319–32.

—— and Zander, U. (1992) 'Knowledge of the firm, combinative capabilities, and the replication of technology', *Organization Science*, 3(3), 383–97.

Konakayama, A. and Chen, T.-Y. (2007) 'Is Hsinchu industrial cluster a planned public policy product?', *Journal of the Faculty of Political Science and Economics, Tokai University*, 39, 91–109.

Koschatzky, K. (2005) 'Foresight as a governance concept at the interface between global challenges and regional innovation potentials', *European Planning Studies*, 13 (4), 619–39.

Kotter, J. P. (1982) *The General Managers*, New York, NY: Free Press.

Kraaijenbrink, J., Spender, J.-C., and Groen, A. J. (2010) 'The resource-based view: A review and assessment of its critiques', *Journal of Management*, 36(1), 349–72.

Krause, D. J. (1996) *Sun Tzu: The Art of War for Executives*, London: Nicholas Brealey.

Krugman, P. (1979) 'Increasing returns, monopolistic competition, and international trade', *Journal of International Economics*, 9(4), 469–79.

—— (1980) 'Scale economies, product differentiation, and the pattern of trade', *American Economic Review*, 70(5), 950–9.

—— (1987*a*) 'Is free trade passé?', *Journal of Economic Perspectives*, 1(2), 131–44.

—— (1987*b*) 'The narrow moving band, the Dutch disease, and the competitive consequences of Mrs. Thatcher', *Journal of Development Economics*, 27(1–2), 41–55.

—— (1990) *Rethinking International Trade*, Cambridge, MA: MIT Press.

—— (1991) *Geography and Trade*, Cambridge, MA: MIT Press.

—— (1994*a*) 'Competitiveness: A dangerous obsession', *Foreign Affairs*, 73(2), 28–44.

—— (1994*b*) 'Proving my point', *Foreign Affairs*, 73(4), 198–203.

—— (1994*c*) 'What do undergrads need to know about trade?', *American Economic Review*, 83(2), 23–6.

—— (1996*a*) *Pop Internationalism*, Cambridge, MA: MIT Press.

—— (1996*b*) 'Making sense of the competitiveness debate', *Oxford Review of Economic Policy*, 12(3), 17–25.

—— (2005) 'Second winds for industrial regions?', in Coyle, D., Alexander, W., and Ashcroft, B. (eds.) *New Wealth for Old Regions: Scotland's Economic Prospects*, Princeton, NJ: Princeton University Press, pp. 35–47.

—— (2009*a*) 'The increasing returns revolution in trade and geography', *American Economic Review*, 99(3), 561–71.

—— (2009*b*) *The Return of Depression Economics and the Crisis of 2008*, New York, NY: W.W. Norton.

—— (2009*c*) 'Increasing returns in a comparative advantage world', Available at http://www.princeton.edu/~pkrugman/deardorff.pdf

—— and Obstfeld, M. (2009) *International Economics: Theory and Policy* (8th edition), Boston, MA: Pearson Addison Wesley.

Krumme, G. and Hayter, R. (1975) 'Implications of corporate strategies and product cycle adjustments for regional employment changes', in Collins, L. and Walker, D. F. (eds.) *Locational Dynamics of Manufacturing Activity*, New York, NY: John Wiley, pp. 325–56.

Kuhn, T. S. (1962) *The Structure of Scientific Revolutions*, Chicago, IL: University of Chicago Press.

Lachmann, L. M. (1956) *Capital and its Structure*, London: London School of Economics and Political Science, University of London, G. Bell and Sons.

—— (1976) 'From Mises to Shackle: An essay on Austrian economics and the kaleidic society', *Journal of Economic Literature*, 14(1), 54–62.

Lagendijk, A. (2006) 'Learning from conceptual flow in regional studies: Framing present debates, unbracketing past debates', *Regional Studies*, 40(4), 385–99.

—— and Cornford, J. (2000) 'Regional institutions and knowledge – Tracking new forms of regional development policy', *Geoforum*, 31(2), 209–18.

Lakatos, I. (1970) 'Falsification and the methodology of scientific research programmes', in Lakatos, I. and Musgrave, A. (eds.) *Criticism and the Growth of Knowledge*, Cambridge: Cambridge University Press, pp. 91–195.

Lall, S. (2001) 'Competitiveness indices and developing countries: An economic evaluation of the Global Competitiveness Report', *World Development*, 29(9), 1501–25.

Lamb, R. B. (ed.) (1984) *Competitive Strategic Management*, Englewood Cliffs, NJ: Prentice-Hall.

Landabaso, M. (2001) 'Clusters in less prosperous places: Policy options in planning and implementation', Draft, Brussels, European Commission.

Langlois, R. N. (2003) 'Strategy as economics versus economics as strategy', *Managerial and Decision Economics*, 24(4), 283–90.

Laudan, L. (1977) *Progress and Its Problems: Toward a Theory of Scientific Growth*, Berkeley, CA: University of California Press.

Lawson, C. (1999) 'Towards a competence theory of the region', *Cambridge Journal of Economics*, 23(2), 151–66.

—— and Lorenz, E. (1999) 'Collective learning, tacit knowledge and regional innovative capacity', *Regional Studies*, 33(4), 305–17.

Leamer, E. E. (1984) *Sources of International Comparative Advantage: Theory and Evidence*, Cambridge, MA: MIT Press.

—— (2007) 'A flat world, a level playing field, a small world after all, or none of the above? A review of Thomas L. Friedman's *The World is Flat*', *Journal of Economic Literature*, 45(1), 83–126.

—— and Levinsohn, J. (1994) 'International trade theory: The evidence', National Bureau of Economic Research Working Paper, No. 4940.

Learned, E. P., Christensen, C. R., Andrews, K. R., and Guth, W. D. (1965/1969) *Business Policy: Text and Cases* (rev. ed.), Homewood, IL: Richard D. Irwin.

Lee, C.-Y. (2009) 'Do firms in clusters invest in R&D more intensively? Theory and evidence from multi-country data', *Research Policy*, 38(7), 1159–71.

Lei, D., Hitt, M. A., and Bettis, R. A. (1996) 'Dynamic core competences through meta-learning and strategic context', *Journal of Management*, 22(4), 549–69.

Leo, J. E. (1982) 'Review of Porter, Michael E.: *Competitive Strategy*', *Industrial Marketing Management*, 11(4), 318–19.

Levitt, T. (1983) 'The globalization of markets', *Harvard Business Review*, 61(3), 92–102.

Lewis, W. (1981) 'Review: [untitled]', *Strategic Management Journal*, 2(1), 93–5.

Lewis, W. W. (2004) *The Power of Productivity: Wealth, Poverty, and the Threat to Global Stability*, Chicago, IL: University of Chicago Press.

Lin, J. Y. (2009) *Economic Development and Transition: Thought, Strategy, and Viability*, Cambridge, MA: Cambridge University Press.

—— and Wang, Y. (2008) 'China's integration with the world: Development as a process of learning and industrial upgrading', Policy Research Working Paper, No. 4799, Washington, DC: World Bank.

Linder, S. B. (1961) *An Essay on Trade and Transformation*, Uppsala: Almquist & Icksell.

Lippman, S. A. and Rumelt, R. P. (1982) 'Uncertain imitability: An analysis of interfirm differences in efficiency under competition', *Bell Journal of Economics*, 13(2), 418–38.

List, F. (1841) *Das Nationale System der Politischen Okonomie*, Stuttgart/Tubingen: J. G. Cotta.

Llewellyn, J. (1996) 'Tackling Europe's competitiveness', *Oxford Review of Economic Policy*, 12(3), 87–96.

Loasby, B. J. (1976) *Choice, Complexity, and Ignorance: An Enquiry into Economic Theory and the Practice of Decision-Making*, Cambridge, MA: Cambridge University Press.

Locke, R. R. (1996) *The Collapse of the American Management Mystique*, New York, NY: Oxford University Press.

Lu, J. W. and Beamish, P. W. (2004) 'International diversification and firm performance: The S-curve hypothesis', *Academy of Management Journal*, 47(4), 598–609.

Lundquist, K.-J. and Olander, L.-O. (1999) 'Firms, regions and competitiveness: A broadbrush approach', *Geografiska Annaler: Series B, Human Geography*, 81(3), 145–64.

Lundvall, B.-Å. (1985) *Product Innovation and User-Producer Interaction*, Aalborg: Aalborg University Press.

—— (1988) 'Innovation as an interactive process – From user–producer interaction to the National System of Innovation', in Dosi, G., Freeman, C., Nelson, R., Silverberg, G., and Soete, L. (eds.) *Technical Change and Economic Theory*, London: Pinter, pp. 349–69.

—— (ed.) (1992*a*) *National Systems of Innovation: Towards a Theory of Innovation and Interactive Learning*, London: Pinter.

—— (1992*b*) 'User-producer relationships, national systems of innovation and internationalization', in Lundvall, B.-Å. (ed.) *National Systems of Innovation: Towards a Theory of Innovation and Interactive Learning*, London: Pinter, pp. 45–67.

—— and Johnson, B. (1994) 'The learning economy', *Journal of Industry Studies*, 1(2), 23–42.

Maddison, A. (2007) *Contours of the World Economy, 1–2030 AD: Essays in Macro-Economic History*, Oxford: Oxford University Press.

Mahoney, J. T. (1993) 'Strategic management and determinism: Sustaining the conversation', *Journal of Management Studies*, 30(1), 173–91.

—— and Pandian, J. R. (1992) 'The resource-based view within the conversation of strategic management', *Strategic Management Journal*, 13(5), 363–80.

Mahroum, S., Huggins, R., Clayton, N., Pain, K., and Taylor, P. (2008) *Innovation by Adoption: Measuring and Mapping Absorptive Capacity in UK Nations and Regions*, London: National Endowment for Science, Technology and the Arts.

Maillat, D. (1995) 'Territorial dynamic, innovative milieus and regional policy', *Entrepreneurship and Regional Development*, 7(2), 157–65.

Malecki, E. J. (1984) 'High technology and local economic development', *Journal of the American Planning Association*, 50(3), 262–9.

—— (1991) *Technology and Economic Development: The Dynamics of Local, Regional, and National Change*, Essex: Longman Scientific & Technical.

—— (1997) *Technology and Economic Development: The Dynamics of Local, Regional, and National Competitiveness* (2nd edition), Essex: Addison-Wesley Longman.

—— (2004) 'Jockeying for position: What it means and why it matters to regional development policy when places compete', *Regional Studies*, 38(9), 1101–20.

—— (2007) 'Cities and regions competing in the global economy: Knowledge and local development policies', *Environment and Planning C: Government and Policy*, 25(5), 638–54.

—— and Hospers, G.-J. (2007) 'Knowledge and the competitiveness of places', in Rutten, R. and Boekema, F. (eds.) *The Learning Region: Foundations, State of the Art, Future*, Cheltenham: Edward Elgar, pp. 143–59.

—— and Varaiya, P. (1986) 'Innovation and changes in regional structure', in Nijkamp, P. (ed.) *Handbook of Regional and Urban Economics*, Vol. 1, *Regional Economics*, Amsterdam: North-Holland, pp. 629–45.

Malmberg, A. and Maskell, P. (2002) 'The elusive concept of localization economies: Towards a knowledge-based theory of spatial clustering', *Environment and Planning A*, 34(3), 429–49.

—— and Power, D. (2006) 'True clusters: A severe case of conceptual headache', in Asheim, B., Cooke, P., and Martin, R. (eds.) *Clusters and Regional Development: Critical Reflections and Explorations*, London: Routledge, pp. 50–68.

—— Sölvell, Ö., and Zander, I. (1996) 'Spatial clustering, local accumulation of knowledge and firm competitiveness', *Geografiska Annaler, Series B, Human Geography*, 78(2), 85–97.

Maneschi, A. (1998) *Comparative Advantage in International Trade: A Historical Perspective*, Cheltenham: Edward Elgar.

—— (2000) 'How new is the "new trade theory" of the past two decades?', Working Paper 00-W27, Department of Economics, Vanderbilt University, Nashville.

March, J. G. and Simon, H. A. (1958) *Organizations*, New York, NY: Wiley.

Marengo, L., Dosi, G., Legrenzi, P., and Pasquali, C. (2000) 'The structure of problem-solving knowledge and the structure of organizations', *Industrial and Corporate Change*, 9(4), 757–88.

Markham, J. W. and Papanek, G. F. (eds.) (1970) *Industrial Organization and Economic Development: In Honor of E. S. Mason*, Boston, MA: Houghton Mifflin Company.

Markusen, A. (1996a) 'Interaction between regional and industrial policies: Evidence from four countries', *International Regional Science Review*, 19(1–2), 49–77.

—— (1996b) 'Sticky places in slippery space: A typology of industrial districts', *Economic Geography*, 72(3), 293–313.

Marshall, A. (1890) *Principles of Economics*, London: Macmillan.

Martin, P., Mayer, T., and Mayneris, F. (2008a) 'Natural clusters: Why policies promoting agglomeration are unnecessary', 4 July, available at http://www.voxeu.org/index.php?q=node/1354

—— —— —— (2008b) 'Public support to clusters: A firm level study of French "local production systems"', CEPR Discussion Paper No. 7102, London: Centre for Economic Policy Research.

Martin, R. and Sunley, P. (1996) 'Paul Krugman's geographical economics and its implications for regional development theory: A critical assessment', *Economic Geography*, 72(3), 259–92.

—— —— (2003) 'Deconstructing clusters: Chaotic concept or policy panacea?', *Journal of Economic Geography*, 3(1), 5–35.

Mascarenhas, B. (1989) 'Strategic group dynamics', *Academy of Management Journal*, 32 (2), 333–52.

Maskell, P. (2001) 'Towards a knowledge-based theory of the geographical cluster', *Industrial and Corporate Change*, 10, 921–43.

—— Eskelinen, H., Hannibalsson, I., Malmberg, A., and Vatne, E. (1998) *Competitiveness, Localised Learning and Regional Development: Specialisation and Prosperity in Small Open Economies*, London: Routledge.

Mason, E. S. (1939*a*) 'Methods of developing a proper control of big business', *Proceedings of the Academy of Political Science*, 18 (Monopoly and Competition in Industry and Labor) (2), 40–9.

—— (1939*b*) 'Price and production policies of large-scale enterprise', *American Economic Review*, 29(Supplement), 61–74.

—— (ed.) (1959) *The Corporation in Modern Society*, Cambridge, MA: Harvard University Press.

May, W., Mason, C., and Pinch, S. (2001) 'Explaining industrial agglomeration: The case of the British high-fidelity industry', *Geoforum*, 32(3), 363–76.

McArthur, J. W. and Sachs, J. D. (2001) 'The Growth Competitiveness Index: Measuring technological advancement and stages of development', in World Economic Forum (ed.) *The Global Competitiveness Report 2001–02*, New York, NY: Oxford University Press, pp. 28–51.

McCann, B. T. and Folta, T. B. (2011) 'Performance differentials within geographic clusters', *Journal of Business Venturing*, 26(1), 104–23.

McCann, P. (2001) *Urban and Regional Economics*, Oxford: Oxford University Press.

—— and Arita, T. (2006) 'Clusters and regional development: Some cautionary observations from the semiconductor industry', *Information Economics and Policy*, 18(2), 157–80.

McDonald, F., Huang, Q., Tsagdis, D., and Tüselmann, H. J. (2007) 'Is there evidence to support Porter-type cluster policies?', *Regional Studies*, 41(1), 39–49.

McGahan, A. M. and Porter, M. E. (1997) 'How much does industry matter, really?', *Strategic Management Journal*, 18(Summer Special Issue), 15–30.

—— —— (1999) 'The persistence of shocks to profitability', *Review of Economics and Statistics*, 81(1), 143–53.

McKiernan, P. (1997) 'Strategy past; strategy futures', *Long Range Planning*, 30(5), 790–8.

—— (ed.) (1996) *Historical Evolution of Strategic Management*, Brookfield, VT: Dartmouth Publishing.

McNair, M. P., Hansen, H. L., and Learned, E. P. (1949) *Problems in Marketing*, New York, NY: McGraw-Hill.

Metcalf, J. S. and Gibbons, M. (1989) 'Technology, variety, and organization: A systematic perspective on the competitive process', *Research on Technological Innovation, Management and Policy*, 4, 153–93.

Mills, K. G., Reynolds, E. B., and Reamer, A. (2008) *Clusters and Competitiveness: A New Federal Role for Stimulating Regional Economies*, Washington, DC: Brookings Institution.

Minford, P. (2006) 'Competitiveness in a globalised world: A commentary', *Journal of International Business Studies*, 37(2), 176–8.

Mintzberg, H. (1973) *The Nature of Managerial Work*, New York, NY: Harper & Row.

—— (1987) 'The Strategy Concept I: Five Ps for strategy', *California Management Review*, 30(1), 11–24.

—— (1990*a*) 'The design school: Reconsidering the basic premises of strategic management', *Strategic Management Journal*, 11(3), 171–95.

—— (1990*b*) 'Strategy formation: Schools of thought', in Fredrickson, J. W. (ed.) *Perspectives on Strategic Management*, New York, NY: Harper & Row, pp. 105–235.

—— (2004) *Managers not MBAs: A Hard Look at the Soft Practice of Managing and Management Development*, San Francisco, CA: Berrett-Koehler Publishers.

—— (2009) *Managing*, San Francisco, CA: Brett-Koehler Publishers.

—— Ahlstrand, B. W., and Lampel, J. (1998) *Strategic Safari: A Guided Tour through the Wilds of Strategic Management*, New York, NY: Free Press.

Mistral, J. (1982) 'Maîtrise da marché intérieur, compétitivité et redéploiement', in Bourguinat H. (ed.) *Internationalisation et Autonomie de Décision*, Paris: Economica.

Moreton, B. (2009) *To Serve God and Wal-Mart: The Making of Christian Free Enterprise*, Cambridge, MA: Harvard University Press.

Morgan, G. (1997) *Images of Organization* (2nd edition), Thousand Oaks, CA: Sage Publications.

Morgan, K. (1997) 'The learning region: Institutions, innovation and regional renewal', *Regional Studies*, 31(5), 491–503.

Motoyama, Y. (2008) 'What was new about cluster theory?: What could it answer and what could it not answer?', *Economic Development Quarterly*, 22(4), 353–63.

Moulaert, F. and Sekia, F. (2003) 'Territorial innovation models: A critical survey', *Regional Studies*, 37(3), 289–302.

Muellbauer, J. (1991) 'Productivity and competitiveness', *Oxford Review of Economic Policy*, 7(3), 99–117.

Murray, A. I. (1989) 'Top management group heterogeneity and firm performance', *Strategic Management Journal*, 10(Summer Special Issue), 125–41.

Nadvi, K. and Barrientos, S. (2004) *Industrial Clusters and Poverty Reduction: Towards a Methodology for Poverty and Social Impact Assessment of Cluster Development Initiatives*, Vienna: United Nations Industrial Development Organization.

Nam, C. W., Nerb, G., and Russ, H. (1990) *An Empirical Assessment of Factors Shaping Regional Competitiveness in Problem Regions*, Main Report, Luxembourg: Commission of the European Communities.

Neffke, F., Henning, M., and Boschma, R. (2009) 'How do regions diversify over time? Industry relatedness and the development of new growth paths in regions', Papers in Evolutionary Economic Geography, No. 09.16, Utrecht: Utrecht University.

Nelson, R. R. (ed.) (1993) *National Innovation Systems: A Comparative Analysis*, New York, NY: Oxford University Press.

—— (1995) 'Co-evolution of industry structure, technology and supporting institutions, and the making of comparative advantage', *International Journal of the Economics of Business*, 2(2), 171–84.

—— (1996) 'The evolution of comparative or competitive advantage: A preliminary report on a study', *Industrial and Corporate Change*, 5(2), 597–617.

—— and Winter, S. G. (1982) *An Evolutionary Theory of Economic Change*, Cambridge, MA: Belknap Press.

Nerur, S. P., Rasheed, A. A., and Natarajan, V. (2008) 'The intellectual structure of the strategic management field: An author co-citation analysis', *Strategic Management Journal*, 29(3), 319–36.

Newfarmer, R., Shaw, W., and Walkenhorst, P. (eds.) (2009) *Breaking Into New Markets: Emerging Lessons for Export Diversification*, Washington, DC: World Bank.

Newman, H. H. (1973) 'Strategic groups and the structure-performance relationship: A study with respect to the chemical process industries', Unpublished PhD dissertation, Harvard University.

—— (1978) 'Strategic groups and the structure-performance relationship', *Review of Economics and Statistics*, 60(3), 417–27.

Noda, T. and Bower, J. L. (1996) 'Strategy making as iterated processes of resource allocation', *Strategic Management Journal*, 17 (Summer Special Issue), 159–92.

Nonaka, I. (1991) 'The knowledge-creating company', *Harvard Business Review*, 69(6), 96–104.

—— (1994) 'A dynamic theory of organizational knowledge creation', *Organization Science*, 5(1), 14–37.

—— and Takeuchi, H. (1995) *The Knowledge-Creating Company: How Japanese Companies Create the Dynamics of Innovation*, New York, NY: Oxford University Press.

Norton, R. D. and Rees, J. (1979) 'The product cycle and the spatial decentralization of American manufacturing', *Regional Studies*, 13(2), 141–51.

O'Driscoll, G. P. and Rizzo, M. J. (1985) *The Economics of Time and Ignorance*, Oxford: Basil Blackwell.

O'Gorman, C. and Kautonen, M. (2004) 'Policies to promote new knowledge-intensive industrial agglomerations', *Entrepreneurship and Regional Development*, 16(6), 459–79.

ODPM (2003) *Cities, Regions and Competitiveness*, London: Office of the Deputy Prime Minister.

—— (2004) 'Competitive European cities: Where do the core cities stand?', Urban Research Paper 13, London: Office of the Deputy Prime Minister.

OECD (1992) *Technology and the Economy: The Key Relationship*, Paris: OECD.

—— (1999) *Boosting Innovation: The Cluster Approach*, Paris: OECD.

—— (2003) *The Policy Agenda for Growth: An Overview of the Sources of Economic Growth in OECD Countries*, Paris: OECD.

—— (2004) *Understanding Economic Growth: Macro-Level, Industry-Level, Firm-Level*, New York, NY: Palgrave Macmillan.

—— (2007) *Competitive Regional Clusters: National Policy Approaches*, Paris: OECD.

Oerlemans, L. A. G. and Meeus, M. T. H. (2005) 'Do organizational and spatial proximity impact on firm performance?', *Regional Studies*, 39(1), 89–104.

Ohlin, B. G. (1933) *Interregional and International Trade*, Cambridge, MA: Harvard University Press.

Ohmae, K. (1990) *The Borderless World*, New York, NY: Harper and Row.

Oinas, P. and Malecki, E. J. (2002) 'The evolution of technologies in time and space: From national and regional to spatial innovation systems', *International Regional Science Review*, 25(1), 102–31.

Oster, S. (1982) 'Intraindustry structure and the ease of strategic change', *Review of Economics and Statistics*, 64(3), 376–83.

Oxford Research (2008) *Cluster Policy in Europe: A Brief Summary of Cluster Policies in 31 European Countries*, Synthesis report for the Europe INNOVA Cluster Mapping Project, Kristiansand: Oxford Research.

Paniccia, I. (2006) 'Cutting through the chaos: Towards a new typology of industrial districts and clusters', in Asheim, B., Cooke, P., and Martin, R. (eds.) *Clusters and Regional Development: Critical Reflections and Explorations*, London: Routledge, pp. 90–114.

Parente, S. L. and Prescott, E. C. (2006) 'What a country must do to catch up to the industrial leaders', in Balcerowicz, L. and Fischer, S. (eds.) *Living Standards and the Wealth of Nations: Successes and Failures in Real Convergence*, Cambridge, MA: MIT Press, pp. 17–39.

Park, S. O. (1996) 'Networks and embeddedness in the dynamic types of new industrial districts', *Progress in Human Geography*, 20(4), 476–93.

Pefeffer, J. and Davis-Blake, A. (1986) 'Administrative succession and organizational performance: How administrator experience mediates the succession effect', *Academy of Management Journal*, 29(1), 72–83.

Peneder, M. (2001) *Entrepreneurial Competition and Industrial Location: Investigating the Structural Patterns and Intangible Sources of Competitive Performance*, Cheltenham: Edward Elgar.

Penner-Hahn, J. and Shaver, J. M. (2005) 'Does international research and development increase patent output? An analysis of Japanese pharmaceutical firms', *Strategic Management Journal*, 26(2), 121–40.

Penrose, E. T. (1959) *The Theory of the Growth of the Firm*, New York, NY: John Wiley & Sons (Fourth Edition, 2009, Oxford, Oxford University Press).

Perroux, F. (1955) 'Note sur la notion de "pôle de croissance"', *Economie Appliquée*, (1–2), 307–20.

Peteraf, M. A. (1993) 'The cornerstones of competitive advantage: A resource-based view', *Strategic Management Journal*, 14(3), 179–91.

—— and Barney, J. B. (2003) 'Unraveling the resource-based tangle', *Managerial and Decision Economics*, 24(4), 309–23.

—— and Shanley, M. (1997) 'Getting to know you: A theory of strategic group identity', *Strategic Management Journal*, 18(Summer Special Issue), 165–86.

Pfeffer, J. (1994) 'Competitive advantage through people', *California Management Review*, 36(2), 9–28.

—— (2007) 'A modest proposal: How we might change the process and product of managerial research', *Academy of Management Journal*, 50(6), 1334–45.

—— and Veiga, J. F. (1999) 'Putting people first for organizational success', *Academy of Management Executive*, 13(2), 37–48.

Phillips, A. and Stevenson, R. E. (1974) 'The historical development of industrial organization', *History of Political Economy*, 6(3), 324–42.

Pietrobelli, C. and Rabellotti, R. (2004) *Upgrading in Clusters and Value Chains in Latin America: The Role of Policies*, Washington, DC: Inter-American Development Bank.

Pigou, A. C. (1922) 'Empty economic boxes: A reply', *Economic Journal*, 32(128), 458–65.

Pike, A., Rodríguez-Pose, A., and Tomaney, J. (2006) *Local and Regional Development*, London: Routledge.

Piore, M. J. and Sabel, C. F. (1984) *The Second Industrial Divide: Possibilities for Prosperity*, New York, NY: Basic Books.

Polanyi, M. (1966) *The Tacit Dimension*, Garden City, NY: Doubleday.

Popper, K. R. (1959) *The Logic of Scientific Discovery*, New York, NY: Basic Books.

—— (1972) *Objective knowledge: An Evolutionary Approach*, Oxford: Clarendon Press.

Porac, J. F., Thomas, H., Wilson, F., Paton, D., and Kanfer, A. (1995) 'Rivalry and the industry model of Scottish knitwear producers', *Administrative Science Quarterly*, 40(2), 203–27.

Porter, M. E. (1973) 'Consumer Behavior, Retailer Power, and Manufacturer Strategy in Consumer Goods Industries', Unpublished PhD dissertation, Harvard University.

—— (1974) 'Consumer behavior, retailer power and market performance in consumer goods industries', *Review of Economics and Statistics*, 56(4), 419–36.

—— (1975) 'Note on the structural analysis of industries', HBS Case # 376-054.

—— (1976a) *Interbrand Choice, Strategy, and Bilateral Market Power*, Cambridge, MA: Harvard University Press.

—— (1976b) 'Please note location of nearest exit: Exit barriers and planning', *California Management Review*, 19(2), 21–33.

—— (1979a) 'How competitive forces shape strategy', *Harvard Business Review*, 57(2), 137–45.

—— (1979b) 'The structure within industries and companies' performance', *Review of Economics and Statistics*, 61(2), 214–27.

—— (1980a) *Competitive Strategy: Techniques for Analyzing Industries and Competitors*, New York, NY: Free Press.

—— (1980b) 'Industry structure and competitive strategy: Keys to profitability', *Financial Analysts Journal*, 36(4), 30–41.

—— (1981) 'The contributions of industrial organization to strategic management', *Academy of Management Review*, 6(4), 609–20.

—— (1983) *Cases in Competitive Strategy*, New York, NY: Free Press.

—— (1985a) *Competitive Advantage: Creating and Sustaining Superior Performance*, New York, NY: Free Press.

—— (1985b) 'Technology and competitive advantage', *Journal of Business Strategy*, 5(3), 60–78.

—— (ed.) (1986a) *Competition in Global Industries*, Boston, MA: Harvard Business School Press.

—— (1986b) 'Competition in global industries: A conceptual framework', in Porter, M. E. (ed.) *Competition in Global Industries*, Boston, MA: Harvard Business School Press, pp. 15–60.

—— (1986c) 'Changing patterns of international competition', *California Management Review*, 28(2), 9–39.

—— (1987a) 'From competitive advantage to corporate strategy', *Harvard Business Review*, 65(3), 43–59.

—— (1987b) 'Changing patterns of international competition', in Teece, D. J. (ed.) *The Competitive Challenge: Strategies for Industrial Innovation and Renewal*, Cambridge, MA: Ballinger, pp. 27–57.

—— (1990a) *The Competitive Advantage of Nations*, New York, NY: Free Press.

—— (1990b) 'The competitive advantage of nations', *Harvard Business Review*, 68(2), 73–93.

—— (1991) 'Towards a dynamic theory of strategy', *Strategic Management Journal*, 12 (Winter Special Issue), 95–117.

—— (1992) 'Capital disadvantage: America's failing capital investment system', *Harvard Business Review*, 70(5), 65–82.

—— (1994) 'The role of location in competition', *Journal of the Economics of Business*, 1(1), 35–9.

—— (1995) 'The competitive advantage of the inner city', *Harvard Business Review*, 73(3), 55–71.

—— (1996a) 'Competitive advantage, agglomeration economies, and regional policy', *International Regional Science Review*, 19(1–2), 85–90.

—— (1996b) 'What is strategy?', *Harvard Business Review*, 74(6), 61–78.

—— (1997) 'Creating advantages', *Executive Excellence*, 14(12), 17–18.

—— (1998a) 'The Adam Smith address: Location, clusters and the "new" microeconomics of competition', *Business Economics*, 33(1), 7–13.

—— (1998b) 'Clusters and the new economics of competition', *Harvard Business Review*, 76(6), 77–90.

—— (1998c) *On Competition*, Boston, MA: Harvard Business School Publishing.

—— (1998d) 'Clusters and competition: New agendas for companies, governments, and institutions', in Porter, M. E. (ed.) *On Competition*, Boston, MA: Harvard Business School Publishing, pp. 197–287.

—— (2000a) 'Locations, clusters, and company strategy', in Clark, G. L., Feldman, M. P., and Gertler, M. S. (eds.) *The Oxford Handbook of Economic Geography*, Oxford: Oxford University Press, pp. 253–74.

—— (2000b) 'Location, competition, and economic development: Local clusters in a global economy', *Economic Development Quarterly*, 14(1), 15–34.

—— (2000c) 'Attitudes, values, beliefs, and the microeconomics of prosperity', in Harrison, L. E. and Huntington, S. P (eds.) *Culture Matters: How Values Shape Human Progress*, New York, NY: Basic Books, pp. 14–28.

—— (2001a) 'Enhancing the microeconomic foundations of prosperity: The Current Competitiveness Index', in World Economic Forum (ed.) *Global Competitiveness Report, 2001–02*, New York, NY: Oxford University Press, pp. 2–26.

—— (2001b) 'Regions and the new economics of competitiveness', in Scott, A. J. (ed.) *Global City Regions*, Oxford: Oxford University Press, pp. 139–57.

—— (2001c) 'Strategy and the Internet', *Harvard Business Review*, 79(3), pp. 62–78.

—— (2003) 'The economic performance of regions', *Regional Studies*, 37(6&7), 549–78.

—— (2004) 'Building the microeconomic foundations of prosperity: Findings from the Business Competitiveness Index', in Porter, M. E., Schwab, K., Sala-i-Martin, X., and Lopez-Claros, A. (eds.) *The Global Competitiveness Report 2003–2004*, New York, NY: Oxford University Press, pp. 29–56.

—— (2005) *Clusters of Innovation Initiative: Regional Foundations of U.S. Competitiveness*, Washington, DC: Council on Competitiveness.

—— (2008*a*) 'The five competitive forces that shape strategy', *Harvard Business Review*, 86(1), 78–93.

—— (2008*b*) *On Competition*, Updated and Expanded Edition, Boston, MA: Harvard Business School Press.

—— and Ketels, C. (2003) 'UK competitiveness: Moving to the next stage', DTI Economics Paper No. 3, London: Department of Trade and Industry.

—— —— (2009) 'Clusters and industrial districts: Common roots, different perspectives', in Becattini, G., Bellandi, M., and de Propris, L. (eds.) *Handbook of Industrial Districts*, Cheltenham: Edward Elgar.

—— and Kramer, M. R. (1999) 'Philanthropy's new agenda: Creating value', *Harvard Business Review*, 77(6), 121–30.

—— —— (2002) 'The competitive advantage of corporate philanthropy', *Harvard Business Review*, 80(12), 56–69.

—— —— (2006) 'Strategy & Society: The link between competitive advantage and corporate social responsibility', *Harvard Business Review*, 84(12), 78–92.

—— and Millar, V. E. (1985) 'How information gives you competitive advantage', *Harvard Business Review*, 63(4), 149–60.

—— and Reinhardt, F. L. (2007) 'A strategic approach to climate', *Harvard Business Review*, 85(10), 22–6.

—— and Sakakibara, M. (2004) 'Competition in Japan', *Journal of Economic Perspectives*, 18(1), 27–50.

—— and Sölvell, Ö. (1998) 'The role of geography in the process of innovation and the sustainable competitive advantage of firms', in Chandler, A. D., Hagström, P., and Sölvell, Ö. (eds.) *The Dynamic Firm: The Role of Technology, Strategy, Organization, and Regions*, Oxford: Oxford University Press, pp. 440–57.

—— and Stern, S. (2001) 'Innovation: Location matters', *MIT Sloan Management Review*, 42(4), 28–36.

—— and Takeuchi, H. (1999) 'Fixing what really ails Japan', *Foreign Affairs*, 78(3), 66–81.

—— and Teisberg, E. O. (2006*a*) *Redefining Health Care: Creating Value-Based Competition on Results*, Boston, MA: Harvard Business School Press.

—— —— (2006*b*) 'Redefining competition in health care', *Harvard Business Review*, 82(6), 64–76.

—— and van der Linde, C. (1995*a*) 'Green and competitive: Ending the stalemate', *Harvard Business Review*, 73(5), 120–34.

—— —— (1995*b*) 'Toward a new conception of the environment-competitiveness relationships', *Journal of Economic Perspectives*, 9(4), 97–118.

—— and van Opstal, D. (2001) *U.S. Competitiveness 2001: Strengths, Vulnerabilities and Long-Term Priorities*, Washington, DC: Council on Competitiveness.

—— Takeuchi, H., and Sakakibara, M. (2000) *Can Japan Compete?*, Basingstoke: Macmillan.

—— Ketels, C., Miller, K., and Bryden, R. T. (2004) *Competitiveness in Rural U.S. Regions: Learning and Research Agenda*, Report prepared for the Economic Development Administration, Department of Commerce, Washington, DC: Department of Commerce.

—— Lorsch, J. W., and Nohria, N. (2004) 'Seven surprises for new CEOs', *Harvard Business Review*, 82(10), 62–72.

—— Council on Competitiveness, and Monitor Company (2005) *Clusters of Innovation Initiative: Regional Foundations of U.S. Competitiveness*, Washington, DC: Council on Competitiveness.

—— Delgado, M., Ketels, C., and Stern, S. (2008) 'Moving to a new Global Competitiveness Index', in Porter, M. E. and Schwab, K. (eds.) *Global Competitiveness Report 2008–09*, New York, NY: Palgrave Macmillan, pp. 43–63.

Posner, R. A. (1996) *Overcoming Law*, Cambridge, MA: Harvard University Press.

Powell, C. P. (1995) 'Total Quality Management as competitive advantage: A review and empirical study', *Strategic Management Journal*, 16(1), 15–37.

Prahalad, C. K. and Hamel, G. (1990) 'The core competence of the corporation', *Harvard Business Review*, 68(3), 79–91.

Pressman, S. (1991) '*The Competitive Advantage of Nations: A Review*', *Journal of Management*, 17(1), 213–15.

Prestowitz, Jr., C. V. (1994) 'Playing to win', *Foreign Affairs*, 73(4), 186–9.

Ramos-Rodríguez, A.-R. and Ruiz-Navarro, J. (2004) 'Changes in the intellectual structure of strategic management research: A bibliometric study of the *Strategic Management Journal*, 1980–2000', *Strategic Management Journal*, 25(10), 981–1004.

Redding, S. (1999) 'Dynamic comparative advantage and the welfare effects of trade', *Oxford Economic Papers*, 51(1), 15–39.

Reger, R. K. and Huff, A. S. (1993) 'Strategic groups: A cognitive perspective', *Strategic Management Journal*, 14(2), 103–23.

Reich, R. (1990) 'But now we're global', *The Times Literary Supplement*, August 31.

Reinert, E. S. (1995) 'Competitiveness and its predecessors – A 500-year cross-national perspective', *Structural Change and Economic Dynamics*, 6(1), 23–42.

Robins, J. and Wiersema, M. F. (1995) 'A resource-based approach to the multibusiness firm: Empirical analysis of portfolio interrelationships and corporate financial performance', *Strategic Management Journal*, 16(4), 277–99.

Rocha, H. O. (2004) 'Entrepreneurship and development: The role of clusters', *Small Business Economics*, 23(5), 363–400.

Rodrik, D. (2007) *One Economics, Many Recipes: Globalization, Institutions, and Economic Growth*, Princeton, NJ: Princeton University Press.

Romer, P. M. (1986) 'Increasing returns and long-run growth', *Journal of Political Economy*, 94(5), 1002–37.

Roquebert, J. A., Phillips, R. L., and Westfall, P. A. (1996) 'Markets vs. management: What "drives" profitability?', *Strategic Management Journal*, 17(8), 653–64.

Rosenfeld, S. A. (1997) 'Bringing business clusters into the mainstream of economic development', *European Planning Studies*, 5(1), 3–23.

—— (2002) *A Governor's Guide to Cluster-Based Economic Development*, Report for the National Governors Association and the Council on Competitiveness, Washington, DC: National Governors Association.

—— (2007) *Cluster-Based Strategies for Growing State Economies*, Washington, DC: National Governors Association and Council on Competitiveness.

Roveda, C. and Vecchiato, R. (2008) 'Foresight and innovation in the context of industrial clusters: The case of some Italian districts', *Technological Forecasting and Social Change*, 75(6), 817–33.

Rugman, A. (1991) 'Diamond in the rough', *Business Quarterly*, 55(3), 61–4.

—— (1992) 'Porter takes the wrong turn: Michael Porter's analysis of the Canadian economy is seriously flawed and should be viewed circumspectly', *Business Quarterly*, 56(3), 59–64.

Rumelt, R. P. (1974) *Strategy, Structure, and Economic Performance*. Boston, MA: Division of Research, Graduate School of Business Administration, Harvard University.

—— (1984) 'Towards a strategic theory of the firm', in Lamb, R. (ed.) *Competitive Strategic Management*, Englewood Cliffs, NJ: Prentice-Hall, pp. 556–70.

—— (1987) 'Theory, strategy, and entrepreneurship', in Teece, D. (ed.) *The Competitive Challenge: Strategies for Industrial Innovation and Renewal*, Cambridge, MA: Ballinger, pp. 137–58.

—— (1991) 'How much does industry matter?', *Strategic Management Journal*, 12(3), 167–85.

—— and Wensley, R. (1981) 'In search of the market share effect', *Academy of Management Proceedings*, 41, 2–6.

—— Schendel, D., and Teece, D. J. (1991) 'Strategic management and economics', *Strategic Management Journal*, 12 (Winter Special Issue), 5–29.

—— —— (eds.) (1994) *Fundamental Issues in Strategy: A Research Agenda*, Boston, MA: Harvard Business School Press.

Rush, H., Bessant, J., and Hobday, M. (2007) 'Assessing the technological capabilities of firms: Developing a policy tool', *R&D Management*, 37(3), 221–36.

Rutten, R. and Boekema, F. (eds.) (2007) *The Learning Region: Foundations, State of the Art, Future*, Cheltenham: Edward Elgar.

Sakakibara, M. and Porter, M. E. (2001) 'Competing at home to win abroad: Evidence from Japanese industry', *Review of Economics and Statistics*, 83(2), 310–22.

Sala-i-Martin, X. and Artadi, E. (2004) 'The Global Competitiveness Index', in Porter, M. E., Schwab, K., Sala-i-Martin, X., and Lopez-Claros, A. (eds.) *The Global Competitiveness Report 2004–2005*, New York, NY: Palgrave Macmillan, pp. 51–80.

—— Blanke, J., Hanouz, M. D., Geiger, T., and Mia, I. (2009) 'The Global Competitiveness Index 2009–10: Contributing to long-term prosperity amid the global economic crisis', in Schwab, K. (ed.) *The Global Competitiveness Report 2009–10*, Geneva: World Economic Forum, pp. 3–47.

Saloner, G. (1991) 'Modeling, game theory, and strategic management', *Strategic Management Journal*, 12 (Winter Special Issue), 119–36.

—— (1994) 'Game theory and strategic management: Contributions, applications, and limitations', in Rumelt, R. P., Schendel, D. E., and Teece, D. J. (eds.) *Fundamental Issues in Strategy: A Research Agenda*, Boston, MA: Harvard Business School Press, pp. 155–94.

Samuelson, P. A. (1948) 'International trade and the equalisation of factor prices', *Economic Journal*, 58(230), 163–84.

—— (1949) 'International factor-price equalisation once again', *Economic Journal*, 59 (234), 181–97.

Sanchez, R. (1995) 'Strategic flexibility in product competition', *Strategic Management Journal*, 16 (Summer Special Issue), 135–59.

Saxenian, A. (1994) *Regional Advantage: Culture and Competition in Silicon Valley and Route 128*, Cambridge, MA: Harvard University Press.

Scharping, R. (1994) 'Rule-based competition', *Foreign Affairs*, 73(4), 192–4.

Schendel, D. (1996) 'Evolutionary perspectives on strategy', *Strategic Management Journal*, 17 (Summer Special Issue), 1–4.

—— and Hatten, K. J. (1972) 'Business policy or strategic management: A broader view for an emerging discipline', *Academy of Management Proceedings*, 32, 99–102.

Scherer, F. M. (1970) *Industrial Market Structure and Economic Performance*, Chicago, IL: Rand McNally.

Scott, A. J. (2006) *Geography and Economy: Three Lectures*, New York, NY: Oxford University Press.

Segerstrom, P. S., Anant, T. C. A., and Dinopoulos, E. (1990) 'A Schumpeterian model of the product life cycle', *American Economic Review*, 80(5), 1077–91.

Selznick, P. (1957) *Leadership in Administration: A Sociological Interpretation*, Evanston, IL: Row, Peterson.

Shapiro, C. (1989) 'The theory of business strategy', *RAND Journal of Economics*, 20(1), 125–37.

Shaver, J. M. and Flyer, F. (2000) 'Agglomeration economies, firm heterogeneity, and foreign direct investment in the United States', *Strategic Management Journal*, 21(2), 1175–93.

Sheehan, N. T. and Foss, N. J. (2007) 'Enhancing the prescriptiveness of the resource-based view through Porterian activity analysis', *Management Decision*, 45(3), 450–61.

—— —— (2009) 'Exploring the roots of Porter's activity-based view', *Journal of Strategy and Management*, 2(3), 240–60.

Shih, H.-Y. (2007) 'Structural analysis of market structure and performance: A new empirical industrial structure method in competitive analysis', *Proceedings of International Conference on Business and Information*, Tokyo, 11–13 July.

Shubik, M. (1983) 'The strategic audit: A game theoretic approach to corporate competitive strategy', *Managerial and Decision Economics*, 4(3), 160–71.

Siggel, E. (2006) 'International competitiveness and comparative advantage: A survey and a proposal for measurement', *Journal of Industry, Competition and Trade*, 6(2), 137–59.

Simmie, J. (2004) 'Innovation and clustering in the globalised international economy', *Urban Studies*, 41(5–6), 1095–112.

—— (2006) 'Do clusters or innovation systems drive competitiveness?', in Asheim, B., Cooke, P., and Martin, R. (eds.) *Clusters and Regional Development: Critical Reflections and Explorations*, London: Routledge, pp. 164–87.

Simon, H. A. (1945) *Administrative Behavior*, New York, NY: Macmillan.

Smith, A. (1976, original 1776) *An Inquiry into the Nature and Causes of the Wealth of Nations*, in Campbell, R. H. and Skinner, A. S. (eds.), Oxford: Clarendon.

Smith, J. E., Carson, K. P., and Alexander, R. A. (1984) 'Leadership: It can make a difference', *Academy of Management Journal*, 27(4), 765–76.

Smith, Jr., G. A. (1951) *Policy Formulation and Administration; A Casebook of Top-management Problems in Business*, Chicago, IL: Richard D. Irwin.

Smith, K. G., Smith, K. A., Olian, J. D., Sims, Jr., H. P., O'Bannon, D. P., and Scully, J. A. (1994) 'Top management demography and process: The role of social integration and communication', *Administrative Science Quarterly*, 39(3), 412–38.

Snowdon, B. (2001) 'Championing free trade in the second age of globalisation: Jagdish Bhagwati on trade, democracy and growth', *World Economics*, 2(4), 53–104.

—— (2006) 'The enduring elixir of economic growth: Xavier Sala-i-Martin on the wealth and poverty of nations', *World Economics*, 7(1), 73–130.

—— (2007) *Globalisation, Development and Transition: Conversations with Eminent Economists*, Cheltenham: Edward Elgar.

—— and Stonehouse, G. (2006) 'Competitiveness in a globalised world: Michael Porter on the microeconomic foundations of the competitiveness of nations, regions, and firms', *Journal of International Business Studies*, 37(2), 163–75.

—— and Vane, H. R. (2005) *Modern Macroeconomics: Its Origins, Development and Current State*, Cheltenham: Edward Elgar.

Solow, R. M. (1956) 'A contribution to the theory of economic growth', *Quarterly Journal of Economics*, 70(1), 65–94.

Sölvell, Ö. (2008) *Clusters: Balancing Evolutionary and Constructive Forces*, Stockholm: Ivory Tower Publishing.

—— Lindqvist, G., and Ketels, C. (2003) *The Cluster Initiative Greenbook*, Stockholm: Ivory Tower Publishing.

—— Ketels, C., and Lindqvist, G. (2008) 'Industrial specialization and regional clusters in the ten new EU member states', *Competitiveness Review*, 18(1), 104–30.

Speed, R. J. (1989) 'Oh Mr. Porter! A re-appraisal of *Competitive Strategy*', *Market Intelligence & Planning*, 7(5/6), 8–11.

Spender, J.-C. (1989) *Industry Recipes: The Nature and Sources of Managerial Judgement*, Oxford: Blackwell.

—— (1994) 'Organizational knowledge, collective practice and Penrose rents', *International Business Review*, 3(4), 353–67.

—— (2007) 'Management as a regulated profession: An essay', *Journal of Management Inquiry*, 16(1), 32–42.

—— and Grant, R. M. (1996) 'Knowledge and the firm: Overview', *Strategic Management Journal*, 17 (Winter Special Issue), 5–9.

Stalk, G., Evans, P., and Shulman, L. E. (1992) 'Competing on capabilities: The new rules of corporate strategy', *Harvard Business Review*, 70(2), 54–66.

Starkey, K., Hatchuel, A., and Tempest, S. (2004) 'Rethinking the business school', *Journal of Management Studies*, 41(8), 1521–31.

Steil, B. (1994) 'Careless arithmetic', *Foreign Affairs*, 73(4), 197.

Steiner, G. A. (1981) 'Book Review: *Competitive Strategy* by Michael Porter', *Journal of Business Strategy*, 1(3), 84–5.

Steiner, M. (ed.) (1998a) *Clusters and Regional Specialisation: On Geography, Technology and Networks*, London: Pion.

—— (1998*b*) 'The discreet charm of clusters: An introduction', in Steiner, M. (ed.) *Clusters and Regional Specialisation: On Geography, Technology and Networks*, London: Pion, pp. 1–17.

—— (2002) 'Clusters and networks: Institutional settings and strategic perspectives', in McCann, P. (ed.) *Industrial Location Economics*, Cheltenham: Edward Elgar, pp. 207–21.

—— (2006) 'Do clusters think? An institutional perspective on knowledge creation and diffusion in clusters', in Asheim, B., Cooke, P., and Martin, R. (eds.) *Clusters and Regional Development: Critical Reflections and Explorations*, London: Routledge, pp. 199–217.

Steinfeld, E. S. (2004) 'China's shallow integration: Networked production and the new challenges for late industrialization', *World Development*, 32(11), 1971–87.

Stiglitz, J. E. (2009) 'The current economic crisis and lessons for economic theory', *Eastern Economic Journal*, 35(3), 281–96.

Stolper, W. F. and Samuelson, P. A. (1941) 'Protection and real wages', *Review of Economic Studies*, 9(1), 58–73.

Stonehouse, G. and Snowdon, B. (2007) 'Competitive advantage revisited: Michael Porter on strategy and competitiveness', *Journal of Management Inquiry*, 16(3), 256–73.

Storper, M. (1995) 'The resurgence of regional economies, ten years later: The region as a nexus of untraded interdependencies', *European Urban and Regional Studies*, 2(3), 191–221.

—— (1997) *The Regional World: Territorial Development in a Global Economy*, New York, NY: Guilford Press.

Stuart, T. E. and Podolny, J. M. (1996) 'Local search and the evolution of technological capabilities', *Strategic Management Journal*, 17 (Summer Special Issue), 21–38.

Tallman, S. (2001) 'Global strategic management', in Hitt, M. A., Freeman, R. E., and Harrison, J. S. (eds.) *Handbook of Strategic Management*, Oxford: Blackwell Publishers, pp. 464–90.

—— Jenkins, M., Henry, N., and Pinch, S. (2004) 'Knowledge, clusters, and competitive advantage', *Academy of Management Review*, 29(2), 258–71.

Tavoletti, E. and te Velde, R. (2008) 'Cutting Porter's last diamond: Competitive and comparative (dis)advantages in the Dutch flower cluster', *Transition Studies Review*, 15 (2), 303–19.

Teece, D. J. (1982) 'Towards an economic theory of the multiproduct firm', *Journal of Economic Behavior & Organization*, 3(1), 39–63.

—— (ed.) (1987) *The Competitive Challenge: Strategies for Industrial Innovation and Renewal*, Cambridge, MA: Ballinger.

—— (2007) 'Explicating dynamic capabilities: The nature and microfoundations of (sustainable) enterprise performance', *Strategic Management Journal*, 28(13), 1319–50.

—— Pisano, G., and Shuen, A. (1997) 'Dynamic capabilities and strategic management', *Strategic Management Journal*, 18(7), 509–33.

Teigland, R. and Lindqvist, G. (2007) 'Seeing eye-to-eye: How do public and private sector views of a biotech cluster and its cluster initiative differ?', *European Planning Studies*, 15(6), 767–86.

Teisberg, E. O., Porter, M. E., and Brown, G. B. (1994*a*) 'Making competition in health care work', *Harvard Business Review*, 72(4), 131–41.

—— —— —— (1994b) 'Finding a lasting cure for U.S. health care', *Harvard Business Review*, 72(5), 62–3.

ter Wal, A. L. J. and Boschma, R. A. (2007) 'Co-evolution of firms, industries and networks in space', Papers in Evolutionary Economic Geography No. 07.07, Utrecht University.

Thomas, M. D. (1975) 'Growth pole theory, technological change, and regional economic development', *Papers of the Regional Science Association*, 34(1), 3–25.

Thomas, H., Beer, A., and Bailey, D. (2008) 'A tale of two regions: Comparative versus competitive approaches to economic restructuring', *Policy Studies*, 29(3), 357–70.

Thompson, J. D. (1967) *Organizations in Action: Social Science Bases of Administrative Theory*, New York, NY: McGraw-Hill.

Thurow, L. C. (1992) *Head to Head: The Coming Economic Battle Among Japan, Europe, and America*, New York, NY: Morrow.

—— (1994) 'Microchips, not potato chips', *Foreign Affairs*, 73(4), 189–92.

Tirole, J. (1988) *The Theory of Industrial Organization*, Cambridge, MA: MIT Press.

Tödtling, F. and Trippl, M. (2004) 'Like phoenix from the ashes? The renewal of clusters in old industrial areas', *Urban Studies*, 41(5–6), 1175–95.

Tylecote, A. (1993) 'Managerial objectives and technological collaboration in national systems of innovation: The role of national variations in cultures and structures', CRTTEC Discussion Paper No. 2, Sheffield: Sheffield University Management School.

UNIDO (2001) *Development of Clusters and Networks of SMEs*, Vienna: United Nations Industrial Development Organization.

Utterback, J. M. and Abernathy, W. J. (1975) 'A dynamic model of product and process innovation', *Omega*, 3(6), 639–56.

Van de Ven, A. (2007) *Engaged Scholarship: A Guide for Organizational and Social Research*, Oxford: Oxford University Press.

Van Den Bosch, F. A. J. and Van Prooijen, A. A. (1992) 'The competitive advantage of European nations: The impact of national culture – A missing element in Porter's analysis?', *European Journal of Management*, 10(2),173–7.

van der Linde, C. (2002) 'Findings from the cluster meta-study', Boston, MA: Institute for Strategy and Competitiveness, Harvard Business School, Available at http://www.isc.hbs.edu/MetaStudy2002Prz.pdf

Vaughn, K. I. (1994) *Austrian Economics in America: The Migration of a Tradition*, Cambridge: Cambridge University Press.

Veblen, T. (1904) *The Theory of the Business Enterprise*. New York, NY: C. Scribner's Sons.

Veendorp, E. C. H. (1978) 'Review: [untitled]', *Southern Economic Journal*, 45(2), 670–1.

Venables, A. J. (1996) 'Localization of industry and trade performance', *Oxford Review of Economic Policy*, 12(3), 52–60.

Verdin, P. J. and Williamson, P. J. (1994) 'Core competences, competitive advantage and market analysis: Forging the links', in Hamel, G. and Heene, A. (eds.) *Competence-Based Competition*, New York, NY: Wiley, pp. 77–110.

Vernon, R. (1966) 'International investment and international trade in the product cycle', *Quarterly Journal of Economics*, 80(2), 190–207.

Verspagen, B. (1992) 'Endogenous innovation in neo-classical growth models: A survey', *Journal of Macroeconomics*, 14(4), 631–62.

Visser, E. (1999) 'A comparison of clustered and dispersed firms in the small-scale clothing industry of Lima', *World Development*, 27(9), 1553–70.

Waits, M. J. (2000) 'The added value of the industry cluster approach to economic analysis, strategy development, and service delivery', *Economic Development Quarterly*, 14(1), 35–50.

Wells, L. T. (1972) 'International trade: The product life cycle approach', in Wells, L. T. (ed.) *The Product Life Cycle and International Trade*, Boston, MA: Graduate School of Business Administration, Harvard University, pp. 3–33.

Wennberg, K. and Lindqvist, G. (2010) 'The effect of clusters on the survival and performance of new firms', *Small Business Economics*, 34(3), 221–41.

Wensley, R. (1982) 'PIMS and BCG: New horizons or false dawn?', *Strategic Management Journal*, 3(2), 147–58.

Wernerfelt, B. (1984) 'A resource-based view of the firm', *Strategic Management Journal*, 5 (2), 171–80.

Wiggins, R. R. and Ruefli, T. W. (1995) 'Necessary conditions for the predictive validity of strategic groups: Analysis without reliance on clustering techniques', *Academy of Management Journal*, 38(6), 1635–56.

Williamson, O. E. (1975) *Markets and Hierarchies: Analysis and Antitrust Implications*, New York, NY: Free Press.

—— (1985) *The Economic Institutions of Capitalism: Firms, Markets, Relational Contracting*, New York, NY: Free Press.

Winter, S. G. (2003) 'Understanding dynamic capabilities', *Strategic Management Journal*, 24(10), 991–5.

—— (2005) 'Developing evolutionary theory for economics and management', in Smith, K. G. and Hitt, M. (eds.) *Great Minds in Management*, Oxford: Oxford University Press, pp. 509–46.

Witt, U. (2009) 'Evolutionary economics', in Durlauf, S. N. and Blume, L. E. (eds.) *The New Palgrave Dictionary of Economics Online* (2nd edition), Basingstoke: Palgrave Macmillan.

Wolfe, D. A. and Gertler, M. S. (2004) 'Clusters from the inside and out: Local dynamics and global linkages', *Urban Studies*, 41(5–6), 1071–93.

World Bank (2004) *World Development Report 2005: A Better Investment Climate for Everyone*, Oxford: Oxford University Press.

—— (2008) *Doing Business 2009*, New York, NY: Palgrave Macmillan.

—— (2009a) *World Development Report 2009: Reshaping Economic Geography*, Washington, DC: World Bank.

—— (2009b) *Clusters for Competitiveness: A Practical Guide & Policy Implications for Developing Cluster Initiatives*, Washington, DC: World Bank.

Ylä-Anttila, P. and Palmberg, C. (2007) 'Economic and industrial policy transformations in Finland', *Journal of Industry, Competition and Trade*, 7(3–4), 169–87.

Zajac, E. (1995) 'SMJ 1994 best paper prize to Birger Wernerfelt', *Strategic Management Journal*, 16(3), 169–70.

Zeng, D. Z. (ed.) (2008) *Knowledge, Technology, and Cluster-Based Growth in Africa*, Washington, DC: World Bank.

Index

Diagrams and tables are given in italics

Lightning Source UK Ltd.
Milton Keynes UK
UKOW07f0621150215

246278UK00001B/2/P